Dramatherapy

Dramatherapy is now an established practice in both education and a variety of clinical settings. The processes and methods of theatre and drama have proved invaluable in working therapeutically with at-risk and vulnerable populations such as people with mental health problems or learning disabilities. Its techniques can be used across the age range, from babies to elderly persons, to help build communication and relationship skills. Its scope and applicability to a wide range of contemporary problems reflect the roots of the profession in the ritual and theatre of ancient arts of healing.

Dramatherapy: Theory and practice, Volumes 1, 2 and 3, together provide a rounded picture of the development of the profession up to the present day. This third volume shows how dramatherapy is evolving its own theory and methodology as well as specific models for supervision and assessment. It tackles key issues in contemporary social relationships and introduces the major new themes of gender, race and politics.

Presenting the latest research and method from an international perspective *Dramatherapy: Theory and practice 3* makes it clear how this powerful method of healing can be beneficially employed in many new fields such as management and training, rehabilitation and aftercare, as well as in the traditional areas of clinical practice.

Edited by **Sue Jennings**, consultant dramatherapist, and Professor in Dramatherapy at the University of Ulster.

This book is dedicated to my fellow pioneer Gordon Wiseman. He led the way in dramatherapy with issues of politics and gender and sustained me when working with very severe learning difficulty in Germany and Belgium.

Dramatherapy
Theory and practice 3

Edited by Sue Jennings

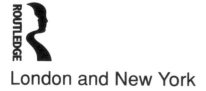

London and New York

First published 1997
by Routledge
11 New Fetter Lane, London EC4P 4EE

Simultaneously published in the USA and Canada
by Routledge
29 West 35th Street, New York, NY 10001

Typeset in Times by
Ponting–Green Publishing Services, Chesham,
Buckinghamshire
Printed and bound in Great Britain by
Biddles Ltd, Guildford and King's Lynn

British Library Cataloguing in Publication Data
A catalogue record for this book is available from the
British Library

Library of Congress Cataloguing in Publication Data
Dramatherapy: theory and practice 3 / edited by Sue Jennings.
    Includes bibliographical references and index.
    1. Psychodrama.   I. Jennings, Sue.
RC489.P7D292   1996
616.89'1523–dc20
95–26386

ISBN   0–415–13140–5 (hbk)
ISBN   0–415–13141–3 (pbk)

Contents

Illustrations

FIGURES

TABLES

Contributors

Terrence Brathwaite is an adaptive arts specialist. He leads workshops and lectures on the cross-cultural potential of dance and music in special education, at institutions including the University of Taiwan, the Laban Centre (University of London), Barbados Dance Theatre and Canada's York University. He was formerly choreographer and principal dancer with the Trinidad Ballet for ten years and toured worldwide. He is currently visiting lecturer in the Department of Drama and Theatre Arts, University of Birmingham, teaching Carnival and street theatre.

Jörg Burmeister, Dr. med. (Germany), psychiatrist, and trainer in psychodrama, is head physician at the Hard Psychiatric Clinic, Switzerland, president of the German Psychodrama Association (DFP) and psychodrama trainer of the Moreno Institute, Überlingen. He uses contrasting models of psychotherapy as a trainer and workshop leader in Europe. He has published several articles on psychodrama.

John Casson, MA, is a dramatherapist, psychodrama psychotherapist and supervisor. He is course leader of the Manchester Diploma Course in Dramatherapy at City College. He is a founder member of the Northern School of Psychodrama.

Dan Baron Cohen is a senior lecturer in theatre studies at the University of Glamorgan in South Wales. Between 1986 and 1994 he coordinated Manchester and Derry Frontline: Culture and Education, community-based organisations which specialised in working-class community theatre. The formation of both cultural organisations arose out of his collaboration with Ngugi Wa Thiong'o (1984) and Edward Bond (1981–1985). Derry Frontline is currently developing and evaluating its work in preparation for a new cultural education programme.

Cecilia Dintino, MA, RDT, is a dramatherapist at Jamaica Hospital Medical Center, New York City and a member of the New Haven Drama Therapy Institute in New Haven, Connecticut. She was formerly a dramatherapist at the National Center for Post-Traumatic Stress Disorder at the West Haven Veterans Affairs Medical Center.

David Fontana, PhD, holds posts in the University of Wales and the University of Minho, Portugal, where he is full professor. He is a qualified counselling psychologist and frequent broadcaster on both radio and television. His eighteen books have been translated into nineteen languages and include *The Meditator's Handbook*, *The Secret Language of Symbols*, *The Secret Language of Dreams*, *Growing Together*, and *The Lotus in the City*.

Alida Gersie is director of studies of the Graduate Arts Therapies Programme, University of Hertfordshire, School of Art and Design. She pioneered the therapeutic storymaking method and has conducted workshops and lectures worldwide. She has published several books including *Storymaking in Bereavement* and *Earth Tales*.

Martin Gill works as full-time dramatherapist for Gwynedd Social Services. He graduated in drama, film and music at Manchester, having spent his early life as a blacksmith and toolmaker. He was founder/director of Street Level Theatre Company, which worked with unemployed people in areas including domestic violence and abuse. He trained as a dramatherapist with the Sesame Institute and has introduced his work at Samadham in India. He has also trained in co-counselling and psychodrama.

Andy Hickson is an actor, theatre practitioner and trainer. He has run courses for social services, the probation service, the Institute of Dramatherapy and the Royal London Hospital, as well as travelling in Africa and South-east Asia. His third play, *The Silent Scream*, on the theme of bullying, has just been performed at the Albany Theatre to widespread acclaim. He has published *Creative Action Methods in Groupwork* and *Groups and Groupwork* (in preparation). He is currently on an MA course in social anthropology at the University of London.

Cyril Ives, B Phil (Ed), DipArts Ther/Ed, CertHealth Ed, FRSA, is cofounder and director of the Lantern Trust – working therapeutically with the arts in educational settings. In addition to his teaching responsibilities he works closely with the university of Greenwich in the development of innovative programmes in the field of life, death and loss studies. He is also curriculum development adviser to the dramatherapy diploma course in Athems, and to the Institute of Psychodrama and Sociodrama in London.

Roland Javanaud holds degrees in literature, philosophy and sociology from the Universities of Oxford, Liverpool and Lancaster. He qualified as a primary teacher in 1977 and as a dramatherapist in 1989. He taught drama at primary, secondary and higher education levels before joining Liverpool MIND in 1983. He is currently employed by Derbyshire Social Services as manager of a community mental health project. His dramatherapy work has principally been with people who have severe, enduring mental ill health. He also has a special interest in the use of dramatherapy for assessment, and regularly runs training workshops for social-work students on this topic.

Marina Jenkyns is a freelance dramatherapist, lecturer, trainer and director. She also has a private therapy and supervision practice. She is particularly interested in the development of supervision training for arts therapists, and in the use of dramatic text as a therapeutic medium: her book *The Play's The Thing; Exploring Text in Drama and Therapy* is published by Routledge (1996). She also explores the interface between dramatherapy and theatre.

Sue Jennings is an actress, broadcaster and author. She is Professor in theatre and dramatherapy at the University of Ulster, senior research associate at the School of Oriental and African Studies (University of London) and visiting dramatherapy professor at New York University and Tel Hai College, Israel. She founded the Institute of Dramatherapy, which is now part of the Roehampton Institute (UK), and helped to establish drama-therapy training in Greece and Israel. She has conducted research in drama-therapy and fertility, and forensic dramatherapy, and is researching her theory of *in utero* drama. She is currently touring a new solo show, *My Dear Emily*, based on the life of Elizabeth Garrett Anderson, the first female doctor to qualify in the UK.

David Read Johnson, PhD, RDT, is associate professor, Department of Psychiatry, Yale University School of Medicine, and Director of the Out-patient Division of the National Center for Post-Traumatic Stress Disorder at the West Haven Veterans Affairs Medical Center. He is the director of the New Haven Drama Therapy Institute, was previously the president of the National Association for Drama Therapy, the chair of the National Coalition of Arts Therapy Associations.

Mahnoor Yar Khan is an activist and a documentary film maker from India. She has innovated a 'drama as therapy' programme in a school in East Jerusalem, working with clinicians and actors. She is presently developing a drama programme with adolescents in the Occupied Palestinian Territories as a means of helping them to articulate and address areas of concern.

James King is lecturer in drama at the University of Ulster where he has developed courses in educational, community and therapeutic drama. He has initiated an in-service training course in dramatherapy in conjunction with the Western Area College of Nursing. He has a special interest in street theatre and environmental presentations and has performed in Belfast, Cork, Kassel in Germany, and frequently in Derry City. He has led workshops throughout Ireland and England.

Demys Kyriacou, MD, DipDth, RDTh, DipHom, is a psychiatrist and homeopath in Salonika, Greece. He is director of the Dramatherapy Institute of Northern Greece, and founder and course director of the Dramatherapy

Institute of Cyprus. He has a particular interest in the use of myths and symbols, particularly from Greek culture. He is currently writing an introductory book on dramatherapy, the first to be published in the Greek language.

Mooli Lahad, PhD, is director of dramatherapy training at Tel Hai College, Israel, and has pioneered the BASIC PH method of assessment through stories. He founded the Community Stress Prevention Centre in Kyriat Shmona, and his work on post-traumatic stress disorder is known worldwide. He is an international lecturer and workshop leader and has published extensively in English and Hebrew.

Robert J. Landy, PhD, RDT, is Professor and director of the dramatherapy programme at New York University. He is also the editor-in-chief of the international journal, *The Arts in Psychotherapy*. He has pioneered the role taxonomy method of assessment and application in dramatherapy, and has written prolifically in this area. His most recent book is *Essays in Drama Therapy: The Double Life*.

Tom Magill was born in Belfast. He is a former prisoner who worked as a drama specialist in HMP Maze with paramilitary prisoners. After training at Birmingham and Leeds universities, he worked as a professional actor. He is currently artistic director of Shankill Community Theatre Company and chair of the Community Arts Forum, Belfast. His research involves looking at applying theatre as a rehearsal for positive change in everyday life.

John D. McGinley is currently consultant forensic psychologist at Ashworth Hospital and has worked in special hospital settings for six years. Previously he worked in the Scottish prison system. He is chair of the training committee of the Division of Criminological and Legal Psychology (DCLP) of the BPsP, an area in which he has published several papers. His doctoral research is on testing and research in forensic settings.

Sue Mitchell is an educational consultant and private therapist. She developed Personagrams when at the Centre for Human Communication in Torquay. Her most recent training has been at Metanoia Psychotherapy Training Institute in London. She has published two books in the field of personal and social development. She also teaches young people with emotional and behavioural problems, and runs personal guidance training workshops for social workers, youth workers, teachers and trainee counsellors.

Roisin Muldoon was born and grew up in West Belfast. After graduating and qualifying in social work she worked in a probation hostel and field probation office in north-east England. After travel and a career break she returned to Northern Ireland as a probation officer in rural Fermanagh, and then joined the Turas Project at its outset in 1991. She is currently employed as a senior probation officer in South Belfast.

Margaret Orr, MbChB, MRCPsych, has been consultant forensic psychiatrist at Broadmoor Hospital since 1988, and during the last three years as director of medical services has promoted forensic psychotherapy and the use of creative arts therapies to enrich the treatment offered to mentally disordered offenders. She trained in psychiatry in Greenock and Knowle Hospital, working with Malcolm Faulk, a pioneer in forensic psychiatry. There she began to appreciate the impact the arts therapies can have in the treatment of mental disorder. She worked for four years in Winchester prison using art and drama to help young men communicate their feelings.

Susana Pendzik, MA, RDT, is a practising dramatherapist in Latin America and Israel. Her involvement with domestic violence began in San Francisco, through her work in *Don't Air Your Dirty Laundry*, a play on abuse. She developed and coordinated a training programme for counsellors of battered women in Mexico, and published a book and articles on this subject. She has led workshops worldwide, and currently lives in Jerusalem and teaches at Tel Hai College.

Crissiie Poulter, BA, MA, is currently lecturer in drama studies at Trinity College, University of Dublin. She is a founder member of Jubilee Community Arts in the West Midlands. She has been involved with community and youth drama in Ireland North and South since 1979, and was a member of the Gulbenkian Enquiry into Arts in Rural Areas.

Katerina Couroucli-Robertson is a dramatherapist and a teacher in special education. As a dramatherapist she works both privately, at Herma Dramatherapy Centre, and as director of studies at the dramatherapy training centre Theatre and Therapy in Athens. She has been involved in the training of dramatherapists since 1987. She coordinates a theatre and music group for people with various disabilities for Very Special Arts Hellas.

Elektra Tselikas, Dr Phil (Switzerland), DipDth, lives in Graz, Austria, and works as a freelance dramatherapist, supervisor and trainer. Besides working clinically, she is engaged in the application of dramatherapy in the fields of language therapy, multilingual/multicultural education, personnel and management development, and soft skills training. Originally a sociologist, she worked in Switzerland, Greece and China. Her special interests include social identity, multilingualism/multiculturalism, and theatricality in organisations. She has published two books and several articles on these subjects.

Lucilia Valente, PhD, is a chartered psychologist and completed her doctoral research in educational psychology. Currently she is Head of Creative Arts in the Department of Early Child Education, University of Minho, Portugal. She studied creative arts and arts therapies at the Conservatory, Lisbon. With David Fontana she has published many dramatherapy articles and book chapters in Britain and America.

Clare Woolhouse, BA, PGCE, DipDth, trained as a dramatherapist at the University of Hertfordshire and specialises in individual and small-group dramatherapy with children. She has a background in drama teaching, theatre-in-education and special education. Currently she works as a dramatherapist and support teacher with Solihull Education Authority's EBD team (for children with emotional/behavioural difficulties). She is a founder member of Dramatherapy Midlands. She works as a freelance dramatherapy workshop leader.

Introduction

Sue Jennings

Dramatherapy: Theory and practice 3 is a collection of chapters by drama-therapists and drama practitioners which opens up new areas of debate and discussion. As well as considering methods and underlying theoretical concepts, it explores new areas of application and research. Practical issues are addressed, such as funding and support, and the problems of 'product' or 'process'. Cross-cultural ideas begin to be examined in relation to the rituals and dramas extant in subcultures and societies. Subject matter derives from theatre and drama as well as psychotherapy, and the various dramatherapists juggle their orientation between these polarities.

The book is divided into four main subject areas, though all interlink at several levels. Part I describes developments in theory and method, and addresses the issue of dramatherapists developing a dramatherapeutic language in supervision and practice. In Part II, based on case-history material involving individuals and groups, several practitioners focus on the importance of evaluation and assessment. Part III focuses on the important area of gender issues both in supervision and practice. Part IV looks at dramatherapy as a means of cultural expression and also of political exploration. This part includes several contributions from areas where there is tension and conflict. The aim of these chapters is not to take sides in the political debate, but to consider how dramatherapy can perhaps be useful as a means of exploration and change. As we can see, some chapters are practical experiments and others are reflective ideas. Several consider the meaning of the word 'therapy'.

Theory and practice 1 is an introductory textbook which considers basic principles in dramatherapy application in training and practice; *Theory and practice 2* opened up new areas for consideration, with important contributions from the USA and Israel. It is interesting that this third volume (the last in the series) includes chapters which make use of the theory outlined in volumes 1 and 2, such as the EPR developmental paradigm.

Dramatherapy is beginning to develop its own theory and methodology as well as models for supervision, assessment and evaluative research. Increasingly dramatherapists are addressing the issue of a continuum of care, where dramatherapeutic ideas are being used preventively as a means of maintaining health, as well as curatively in various therapeutic interventions for ill health.

Dramatherapy is firmly established in many countries, as the international diversity of the contributors illustrates. Furthermore, countries that started dramatherapy training from UK models are now developing their own programmes, addressing their own cultural and clinical needs. As a pioneer in the field, this is a source of constant delight to me.

IMPORTANT NOTE

Whereas all the methods and techniques described in this book have been applied in supervised and professional contexts, the authors do not take responsibility for their being practised without the appropriate training. Dramatherapy is a dynamic medium which can take people unawares. All dramatherapists adhere to a code of practice and ethics after their training and registration. Dramatherapy is recognised as a profession by the Department of Health. (Detailed information is available from: The British Association for Dramatherapists, 5 Sunnydale Villas, Durlston, Swanage, Dorset BH19 2HY.)

Part I

Developments in theory and method

Chapter 1

'Knocking at the gate'

Dramatherapy and the critical tradition

Roland Javanaud

INTRODUCTION

Dramatherapy has reached a point in its development where it is sufficiently well established and mature for us to to stand back and examine not only its achievements but also the current gaps in theory and practice. This chapter explores one such neglected area – namely, the relevance to practising dramatherapists of the great English literary critics.[1]

Dramatherapy is an eclectic discipline, one of its greatest strengths being its ability to draw inspiration from a wide range of source materials. Ordinary, everyday experiences, such as watching soap operas on television, and more esoteric pursuits, such as exploring *The Tibetan Book of the Dead*, *The Divine Comedy* or the Tarot Pack, can equally be used to form the starting point of valuable dramatherapeutic activity – and indeed all these subjects have recently been the focal point of dramatherapy workshops or published articles. It sometimes seems that for dramatherapy, as for the drama itself, there is no area of human experience which lies outside its remit. Dramatherapists arrive at the sessions they are to facilitate carrying a bag, either figurative or literal, full of the most bewildering variety of ideas and artefacts, which they take out and use, as and when the process requires.

This being the case, it oughtn't to be too difficult an enterprise to provide examples of ways in which a study of the great English literary critics could prove beneficial to practising dramatherapists. However, my aim in what follows is to do rather more than simply that. There is, it seems to me, an important distinction to be drawn between those subjects, on the one hand, which can be used to provide materials for dramatherapy (*EastEnders*, Dante, etc.) and those, on the other, with which we need to be familiar in order fully to understand the origins and process of dramatherapy itself. Students on dramatherapy training courses are usually required to spend some time studying the ancient theatre, healing rituals of non-European cultures, children's play and the literature of psychotherapy. These topics do not appear arbitrarily on the syllabus of training courses, as an alternative to any number of other topics which would have done just as well, but because students must know something about them if they are to arrive at an understanding of what dramatherapy is. In this sense, the study of Aristotle, Moreno and Slade is fundamental for the dramatherapist, whilst seeking out useful material from, say, *Coronation Street* or delving into the *I Ching* may be regarded as optional, if worthwhile, sidelines. I hope to be able to show that at least some of the work of the critics I shall be discussing below falls into the category of 'essential basic reading for the dramatherapist' rather than into that of 'might be handy for a one-off workshop', and I shall leave it to readers and, who knows, perhaps to reviewers (see note 1) to judge to what extent I am successful.

THE CLASSICAL UNITIES

Dr Johnson's great edition of Shakespeare appeared in October 1765, the monumental product of nine long years' laborious study. Johnson's edition provided the most reliable version of Shakespeare's text produced up to that time, restoring to their original First Folio form many of the 'corrections' and 'improvements' mistakenly or wilfully made by previous editors. Extensive explanatory and critical notes on particular passages and an overall *General Observation* on each of the plays constitute in themselves a major critical enterprise, for which future generations of Shakespeare scholars have had good reason to feel indebted. Only when he had completed the arduous task of preparing and annotating the text did Johnson sit down to write his famous *Preface to Shakespeare*, one of the glories of English literary criticism. 'At that time', writes John Wain, in his splendid *Samuel Johnson*,

> Johnson must have come close to knowing the entire text of Shakespeare by heart. The strongly confident generalizations of the preface are rooted in the line-by-line analysis of particular passages. Having commented on, explained, as a last resort even conjectured, thousands of times, he is ready with a grand over-all view which is like the summing-up of some great judge.
>
> (Wain 1980, p. 255)

One of the subjects which occupied Johnson in his *Preface* was that of Shakespeare's disregard of the supposedly Aristotelian unities of time, place and action. Almost a hundred years earlier, in his essay *Of Dramatick Poesie* (1668), John Dryden had asked a pair of related questions: were the dramatic works of the classical writers to be preferred to those of the moderns, and could a consideration of the extent to which they respectively adhered to the unities help to resolve the issue? Dryden's essay takes the form of a dramatic dialogue, each of the four speakers presenting a contrasting viewpoint. The bulk of the debate on the issue of the unities is contained in an interchange between two of the protagonists – Crites, who argues for the superiority of the ancients, and Eugenius, who defends the moderns.
  Crites begins by stating what the unities are. 1. Time: ideally the length of

time it takes to perform a play should correspond to the length of time taken up by the actions the play represents, or, at the very least, the time imagined as passing in the course of a performance should not exceed twenty-four hours. 2. Place: 'That the Scene ought to be continu'd through the Play, in the same place where it was laid in the beginning.' 3. Action: a play should have a single main plot, to which any so-called 'underplots' are clearly both related and subservient.

'If by these Rules', claims Crites,

> we should judge our modern Plays; 'tis probable, that few of them would endure the tryal: that which should be the business of a day, takes up in some of them an age; instead of one action they are the Epitomes of a mans life; and for one spot of ground (which the stage should represent) we are sometimes in more Countries than the map can shew us.

> (Dryden 1964, pp. 48–49)

Eugenius, in response, contests that, despite what is popularly supposed, the unities ever formed part of the prescribed classical rules of drama. Those of time and action may possibly have, though even that is far from certain, but

> The Unity of Place, how ever it might be practised by them, was never any of their Rules: We neither find it in Aristotle, Horace, or any who have written of it, till in our age the French Poets first made it a Precept of the Stage.

> (p. 55)

Finally, even if the unity rules were accepted by classical dramatists, observation of actual plays shows that in practice they were less rather than more governed by them than many playwrights of the modern period.

The reader of Dryden's *Essay* is likely to derive much enjoyment from the author's ability to depict a range of divergent opinions, all equally strongly argued and with an equally vivid, at times even pugnacious, turn of phrase. In this respect Dryden is comparable to the sensitive psychodrama director, or group member, doubling accurately and in turn for a series of auxiliaries who may be at variance or in conflict with each other. This is so much of a pattern that it is hard to say for certain at any point to which of his speakers' positions Dryden himself inclines. It is probable, however, that Dryden, founder member of what later came to be called the neo-classical movement, believed that 'the French Poets', Racine and Corneille, were right to keep step with what they took to be classical guidelines, whether or not Greek or Roman authors had either known or followed them. Certainly Dryden's own *All For Love or The World Well Lost* (1678) provides an extraordinary example of how a work as unregardful of the classical rules as any censured by Crites – in this case Shakespeare's *Antony and Cleopatra* – could be turned into one exemplifying them all; though whether the transformation constitutes an improvement is a question which has long since ceased to be regarded as one worth asking, Shakespeare's play continuing to absorb audiences, listeners and readers on a worldwide basis, whilst Dryden's carries the status of a historical curiosity.

Johnson takes a very different and, in the light of what had gone before, wholly refreshing approach to the issue. He begins by frankly acknowledging that Shakespeare's plays fail entirely to accord with the rules of unity, most notably those of time and place:

> To the unities of time and place he has shown no regard; and perhaps a nearer view of the principles on which they stand will diminish their value and withdraw from them the veneration which, from the time of Corneille, they have very generally received, by discovering that they have given more trouble to the poet than pleasure to the auditor.
>
> (Johnson 1969, p. 69)

Johnson then restates the argument in favour of the unities, in terms not markedly different from those Dryden had put into the mouth of Crites:

> The necessity of observing the unities of time and place arises from the supposed necessity of making the drama credible. The critics hold it impossible that an action of months or years can be possibly believed to pass in three hours; or that the spectator can suppose himself to sit in the theatre while ambassadors go and return between distant kings, while armies are levied and towns besieged, while an exile wanders and returns, or till he whom they saw courting his mistress shall lament the untimely fall of his son. The mind revolts from evident falsehood, and fiction loses its force when it departs from the resemblance of reality.
>
> (p. 69)

Having presented the argument thus, fairly and even forcibly, Johnson now proceeds, in one of the most sparkling passages in the whole of English prose, to tear it to pieces. I make no apology for quoting at length.

> The objection arising from the impossibility of passing the first hour at Alexandria and the next at Rome, supposes that when the play opens the spectator really imagines himself at Alexandria and believes that his walk to the theatre has been a voyage to Egypt, and that he lives in the days of Antony and Cleopatra. Surely he that imagines this may imagine more. He that can take the stage at one time for the palace of the Ptolemies may take it in half an hour for the promontory of Actium. Delusion, if delusion be admitted, has no certain limitation; if the spectator can once be persuaded that his old acquaintance are Alexander and Caesar, that a room illuminated with candles is the plain of Pharsalia or the bank of Granicus, he is in a state of elevation above the reach of reason or truth, and from the heights of empyrean poetry may despise the circumscriptions of terrestrial nature.

There is no reason why a mind thus wandering in ecstasy should count the clock, or why an hour should not be a century in that calenture of the brains that can make the stage a field.

(p. 70)

The old argument for the unities had been basically a logical one. If we believe ourselves to be in a particular time and place at the start of the action, it is illogical to expect us to imagine ourselves elsewhere at some later point. Johnson takes the line of contesting the initial premise. Thereafter, even if the argument following from it is valid, the conclusion it delivers will be false. What makes Johnson's approach so startlingly innovative, however, really has nothing to do with logic. The question which interested him is in fact a psychological one: what processes are going on in the minds of those present at, and perhaps absorbed by, a dramatic performance? The answer which he provides is perhaps the earliest statement of the engagement/ distancing synthesis which lies at the heart of dramatherapy theory and practice. Johnson clearly understood that the spectators at a play, and, one might add, the performers, simultaneously know that they are not present at the time or in the places the play represents and yet, in some sense, believe and even respond as if they were.

Sixteen years prior to the publication of Johnson's *Preface*, Henry Fielding included in his novel *Tom Jones* (1749) a hilarious chapter which gives an account of a visit by Partridge, an uneducated countryman, to a London theatre for a performance of *Hamlet*. Partridge provides a perfect example of the 'mind wandering in ecstasy' referred to by Johnson. Throughout the performance he remains incapable of differentiating between the representation and the thing represented. At each appearance of the ghost of Hamlet's father he disrupts the performance and distracts the audience by his cries of fear and alarm. This is all good slapstick humour, in Fielding's richest vein, but it raises important issues for the dramatherapist.

On many occasions, in different dramatherapy groups, I have used an exercise which I call 'Jungle Escape', first introduced to me by David Powley when I was a student on the York Dramatherapy training course. Group participants are invited to imagine that their plane has crashed in the middle of a jungle and that they have been captured and imprisoned by hostile natives. They are told that a guard stands outside their place of confinement, and that beyond him lies a high wall. Past the wall lie a series of further obstacles, including a crocodile-infested swamp, a waterfall, a desert, a mountain range, etc. Before the improvisation starts they are given time, as a group, to select three items to take with them on their bid for escape.

This can be a very powerful, absorbing and at times even frightening exercise. As a participant in it, I remained aware throughout that we were in fact in the drama studio; at another level, however, the bare floorboards and plain walls seemed to have turned into stepping stones across perilous fast-flowing rivers or into vast sand dunes. Other participants, actually my colleagues, became either staunch allies or mortal enemies. I have since seen the same experience replicated countless times amongst participants in groups where I have facilitated the exercise. The role of the facilitator is that of encouraging engagement in the activity, whilst at the same time remaining alert to the genuine risk, at a time when emotions are prone to be running high, of groups members becoming so taken up by the fantasy that they lose sight of the line which divides it from reality. It is sometimes helpful for the facilitator to take a small, occasional part in the improvisation (e.g. friendly spirit), from where he or she[2] can steer the action at critical or dangerous moments, without disrupting the spell.

Similar concerns around the issues of engagement and detachment are of course very much the business of the psychodrama director. The protagonist who is exploring her current difficulties needs to get emotionally close enough to their origins to be able to work effectively; too close, however, and there is a risk of retraumatisation and real psychological harm. The skilful director knows how and when either to engage the protagonist in the drama or distance her from it; he knows when it is important for the protagonist to be there, then, and when here, now; he knows when it is vital to remain in London and when a trip, at least part of the way, to Alexandria will be therapeutically beneficial. And the ultimate source of this knowledge about distancing is none other than Samuel Johnson.

Before finally moving on from the question of the unities, I cannot resist pointing out that whilst there is no logical or psychological reason why the dramatist or dramatherapist should feel bound by such restrictions, there is, equally, no reason why she should not at times choose to observe them. After a series of sessions devoted to wide-ranging improvisational exercises (such as 'Jungle Escape'), it may be settling and focusing for a group to work on some more highly structured, unified, material.

A group of people with severe enduring mental ill health had been through a month's sessions of very free improvisational work. They had enjoyed the freedom this had given them, the sense they had of being able to take up and drop themes at will, without feeling dictated to by a predetermined plan or form, and without the need for rehearsal or repetition. Towards the end of the final session of this sort, however, I felt that the group's energy was running low, almost that the members had become exhausted by their own creativity and sense of fun.

For the following session I introduced a poem entitled 'The Moon' from Robert Louis Stevenson's *A Child's Garden of Verses*:

> The moon has a face like the clock in the hall;
> She shines on thieves on the garden wall,
> On streets and fields and harbour quays,
> And birdies asleep in the forks of the trees.

The squalling cat and the squeaking mouse,
The howling dog by the door of the house,
The bat that lies in bed at noon,
All love to be out by the light of the moon.

But all of the things that belong to the day
Cuddle to sleep to be out of her way;
And flowers and children close their eyes
Till up in the morning the sun shall rise.

Line by line, with much concentration and much repetition, we put the whole together into a dramatic performance:

Line one: One of the group members becomes the clock in the hall, her arm a swinging pendulum. She is flanked by two other group members – one 'tick', one 'tock'. At the end of the line, the moon rises up on a chair above and behind the clock.

Line two: Two thieves enter, equipped with swag bags, and climb on the garden wall, made up of chairs. 'Let's get this job done, Bert', says one to the other.

Line three: A harbour scene, complete with fishermen, boats and the sounds of the sea.

Line four: On the opposite side of the room, a little bird tweets and puts its head under its wing.

Line five: A group of squalling cats position themselves on the wall vacated by the burglars. One of them chases a squeaking mouse past . . .

Line six: . . . the howling dog at the door of the house.

Line seven: A bat gets out of bed, stretches and begins to flit about the room.

Line eight: Chorus of noises from all those who love to out by the light of the moon.

Lines nine and ten: Three flowers close up and droop their heads.

Line eleven: Three children are tucked up in bed and are read a story by dad.

Line twelve: The moon sinks down on the chair behind the clock, whilst, on the opposite side of the room, the sun rises. The flowers straighten up and open up. The children jump out of bed and begin to play 'Ring a Ring o' Roses'. When they get to 'all fall down', everyone, except the clock and the sun, falls down. The clock begins to falter – there are a few halting 'tick tocks', followed by total silence.

After the romps of the previous weeks, the group seemed to benefit from and to appreciate the opportunity to work intensely on a single, structured piece. Afterwards it occurred to me that Stevenson's poem, and indeed our dramatisation of it, follows all the classical unities.[3] The action covers no more than a twelve-hour span between the rising of the moon and that of the sun. In one sense the piece could be said to be set in a multitude of places, but if one takes the moon's range of vision as the determining factor, everything occurs at the same spot, and the same point could be made with regard to the action.

I am not of course suggesting anything so ludicrous as that dramatherapists should construct any of their sessions with the intention of according with the unities – and I don't suppose I would have thought of this myself had not this particular session happened to coincide with my work on this chapter. A far more general point worth making, however, is that the practising dramatherapist does well to vary the form and at times to intersperse moments of classical focus and restraint into the more exuberant (Shakespearean) style with which he is, perhaps, more likely to be familiar.

'KNOCKING AT THE GATE'

When one moves on from the critical writings of eighteenth-century writers like Johnson to those of the nineteenth-century Romantics (Coleridge, Lamb, Hazlitt, De Quincey), one is struck by the extent to which the stage, and the dramatic process, is moved out of the central frame of reference. Shakespeare, in particular, is now far more likely to be viewed as a great poet than as a great dramatist. His compositions are works of literature, to be commented on by the critic, far more than they are plays to be performed. Lamb even went so far as to condemn the very idea of performance:

> Never let me be so ungrateful as to forget the very high degree of satisfaction which I received some years back from seeing for the first time a tragedy of Shakespeare performed, in which . . . two great performers sustained the principal parts. It seemed to embody and realise conceptions which had hitherto assumed no distinct shape. But dearly do we pay all our life after for this juvenile pleasure, this sense of distinctness. When the novelty is past, we find to our cost that instead of realising an idea, we have only materialised and brought down a fine image to the standard of flesh and blood. We have let go a dream, in quest of an unattainable substance.
>
> How cruelly this operates upon the mind, to have its free conceptions thus crampt and pressed down to the measure of a strait-lacing actuality, may be judged from that delightful sensation of freshness, with which we turn to those plays of Shakespeare which have escaped being performed, and to those passages in the acting plays of the same writer which have happily been left out in the performance . . .
>
> It may seem a paradox, but I cannot help being of the opinion that the plays of Shakepeare are less calculated for performance on a stage, than are those of almost any other dramatist whatever. There is so much in them, which comes not under the province of acting, with which eye, and tone, and gesture, have nothing to do.

(Lamb 1833, pp. 102–104)

Lamb's comments here bring to mind the howls of protest which never fail to be sent up on any occasion a Dickens or a George Eliot novel is dramatised as a television serial. Lamb's remarks, however, seem even harder to sympathise with. It is after all quite true that large parts of, say, *Middlemarch* are inevitably and irretrievably lost in a television dramatisation, and viewers who felt that, having seen the television performance, they knew the work would be sadly deluded. But to say that Shakespeare's text best remains locked up in the pages of books seems scarcely more absurd than to suggest the works of Beethoven are too sublime actually to be heard, and should instead be read, in silence, by musicologists.

It is perhaps worth considering that the Romantic critics' distaste for seeing Shakespeare performed may have as much or more to do with with socio-political factors as it does with aesthetics. Looking back in early middle age to the first period of the French Revolution, when it seemed that not merely poetry but society itself stood on the verge of radical and permanent transformation, Wordsworth, in his long autobiographical poem, *The Prelude* (1805), remembered how

Bliss was it in that dawn to be alive,
But to be young was very heaven . . .
    (Wordsworth 1960, p. 196)

and he goes on to compare the experience of being in France at this time of cultural and political change to that of inhabiting a dream or visiting a 'Country in Romance'. The bright hopes for a changed society were dispelled by the later brutalities of the Revolution, a long European war and an extended period of political reaction at home. Whilst Wordsworth himself, like his one-time friend and collaborator Coleridge, took refuge in increasingly right-wing political positions, the younger generation of Romantic poets (Shelley, perhaps, excepted) ceased to believe in revolution in anything other than an artistic sense. The attempt to turn the dream of a brave new world into a reality had been a disappointing failure, and the will to try again was absent. In this context, Lamb's resistance to the enterprise of performing Shakespeare becomes easier to understand. Dramatherapists, however, or those using its methods (one thinks of Boal's work in using drama as a way of raising political consciousness and prompting social transformation) need, for their clients' sakes, to retain a commitment to the belief that change is possible, that dreams can be embodied and that, so to speak, the Shakespearean word can become theatrical flesh, without a diminishment of magic or power.

The propensity of the Romantic critics to shy away from performance, particularly of Shakespeare, does not however mean that their writings are without relevance to the dramatherapist, and I should like to look now at three passages which I feel are particularly instructive.

In his famous essay 'On the Knocking at the Gate in *Macbeth*' Thomas De

Quincey sets out to answer a question which, he states at the outset, had perplexed him since his youth:

> The knocking at the gate, which succeeds to the murder of Duncan, produced to my feelings an effect for which I could never account. The effect was, that it reflected back upon the murder a peculiar awfulness and a depth of solemnity; yet, however obstinately I endeavoured with my understanding to comprehend this, for many years I never could see why it should produce such an effect.
>
> (De Quincey 1909, p. 144)

De Quincey goes on to state, in the best dramatherapeutic tradition, that the intellect or understanding is often a very unhelpful guide, and that in cases such as the one he is discussing, it is only by becoming more aware of our emotional or intuitive responses that we shall ever arrive at the truth.

De Quincey then draws a parallel between the knocking at the gate scene and two other imagined moments of emotional intensity. Consider, he says, a situation in which a loved one is perceived to be in danger, perhaps from a fainting fit. It is at that moment when a sigh or a stirring announces that the danger is past that the witness to the scene is most affected by emotion. Or, he goes on,

> if the reader has ever been present in a vast metropolis, on the day when some great national idol was carried in funeral pomp to his grave, and, chancing to walk near the course through which it passed, has felt powerfully in the silence and desertion of the streets, and in the stagnation of ordinary business, the deep interest which at that moment was possessing the heart of man – if all at once he should hear the death-like stillness broken up by the sound of wheels rattling away from the scene, and making known that the transitory vision was dissolved, he will be aware that at no moment was his sense of the complete suspension and pause in ordinary human concerns so full and affecting, as at that moment when the suspension ceases and the goings-on of human life are suddenly resumed.
>
> (p. 148)

Likewise, he concludes, it is not until the knocking at the gate in Shakespeare's play is heard that the spectator is awakened from a trance-like condition and, as the ordinary concerns of life reassert themselves, becomes aware, in its full horror, 'of the awful parenthesis that had suspended them' (p. 148).

De Quincey's insights here have a bearing on our earlier discussion on engagement and distancing. The knocking at the gate, the sigh or stirring and the rattling wheels are the archways through which we pass from high-level involvement in a dramatic process, with attendant high emotions, back to the world of normal consciousness and everyday concerns. Those taking others on such journeys (that is, dramatherapists) need to able to bring them safely back and would do well to remember De Quincey's warning that it is at the moment of transition, at the point when the voyage seems to be completed, that the traveller is most at the mercy of the emotions it has exposed.

It is interesting to note that the scene which begins with the knocking at the gate is the only genuinely comic one in the whole of *Macbeth*. De Quincey does not comment on that in this essay, but in another one, edited by H. Darbishire under the title of 'Law of Ebb and Flow in Works of Art', he looks in some detail, focusing on this occasion on the works of Homer and Milton, at the aesthetic necessity of juxtaposing passages of poetic intensity and concentration with those of humour, relaxation and relief. Here again are valuable messages for the dramatherapist. Once on the wing, in a single session or over a series of them, the therapist may experience an urge to remain in flight, to complete the therapeutic work, so to speak, at full throttle. She needs to remember that the therapeutic medium in which she is working is an art form, and that that which is wrong for the art cannot be right for the therapy. Moments of low intensity, repose and comic relief are as integral a part of the therapeutic process as they are of a tragedy or an epic poem.

In his *Lectures on the English Poets* (1818) William Hazlitt pays tribute to the genius of Shakepeare. It is a wonderful passage and I quote it at length below, with no other comment than that of inviting the reader to substitute for the word 'Shakespeare' each time it occurs some such phrase as 'the ideal dramatherapist' and to consider how adequate a description it then becomes:

> The striking peculiarity of Shakespeare's mind was its generic quality, its power of communication with all other minds – so that it contained a universe of thought and feeling within itself, and had no one peculiar bias, or exclusive excellence more than another. He was just like any other man, but that he was like all other men. He was the least of an egotist that it was possible to be. He was nothing in himself; but he was all that others were, or that they could become. He not only had in himself the germs of every faculty and feeling, but he could follow them by anticipation, intuitively, into all their conceivable ramifications, through every change of fortune or conflict of passion, or turn of thought. He had a mind reflecting ages past and present: – all the people that ever lived are there. There was no respect of persons with him. His genius shone equally on the evil and the good, on the wise and the foolish, the monarch and the beggar. . . . The world of spirits lay open to him, like the world of real men and women.
>
> (Hazlitt 1910, p. 47)

Reading through the notes on particular passages in Shakepeare's plays in Johnson's great edition, or the equally fine notes by Coleridge, one is struck again and again by the immense care and attention these critics bring to their work. Explaining a difficult phrase, drawing attention to a previously unnoticed train of imagery, uncovering a lost irony – these are the tasks they undertake with astonishing persistence and devotion. By the time we reach a writer like A.C. Bradley, writing towards the turn of the century, the study has become even more meticulous. Bradley wants to know the answer to questions such as 'What was the exact sequence of events before the opening of the action in *Hamlet*?' or 'Did Lady Macbeth really faint?', and he very often, perhaps to the reader's surprise, finds evidence from the actual text to support whatever view he adopts. Bradley recognises that there are occasions when Shakepeare's writing is sloppy or defective, but, he claims, though 'it is possible to look for subtlety in the wrong place in Shakespeare . . . in the right places it is not possible to find too much' (Bradley 1904, p. 60). The general consensus, then, was that the works of Shakespeare both merit and reward detailed critical scrutiny, and that the more we seek in them the more we shall find.

Shakepeare's plays certainly are remarkable in this respect. The spectator (or the reader) has a sense of the uniqueness of practically each character, as manifested by idiosyncratic turns of phrase, thought patterns or strands of imagery. He has a strong feeling that what we are witnessing is merely part of a much larger whole – that events contemporaneous with the drama are being enacted, so to speak, in the wings, and that the characters, or the history, went on before and will go on after the curtain rises and falls. It is this sense, no doubt, which has prompted other writers to make an attempt to fill in the gaps, the parts we feel somehow are there, but never actually see – for example Tom Stoppard in *Rosencrantz and Guildenstern are Dead*.

No praise for an author capable of creating such impressions can be too high, but it is essential to note that, whilst other literature rarely evokes the same responses, life itself constantly does so. Shakespeare is to be revered, not for creating an impression of profundity in the plays greater than is present in life, but in enabling us to recognise that it is there. It's like the famous pauses and patterns of broken speech in the early plays of Pinter. To begin with audiences were outraged. 'People simply don't speak like that', they said. But what they meant was, people in plays didn't, or hadn't till Pinter. It took the critics to point out that Pinter had simply chosen to replicate the speech of actual life, rather than that of theatrical convention.

I think the reader will by now see where I am leading. It was not until the critics, through painstaking attention to the minutest detail, had shown how it was possible to draw meaning from a text – and the text of Shakespeare was pre-eminently suitable for this task – that the psychologists, the analysts and the therapists could begin to do the same from actual human interaction, in one-to-one therapeutic work or in groups. The dramatherapist must have the same astute eye and attentive ear, the same ability to make inspired links between different strands of a plot and the same determination resolutely to read beneath the surface as did Johnson, Coleridge or Bradley. In this sense the debt we owe to the critics is immeasurable.

CONCLUSIONS

What then, by way of summary, can we say of the contribution of literary criticism to the the theory and practice of modern dramatherapy?

The arguments around the unities highlight the need for an approach which, as the situation requires, can be either free-ranging and intensely varied on the one hand, or focused and highly structured on the other.

Johnson (and also Fielding) underline the importance of understanding the nature of engagement and distancing in our experience of drama. A failure to differentiate between what the drama is and what it means can be fatal to the therapeutic process.

The Romantic critics' distrust of performance should be seen in a socio-political, as well as an artistic, light and should act as a warning to dramatherapists of the extent to which cultural factors, often unconsciously, affect what purport to be argued choices.

De Quincey's observations on the role of emotion and intuition in critical and artistic appreciation are of immediate and obvious relevance to drama-therapists. His metaphor of 'knocking at the gate' – that is, managing liminality – could become a key text in the study of an area which to date has begun with the ideas of Van Gennep (1908, trans. 1960). His remarks on the importance of varying the levels of intensity in the production of works of art are equally appropriate within the context of therapy.

Much of what Hazlitt says of the genius of Shakespeare is startlingly applicable to the 'genius' of dramatherapy, and perhaps this is less of a coincidence than one might at first think.

Finally, and perhaps most importantly, the literary critics, in their often passionate quest to uncover meaning and discover connections, both within individual works and between the writings of different authors, act as a model and inspiration for the conscientious and creative dramatherapist.

This chapter has been a brief introduction to an area of study which could certainly be profitably developed, and I have no doubt that further research into the works of the writers we have been considering could produce a wealth of interesting material. In the end, though, perhaps the issue is as much one of acknowledgement as it is of applicability. We may very well be able to function effectively and sensitively as dramatherapists without ever having heard of, let alone read, Dryden or De Quincey – but I doubt that drama-therapy would be quite what it is had they never written. It's a matter, at the last, of 'credit where credit's due'.

NOTES

1 The original impetus for this chapter came from a review of *The Handbook of Dramatherapy* which I wrote for the *Dramatherapy Journal* (Javanaud 1994). In that review I remarked that a study of the works of Johnson, Hazlitt and Coleridge, amongst others, could prove fertile ground for the dramatherapy theorist. Shortly

after the review appeared, Sue Jennings, co-author of the *Handbook* and editor of the present collection, prompted by my friend and colleague, John Casson, invited me to write a piece which would set about filling this particular gap.

2 For the sake of convenience I alternate masculine and feminine forms in the rest of the chapter.

3 In a letter to a friend Stevenson (1952, p. 11) describes his children's poems as 'rhymes' and 'jingles' and, curiously enough, goes on to remark that he doesn't 'go in for eternity or the three unities . . .' – an example, surely, of the poet's self-effacement, rather than an accurate account of his artistic intent.

REFERENCES

Bradley, A.C. (1904) *Shakespearean Tragedy*, London: Macmillan.

Coleridge, S.T. (1906) *Biographia Literaria*, ed. A. Symons, London: Dent.

—— (1960) *Shakepearean Criticism*, ed. T. Middleton Raysor, London: Dent.

De Quincey, T. (1909) *Literary Criticism*, ed. H. Darbishire, London: Frowde.

Dryden, J. (1964) *Of Dramatick Poesie*, ed. J.T. Boulton, London: Oxford University Press.

Fielding, H. (1966) *Tom Jones*, Harmondsworth, UK: Penguin.

Hazlitt, W. (1910) *Lectures on the English Poets*, London: Dent.

Javanaud, R. (1994) Review of S. Jennings *et al. The Handbook of Dramatherapy* in *Journal of the British Association for Dramatherapists* 16(1): 24–25.

Jennings, S., A. Catlanach, S. Mitchell, A. Chesner and B. Meldrum (1994) *The Handbook of Dramatherapy*, London: Routledge.

Johnson, S. (1969) *On Shakespeare*, ed. W.K. Wimsatt, Harmondsworth, UK: Penguin.

Lamb, C. (1833) *Prose Works*, London: Moxon.

Stevenson, R.L. (1952) *A Child's Garden of Verses*, Harmondsworth, UK: Penguin.

Stoppard, T. (1967) *Rosencrantz and Guildenstern are Dead*, London: Faber & Faber.

Van Gennep, A. (1960) *The Rites of Passage*, trans. M.B. Vizedom and G.L. Caffee, London: Routledge.

Wain, J. (1980) *Samuel Johnson*, London: MacMillan.

Wordsworth, W. (1960) *The Prelude*, ed. H. Darbishire, London: Oxford University Press.

Chapter 2

Assessing client progress in dramatherapy

Lucilia Valente and David Fontana

WHAT IS PSYCHOLOGICAL HEALTH?

The meaning and nature of psychological health present some of the most taxing issues facing those involved in the psychotherapeutic process. Even in an area such as dramatherapy, where the client can be observed in an expressive as well as in a verbal context, assessment of his or her progress presents a number of major problems to the therapist. These stem at base from the prior lack of any universally agreed definition among psychologists and psychotherapists of what is meant by psychological health. In the absence of such a definition, it can become difficult to define clear therapeutic goals, and thus to monitor progress within an appropriately objective context.

This is not to deny the fact that all clients are individuals, and that therapeutic objectives must be tailored to the concept of specific as opposed to generalised needs; nor is it to deny the right of the clients themselves to identify appropriate therapeutic aims. Except in rare instances, therapy should never be therapist-driven, and there can be dangers in any attempt to impose upon clients our own interpretation of what it means to be a psychologically whole person. Clients may in any case disagree with this interpretation, or may need time and space in which to arrive at an interpretation of their own. In addition many clients, when entering therapy, are unsure of where they want to go, and of what it would feel like to get there, and need time and space in which to clarify their personal therapeutic goals. Other clients may favour a process-orientated therapeutic experience from which goals may or may not in due course arise.

However, few therapists subscribe these days to the extreme existentialist view popular in the 1960s and 1970s (see for example Boss 1977) that the client must be given complete freedom to define his or her own *being-in-the-world*. Most accept that there are a wide range of clues that we use to monitor client progress, and a wide range of outcomes that we regard as having preference over others. Furthermore, unless the dramatherapist can clarify what is meant by good therapeutic consequences, it will remain difficult to shape research capable of demonstrating to other professionals the efficacy of dramatherapeutic experience (Payne 1993). In the absence of an objective profile of psychological health, any assessment of the client's current state of being must remain worryingly partial. Johnson (1988) supports Bruscia in affirming that assessment in the creative arts therapies helps the therapist respectively to describe clients' behaviour more exactly, to determine an accurate diagnosis, to point towards appropriate treatment methods, and to extend both empirical and theoretical knowledge.

Freud's criteria

One of the most succinct descriptions of psychological health was that of Freud (1957), namely that the psychologically healthy person is one who has the ability to *work* and to *love*. By this Freud meant the ability respectively to engage in productive and self-fulfilling activity, and to sustain emotionally warm and supportive relationships with others and with oneself. Discussing this abbreviated criteria, Allport (1961) added a third variable, namely the ability to *play*, that is to enjoy non-serious activity which is entertaining and recreational, and not driven primarily by extrinsic goals or objectives.

We have suggested (Fontana and Valente 1991) that this three-fold model should be supplemented by a fourth criterion, the ability to *pray*. The word *pray* is not used in any narrowly religious sense, but to stand for the ability to appreciate the numinous quality of life, the beauty and mystery that can hold us spellbound, expressed through the creative arts and the mystical and spiritual literature of the world. As we shall see shortly, this ability links with the *peak experiences* and the *unifying philosophy of life* referred to respectively by Maslow (1970) and by Allport (1961), and at its deepest level it also includes gratitude for the gift of our individual human lives (Maslow's *life appreciation* variable). In our experience, this gratitude reflects itself in such qualities as a generally positive and optimistic attitude towards life, and a readiness to meet and place in perspective the challenges it has to offer.

It should also be pointed out that, in most instances, the ability successfully to *work*, *love*, *play* and *pray* subsumes an ability to *communicate*. In each of these four areas, information, ideas, emotions, feelings, appraisals, needs, expectations, interests and insights frequently require to be shared with others. Indeed, in most cases, sharing can define and enhance the cognitive or affective experiences concerned, and render them part of the commerce of social living. In addition, communication, whether verbal or through touch, body language or visual expression, reassures the individual of his or her own humanity, and invites responses from others which can be variously educative, stimulating, provocative, healing or diverting. The ability to communicate psychologically healthy levels of being also allows the individual to serve as a valuable role model, and thus to modify and enhance the broad texture of social and cultural living.

Maslow and self-actualisation

Freud's attempt to define psychological health was a valuable initiative in that it demonstrated that what at first sight seems an imponderable, can actually be represented in objective psychological terms. It is Maslow. however, rather than Freud, who is most clearly associated with attempts to define psychological health. In the course of his research into the concept, Maslow (1970), individually interviewed a sample of men and women nominated by their peers as markedly psychologically mature. The results suggested to him that such people appear to have achieved a state which he called *self-actualisation*, and which indicates that they have reached much of their full potential as human beings (Jung would have said they were in proper contact with all their psychological functions, instead of living in a restricted part of their inner being). Self-actualised people were found by Maslow to be perceptive, emotionally open, natural and spontaneous, problem-centred in their approach (as opposed to self-centred), happy with their own company, autonomous (i.e. independent rather than under the control of events or of other people), accepting of self and others (as opposed to being over-critical and judgemental), appreciative of life, capable of deep relationships with loved ones, humorous, creative, ethical, goal-orientated, democratic and consistent.

Reassuringly for the rest of us, Maslow discovered that they also share certain imperfections, some of which arise paradoxically from their strengths. For example, their independence and goal-orientation may make them sometimes appear ruthless or anti-social, while their compassion can lead them to become too closely involved with neurotic and over-demanding people. They are also by no means free of the guilt, anxieties, sadness, self-blame, internal strife and conflict suffered by the rest of the human race, but the difference is that in their case these states of mind are related to realistic appraisals of life events rather than to imaginary or exaggerated problems, and are not allowed to dominate thinking, to become obsessional, or to interfere with personal effectiveness.

Maslow also noted that his sample of self-actualised people frequently reported what he called *peak experiences*. These were moments of ecstasy and wonder and awe when they felt themselves to be outside time and space, experiencing limitless horizons and the certainty that something transforming and extraordinary had happened to them which lent strength to their lives. Such moments appear to be akin to mystical experiences, and are often associated with spiritual or philosophical insights, with artistic enjoyment or inspiration, and with feelings of self-transcendence and of universal unity and love.

Allport (1961), in another classic study, recognised that few people achieve full self-actualisation, and accordingly proposed the term *mature personality* to designate those whose psychological development appears to be headed in the appropriate direction. Among the qualities he identified as characterising the mature personaliity are consistency, an extended sense of self (which enables one to care as much for others as for oneself), realistic appraisals (which lead one to be a good judge of people and events), self-insight, a sense of humour (which allows one to laugh at oneself), and a unifying philosophy of life (which gives meaning and purpose to existence).

HOW DO DRAMATHERAPISTS ASSESS CLIENT PROGRESS?

Dramatherapists, together with other psychotherapeutic practitioners, may argue that they have no such lofty aims for clients as the attainment of self-actualisation or even of maturity of personality. The majority of clients come into therapy with fairly basic survival needs, and few of them remain long enough to complete the long journey into a fully realised human being. In addition, each client operates at his or her own level. What may represent the ability to work or love or play or pray for one client, may be beyond the reach of another, or altogether too prosaic for a third. Other clients may only be concerned with achieving certain aspects of self-actualisation, and may exhibit a lack of interest or even hostility towards all the rest.

In addition, dramatherapists are themselves important variables in the equation. They may feel able to facilitate and monitor progress in certain of the areas listed above, but less confident in others. Alternatively, they may be confident in all the various areas when working with some of their clients, but not when working with others. As Jennings (1987) points out, drama-therapists interact professionally with a much wider range of clients than is usual in many other forms of psychotherapy. They can, for example, be called upon to operate with children and adults with learning disabilities, with disturbed adolescents, psychiatric patients, the elderly, and with individuals and groups presenting psychological and social problems as diverse as infertility, family dysfunction, personal identity, stress management, self-assertion, gender difficulties and role confusions.

It can also be argued that dramatherapy finds its theoretical base in a very diverse range of psychological theories, and that not all of these address themselves to the full complement of variables identified as constituting psychological health. Dramatherapists working within the context of theories which fail to address the whole complement may find their attempts to formalise their thinking in certain areas somewhat handicapped in consequence. For example, Valente (1993) has shown that dramatherapy calls upon theories that range from psychoanalysis and analytical psychology, through humanistic and client-centred theories, to psychosynthesis, Gestalt and transpersonal psychology. In several useful ways it even links to aspects of behavioural theory, and to newer personality theories such as reversal theory (Fontana and Valente 1993a and b).

An array of qualifications and reservations arising from the above considerations must therefore be attached to any pronouncements upon assessment in dramatherapy. Nevertheless, such pronouncements are vital if dramatherapy is to improve its effectiveness, and to be recognised by other professionals as a fully-fledged member of the psychotherapeutic family. Accordingly, having established from the work of Freud, Maslow and others that psychological health appears to be a concept that can be operationalised, set out, as part of a wide-ranging research study into theory and practice in dramatherapy (Fontana and Valente 1991), to identify the variables that dramatherapists currently take into account in assessing their clients. The identification of such variables allows us not only to establish the assessment priorities operated by dramatherapists, but to observe the extent to which these priorities match the criteria of psychological health proposed by Freud and others.

THE THREE STAGES OF ASSESSMENT

In any therapeutic process assessment has three stages, namely *initial assessment, ongoing assessment,* and *final assessment. Initial assessment* screens those clients suitable for acceptance into a particular therapeutic programme; *ongoing assessment* monitors progress and provides the therapist with clues as to what changes if any need to be made to what is being done; and *final assessment* establishes the point reached at the close of therapy, and provides guidance as to what needs to be done in the future. It is of course *final assessment* that relates most closely to psychological health variables. Our research sought details from dramatherapists on the client variables taken into account at each of these three stages.

As described fully elsewhere (Fontana and Valente 1991), we were able to obtain relevant data from 86 per cent of the population of qualified British dramatherapists, and these data therefore provide us with a comprehensive picture of good current practice. It must be made clear that the questions on assessment that we put to dramatherapists (all of which were derived from the material yielded by semi-structured interviews with a panel of leading dramatherapists) were not concerned with how dramatherapy can be used to assess psychological or psychiatric disorders, although work such as that by Kramer and Iager (1984) and by Goodman (1989) indicates that the creative arts therapies can be utilised effectively for this purpose. Nor were these questions designed to identify the specific assessment tools (if any) used by dramatherapists to achieve their assessment aims. Such tools, which include instruments like Johnson's *diagnostic role-playing test*, are described fully elsewhere (e.g. *The Arts in Psychotherapy* special issue on assessment, 1988). Our concern was solely with what qualities *in the client* are taken by the dramatherapist as indicative of current psychological states.

The three stages of assessment can be looked at in turn.

Initial assessment

All clients are individuals, and some are more suited to dramatherapy than others. Dramatherapy is, by nature of the richness and variety of the therapeutic experiences it has to offer, more accommodating than most psychotherapies, but even so there are clients who are likely to be resistant to its methodologies, or who are unsuited to group work, or who by virtue of temperament or previous life experience are likely to make more rapid progress within alternative therapeutic environments. Table 2.1 lists those variables which our sample regard as indicating that clients *are* likely to benefit from dramatherapy, and likely to prove amenable to what the dramatherapist has to offer. The variables are arranged in rank order: that is, the ones at the top of the list were those given the highest mean rating of suitability (on a scale from 1 to 4, with 1 representing maximum suitability) by the sample, while those lower down the list were given a less favourable rating. However, all the variables attracted some degree of support, and therefore all may feature in the assessment repertoire of dramatherapists from time to time. The differences in mean ratings between some of the variables is small, but the appropriate statistical technique showed that, overall, ranking was a justifiable procedure.

Table 2.1 Factors relevant for initial client assessment by dramatherapists

Rank order	Variable	Mean suitability rating
1	Motivation	1.49
2	Therapist's ability to work with client	1.55
3	Client's willingness to work with therapist	1.56
4	Willingness to change	1.68
5	Personal/social background	1.99
6	Willingness to observe limits and boundaries	2.04
7	Willingness to play creatively	2.05
8	Willingness to use creative media	2.11
9	Willingness to remain in therapy	2.12
10	Ability to fit in with dramatherapy group	2.22
11	Clinical history	2.40
12	Willingness to play in role	2.41
13	Absence of long-term reality-altering drug therapy	2.56
14	Previous experience in therapy	2.62
15	Apparent absence of psychosis	2.65
16	Absence of acute insight into personal problems	2.98
17	Reasonable ability to articulate	3.03
18	Logical, rational, focused thinking	3.17
19	Understanding of creative process	3.31

Table 2.1 indicates that *motivation* carries the highest mean rating, followed by *therapist's ability to work with client* and *client's willingness to work with therapist*. These two variables suggest that dramatherapy is very much a two-way process, with both therapist and client responding to, and being influenced by, the other. The next item, *willingness to change*, is a pre-requisite of most if not all therapies, and indeed only one variable among the nineteen is specific to dramatherapy, namely *willingness to play in role*, which appears in twelfth place. However, general items connected with the creative process such as *willingness to play creatively* occupy high positions, as does *willingness to use creative media* (eighth place). Nevertheless, *understanding of creative process* appears at the bottom of the list, stressing perhaps the importance of action and doing rather than of more intellectual levels of comprehension.

Ongoing assessment

During the dramatherapy process, the monitoring of client progress provides the therapist with the feedback needed if the therapeutic process is to remain sensitive to the client's current needs. It also gives clues as to the required duration of therapy, and allows the therapist to share with the client appropriate insights into the latter's condition at any given time.

Table 2.2 shows that the client's ability to *express feelings* appears to be the dramatherapist's prime clue to a client's progress, followed by his or her ability to *become acquainted* with the therapist and with other members of the group. In this list the mean ratings are all relatively high, with none below 2.85. This indicates the importance of all the variables concerned, and would seem to indicate that practitioners think of dramatherapy processes in a gratifyingly cohesive way. Table 2.2 can thus serve as an appropriate inventory or checklist for the purposes of ongoing assessment. Its use should help professionals to be systematically aware of what is actually happening to their clients, although not all items would be relevant to all client groups.

After *express feelings*, which links with the relatively high placing of *be spontaneous* (seventh), the pattern that emerges indicates that the drama-therapist consistently attempts to help clients place their individual psycho-therapeutic progress within a social context. Variables near the top of the table such as *become acquainted* (second), *find communality with group* (fourth), *accept feelings of others* (third), and *make contact with therapist* (fifth) all point in this direction, while variables connected with more individual and cognitive factors, such as *understand transference*, *effect transference* and *reconstruct personal myths and rituals*, come near or at the bottom of the table.

In addition to the variables observable in individual clients, we asked our sample to indicate the relative importance they attach to various whole-group factors during ongoing assessment. Table 2.3 lists their responses.

Table 2.2 Factors relevant for ongoing client assessment by dramatherapists

Rank order	Variable	Mean suitability rating
1	Ability to express feelings	1.51
2	Ability to become acquainted	1.63
3	Accept feelings of others	1.66
4	Find communality with group	1.68
5	Make contact with therapist	1.69
6	Reintegrate self positively	1.79
7	Be spontaneous	1.84
8	Take risks	1.85
9	Explore potentialities through role	1.90
10	Identify expectations	1.93
11	Handle fears and insecurities	1.99
12	Identify potential social contributions	2.03
13=	Identify own problems	2.07
13=	Share differences with others	2.07
15	Self-disclose	2.17
16	Explore personal pain	2.25
17	Relate symbolic roles to personal experience	2.33
18	Heal own spirits	2.34
19	Contain own emotions appropriately	2.51
20	Reject others' feelings when appropriate	2.53
21=	Recognise personal instability	2.58
21=	Effect transference	2.58
23	Understand transference	2.80
24=	Play a single role effectively	2.84
24=	Experience catharsis	2.84
26	Reconstruct personal myths and rituals	2.85

Table 2.3 Factors relevant for ongoing group assessment by dramatherapists

Rank order	Variable	Mean suitability rating
1	Group involvement	1.48
2	Group cohesion	1.75
3	Group risk-taking	1.80
4	Group spontaneity and creativity	1.81
5	Level of group work	2.12
6	Movement from mundane to dramatic reality	2.14

There are no surprises in Table 2.3, although it is interesting to note that the two variables which relate to performance, namely *level of group work* and *movement from mundane to dramatic reality*, are placed after the four variables relating to the group's affective tone.

Final assessment

No therapist would claim that healing is ever finally accomplished. To be alive is to meet problems. But all good psychotherapy helps the individual to understand more fully the real nature of his or her own being, and to cope with daily living more effectively. Our research, together with our study of the literature, showed us however that in dramatherapy there appears to be no systematic way of assessing how far healing has progressed by the end of therapy, and how closely this level of healing equates with concepts of psychological health. Nevertheless, we were able to identify the wide range of variables used by dramatherapists, together with the degree of importance attached to each of them. Table 2.5 presents these variables (which are also presented and discussed in Valente and Fontana 1994), and if future research can show us how each of them is recognised in client behaviour, we should be able to take an important step forward in demonstrating the effectiveness of dramatherapy outcomes.

We first demonstrate the importance of such recognition by giving Table 2.4, which shows the results of our research into the methods used by dramatherapists during final assessment. It will be seen that observation of *behaviour* comes in first place, which links with our emphasis upon the usefulness of behavioural models as additions to the other psychological theories that underpin dramatherapy (Fontana and Valente 1989).

Table 2.4 Methods relevant for final assessment by dramatherapists

Rank order	Variable	Mean suitability rating
1	Observation of client behaviours	1.32
2	Client self-reports	1.68
3	Reports from other professionals	2.23
4	Projective techniques	2.34
5	Clients' use of diagnostic dramatherapy media	2.72
6	Reports by other group members	2.82
7	Kelly's repertory grid	3.34

Although *observation of client behaviours* comes at the top of the list, we found elsewhere in our research that dramatherapists generally give a very low rating to behaviourism, which modern scientific psychology shows is in fact the basis of much informed observation. We share of course the view that behaviourism is only one part of psychology, and that psychologists made a grave mistake during past decades when they assumed that their subject should be *nothing but* behaviourism. Current thinking has turned against this view. The objective observation of behaviour is only one tool in the psychologist's armoury, but its high placing in Table 2.4 suggests that dramatherapists should perhaps be better acquainted with modern developments within the area.

Placed second in Table 2.4 is *client self-reports*. This is an important means of assessment – provided the client is helped in methods of self-observation and analysis – and accords with Kelly's well-known first principle that 'if you want to know what is happening to the client why don't you ask him – he might just know'. *Kelly's repertory grid* does, however, come bottom of the list! In fact many of our sample indicated to us that they have no knowledge of this invaluable assessment tool. This surprised us, as there is already some valuable dramatherapy research done in Britain using the repertory grid (Grainger 1987), and one might therefore expect some corresponding knowledge of it amongst practitioners.

One interesting omission from Table 2.4 is any reference to the observation of clients in roles. The work of Landy (e.g. 1990) would seem particularly appropriate in this context, but it may be that roles, together with other aspects of the dramatic repertoire, are subsumed under the general categories of *observation of client behaviours* and *clients' use of diagnostic dramatherapy media*.

As already indicated, Table 2.5 gives the responses of dramatherapists to the question 'What does one look for when assessing client progress?' The variables listed within it carry a dual value, in that not only do they tell us much about final assessment, they also highlight the qualities that practitioners feel are most amenable to development by dramatherapy. The most striking feature of Table 2.5 is the cluster at the top of variables to do with the self. *Self-esteem, self-awareness, self-acceptance* and *self-confidence* are seen as the important qualities most amenable to development through dramatherapy and most apparent in final assessment. We could hardly have a more graphic illustration of the power for psychological change of the dramatic experience. Also prominent is *self–other awareness*, as are *hope, communication, initiative, concentration, imagination, courage* and *reduced depression* – all of them again variables strongly associated with psychological health.

It is interesting to note that *dramatic repertoire* comes at the bottom of the table, although in the list of dramatherapy techniques revealed elsewhere in our research, *script work* is very highly rated. This suggests there may be some confusion amongst dramatherapists as to the way in which drama *per se* actually influences what happens in dramatherapy. But that is another matter, and beyond the scope of this chapter.

Table 2.5 Factors relevant for final assessment by dramatherapists

Rank order	Variable	Mean suitability rating
1	Self-esteem	1.34
2	Self-awareness	1.45
3	Self-acceptance	1.50
4	Self-confidence	1.53
5	Hope	1.54
6	Communication	1.56
7	Trust	1.57
8	Self–other awareness	1.65
9	Spontaneity	1.67
10	Social interaction	1.78
11	Creativity	1.79
12	Initiative	1.84
13	Concentration	1.90
14	Imagination	1.91
15	Courage	1.98
16	Reduced depression	2.07
17	Fewer delusions	2.25
18	Realistic world-view	2.28
19	Self-disclosure	2.34
20	Social self-control	2.35
21	Metaphor change	2.45
22	Physical appearance	2.47
23	Use of language	2.51
24	Social disinhibition	2.70
25	Healing myths	2.77
26	Dramatic repertoire	3.07

FINAL ASSESSMENT AND PSYCHOLOGICAL HEALTH

If we now set the variables shown in Table 2.5 against the various criteria of psychological health given earlier in the chapter, we can give an estimate of the accord between the two sets of attributes.

If we take first of all the four psychological health variables based upon Freud, we can say that the ability to *work* is reflected in Table 2.5 by such attributes as *creativity, initiative, concentration, realistic world-view,* and (though to a lesser extent) by *social self-control, courage* and *use of language.* There is nothing in Table 2.5, however, about life goals, motivation and effort, all of which would seem important within the context of a successful working life.

The ability to *love* seems well-represented in Table 2.5. The first four variables in the table all play an essential part in the ability to love oneself, while the ability to love others is implicit in *trust, self–other awareness, social interaction, self-disclosure* and *social disinhibition*. The ability to *play* would seem to be bound up with *spontaneity, creativity* and *social disinhibition*, but it is noticeable that there is nothing in Table 2.5 directly related to joy or to humour or to non-seriousness.

Finally, the ability to *pray* seems markedly under-represented in the table. *Imagination, metaphor change* and *healing myths* may be pointers in that direction, but there is nothing relating to an enhanced awareness of the wonder and mystery of life, or to a developing sense of meaning and purpose behind living.

If we turn now to Maslow's criteria, the dramatherapist would certainly seem to be assessing clients for what Maslow refers to variously as emotional openness, perception, spontaneity, self- and self–other acceptance, and creativity. But again we notice some omissions in Table 2.5, in this case the absence of a greater appreciation of life, of humour, of ethics, of peak experiences (though perhaps this is understandable), and of autonomy and independence. Similarly, if we look at Allport's criteria for the mature personality, we find a lack in Table 2.5 of any reference to consistency, to an extended sense of self, and to a unifying philosophy of life.

The variables listed in Table 2.5, as in the previous tables, were generated initially by our panel of experts, and then individually rated for suitability by the overall sample. The members of the latter were invited to contribute further variables of their own choosing if they so wished, but in no case did they avail themselves of this invitation. We can conclude therefore that Table 2.5 is reasonably representative of the final assessment criteria used by dramatherapists, and in the context of the missing psychological health variables this leaves us with three possibilities. First, dramatherapists may by training and inclination not be concerned with the development of these missing variables. Second, the clients who come into dramatherapy may not usually be at a level of being which allows them to advance to the personal qualities which these variables represent. And third, these variables may not be amenable to development by dramatherapy, for all its great richness and variety as a psychotherapeutic process.

There are a number of variables in Table 2.5 which do not appear in the list compiled by Maslow and others. *Hope* and *reduced depression* (which link with the optimistic approach to life to which we drew attention earlier in the chapter), are examples, as are *metaphor change, physical appearance, use of language, healing myths*, and of course *dramatic repertoire*. However, these additional variables represent in general the abandonment of negative qualities, and are thus more appropriate to specific psychotherapeutic objectives than to the broader goal of full psychological health.

CONCLUSION

Assessment is all to do with attempts to answer the question 'Is your client getting better?' There have long been arguments, particularly within the context of psychoanalysis (e.g. Fisher and Greenberg 1985), as to whether psychotherapy is 'scientific' or not, and whether it aims to heal or simply to help people live more peacefully with their neuroses. But the fact of the matter is that clients do feel themselves helped by psychotherapy, and do communicate their improved sense of being to the therapist in a wide range of ways. Many of these ways have been covered in this chapter; others are more subtle, and may call more upon the therapist's intuition than upon his or her objective clinical judgement. But taken together they do enable us to answer the question 'Is your client getting better?', and to provide feedback which serves to further refine and develop the dramatherapist's professional skills.

It is hoped that dramatherapists will find the results detailed in this chapter of help to them in reflecting upon their individual assessment skills. In particular, it is hoped that the results will enable them to pose questions relating to these skills. The good therapist is always functioning in the role of a researcher, observing and learning from client responses, and from his or her own application of therapeutic techniques. Such research depends crucially upon the ability to formulate research questions that probe deeply into the effectiveness of what one is doing, and to identify perceptive and appropriate responses to these questions.

As assessment in dramatherapy becomes more precise, so the subject will take on a higher profile within the therapeutic family. Our research has left us in no doubt that assessment is an important concern for dramatherapists, and that the great majority of them are working progressively towards the achievement of greater precision. We shall never be able to turn assessment in any of the psychotherapies into an exact science. But we can be confident that dramatherapy, by virtue of the opportunities it gives to clients for direct social expression, and the opportunities it gives to therapists to observe this expression instead of merely listening to what the client says, has the potential to come closer to this exactitude than many of its sister therapies.

REFERENCES

Allport, G.W. (1961) *Pattern and Growth in Personality*, London and New York: Holt, Rinehart & Winston.

Arts in Psychotherapy, The (1988) Special issue on assessment in the creative arts therapies, *The Arts in Psychotherapy* 15 (whole issue).

Boss, M. (1977) *I Dreamt Last Night*, New York: Gardiner.

Fisher, S. and Greenberg, R.P. (1985) *The Scientific Credibility of Freudian Theories*, New York: Columbia University Press.

Fontana, D. and Valente, L. (1989) 'Monitoring client behaviour as a guide to progress in dramatherapy', *Dramatherapy* 10: 10–17.

—— (1991) 'Drama as pre-therapy', *Speech and Drama* 40: 35–40.

—— (1993a) 'Dramatherapy and the theory of psychological reversals', *The Arts in Psychotherapy* 20: 133–142.

—— (1993b) 'Reversal theory and dramatherapy', in J. H. Kerr, S. Murgatroyd and M. J. Apter (eds) *Advances in Reversal Theory*, Amsterdam, Holland and Berwyn, PA: Swets & Zeitlinger.

Freud, S. (1957) *Two Short Accounts of Psychoanalysis*, Harmondsworth, UK: Penguin.

Goodman, K. (1989) 'Music therapy assessment of emotionally disturbed children', *The Arts in Psychotherapy* 16: 179–192.

Grainger, P. (1987) *The Use of Dramatherapy in the Treatment of Thought Disorder*, unpublished M.Phil. thesis, Huddersfield Polytechnic, Council for National Academic Awards.

Jennings, S. (1987) Introduction to S. Jennings (ed.) *Dramatherapy: Theory and Practice for Teachers and Clinicians*, London and New York: Routledge.

Johnson, D.R. (1988) Introduction to the special issue on assessment in the creative arts therapies, *The Arts in Psychotherapy* 15: 1–3.

Kramer, E.S. and Iager, A-C. (1984) 'The use of art in assessment of psychotic disorders: changing perspectives', *The Arts in Psychotherapy* 11: 197–201.

Landy, R.J. (1990) 'The concept of role in drama therapy', *The Arts in Psychotherapy* 17: 223–230.

Maslow, A.H. (1970) *Motivation and Personality*, New York: Harper & Row.

Payne, H. (1993) 'From practitioner to researcher', in H. Payne (ed.) *Handbook of Inquiry in the Arts Therapies: One River, Many Currents*, London: Jessica Kingsley.

Valente, L. (1993) *Therapeutic Drama and Psychological Health: An Examination of Theory and Practice in Dramatherapy*, unpublished Ph.D. thesis, University of Wales, Cardiff.

Valente, L. and Fontana, D. (1991) 'Dramatherapy and psychological change', in G. Wilson (ed.) *Psychology and Performing Arts*, Amsterdam, Holland and Berwyn, PA: Swets & Zeitlinger.

—— (1994) 'Drama therapist and client: an examination of good practice and outcomes', *The Arts in Psychotherapy* 21: 3–10.

Chapter 3

The story as a guide to metaphoric processes

Mooli Lahad

INTRODUCTION

'Supervision' comprises the two words – super and vision. Bernard and Goodyear (1993) suggest that one of the main skills of the supervisor is the ability to have this view over a range of perspectives in order to assist in understanding and evaluating a situation.

Kadushin's (1992) approach to supervision is integrative. He defines three aspects of supervision: administrative, educational and supportive. Hawkins and Shohat (1989) define the supervision process as intended to develop the personal and vocational skills of the supervisee. Supervision of art therapists intends to do just this, but most of it is carried out in an adapted 'language'. That means to say that in many cases, supervision of arts and dramatherapists is conducted using psychological language and concepts. It is very important for the development of dramatherapy as a profession for it to develop its own language, theories, set of concepts and supervision language. This does not mean alienation from the world of psychology and psychotherapy, rather that these languages should be incorporated into dramatherapy as an arts profession.

If we adopt Proctor and Inskip's stages, then we need to formulate supervision concepts and models for dramatherapy. We have to develop normative processes in order to be able to follow some guidelines as to what dramatherapy should include, and restorative processes whereby drama-therapists receive support in their work through the various media of dramatherapy.

The intention of this chapter is to attempt to focus on one particular aspect of dramatherapy – the use of and understanding of stories themselves as the supervisor.

Over the years, in my role as a supervisor of dramatherapists and psychotherapists, and through my work in bibliotherapy and dramatherapy, I have listened in depth to many stories and descriptions. I have developed a supervision technique using the comprehension of the greater story as a guide to understanding the individual's or the group's place in the therapeutic process, as well as using the 'great story' as a supervisor and guide.

This method is based upon Jungian theory, together with theories on the use of metaphors in therapy. The theory of stories and legends uses the model of the journey of the soul and the inner hero. Legends not only symbolise quests or conflicts, they also represent the developmental stage of the individual or the group.

The act of listening to this therapeutic process introduces into the supervision session an additional mentor: ancient, not only bearing timeless wisdom, but also providing the opportunity for a wider and multidimensional dialogue between the supervisor, the supervisee and the wise old mentor.

The greatness of this wise old person lies in his or her ability to suggest, in a manner that meets little or no resistance, options that the eyes of the 'here and now' are unlikely to perceive. The mentor demonstrates alternatives for coping with problems that invariably lead to generating 'second-degree solutions'.

THE USE OF METAPHOR IN SUPERVISION

The use of stories and metaphors as therapeutic tools is reported widely in the professional literature. Hammond (1990) reviews the accumulated knowledge regarding the use of metaphors, mainly emphasising how they are integrated in suggestive, hypnotic processes. Erickson and Rossi (1979), Haley (1973) and Mills and Crowley (1986) deal with the connection between the use of metaphors and circumventing defence mechanisms and unconscious learning. Siegellman (1990) focuses on the use of metaphors in imagination-oriented psychotherapy. Elitsur (1992) emphasises the use of metaphors produced by the client. Achterberg (1985) reviews many therapeutic approaches in psychotherapy and medicine which make use of the imagination for achieving a wide range of aims, including changes in behaviour, attitude and emotions. Ankori (1991) suggests that the quest of the hero is in fact the story of the psyche and the issues appropriate to the developmental age. Bion (1968) suggests that there is a group unconscious that manifests itself through the story of the group.

In spite of the reports existing in the literature about combining metaphors and stories in the therapeutic process, there is practically no reference made to tools and techniques from this area in supervision.

Ekstein and Walerstein (1972) distinguish between three directions in supervision:

1 patient-centred supervision
2 therapist-centred supervision
3 process-centred supervision.

Supervisor and supervisee can deal with theories, techniques and diagnosis, and can decide upon a line of treatment and give the supervision session a consultative tone. They can deal with the feelings and requests of the supervisee and give the supervision session a more treatment-oriented tone. Furthermore, they can deal with any ongoing interactions and focus the supervision on interpersonal processes and other parallel processes.

Many times in supervision, after taking a decision with regard to the direction and desired content, I find myself debating a further dilemma: should I stay within the realms of thought and logic (left hemisphere of the brain) or should I expand to the realms of imagination and experience (right hemisphere) and develop the dialogue between the two realms? As a therapist, this extension is quite acceptable to me and I find it of great benefit. This generalisation into the area of supervision demands additional thought, and this chapter illustrates this way of working by examples. It is important to stress that the use of stories and metaphors is not offered as a substitute for other methods of supervision; it does not come in place of theoretical understanding and does not prevent the defining of therapeutic aims, but only provides different ways of looking at things. The way of work that I will describe is likely to help in many supervision situations, from making a diagnosis and deciding upon a therapeutic approach to understanding the therapeutic process and the therapist–client relationships. I have found this particularly suitable in situations where the supervisee is 'stuck', there is resistance or there is a tendency to rationalisation. In these types of situation, this approach can be used to enlist powers and cope with difficulties, by strengthening inner concentration and the visualisation of concepts and problems, by creating experiential-emotional feelings in supervisees who tend to intellectualise, by finding internal resources and by strengthening the feeling of control.

The use of stories and metaphors, whether in the therapeutic or in the supervisional process, is based on the assumption that a story or image can represent the objective or subjective perception of internal or external reality. Relating to the representative image is likely to change internal reality, or can bring about a change in perceiving the external reality, but does not aspire to achieve change in the objective reality itself.

During the course of supervision, once the decision has been made to use metaphors, it should be explained to the supervisee how it works. The 'rules of the game' and teaching the metaphoric way of thinking should explain the journey of the hero as a way of understanding the journey of the psyche. Locating the 'great story' and transcending into the fantastic reality can help the supervisee to observe a situation, widen alternatives, devise some ways of preventing something from happening and enable the transition from a current situation to a desired one. During the supervision session, it is possible to stay within the realm of images and metaphor and not to concern oneself with explanations and interpretations, or to use the products of the unconscious in order to broaden one's consciousness. Supervisors and supervisees who are interested in this can find the real counterparts and 'translate' the language of images into the language of reality.

THE SLEEPING BEAUTY: A GROUP ON ITS WAY TO OVERCOMING ITS PROBLEM

The group described here is an open dramatherapy group of patients in a day-care psychiatric unit. The two dramatherapists brought to the first session a description of a meeting in which the clients took part in the 'Olympic Games'. The group was varied and all sorts of competitions took place. On hearing the account, it became clear that over and above the different roles taken by men and women, there was an atmosphere of competition between two men in the group, one older, the other younger. As we listened to their stories, the legend of the old king who must make way for the young prince became apparent. The young prince usually has to prove himself by fulfilling some kind of task, often resulting in finding the princess. As a developmental stage, this represents adolescence. When we examined several stories of that nature and established an understanding of the psyche's quest, we could speculate on the possible process of searching for the princess and the journey to maturity which will entail the struggle between young and old.

In the second supervisory session, the dramatherapists brought a description of a meeting in which the group decided to enact part of the story from the book of Esther, as it was just before the festival of Purim. This festival is based on the miraculous salvation of the Jews of Persia by Queen Esther, who married the Persian king, Ahasuerus. Nowadays, as part of the celebrations, children dress up in fancy dress. The part of the book they chose was where all the women were preparing to be chosen as queen: the contest, or as they called it, 'The Miss Shushan the Capital Competition'. A number of patients decided to play the parts of the women (including Vashti, the original queen) and one of them asked to be Esther. The preparations for the ceremony went on and on, and despite the prodding of the therapists none of the participants reached the stage of the actual selection.

In trying to understand the dynamics of these stories, we arrived at the tales of the reluctant princess, unsure as to whether she really wants to get married to this prince, or even to grow up. The discussion this time investigated the different stories about the heroine's journey to maturity (Cinderella, The Sleeping Beauty). Whilst examining these stories, we examined a few of the possible alternatives for group development, such as avoidance of male–female contact, passivity of female members, seduction, etc. In the third supervisory session, the dramatherapists described a meeting in which they used small puppets. Everyone joined in, apart from one girl who remained lying on the bench, rocking away. She said that was the way she fell asleep. One of the therapists tried, using techniques such as pacing and leading (imitating the young woman's movements and joining in with her), to make her rock even quicker and then lead her into a dance, or at least to stop her lying down. These attempts lasted only a short while and eventually the patient went and lay down again.

The two therapists were exceedingly frustrated, and furthermore they were unable to agree on how to deal with the patient's behaviour. It took them some time to answer my question about which tale this situation reminded them of. They finally identified the Sleeping Beauty, the heroine who not only did not want to take part in a competition to see who would marry the prince, she even stopped growing up and went into a deep sleep. We then tried to understand what was happening to the group in which the princess wanted to fall asleep, what were the open behavioural processes and what were the internal processes pulling her back, the suspension, the awakening sexuality. We predicted that the next dramatherapy session would develop along the lines of avoidance, suspension of all decisions regarding new material, low energy levels and slowness.

The fourth supervision session also focused on the patient who preferred to rock. This time the therapists allowed her to do so and brought the group to participate in rocking the patient. In the following dramatherapy session, one of the therapists tried to check if the princess was really asleep, and if it was possible to wake her up.

In a guided fantasy process, the therapist described to the group a journey in which everyone had to pass through a forest in order to reach an enchanted castle.

That day there were five participants in the group. The first one entered the forest, met a monster and retreated. The second went in, fell into some deep tunnels and got lost. The third entered on horseback, reached a desert and fell asleep in the shade of the horse. The fourth crossed the forest and reached the bridge leading across the river to the castle. Two guards were waiting at the other side with two conundrums. Only those giving the correct answers could cross the bridge and since he did not know the right answer, this participant was not allowed across. The last one, the patient who had made most progress, and was just about to be discharged, said that she did manage to cross the forest and reach the castle that was still fast asleep. She woke up the guards and . . . the story ends.

The therapist was astounded to discover that it was impossible to waken the sleeping beauty before her time was up. The group was still at the stage of the sleeping beauty, and the therapist's guiding attempts to waken it were of no avail. Even the patient who was about to be discharged the next week was unable to function beyond the place where the group was.

In the fifth supervision session we observed how the group slowly awakened, and as in the fairy tales, the process of courtship began between the princess and the prince. In one of these dramatherapy sessions, the young male whom we mentioned earlier as being in competition with the older male was dancing a very sensual dance with a stick, in a ritualistic, performance-like manner. The recurrent themes in these sessions were: going to the café, dance parties, and meals out. Occasionally the old rivalries between the 'old king' and the 'young prince' resurfaced.

During the following stage the kind of stories that appeared were those that involved becoming established, such as the search for the fountain of eternal youth and attempts to learn to live together, as well as adventure stories.

Conclusion

The sessions decribed above are an example of a process whereby translation of the group behaviour and dynamics into fairy tales helped us to understand the group psyche, predict potential developments in the group and help the therapists see the group from a different slant, thus introducing perspective and alternative understandings of the group's life. The process was more significant in this case as the group was an open group with no apparent 'life of its own'. Moreover, this was a group of post-psychotic patients, in which many therapists have difficulties in finding any meaning beyond the usual interpretation of human behaviour. Thus, using the language of fairy tales and understanding the inner journey of the group through the metaphoric events helped therapists to see a journey of growth and change in the life of an otherwise 'usual' group.

ONE-SESSION SUPERVISION – HEIDI THE MOUNTAIN GIRL

I was recently invited to give a seminar to some Bosnian therapists, psychologists, social workers, teachers and physicians who came to Israel to learn about crisis intervention with children and the community in a situation of ongoing war. This seminar combined theory, skills, models and supervision. One of the models that we discussed and that was later adopted extensively by the participants in their clinical work was the BASIC Ph model (Lahad 1992).

BASIC Ph assumes that people cope with life in a variety of ways, but that with time, everyone adopts their own particular preferred modes of coping. BASIC Ph is an acronym for the six underlying coping modes: Beliefs, Affect, Social support, Imagination, Cognition (reality) and Physical activity. For most people, all these modes are present in greater or lesser degrees, but with some insight and testing it becomes apparent what a person's particular BASIC Ph make-up is. For example, one can be predominantly C, Ph, signifying the type of person who will wish to understand his or her problem then do something practical about it; or A, S, signifying the type of person who will wish to talk about his or her problem, and solve it preferably with others' help or within a defined social setting.

These predominant modes of coping constitute the language (in BASIC Ph terms) with which the person meets the world. In times of stress, it is important to adopt the client's personal language in order to create rapport and devise means of crisis intervention and practical support. Once other less strong modes of coping are identified, then further suggestions for treatment can be developed.

One of the Bosnian participants, a paediatrician, described the case of a young girl rushed to hospital after an air raid with epileptic symptoms. All tests were satisfactory and after a few days she was about to be sent home; however, she was in a state of high anxiety. All the staff's attempts at calming her down were in vain. The girl had two parents and two brothers, one older and one younger. The parents were in favour of letting her stay in the hospital. After the parents had promised that they would move to another village, the girl left the hospital. The doctor was very worried at the possibility that the girl might stay; she said that there were many other children who really needed care and there were not enough beds and food for all of them, not to mention medicine.

A few days passed, and following another bombardment the girl was once more rushed to the hospital with the same epileptic symptoms. The parents left her in the hospital for the doctors to take care of, but once again, after extensive examination, they found nothing wrong. This time, the girl refused to leave, the parents did not come to take her, and the staff members were at a loss as to what to do with her. With the girl still in hospital, the attempts of the supervision group to understand what was going on and to advise were met with the doctor's comment, 'We tried, but it didn't work.' My attempts at understanding the systems at work and the girl's outlook on the world did not advance progress. The one new thing that we did understand was that the symptoms were in effect the girl's language of expression. Use of the multi-modal BASIC Ph model gave us some guidance. We understood that the girl was using Ph, C, S, but it seemed as if the doctor was finding difficulty in hearing the group's advice. I turned to the group and asked if anyone could think of a story or legend in which something physical happens to a girl and she is sent away from home, and no one comes to take any interest in her fate. After a short silence, one of the participants said 'Heidi'. I asked her to relate the story as she remembered it and I then asked, 'What do you think helped Heidi?'

She answered that Heidi helps another girl. I asked the doctor if that gave her any leads. She started to smile. 'It sounds right, we will give her something to do.' Other group members added that this would change her from being passive and dependent to being active and significant. The final suggestion was to promise the girl that she could come and take care of other children whenever she wanted to do so, but each time only for two or three days at most. In this way a number of things could be achieved:

1 There would be no need for an epileptic attack: every time she wished to come to the hospital she was free to come.

2 There would be no need for her to be passive and sick in order to receive attention.

3 She would have a role and she could help. This constitutes a change from an internal focusing on worries to an external one, worrying about the needs of others.

4 Her regression would be structured to a period defined as active.

5 She would acquire control over the symptom.

6 Her situation would be reframed, from being a patient to being an assistant.

It was obvious that a second-degree solution had been found.

Conclusion

One needs to understand the desperate situation in Sarajevo in order to appreciate the sort of work these people are doing. I believe that over and above what we call resistance (to authority) in supervision, the exhaustion of the staff and the daily encounter with disaster made it very difficult for the physician concerned to accept any advice from the group even though she herself asked for it.

BASIC Ph as a model for understanding human encounters with the world was very well received but did not open her up to listening to any new solutions or alternatives. The story as a neutral, indirect tool did not threaten her status or emotions. She found it amusing to listen to the story of Heidi and became receptive to Heidi's solutions. Only then was she open to accept different interpretations of Heidi's solution, connecting it to her client's situation.

We countered the doctor's resistance by offering advice from the group by means of a story, seemingly distant and non-threatening.

THE LUCKY DRAW CLUB

I was supervising a group of sophisticated, senior group facilitators, highly experienced people, and it was clear to me that avoidance would be the name of the game. The participants were reluctant to raise difficult issues and were very protective. One day, no one brought up any subject and resistance was obvious. I then asked them if they could think of a story or film which could describe the supervision group. One of the group members said 'The Lucky Draw Club'. I could feel people paying attention now. The member then started to describe how the story, and even more so the film, was so much like them. She said 'You remember the old Chinese woman who said that Jews do not know how to play Mah Jong?' I asked her 'Do you know how to play Mah Jong?' and she smiled and said: 'I have this game at home and it is very difficult to play. It took me quite a while, it is from a different culture and philosophy.'

Other members of the group told what they remembered of the film 'The Lucky Draw Club', describing their opinions and impressions. They mentioned the need to continue playing the game – 'the show must go on'; the secrets that are so difficult to tell; the need to pretend and make-believe about the difficulties of settling in a new country; the question of translation (in the story the main character does not read and write Chinese and she needs assistance from one of her late mother's friends).

I then said to the woman who chose the film: 'So you think of us as the Lucky Draw Club.' There was great laughter. Another member said 'Yes, we don't know how to play Mah Jong, do we?' I repeated 'We don't know how to play Mah Jong.' Another member said 'We have difficulty in translation' and someone else added 'It is difficult to open secrets here.' We continued to talk about the similarities and differences between us and the story. From then on, we were known as the 'Lucky Draw Club'. I must add that the name of the film in Hebrew can mean 'The Club of the Merry Luck'. It had changed the group into a much happier, much more active and vibrant group in which people opened up things and contributed willingly to the process.

DIFFERENT APPROACHES

For many years, dramatherapists were made to believe that supervision should be focused on understanding the process of the interaction of the symbols in the psychological framework. What I have described here is the use of an artistic tool, the story or the metaphor as the frame of reference through which we can understand the process, make assumptions and draw conclusions. Calling upon the treasures of the arts and the ancient wisdom of legends helps to widen our spectrum. It calls upon the material stored in the right hemisphere of the brain, a stock of images, impressions, sounds, smells, pictures and knowledge of a different sort, other than the rational/sequential processes of the left hemisphere.

The combination of stories and metaphor in supervision can be applied in varied and different ways, by suiting them to tendencies, to theoretical perspectives, and to the personality and the needs of the supervisor and the supervisee. These tools are particularly suitable for dramatherapists interested in understanding the metaphor in their clinical work, or for those who accept treatment methods in which the client is not barred from taking an active role, initiating or directing the show. In this situation there is an overlap between the processes learned in supervision sessions and those required in the course of therapy, from the point of view of both content and procedure.

A further characteristic which influences the degree of matching is the limited ability of some supervisees to use their own banks of images and stories or to think metaphorically. There are many reasons for this: an unwillingness to relinquish any control or logical thinking; resistance; a lack of experience or a tendency to imitate the psychologists' and social workers' model for understanding the therapeutic session, process and interactions. It is true that most dramatherapists are supervised by these professionals and most clinics are governed by the psychosocial and psychiatric professions. There is therefore a vital need to develop a distinct language for the dramatherapist in order to conceptualise and understand the therapeutic process. This is so that professional identity can be developed and the unique contribution of the dramatherapist in the multidisciplinary team in the mental health system can be recognised.

Understanding the 'Great Story', the message and the alternative solution it raises, and sharing it with the team, bring a new dimension to the creative process within the arts.

Different ways of looking at this approach can also be found amongst supervisees who do not have any difficulty with the procedure. Some who work in the world of images and imagination intuitively and creatively are satisfied with this and do not need 'translation' into reality. Others, who claim that this approach does not add anything to their knowledge drawn from the world of reality, say that they can even be misled. There are some supervisees who need to practise metaphorical thinking before the instruction session, and others for whom it is important to understand precisely its context in reality before the supervision ends.

DANGERS, RESTRICTIONS AND RECOMMENDATIONS

Since the procedure of using metaphors calls for circumvention of rational thinking and forays into less conscious realms, their use sometimes leads to situations akin to therapy. For example, one can meet problematic behaviour, difficult situations from the past or present and intense emotional involvement. A supervisor who uses these tools must be aware of these possibilities and the choices for making use of them for therapeutic purposes, for when giving supervision one needs to stick to the contract fixed with the supervisee.

There is a distinction between therapy and supervision, but inevitably there are many areas of similarity and overlap between the two. Like the dramatherapy sessions, we move here between reality and dramatic reality and sometimes experience both at the same time. The supervisor has the means to act very positively or very negatively. These means could be used manipulatively, in order to satisfy personal needs, ignoring either consciously or unconsciously the supervisee's needs.

An additional danger stems from the fact that there are some supervisors and supervisees who prefer to use metaphors and stories, usually on an unconscious level, to avoid direct confrontation with some hard reality or difficult feelings. Sometimes this avoidance masks certain situations: at other times it is vital as a defence mechanism. Correct utilisation of these tools will not strengthen unnecessary avoidance, but will serve as a springboard when encountering less conscious properties and difficult, embarrassing or emotion-laden situations.

There are supervisees who labour under the delusion that this is an easy option and one can always use it to reach solutions and obtain quick changes. The use of guided imagery and metaphors can often bring about quick and dramatic developments. It is liable to create the mistaken impression that we are talking about a 'box of magic' which the therapist can use to sort out every problem met. It is superfluous to state that this is not so. Sometimes, the use of this tool is not appropriate and it cannot be of assistance. It can be that the overstating solutions obtained with this tool can be misleading and can cause other more suitable directions of work to be ignored.

After having learned to use the described tools, many supervisees create their own metaphors and 'enter into' a metaphoric world on their own initiative. In these situations all that is required of the supervisor is to be aware of this and to cooperate, and not to miss opportunities to help the supervisee achieve the maximum in learning. However, even when the supervisor initiates and directs this type of work, it should be made clear that the supervisee does not see the experience as anything more than a different way of looking at things. In this type of instruction, there is more encouragement towards creativity and the search for internal unconscious resources, and getting to know one's inner world, through the encounter with the ancient storyteller. The function of the supervisor, when including this method in his or her way of work, is to provide a framework and tools. The supervisee is the one responsible for the content and for filling the framework.

The use of imagination and metaphors is liable or likely (depending on one's point of view) to change the internal balance or to 'shake' the defence mechanisms. Bearing this in mind, it is important to check at the beginning of the process the contingencies for such an outcome and then, at the end, to return the balance to its original state (derole) or create a new balance (learn a new role).

Supervisors and supervisees who have learned to adopt this method in their sessions generally report satisfaction and a feeling of effectiveness. Although this is subjective evidence, it is enough to reinforce the approach that views metaphoric thinking and the use of stories as additional tools at the disposal of the dramatherapy supervisor. It should be remembered that these tools, like other techniques and tools, have both advantages and restrictions, and their combination in supervision sessions should be considered according to the circumstances.

REFERENCES

Achterberg, J. (1985) *Imagery in Healing*, Boston and London: New Science Library.
Ankori, M. (1991) *And This Forest Has No End: A Comparative Study in Jewish Mysticism and Depth Psychology*, Tel Aviv: Ramot Publishers.

Bernard, J. and Goodyear, R. (1993) *Fundamentals of Clinical Supervision*, Boston: Allyn & Bacon.

Bion, W. (1968) *Experiences in Groups*, London: Tavistock Publications.

Ekstein, R. and Walerstein, R.S. (1972) *The Teaching and Learning of Psychotherapy*, New York: International Universities Press.

Elitsur, A. (1992) 'Birds in the head, butterflies in the stomach and other animals, use of metaphors in the therapeutic process', *Sichot* 6(2): 157–166 (in Hebrew).

Erickson, M.H. and Rossi, E.L. (1979) *Hypnotherapy: An Exploratory Casebook*, New York: Irvington.

Haley, J. (1973) *Uncommon Therapy*, New York: Norton.

Hammond, D.C. (ed.) (1990) *Hypnotic Suggestions and Metaphors*, New York: Norton.

Hawkins, P. and Shohat, R. (1989) *Supervision in the Helping Professions: An Individual Group and Organisational Approach*, Milton Keynes, UK: Open University Press.

Kadushin, A. (1992) *Supervision in Social Work*, Columbia, Mo.: Columbia University Press.

Lahad, M. (1992) *Story Making as an Assessment Method for Coping with Stress*, in S. Jennings (ed.) *Dramatherapy: Theory and Practice 2*, London: Routledge.

Mills, A. and Crowley C. (1986) *Therapeutic Metaphors for Children*, New York: Bruner & Mazel.

Siegellman, E. (1990) *Metaphor and Meaning in Psychotherapy*, New York: Guildford.

Chapter 4

The therapeusis of the audience

John Casson

INTRODUCTION

The first theatre audiences who attended shamanic ceremonies, Greek tragedies, mystery plays and dramatic rituals did so for more than entertainment: these theatres were for healing purposes, for spiritual uplift, fertility, catharsis and community benefit. Entertainment was important but these events also contained symbolic processes that spoke to deeper aspects of the individual and collective consciousness of the audience with the intent of providing relief from psychological and social tensions. Modern theatre audiences seek many things in theatre and find satisfaction of various needs ranging from the erotic to the political. Is theatre still a healing art form? If the answer to this question is yes then how is theatre therapeutic and what therapeusis might an audience experience? This chapter will explore the therapeutic processes in theatre for the audience. Dramatherapists must pay attention to these processes if their work is to be effective. I will consider the following issues: the value of pleasure; the heightened awareness that theatre brings; projection and transference; catharsis; fusion and separation; the story: structure and insight; and the client and the therapist as audiences of each other and their potential for mutual therapeusis. Let us first hear from a member of a theatre audience.

THE WITCH AND THE WITNESS

I found the play inspiring and helpful. I arrived at it after a staff training meeting at my school. We had been lectured in government national curriculum jargon about 'managing the learning of the client group' by an inspector. In the wake of our union calling off the boycott of national curriculum standard testing I had been feeling isolated. I wondered if it would be in my class's best interests to cave in and 'teach to the tests' while trying against all the odds not to kill off self-expression, inspiration and spontaneity. This dilemma, the glibness of the inspector, and a friend pointing out that the scheme of work I had spent many hours on was restrictive and unneccesary, left me howling tears of rage and frustration half an hour before seeing 'Alyson'.

Having watched the play and been reminded that it is very usual for a wise woman to be isolated, swimming against the stream, and correct, I felt much calmer. Often when no-one else is expressing opposition to the dominant orthodoxy I feel 'is it only me?' I also know that in the group it is very hard and dangerous to speak out against what the management are saying. I felt inspired by Alyson because of her self-confidence. She did not alter the way she was in order to fit in with the dominant group's (male) expectations.

These realisations made me act in a much more confident way than my usual pattern of behaviour. Normally I would have continued angry and upset. I would have muttered and mumbled and found other people to agree with me about how awful the government and management are. This time I took note of my dilemma as to how best to help my class and charitably gave the headteacher credit for also wanting the best for them. I then went and discussed with her in an equal, adult and intellectual fashion the practical and theoretical issues involved. This helped me release my tension and anger and reduce the polarity of our positions. I also told my friend that I had been upset by her dismissal of my efforts, but mainly because I agreed with her.

This play had the power to recharge my determination and self-confidence.

(A member of the audience reviewing Sue Emmy Jennings's performance as 'Alyson the Green Witch')

THE AUDIENCE IN THERAPY

Dramatherapists work with clients using drama to facilitate the therapeutic process. If we turn the spotlight from the active members of the group, from the performers to the client who watches the performance, the person who is not apparently active but who witnesses, what therapeutic experiences might that person have whilst watching other people in the group? Dramatherapists might anxiously wish all to be actively involved in the drama process; but if we respect that a client may for any reason wish to sit and observe, to simply be present as a witness, what therapeusis might that person gain from being 'in the audience'? If theatre is therapeutic what kinds of experiences do members of an audience have that could be regarded as therapeutic?

The pleasure principle

Adrian Noble, writing in the preface to *Shakespeare as Prompter*, asserts that Shakespeare's 'poetry has the energy and the power to change the individual; and that in a performance, shared by many hundreds of people, something can happen that is infinitely enriching, invisibly healing' (Cox and Theilgaard 1994, p. xiii)

Theatre energises and delights: even tragedy, as Aristotle pointed out, gives us pleasure. The traditional, therapeutic, community theatre rituals I witnessed in Sri Lanka (Casson 1984, p. 11) were intended to delight their audiences with a mixture of excitement, even terror, outrageous obscene comedy, religious awe and beauty to counter the forces of sterility, disease and death. The opening dance of a recent performance of traditional Tibetan dance/drama was 'Sha-nag' (black hat dance), the stated aim of which was to counter the negative, evil forces. Live Theatre (as opposed to deadly theatre, *pace* Brook 1976) is of necessity on the side of life. It is erotic in the deepest sense. (By using the word 'erotic' I do not mean simply sexually stimulating but rather the wider sense the word can have of sensual stimulation, warmly enriching, pleasure giving.) For a depressed person, who is anhedonic, pleasure at witnessing a performance might well be therapeutic: the libidinal energy and stimulation of theatre may well enrich an emotionally impoverished client, enlivening and lifting their spirit. We must not, as the Puritan did, downplay the pleasurable as a source of healing. Here I must acknowledge a debt to Don Feasey, who in his answer to my paper 'The therapeutic elements in drama' (Casson 1994) wrote: 'Drama promotes the use of energy and this is often felt as pleasure and stands in determined opposition to the destructive forces of death and depression' (Feasey 1994, p. 11).

My reference above to eroticism conjures up the god Eros. If Psyche and Eros are a central myth for psychotherapists (James Hillman – see Moore 1990, p. 266) then it is important that dramatherapists acknowledge the impact of the multiple sensory stimulation that theatre provides. Theatre is the magical palace that delights and entrances Psyche. Eros, like Peter Pan and Puck in *A Midsummer Night's Dream*, takes us into the imaginal world of play: to the land of the amending imagination.

Aphrodite, mother of Eros, is the laughing goddess. Simply smiling may be therapeutic: Norman Cousins laughed himself better from crippling ankylosing spondylitis by watching comic films (Hodgkinson 1987, p. 85), and when I was depressed recently, following a broken leg, a video of Fawlty Towers did lift my spirits! Comedy can be healing, laughter cathartic, liberating, releasing us from blocks, heaviness, the prison of over-seriousness.

The audience's pleasure is not just cerebral but felt in the body. Witnessing Chi Kung practice (slow-motion Chinese breathing/movement exercises) I begin to relax: the rhythm and graceful movements call forth in my body a sympathetic response; I begin to breathe with the performers, my body responding as if through some animal magic. At a performance of the Balinese Theatre I notice my body vibrating with the gamelan, the gongs and drums directly speaking to my guts, my feet, my buttocks. The dancers and their embodied rhythms invite my active participation. At a concert of the Japanese Kodo drummers I had the impression that the vast drum at the centre was affecting my heart, the pounding rhythm shaking me to the core. Drumming, the shamans discovered, can affect both body and mind, psyche and soma. Margo Lee Sherman reports the spontaneous remission of back pain whilst listening to Colin Walcott drumming during a theatre performance. In Sri Lanka members of the audience dance and go into trance during healing rituals accompanied by continuous drumming. My point is that not only sounds and rhythms affect the audience: images pass straight into the soma and thence into the psyche through the associations, memories, ideas and emotions thereby aroused.

'Living Memory' is a theatre that performs exclusively to elderly people. Paul Sneddon says:

> The work is a stimulus to long-term memory. It also enables people to establish their own identity, which has often been taken away from them . . . . It's also a good way of people getting to know each other. They feel they have some common ground.
>
> (*Guardian*, 8 June 1993)

So theatre can provide strong stimulus to body, mind, emotions and memory, and thereby open up channels for intra-psychic and inter-psychic therapeusis.

The active witness: on becoming aware

Pamela Corti has written about the importance of the witness, the audience that the therapist, or other members of the group, provides to clients (Corti 1993). This function of an audience, witnessing, is not simply passive. Margo Lee Sherman states:

> The audience is not the passive recipient. We actually take part. . . . It's not only the performer but the audience that creates the artistic experience . . . I feel that exchange very viscerally when I'm on stage: a sending and receiving that goes back and forth continually during the performance. Every performance has a different chemistry.

She quotes Mary Krapf (actor, director and member of the Living Theatre): 'There are the actors and the audience, and if the audience doesn't play their role, it's not much fun for us' (personal communication).

What then is the role of the theatre audience? Theatre invites us to enter the imaginal realm in which anything is possible, in which energies are liberated, conflicts enacted, emotions released, secrets revealed, wonders, terrors and beauty presented. Sometimes we are invited to suspend our disbelief, on other occasions to be aware of the artifice and think about the experience. What these different forms have in common is that they insist on our attention: that we are conscious of experiencing. As all art is an invitation to be aware so theatre can bring us into altered states of consciousness, making us aware of feelings, images, ideas, patterns, colours, struggles, revelations. It is a strong stimulus and able to bring into consciousness things we have either not experienced or have avoided or repressed. We may then be confronted with the shock of an encounter with both intra-psychic and inter-psychic material that challenges us, facing us with imaginal and real truths. This was certainly the experience of the audience in Broadmoor Hospital who watched the Royal Shakespeare Company's productions of *Hamlet* and *King Lear*. Amongst the statements Murray Cox reports from members of that audience are the following:

> This made me think how unaware I was about other people's feelings when committing my crimes . . . . I asked one of the actors how he put his heart into the role. He said to me, 'Understand the character and feel what he must have felt like.' I had to think of my victims how they felt. It was an experience I will never forget.
>
> (Cox 1992, p. 143)

> When you picked up the skull it really got to me; hit me right in the stomach; I've killed a person and I've done a lot of work on how the relatives must feel, I've played the role of the relatives; but it never crossed my mind until now that there is a corpse somewhere of the person I killed. I have never thought about the corpse before.
>
> (Cox 1992, p. 148)

Long before psychiatrists discovered that ECT had a therapeutic effect shamans were utilising shock in healing ceremonies. In the Thovil exorcism drama of Sri Lanka the patient is suddenly confronted with the demon (a masked actor) that is possessing her. The exorcist stated to me that shock was essential to the healing: if the patient was not terrified there could be no cure. Moreno used 'psychodramatic shock' on occasion to facilitate the healing of traumatic experiences:

> The technique is a kind of implosive therapy and deconditioning, replaying a traumatic scene until it loses its negative power. For example, there is the actual case of a woman who became very angry at the dinner table and told her father to drop dead – and he did. The scene was reenacted repeatedly to allow her to integrate it into her life.
>
> (Blatner 1988, p. 173)

The above insists that we no longer view the audience as passive but recognise that they are actively, even viscerally, involved in a confrontation with self: that theatre is the mirror that helps us face ourselves.

Projection and transference: 'a mirror held up to nature'

A member of the audience of a Playback Theatre performance who witnessed her story enacted reported: 'I was absolutely amazed at the instant improvisation. It made good therapy too, because to see what was, for me, a traumatic event re-enacted, helped me to exorcise the ghosts that still haunt me' (from Manchester Playback Theatre publicity leaflet). Playback is a form of theatre that specifically offers its audiences a therapeutic experience in using the mirror technique from psychodrama. An audience member tells a story from his or her life and a group of actors spontaneously re-create that story and 'feed it back' to the teller. In this process the story can be transformed and the teller can see things from a different perspective. Pam Corti gives a good example of this:

> One Teller laughed as she told the story of a car crash in Arizona, recounting the comic foibles of a fellow passenger's reactions. On seeing the drama unfold she burst into tears as she re-experienced the terror and subsequently chose an alternative ending in which she was rescued. A group member remarked, 'I've heard you talk about that several times but you always laughed it off so I had no idea what a terrible experience it really was for you.'
>
> The power of a dramatic re-enactment, rather than an anecdotal recounting of the experience, is that when given movement, voice and a living context the dynamic becomes potent and has a life of its own which is far less easy to control or censor. Actors, Teller and Audience are drawn into a mutual relationship generating an emotion which cannot easily be circumscribed by denial or disassociation.
>
> (Corti 1993, p. 15)

Phil Jones in his excellent article 'Dramatherapy: five core processes' (1991) writes: in 'theatre . . . we see ourselves writ large . . . we see and comprehend ourselves; to come to see oneself is to effect change in oneself in the very act of seeing'.

Moreno also pointed out that the members of the audience, recognising their own problems in the protagonist's enactment, could experience a vicarious therapeusis. In psychodrama he also developed the mirror technique in which the protagonist withdraws from the action and becomes an audience, watching as someone else plays her role. Getting some distance from the action she is often able to see things more clearly and release herself from the bind she was in.

As well as offering a mirror that shows us the outside, our behaviour and interpsychic world, theatre offers a mirror that shows us that which is within: the inner scenario. The theatre is a mirror in which

> the therapist and actor serve as projective figures. The transference does not represent a real object relationship, but it is one in which the therapist/actor serves as a target upon which the patient/spectator transfers and projects feelings stemming from important figures (objects) from the past. A mutual exchange takes place in this intermediary area, which is the space in-between therapist and patient, actor and spectator, and which is

also in-between the conscious and unconscious mind .... This 'transference illusion' as Winnicott (1953) called it, resembles 'the-play-within-the-play' situation, an interior world of imagination, so often used by Shakespeare. He dissolves problems within the transitional space of the theatre .... Shakespeare's themes of conflicts, which range from the everyday to the most bizarre, make the projection possible. By experiencing dramatic material mirroring personal conflicts, thoughts, fantasies and feelings are projected onto fictive objects. Contact is thereby made between conscious and unconscious material, so that a higher degree of integration becomes possible. This is one of the therapeutic benefits of witnessing the plays in live performance.

(Cox and Theilgaard 1994, pp. 266–267)

Shakespeare's paraclinical presentation augments the intensity of attending, not only to the text, but also to the subtext, which is so often linked to individual and corporate unconscious material. This is one reason for the unrivalled hold Shakespeare has upon the theatre audience, because buried affect is 'carried across' – through transference and metaphor – and is therefore communicated directly to the unconscious of each individual and to the corporate unconscious of the audience-as-a-whole.

(Cox and Theilgaard 1994, p. 185)

The authors go on to relate the audience to the therapy group. In ancient Greece theatre was seen as a healing place.

Catharsis

Aristotle was the first writer to point out that Tragedy had not only an aesthetic, pleasurable effect on audiences but also a healing release or purgation of emotions: 'A tragedy, ... with incidents arousing pity and fear, wherewith to accomplish its catharsis of such emotions' (Fyfe 1967, p. 16).

Commenting on this passage Fyfe writes:

Aristotle, realising the risk of inhibition, replies that this effect is not only pleasurable but also beneficial. Tragedy is a sort of nervous specific which provides Catharsis – we might say 'a good clearance' – of emotions which might otherwise break out inconveniently. It saves us from psychical distress by providing an emotional outlet.

(Fyfe 1967, p. 15)

Moreno was inspired by the ancient Greek theatre. He considered the audience to be an essential instrument of the healing power of psychodrama. He referred also to the therapeusis of the audience. During a psychodrama members of the audience, identifying with the protagonist, may well see their own tragedy, conflict, anger, grief revealed and experience catharsis. He refined his method to facilitate such cathartic therapeusis of the audience by instituting a period of sharing after the main enactment was over in which members of the audience share with the protagonist what the drama touched in them, what they recognised from their own life (Pitzele 1992, p. 3).

Murray Cox reports on the cathartic effect of watching Shakespeare's tragedies in Broadmoor Hospital: one patient stated:

> What affected me most was the sad and violent deterioration of Lear himself . . . . When Lear died I felt an overwhelming sense of loss and tears riding down my cheeks. I desperately wanted to go over and hug Lear's corpse. I felt a sense of union in death between Lear and his daughters. Also the sense of peace and wholeness in the deaths . . . . Having killed and abused ourselves, we are able to understand the madness and violence and the many ranges of emotions in Shakespeare's tragedies because it is close to our heart.
>
> (Cox 1992, p. 140)

Fusion and separation, proximity and distance

Successful therapy involves a process within which the client finds a safe space to trust, depend, grow and individuate: the potential therapeutic space is a womb-like container within which the client might first have an experience of merging with (and transferring upon) and later separating from the therapist. Indeed it could be argued that unless there is some joining with the therapist the client will not feel sufficiently held for there to be therapeusis. The counter-transference is the therapist's experience of this fusion. This process of fusion/separation is first experienced with the good enough parent who enables the child to play in the space that is at once near enough for the child to feel secure (held) and yet separate enough to support a feeling of having a private space in which he or she can become absorbed in the dramatic reality of play. Theatre is a place within which the audience experience a temporary fusion, both with each other in the 'audience-as-a-whole' and with the actors upon whom they may project or with whom they may identify (see Jones 1991, p. 9). Peter Brook sees this as one of the healing elements in theatre: at a recent seminar in Manchester (during the 1994 City of Drama Festival) he reflected that 'the theatre audience came to the play as isolates and that a successful play joined people together, giving them an experience of communality, even communion: a sense of shared wholeness' (Casson 1995, p. 12).

Theatre, as an art, invites a merging and emerging of conscious and unconscious material. As the scenery shifts and characters interact the audience are able, vicariously, to explore and encounter different aspects of themselves and the world, temporally merging, fusing with the fiction, to emerge as the curtain falls enriched by the experience. We come blinking into the street, feeling slightly strange as we reorientate ourselves back to our everyday selves in ordinary reality.

'Art, therefore, by encouraging a fusion with the aesthetic object, allows the audience to enrich and revivify the adult and differentiated self with the emotional gain of that fusion' (Stockholder quoted in Cox and Theilgaard 1994, p. 268). Sue Jennings quotes 'Wilshire's description of enactment in the theatre when he says that the actor and audience are engaged in a dramatic encounter which is brought about by giving up, or holding constant, the conscious self'. She continues:

> To articulate fusion and engulfment, the actor allows artistically controlled engulfment with his audience to occur. As they feed off his characterisation, he feeds off their passivity, their fusing and their objectivity in regard to the character before them. His artistry consists in maintaining a precarious balance between abandonment to archaic fusion authorised by the audience, and artistic control of what enactment is allowed.
>
> (Jennings 1995, p. 186)

Roger Grainger writes:

> Drama itself is largely concerned with the experiences of separation and involvement (or alienation and engulfment), and with the achievement of a healthy balance between them, by which is meant one which reflects and explores an individual's sense of social identity. I have claimed elsewhere (1990) that it possesses the ability to strengthen human personhood by using imaginative involvement in other people's lives as a way of validating the self and I have suggested that this may be a reason why people with a tenuous sense of their own separate individuality show signs of an enhanced ability to think clearly about other people understood in relation to themselves.
>
> (Grainger 1992, p. 177)

Dramatic distance not only provides safety but also enables the client to achieve an objective subjectivity: to be a witnessing audience through others to the self. One of the Broadmoor patients, reflecting on the experience of watching *Hamlet*, wrote:

> For me it was a journey of self recognition through madness, and it was healthy for me to experience. Several times I saw myself in the guise of these brilliant actors and actresses. True, parts were traumatic, but somehow it was a positive calling up of my own savage memories. They could be viewed rationally from a distance, like in a play.
>
> (Cox 1992, p. 142)

The story: structure and insight

When Othello's love for Desdemona is threatened, when that central pivotal structure of his life is undermined, he says: '. . . and when I love thee not, Chaos is come again' (III, iii, 92–93). Another aspect of the therapeusis of the audience, Di Adderley writes, is

> to do with learning to structure one's own experience. Life is a chaotic continuum and sense (and connection) can only be made by editing, structuring, perceiving (with some degree of objectivity) and sharing with others the insights gained. In Playback Theatre a very important part of the conductor's job is aiding the teller to structure their story – this is simply done by asking, 'When and where does your story take place, who is in it, what happens, how did you feel at the end?' Many tellers come to the chair saying 'I don't think this is really a story but . . .' I think what they mean is: 'I can't see the wood for the trees – I know there's something there but I'm not sure what it is. Can you help?' The structuring of experience is in itself therapeutic. Art structures experience even when it is chronicling chaos: e.g. Picasso's Guernica.
>
> (personal communication)

Through such art, through watching a play, we learn to structure in our own way. Traditional stories have archetypal deep structures that resonate with us below the floor level (beneath the stage) of consciousness. So fairy stories with their 'happy ever after' endings are deeply satisfying even if our modern consciousness is cynical of such simple conclusions in our fractured, tragic world of relativity. We, like Othello, are only too aware of the threat of chaos. In the performance of a play we have the reassurance that the playwright has done the structuring for us: he or she has done the editing, made the choices. We can enjoy the coherence of the story. Nevertheless we also do our own editing through selective attention determined by projective processes, so that each member of the audience can have a different perception of the same play. Thus a multifaceted work of art can speak to each member of the audience and their inner world. Di Adderley believes we can learn from such experiences in art 'to apply selectivity to our own stories. Sometimes our selection process may be for self presentation and we may need to re-structure that part of our story at a later date', possibly in therapy.

Learning to structure and edit experience is also crucial in therapy: being clear what is the main road and what are the diversions for this particular time is essential if the client and therapist are not to get lost/stuck/confused. A play has a through line, and this is also essential in creative dramatherapy where together the clients and therapist must seek the emerging structure and meaning in the process. The dramatherapist through training learns when to structure and when to follow the clients' process. In a psychodrama both protagonist and therapist are continually faced with multiple choices about which of the myriad facets of an emerging story are the right ones to follow at this particular moment; the guiding principles for the selection of the right direction include following the protagonist, remembering the contract for the psychodrama and achieving a sense of completion through circular form. Art celebrates its triumph over the chaos of life through form and the completeness of unity: the satisfaction of a completed Gestalt. The audience has the pleasure of enjoying the wholeness implicit in a finished work, whereas in life we are often struggling with unfinished business.

The client

In individual therapy the client is the audience of the therapist's performance. Therapeusis might result from many factors in that performance. One incident from my own practice where I performed, as if a mirror for the client, must suffice as an example here. I had invited her to make a pattern with buttons on a white sheet of paper. She created an 'S' shape. I asked what associations she had with the letter S. She said her name, Silence, Secrets, Scream, Snake. I invited her to move as the shape. We moved together: I mirrored her movement. I noticed that her hands snaked from side to side, as if brushing someone or something away, to give her space. She stopped and said she felt stupid. We added that to the list of S associations and laughed. I then invited her to watch me do the movement and reported to her what I felt/imagined about the movement. This immediately triggered a memory of a recent incident in which she had wanted to claim more personal space and subsequently recalled other important material. These insights were the result of my performing the action for her so that she did not feel self-conscious or stupid: at the safe distance of the role of audience she was more able to connect with the meaning inherent in the action.

The therapist

As we witness our clients' theatre of therapy do we as therapists benefit? Are we, sometimes in an audience of one, helped by the performance? Supervision is the place we take our doubts, anxieties and problems in the work. It is also a place we celebrate when things go well. As I witness the clients I work with struggling, growing, triumphing, I do benefit. My self-esteem is raised by work well done. I benefit from vicarious joy. I learn. I grow. I am healed.

ACKNOWLEDGEMENTS

For their contributions to this chapter I am grateful to the following: Di Adderley, actor, Playback Theatre Director, Manchester; Margo Lee Sherman, actor, New York; Jill Wallis, dramatherapy trainee, Manchester.

REFERENCES

Blatner, A. with Blatner, A. (1988) *Foundations of Psychodrama*, New York: Springer Publications.

Brook, P. (1976) *The Empty Space*, Harmondsworth, UK: Penguin.

Casson, J. (1984) 'The Therapeutic Dramatic Community Ceremonies of Sri Lanka', *Journal of the British Association for Dramatherapists* 7(2) (Spring): 11–18.

—— (1994) 'The therapeutic elements in drama', *Newsletter of the British Association for Dramatherapists* (Spring): 10–11.

—— (1995) 'The therapeutic value of performance', *Newsletter of the British Association for Dramatherapists* (Summer): 10–13.

Corti, P. (1993) 'Bearing witness', *Journal of the British Association for Dramatherapists* 15 (3) (Winter): 12–16.

Cox, M. (1992) *Shakespeare Comes to Broadmoor: The Performance of Tragedy in a Secure Psychiatric Hospital*, London: Jessica Kingsley.

Cox, M. and Theilgaard A. (1994) *Shakespeare as Prompter*, London: Jessica Kingsley.

Feasey, D. (1994) 'A response to John Casson's paper' (*'The therapeutic elements in drama'*), *Newsletter of the British Association for Dramatherapists* (Spring): 11.

Fyfe, W.H. (1967) *Aristotle's Art of Poetry*, Oxford: Clarendon Press.

Grainger, R. (1990) *Drama and Healing: The Roots of Dramatherapy*, London: Jessica Kingsley.

Grainger, R. (1992) 'Dramatherapy and thought disorder', in S. Jennings (ed.) *Dramatherapy Theory and Practice 2*, London: Routledge.

Hodgkinson, L. (1987) *Smile Therapy*, London: Optima.

Jennings, S. (1995), *Theatre, Ritual and Transformation: The Senoi Temiars*, London: Routledge.

Jones, P. (1991), 'Dramatherapy: five core processes', *Journal of the British Association for Dramatherapists* 14(1) (Autumn): 8–15. (See also Jones, P. (1995) *Dramatherapy – Theatre as Living*, London: Routledge.)

Moore, T. (ed.) (1990) *The Essential James Hillman*, London: Routledge.

Pitzele, M. (1992) 'Moreno's chorus: the audience in psychodrama', *Journal of the British Psychodrama Association* 7(1) (Summer): 3–8.

Chapter 5

Personagrams

The exploration of our inner world through group sculpting

Sue Mitchell

Our remedies oft in ourselves do lie.

All's Well That Ends Well

INTRODUCTION

Many years ago as a drama teacher and someone involved in personal development, I was struck by the need to find a way of resolving inner conflicts which used the body and avoided ego-confrontation. It was also crucial that such a technique should be both powerful and non-threatening and one that could be used by any group.

The result of this quest was the birth of Personagrams. In this chapter I shall outline what Personagrams are, how they work in action and what mechanisms are operating which make them effective and illustrate some further applications for this technique.

WHAT IS A PERSONAGRAM?

A Personagram is a group activity, using sculpting[1] to look at the multifaceted aspects of ourselves which make up 'me'. Personagrams do not depend on a theory of personality to unravel the psyche, but take the individuality of each of us at a particular moment as their basis. In a Personagram a group member is invited to sculpt the various aspects of his or her[2] personality, using the members of the group to embody them. The aspects are defined and described as a physical sculpture and placed in the Personagram in particular spatial relationships with each other and the 'world out there'.

The word Personagram is formed from two words – personality and hologram. This etymology is very important to the understanding of what I envisaged a Personagram to be. A Personagram is about gaining insights into the different parts of our persona, and a three-dimensional sculpture can be likened to a hologram, a three-dimensional image of an object.

The Personagram involves a projection of the different separated aspects of someone's personality on to other people in the group, who then reflect back, as mirrors, to the originator what they are like and, through creating a group sculpt of these, a three-dimensional picture of the whole is created.

It was important to me when devising a technique to look at our inner life that it should include within the process something which emphasised that the personality was not merely a sum of its parts, but that each aspect was inextricably and inevitably affected by each of the other aspects. The hologram seemed a fitting analogy. If a holographic photograph is broken or fragmented, each tiny part of the photographic plate, no matter how small, contains not just that specific part of the original picture, but the whole of it. Correspondingly a Personagram involves fragmenting the personality to see more clearly what its aspects are, yet each aspect does indeed contain the whole, because its very nature is determined by its relationship to all the other aspects which create that unique individual. The existence of an aspect and its status within a person depends on what else is happening within.

Two further analogies are present. A hologram is a representation caught in a moment of time when the photograph is taken; a Personagram is a reflection of the person as she is here and now and is therefore open to change and movement. Finally, it is important to remember that the hologram may look very real, but it is not the original; just so, the Personagram is not the person herself, she has stepped aside and is there looking at this hologram of herself.

At first view Personagrams have many similarities to the visual dynamic techniques of sculpting and spectograms described by Sue Jennings in her book *Creative Drama in Groupwork* (1986), and to the sculpting techniques used in the sociogram of classical psychodrama, recently described as intrapsychic psychodrama by Peter Pitzele (1991), and in family therapy. However, valuable as these particular techniques are for the purposes they are exploring, they do not tackle the problem that I witnessed of the dominant aspect of a person ordering and censoring what was being expressed by that person. Hence, although the initial stages of setting up a Personagram will be familiar to those people who are conversant with these techniques, there are inherent differences in the action which create a different outcome.

A PERSONAGRAM IN ACTION

How is this holographic image of a person set up, and what does it look like in action? The Personagram requires a facilitator; a sculptor, who is the person who chooses to set up the Personagram; a group of people; and a 'stage' area for the Personagram to be positioned, which is quite simply one end of the room in which you are working. It is not necessary for the group to know each other. In fact this can be a disadvantage, because it can bring previous images and ideas about others into play, thus making it more difficult for people to get out of their heads. Nor is it necessary for any of the group to have previous experience either in group work or role-play work of any kind. Indeed it is vital to stress that the work in no way demands acting skills.

When the facilitator feels that the group is warmed up and there is a state of readiness and trust, she will set the scene for action, clarifying the 'stage' area, the sculptor's inner world, where the Personagram will be created, and defining the outer world – the 'out there' where other people are. The two worlds are delineated by the interacting edge where communication with others takes place. The outer world area is where the group will sit and those not involved in the Personagram will remain as witnesses.

Prior to inviting a group member to try out a Personagram, the facilitator needs to clarify two things with the group: first that there will be a respect of confidentiality agreed by all in the group, and second that everyone is prepared to participate in another person's Personagram if they are chosen as any aspect. If anyone would rather be a witness this is absolutely fine and this should be made very clear to the group, but it is very important to ascertain this *before* the sculptor begins to choose. It could be damaging for a sculptor to be refused by a group member, thereby bringing up issues of rejection or lack of self-worth.

Once the sculptor emerges from the group and joins the facilitator in the 'stage' area, the facilitator must be constantly aware of the sculptor's state of being. This sensitivity and support for the sculptor are the primary role of the facilitator. I mention it here because as the Personagram unfolds it does take on a life of its own and it is all too easy to lose sight of the sculptor as this happens.

FIRST STAGE: SETTING UP THE PERSONAGRAM

The sculptor is asked to begin by selecting some aspects of his personality. Often people are stumped by this question, but if there is a difficulty the facilitator can help by focusing the sculptor's attention on some 'non-threatening' aspect which was evident during the 'warm-up' period. The skill of the facilitator at this point is to ensure that just one distinct trait is selected and not a number of traits rolled into one. Having singled out an aspect the sculptor then chooses someone from the group to become that part of himself. The facilitator then suggests that the sculptor mould this person into a posture which typifies, symbolically, the aspect which is being embodied. Often the sculptor, especially if this sort of work is a new experience, will show concern at this and say that he does not know how this person should pose. Interestingly, whenever this has happened, when I, as facilitator, have stepped in and made a suggestion, and some sort of pose is initiated, the sculptor has immediately intervened with 'Oh yes' and unhesitatingly added to it, or more usually 'Oh no, not like that. It's like this', and has intuitively known exactly what attitude should be adopted, whether on a chair or table, huddled in a corner, arms outstretched, head at a particular angle, or even whether a finger should be crooked or straight. The person being moulded is now an 'Aspect' in terms of the Personagram. The Aspect is now placed spatially in relationship to the 'outside world'. In other words, is this facet of the sculptor's personality 'up front', or does it not interact with others very much, or not show itself to the world out there very readily?

Once one Aspect is in position the sculptor is invited to select other traits of his personality. With each facet the same procedure occurs, usually this time with no hesitation by the sculptor. Of course, like all artists he will stand back from time to time and adjust a hand here or a leg there. The key difference between the first and subsequent Aspects is that they are placed not only in relationship to the outside world, but also in a spatial relationship to each other. Are they close to any other Aspect, placed above or below any, are they touching any other Aspect, looking at any other? In this way, with the help of the facilitator to remind the sculptor of the finer points of his sculpture, for example where the eyes are directed, the Personagram is created. Aspects are added until the sculptor feels satisfied. This completes the first stage and the sculptor and facilitator move out of the stage area and join the witnesses. Thus the sculptor has put himself out there and can now sit back and have a good look!

SECOND STAGE: REVEALING THE FEELINGS AND INNER CONFLICTS

It is now the turn of the Aspects to express their feelings. This is the key point of differentiation from other sculpting techniques mentioned above. In those the person who has set up the sculpt will direct or correct the statements that those in the sculpture might make. In a Personagram the sculptor listens *without any intervention at all*. The reason why this is so crucial to the effectiveness of the Personagram will be detailed in a later section.

The facilitator asks the Aspects to hold their positions exactly as they were placed for a little time in silence. (As the Personagram is building it is advisable to allow the Aspects to relax from their postures occasionally.) Each Aspect is then asked, in the order that they were positioned, how they feel. The facilitator may help the Aspects to begin by guiding them to express how they feel physically in the posture. The Aspect thus has something concrete to start with. It has been my experience that the physical sensations, feelings, are a metaphorical insight into the psychological feelings, emotional world, of the Aspect. Examples of this from past Personagrams are comments like 'I feel constricted' or 'I feel utterly stuck here', or, as an Aspect embodying a 'loving' aspect said, 'I can't feel anything – I feel completely numb.' This was an insight for the sculptor, who suddenly realised that in order to survive a very difficult period she had desensitised her loving feelings and this had resulted in problems in forming new relationships.

Having talked about how an Aspect feels about herself, the facilitator will draw the Aspect's attention to the others in the inner world and then the outer

world. How does she feel about them? Again the physical state seems to be
the key to, and the mirror of, the psychological state. An Aspect 'up front'
has said: 'I can't see any of them. I'm totally oblivious to anyone else. I just
have to keep up a good front to the world.' Or: 'I can't see anyone, but I am
vaguely aware of an irritating person behind who is breathing down my neck.'
Aspects who are placed behind another Aspect vary in their comments from
'I feel a great sense of comfort from this Aspect. I feel that she is shielding
me from the world', to 'I feel blocked from the world by this Aspect and just
can't be seen, which makes me feel very angry towards him.' Aspects which
are very close to others, or actually touching have made comments like 'I feel
that I can't breathe properly because of this Aspect; I'm being suffocated by
her.' Alternatively, others have said 'I feel very supported by this Aspect; he
is protecting me from Loudmouth who is glaring at me.'

It is worth noting that the various Aspects are usually given appropriate
names by the sculptor as they are chosen, like Loudmouth, Floppy, Secretive,
Fun-packed, Vulnerable, Energy, and they are referred to by each other and
by the facilitator by these names.

As each Aspect expresses her feelings about herself, the other Aspects in
the Personagram and the outer world, inner conflicts emerge and internal
support mechanisms are revealed. The clarity of these is quite awe-inspiring
to behold, and often for the sculptor confirm vague feelings which he has not
previously been able to bring into awareness because of the confusion of
messages going on inside, or because certain Aspects have been silenced by
more dominant Aspects.

The basic Personagram is now complete, although the process is by no
means over as there is a developmental stage. At this point, however, the
facilitator breaks proceedings by allowing the Aspects to relax from their
positions, but not to leave the 'stage' area, and turns her attention solely to
the sculptor. As the Aspects have been speaking, the sculptor may have been
feeling vulnerable. There may be parts of his personality on show which may
never have been exposed before. The facilitator must be aware of this and be
sensitive to the sculptor throughout, ready to give support. I usually sit next
to the sculptor during the witnessing and give support when it is needed.

THIRD STAGE: THE DEVELOPMENTAL STAGE

The developmental stage of the Personagram is when the possibilities for
change and resolution of conflicts can be seen.

There are two main ways in which a Personagram can develop:

1 The Aspects move

During the second stage some of the Aspects may state that they feel varying
degrees of discomfiture in the position they are in. The facilitator can suggest

to the Aspects that, without words, they move until they feel happier or 'more comfortable' with each other and the 'world'. The Aspects begin their 'ballet' – moving from place to place with reference to the other Aspects and the 'world'. Within a short space of time a new Personagram emerges, based on the energies felt by the Aspects themselves.

After the movement there is much more connection with the other Aspects, and the isolate is generally no longer so isolated. Sometimes the difference is striking and the resulting picture very moving to witness because it seems to reveal that, with some changes of attitudes to ourselves, we can indeed resolve our inner conflicts. Just prior to the Aspects' moving I quietly whisper to the sculptor to watch carefully who moves first and who resists change. After facilitating many Personagrams it has struck me that these things may be a clue for the sculptor in initiating changes in her life. One sculptor did remark with acute awareness that her Personagram when moving seemed to go into a state of chaos before the Aspects seemed ready to resolve their differences and find more conducive places to be and she was able to see which Aspect was making the changes difficult. 'I now know the area to work on, and I know it won't be easy!' she remarked. Gestalt therapy also states that a state of chaos can often be the precursor to profound change.

Once the Personagram has made this new still picture, the Aspects are again asked how they feel themselves, about the other Aspects and the 'world'. The responses vary, and of course not everyone has found their ideal position and the Aspects often have a great deal to say about 'pushy' Aspects, but there is always a more positive feeling about the whole and usually a feeling of togetherness which was not apparent before. Negative Aspects often take on a positive role, although the fundamental intrinsic nature of the Aspect is the same. Does this indeed highlight the view that there are no truly negative traits of personality, only traits which have not been able to show their potential usefulness and it is just our attitude which makes them positive or negative? I believe that 'There is nothing either good or bad, but thinking makes it so' (*Hamlet*). An interesting feature of changes of this nature is that Aspects will say that their names have changed. This has now become a question which I may pose as the facilitator.

2 One Aspect is chosen to initiate the movement

It may emerge that one particular Aspect 'sticks out like a sore thumb' and seems to be influencing every other Aspect in a negative way, or is very isolated from the rest who are in harmony. If the facilitator feels that it is appropriate she may ask the sculptor if the sculptor would like to see what would happen if such an Aspect moved. This Aspect will then move first to another place, and the other Aspects will then wish to move to adjust to this new position, so the 'ballet' begins. The development then continues as indicated above.

Example

A Personagram when first set up included a very dominant Aspect raised high on a chair, placed on a table, towering above everyone else. All the Aspects were highly aware of this Aspect, afraid of it, or defiant. This dominant Aspect was asked to move, which incidentally she was happy to do, for although she had felt that she was the kingpin in the personality, she also felt very isolated in her lofty position. The Aspect did remain central, but came down to ground level. All the other Aspects then moved, and each one of them became more positive.

I stress this point because in the initial Personagram many Aspects were depressed, aggressive or completely closed in upon themselves. For example, a passive–aggressive Aspect, who was called Desperation, became a pillar of strength and support for a sensitive Aspect who had not previously dared to show his face, and changed his name to Warrior Guard.

This can also be particularly helpful to the sculptor who can see clearly what could happen if she changed one aspect of herself. For example, the sculptor of the Personagram cited above had believed that unless this lofty aspect of his personality totally dominated his approach to himself and others, he would 'crumble' as a person even though he did not like the way he was. Through watching what happened, he saw that if anything the reverse was true and he was reassured that a change was possible.

It is at this point that the Personagram is usually completed. Occasionally more changes will follow, but this should only happen in very exceptional circumstances. If too many changes take place the sculptor can lose sight of herself. It may be possible to create a Personagram which appears completely harmonious by allowing a series of re-adjustments and realignments, and, as previously mentioned, the Aspects, facilitator and witnesses can often see how these adjustments could be made, but the sculptor has to be able to accept herself as she is now. She must be able to see *how* she can change if there is a wish to do so. To present a sculptor with a Personagram, which through several developments appears to be an alien personality to the person she is now, can create a feeling that this is an impossible goal and can lead to a feeling of worthlessness. The sculptor has to live with herself now, not with a Utopian vision of what she might be after fifteen years of constant change. If we are not totally happy with ourselves, and few of us are, we need to see the first few steps we can take to change ourselves. Hence there is a need for the facilitator to be sensitive to the sculptor and aware that the Personagram can take on a life of its own, with the danger that the sculptor can be marginalised. I have had to stop a Personagram when the Aspects started to 'take over' and demand further refinements to sort out some minor conflicts which still remained to be resolved.

STAGE FOUR: DEBRIEFING AND DEROLING

In this closing stage of a Personagram, when the 'stage' area is cleared and we are a group again, the need to avoid intellectual discussion is paramount. I have indeed dissipated the dynamic effect of a Personagram by allowing the group to enter into a discussion about what has happened, the accuracy or otherwise of the Aspects and the mechanisms involved. Immediately, the sculptor felt the need to justify the way the Personagram had been set up, and defence mechanisms came into play in this analytical discussion. I have since found the kind of 'sharing' which takes place after a psychodrama to be the most valuable approach to debriefing. In other words the sculptor can share or not share his feelings, and the witnesses may share similar feelings they might have about themselves. When the sculptor and witnesses have shared as much as they feel they need to, the facilitator must turn her attention to the Aspects.

The participants who have embodied an Aspect have been in this 'role' for a considerable period of time and need to go through a process of deroling. There are many ways to do this, and how much time is devoted to this will often depend on how much experience the participants have had in 'role-playing. Because a Personagram is a physical activity I usually suggest that the Aspects move around the room, putting their bodies into different shapes, thereby releasing the energies from their designated positions. In fact I normally include the whole group in this activity as the rest of the group have also been static for some time. I encourage the group to make sounds as they move around the room, again as a means of releasing any locked energies. Finally, when the group is again seated, I invite the Aspects to state their own names and let go of the Aspect they were embodying.

Once the deroling is complete I allow space for the Aspects to comment on anything they feel they might have gained personally from being the Aspect they were chosen to embody. In many instances the Aspects have gained insights into themselves and the way that particular aspect of themselves interacts: one person encapsulated this by saying 'I know I was your Nurturing, but this was also about me!' Others may not wish to see the connections with themselves and it is vital that the facilitator respects this.

THE MECHANISM AND EFFECTIVENESS OF PERSONAGRAMS

How and why are Personagrams effective in so clearly revealing the inner world of a person? Why do they seem to be so accurate? What factors come into play in this specific technique?

The imagination, intuition, and the spontaneous expression of feelings, by using a body-language technique, seem to be the keys to what happens in a Personagram.

How does the element 'imagination' fit in? The Aspects themselves are 'images', sculptures created by a sculptor who is using her image-making faculties to place in a particular shape an abstract quality within herself. Because she is not attempting to analyse verbally, nor talking at any length about these qualities, the reasoning areas of her mentality do not come into play. She is in a sense forced to use those areas of the brain not connected with language – the right-hand side of the brain, which is accepted by many as being the side concerned with spatial abilities. The right-hand side of the brain is also related to our creative, intuitive areas. A Personagram is not an intellectual analysis of our personality. Indeed, in a Personagram the intellect has to take a back seat. An interesting example of this occurred during a workshop, at which a participant who had some prior knowledge of the technique from a friend set up his Personagram. He related to the group later that he had come to the workshop already prepared for this and had thought carefully about the aspects he would include and how they would be – an intellectual exercise. What astonished him was that, although the basic shape was as he had planned, the minutiae of the sculpting gave the Personagram an unexpected dimension, so that when the Aspects were given voice they reflected his emotional life which he had previously found difficult to access. This astonished him and yet it resonated for him.

The element of intuition mentioned above plays a part in the mechanism of a Personagram, in that once the imagination is fired the sculptor spontaneously and intuitively moulds the Aspects into the appropriate attitudes. The setting up of a Personagram does not take long, once the initial move has been made. It is quite clear to an observer that normal 'thinking', in terms of working out intellectually and rationally where and how each Aspect should stand, is not happening – the activity of the sculptor is not concomitant with that mode of behaviour. Rather, it is as if the image is there and the intuition knows how to create it. The parallel I find when observing the sculptor setting up a Personagram is that of Michelangelo, who chipped away the marble to reveal the statue which he was seeing within it. It is as sure-footed as that.

The intuition also plays a part in the selection of the Aspects. Instinctively the sculptor seems to select the 'right' people to embody very different aspects of her personality. Generally she has only had a short time together with these people and yet the choice seems to be precise. One example which particularly stands out is when a sculptor chose probably the mildest, most timid member of the group to personify her 'anger', positioning her in a classic pose, with clenched fists and set jaw. I remember thinking that for me she would have been the last person I would have chosen. Yet when her anger spoke it became abundantly clear that this person was perfect to express the repressed and stifled anger within the sculptor. And, as already mentioned, the Aspects have frequently stated that their aspect had a relevance for them. There is a linking taking place, with some particular energy within the person recognised intuitively by the sculptor.

The use of body language is integral to the mechanism of a Personagram. The adoption of a particular pose not only creates a physical feeling in someone, but also changes the energy flows within, and this in turn creates a certain state of mind. In our daily lives this chain reaction is seen in reverse. In other words, we are in a particular state of mind, our energy flow follows suit, and we find ourselves sitting or standing in a posture which reflects our state of mind: our mental attitude creates our physical 'attitude'.

The interlinking of body and mind is upheld by many different schools of thought. Initially I became aware of it through Eastern philosophies and practices, such as acupuncture and yoga which assert that the body and mind are inextricably linked. 'By seeing the body in a particular mood and attitude, one can study the emotional state of mind because mind is like an engine which impels the body to adopt a specific posture' (Mishra 1972, p. 90).

Those who work closely with the body say the same: Ken Dychtwald, when analysing these links, called his resulting book *Bodymind*, and Debbie Shapiro states in *The Bodymind Workbook*: 'we have to recognize that the mind and body are one . . . our bodies . . . manifest the unconscious energies which underlie our every action' (Shapiro 1990, p. 90). In Gestalt therapy, through awareness of what is happening with the client physically, the feelings which are being censored by the mind can be accessed.

Thus in a Personagram the emphasis is always on the Aspects' versions of how they are. Whatever they choose to say is not corrected by the sculptor. The reasons for this emphasis are:

1 The sculptor may often find it too difficult or painful to express his feelings. An Aspect, because she does not have the same emotional investment, i.e. she is being a part of someone else, can express deeper, perhaps more 'dangerous' feelings more freely and fully.
2 The sculptor speaks from his whole persona whereas within the Personagram a different person is embodying each single facet.
3 Within the sculptor's usual persona there may be one dominant aspect, for example the intellect, or a childhood introject, or message, for example 'appear to be happy'. This dominant aspect or message will override less confident parts of his personality or aspects which don't fit in to the image which the person is trying to project, so these aspects never get a 'look in' or a chance to express themselves in his communication with others.

In the second and third stages each Aspect expresses how she feels. Each one has an equal chance to speak; no one is overridden or censored by any other. It is interesting to observe that Aspects are often *physically* blocked by other more dominant Aspects, but the process prevents them from being *verbally* blocked or silenced. Certainly an Aspect which in the sculptor's personality has never had the chance to express itself will undoubtedly say so. Such Aspects are usually found crouched somewhere at the back of the 'stage' area, with their backs to the 'world'. Maybe for the first time during a Personagram a frightened, vulnerable part will be given voice to express its feelings of vulnerability, or possibly anger at being shoved to the back, unable to play a positive part in the personality.

During the second and third stages the sculptor does not interject; he absorbs. There is no requirement for him to explain or justify what is being presented; it simply is.

In this way, the sculptor is finding out about himself, and perhaps most importantly about the conflicts which exist within, by highlighting the feelings of the Aspects towards each other. Here again the key is the physical, spatial relationships reflecting the psychological relationships. The inner battles which we feel going on inside us are very difficult to unravel, but the structure of the Personagram gives an immediate picture of this inner state. The feelings expressed by the Aspects put on to this picture the deeper points, usually through metaphorical language that a silent overview alone cannot. Finally the developmental stage reveals ways in which the inner conflicts can be resolved.

APPLICATIONS OF PERSONAGRAMS

In addition to the classical use of Personagrams as a tool for understanding ourselves and our inner conflicts, and thence illustrating possible ways of having a positive inner dialogue, Personagrams can be adapted to a number of different situations.

Resolving a specific conflict

A Personagram can be used to highlight a specific inner conflict, by setting up the Aspects directly felt by the sculptor to be at loggerheads. In such a Personagram two or maybe three Aspects are selected and they have a conversation with each other, revealing their resentments and their motivations for feeling as they do. On most occasions the polarity is so great that it is impossible for the conflicting Aspects to resolve their differences alone. At this point I, as the facilitator, will intervene and ask the Aspects if there is anything which would make them feel able to find a way of coexisting, help them to understand the other's point of view so that their differences might be resolved. In other words what kind of mediator would they listen to? The choice has varied from someone with a sense of humour, to a nurturing, loving individual. The sculptor is then invited to chose an Aspect of herself who is like this, and this Aspect is then introduced into the Personagram. This Aspect acts as mediator. This kind of application tends to have more free-flowing movement within it and is a more advanced use of Personagrams by the facilitator, so should only be undertaken after considerable experience of the usual form of Personagrams.

Resolving an interpersonal conflict

Personagrams can be used to resolve a conflict with someone in the world out there. The Personagram is created in the usual way and the development is that the person with whom the sculptor is having difficulties stands in front of the Personagram and the Aspects say how they feel about this person. (The sculptor is the one who takes the place of this person.) It soon becomes evident which traits of the sculptor's personality are at odds with the person. Moreover, it becomes evident which traits the other person involved is exploiting.

Example

The sculptor was having problems with someone at work. When her Personagram was completed she was invited to address 'her-selves' in the role of her 'difficult' colleague. At first she thought this was impossible (she had never been involved in this kind of work previously), but with encouragement and support she finally did so. When asked what she thought about this personality in the role of her colleague, she replied spontaneously, 'What a mess!' It transpired that the colleague only related to three Aspects and dismissed the others, relating to her as if they did not exist. In her attempts to communicate with her colleague the sculptor had suppressed all but these three Aspects. It was shown through the interactions between these Aspects and the colleague that he was able to manipulate the Aspects. The sculptor had not fully realised what was happening, although she had felt that her leadership position with this person was being somehow eroded. When this was revealed, other Aspects, now on the sidelines having been dismissed and silenced, came back into the Personagram to act as supports to the other three. This enabled these three to be much stronger and less easy to manipulate.

I met this sculptor some months later and she said that this piece of work had effectively enabled her to change her relationship with her colleague.

Resolving an inner motivational conflict

Often we wish to do something but have a conflict within ourselves so we feel stuck and do nothing, for example changing jobs, or changing a particular behaviour. We may not be able to tell what it is that is holding us back. We can, in a similar way to the previous example, present the task to our Personagram. The Aspects each say what they feel about the task. In this way we reveal to ourselves which Aspects are holding us back; our inner conflict is made clear. We can then decide whether we wish to change our alignment, our attitude, so that these Aspects do not hamper us any more. Similarly we can present a problem to 'our-selves' and very often the Aspects' reactions to it can show us the way to resolve it.

Example

A sculptor was feeling frustrated that, despite doing some therapy on a childhood trauma, she was still not 'getting on' with her life as she felt she should. She set up her Personagram to see what might be preventing this. She stood in front of her Personagram and asked why. All the 'up front' Aspects were positive about moving on and letting go of the past; they felt that they had a clear awareness of what had been the problem and could move on. But at the back, apart from the other Aspects, were two Aspects clinging on to each other: Hurt and Vulnerability, looking like the 'Babes in the Wood'. They said that even though they had been seen and heard in the therapy, they now felt exposed and they needed to be nurtured by other Aspects of the personality before they could feel healthy.

The sculptor was very moved by their testimony and realised that she had been trying to push herself too quickly once the cause of her problem had been discovered in therapy. She resolved to herself to take time to nurture herself.

Personagrams in family therapy

A Personagram can be set up in a family therapy session, with the members of the family embodying the Aspects of one of the family's personality. This may seem a strange departure from the usual form of family sculpting, but it can have a bonding effect as well as enabling the participating family members to experience what that particular aspect of their relation is like.

Example

A 17-year-old, who had several times been in trouble with the police and was estranged from her family, agreed to a meeting with her family as part of her intermediate treatment programme. The whole family agreed to try out a Personagram, with the girl as the sculptor. She used each member of her family, including brothers and sisters, as Aspects of her self. The resulting Personagram was very moving, and at the end, for the first time in four years, the mother felt able to hug her daughter.

I was told that this had been the beginning of the girl's rehabilitation. After eleven months she had not reoffended and was still in positive contact with her family, dating from this meeting.

Other applications

I have used this technique to explore work groups, Social Services' case conferences and family dynamics. These are not strictly Personagrams as the inner personality is not being sculpted, but members of a team, or case history or family, who are not present. The element of giving the sculpted team/case/family uncensored expression, without guidance from the sculptor, does allow the sculptor to gain insights, perhaps previously not understood by her.

Example

A leader of a team wished to look at his team's dynamics. The most important insight for him was that one of his new members, to whom he thought he was giving support, actually felt 'crowded' by him and felt that because of his protective attitude towards her, he thought that she wasn't 'up to the job'. Once this had been expressed the leader could understand the rather strange way she had been behaving towards him at work and realised he needed to change his attitude towards her.

CONCLUSIONS

Personagrams are about personal insights into the nature of oneself; they are not, however, a therapy. The sculpture which emerges may stimulate change and it may be an emotional experience for the sculptor, but any changes have to be made by the sculptor in her own life. Unlike psychodrama, and other therapies, a Personagram delves only into our at-the-moment personality and possible next steps in our development. Moreover there is no requirement for the sculptor to accept what she has been presented with. With a very fragile person whom I was initially reluctant to accept as a sculptor, but eventually conceded as he was very keen, I observed that he was oblivious to the metaphorical messages that were quite clear to the other members of the group. I felt that he was not in an emotionally stable enough condition to have any of these pointed out to him at this time, and so I vetoed any attempts by the group to do so. In such a case the overall picture seemed to give the sculptor what he wanted at this time. At the other extreme sculptors have been keenly aware of the messages given by the Aspects and these have been the catalysts for a radical change.

The use of metaphor and projection on to others are the safety catches for the client; factors which make Personagrams a non-confrontational, non-threatening technique. As indicated above, the sculptor can choose not to hear the messages, and because he has projected himself out there he can choose to decide that the Aspects are not being accurate. This rarely happens, however, as the very act of distancing himself from himself does, I believe, allow the sculptor to accept what he sees, because he is not having to defend himself; he himself is not being questioned.

Another feature which reinforces the impression that Personagrams are a non-confrontational, non-threatening approach to self-discovery and conflict-solving, is that a Personagram leaves the sculptor with a greater sense of personal worth. At first, as the Personagram is created with all its disharmonies and apparently conflicting Aspects, some of whom are wretched creatures, or overbearing, or impotent, it would seem that the contrary would be true. But this is not so. This is partly because during the Development stage there is movement and change and these Aspects become positive, or at least a potentially positive face to them is revealed. Hence the sculptor is left with a sense of completeness, with the feeling that all his personality traits are needed: he need no longer feel that he has to suppress certain feelings or facets, or mask them by dominating them with others, and thus distorting even these Aspects from their true natures; he just needs to look at himself in a different way.

Moreover the very fact that these other group members have focused on the sculptor adds to his sense of worth. The feeling towards the sculptor on the part of the Aspects at the end of a Personagram is one of closeness and tenderness, which is experienced directly by the sculptor. As has been said to me by an Aspect, 'It is impossible to feel cold and indifferent towards someone when you have been a part of them.' Another person said, 'This is the quickest way of creating group bonding I have ever come across', and this person had extensive experience of other group activities.

What I have described has been the result of many years experience of Personagrams. I do feel that this technique is particularly suited to drama-therapists who predominantly work in a group setting and wish to work in an active mode, often using the metaphor as the catalyst to awareness and in a way which is non-threatening to the client. I hope that dramatherapists will find Personagrams another meaningful way of working with groups.

REFERENCES AND FURTHER READING

Clarkson, P. (1995) *On Psychotherapy*, London: Whurr Publications.

Clarkson, P. and Mackewn, J. (1993) *Fritz Perls*, London: Sage Publications.

Dychtwald, K. (1978) *Bodymind*, London: Wildwood House.

Greenberg, I.A. (ed.) (1975) *Psychodrama Theory and Therapy*, London: Souvenir Press.

Jennings, S. (1986) *Creative Drama in Groupwork*, Biscester, UK: Winslow Press.

—— (1990) *Dramatherapy with Families, Groups and Individuals*, London: Jessica Kingsley.

Kingsland, K. and V. (1977) *Hathapradipika*, Torquay, UK: Grael Communications.

Mishra, R.S. (1972) *The Textbook of Yoga Psychology*, London: Lyrebird Press.

Pitzele, P. (1991) 'Adolescents inside out: intrapsychic psychodrama', in P. Holmes and M. Karp (eds) *Psychodrama Inspiration and Technique*, London: Routledge.

Shapiro, D. (1990) *The Bodymind Workbook*, Shaftesbury, UK: Element Books.

NOTES

1 Sculpting is a technique whereby a member of the group is placed and moulded as if she is a piece of clay and thus body, limbs, head and facial expressions take up specific shapes, in a specified position.
2 In the remainder of this chapter I shall at times use the masculine pronoun and at others the feminine, as this is much less cumbersome.

Chapter 6

The mask of self

Cyril Ives

'Tis certain that there is no question in philosophy more abstruse than that concerning identity and the nature of the uniting principle which constitutes a person.

D. Hume, 1888

The Lantern Trust is a small educational charity which has been working since 1988 in the fields of HIV education, loss, bereavement and palliative care, using a creative arts approach. This chapter outlines some of the reasons why this direction was chosen and the formidable tasks which confront educators when working with the twin taboos of sex and death.

The increasing incidence of the Human Immuno-Deficiency Virus (HIV) and Acquired Immune Deficiency Syndrome (AIDS) throughout the world has presented health-care workers with not only a professional challenge but also a personal one. Attitudes towards people with an illness as a result of a virus which appears to be largely sexually transmitted can no longer be considered separately from objective professional opinion, and care professionals have often experienced intense anxiety when asked to care for patients with HIV in institutions and settings of all kinds.

The early HIV information campaigns reinforced the belief that infection was confined to people in so-called 'high risk groups', and homosexual and bisexual men were 'blamed' for the spread of the virus. This emphasis drew attention away from the risks in heterosexual contact, which is now increasing at a rate higher than that in any of the so-called risk categories.

Ignorance of the facts of transmission, and political and public squeamishness when faced with the need to talk openly about sexual activity, delayed the implementation of essential health education campaigns, and it was left to the voluntary organisations to respond in a direct and challenging way. The Terrence Higgins Trust was the first organisation in the UK to spell out the need for safer sex and to emphasise that this is not a 'gay disease'.

The essential facts are simple enough. The virus is transmitted in only three ways: through infected semen entering the body during penetrative sexual acts, vaginal or anal; through infected blood directly entering the circulation of another; or from an infected mother to an unborn child. In the latter case, the likelihood of transmission in this way is thought to be as low as 15 per cent.

Understanding basic health and safety precautions is enough to prevent the transmission of the virus, which is extremely fragile and dies almost immediately on contact with the atmosphere outside the human body. This makes nonsense of the media scare stories of infected needles lying on the beach and transmission through social contact. It is more difficult to be infected with HIV than with many other more common agents, Hepatitis B for example.

Confusion also exists in the public mind between HIV, the virus or organism which attacks the immune system lowering resistance to infection, and AIDS, which is the collective name given to infections which may occur as a result of the presence of the virus.

Knowledge of the facts of transmission has not been enough, however, to allay the fears of the public or many of the professionals involved in health care. In 1991, Akinsanya surveyed the attitudes of nurses in the United Kingdom and found that given the choice, 40 per cent of a substantial sample would choose not to care for people with HIV infection or AIDS. This was even true in cases where responses to a factual questionnaire indicated high levels of knowledge about the means of transmission and the precautions to be taken in clinical settings.

The pioneering work of voluntary educators in the United States demonstrated that a creative approach to education is essential if issues which are considered taboo, or too fearful to contemplate, are to be worked with. It was my own interest in the arts therapies that encouraged me to explore ways in which the therapeutic potential of the arts could be integrated into the mainstream education of workers in the fields of health and social care.

Initially it seemed that the greatest need was to confront the dragons of fear and ignorance and to offer a serious challenge to the homophobic and racist attitudes which fuelled the myths of AIDS. Many of the first HIV educational programmes were set up by those most affected in the early 1980s, the majority of whom were gay men. The self-transcendence characteristic of humans to reach out beyond themselves and discover or make meaning of their lives has been well described by Frankl (1963) and clearly evidenced in the responses of gay men to the impact of AIDS in their lives. Support groups, self-help initiatives and major schemes which led to the setting up of the AIDS hospices and day centres were early attempts to make sense of the invasive and potentially devastating pandemic.

It is true that large sums of money were provided in the UK by central government for programmes of HIV prevention and education, but television commercials brought the metaphor of tombstones and icebergs into the living rooms of the nation in a way which instilled fear, rather than a sense of responsibility.

Warming to the theme of a creative approach, I was able to research the training needs in the front line of care through a bursary from the Rowntree Foundation, and in 1988 was involved in the setting up of an educational charity, the Lantern Trust, to implement programmes designed to address the main themes of HIV and AIDS.

Initial research into the training needs of nurses and social-care workers had to be directed through the budget holders in health and local authorities, many of whom clearly believed that 'sex = AIDS = death' was a suitable slogan for a programme of education. Large budgets did not necessarily indicate large amounts of creative thinking!

Most of the early HIV awareness programmes focused on safe (now called safer) sex and overlooked the impact of the twin taboos of sex and death when considered together. Many care professionals could only contemplate HIV as something which affected 'others', and would only take part in training which distanced the issues in this way, shying away from anything which might touch on their own emotions.

BEHEADING IN THE MARKET-PLACE

The course which I designed facilitated the expression of feelings as well as providing clear factual information about HIV and its routes of transmission. The initial planning included several people who were themselves living with the virus, as it was then widely believed that this 'consumer input' was the most effective way of bringing the issues home to others. It did, however, have very great consequences in terms of the emotional impact on both facilitators and group members faced with a young man who openly stated his own positive HIV status, his fear of death and his experience of homophobia at the hands of nurses. It was too much to bear. Groups of nurses, doctors and others regularly implied that although it was 'nothing personal' my friend and colleague Paul must have known what he was doing, with the clear implication that he only had himself to blame for his HIV status. Inevitably tempers flared and the role of the facilitator became that of victim who under such provocation then became a persecutor. Sessions often ended with students and staff in distress, and it became clear that this full-frontal confrontation could not continue.

The final straw for Paul was a reference to beheading in the market-place as a suitable fate for homosexuals which would certainly befall him in the country of origin of the speaker (a local GP).

Judgements of this kind have been, and still are, a feature of the response to HIV and AIDS in the Western world, and the inability to separate moral judgements from the capacity to care has been a major challenge to educators in the field. The contradictions inherent in offering care and support as a professional caregiver and personal moral values which condemn others' sexual behaviour and lifestyles have been played centre stage on many occasions. In taking the risk of appearing in a group and declaring their positive HIV status, men and at first women have been received with admiration and caution and then condemned for their folly in exposing themselves to the virus in the first place. Offering themselves as educators in the field seemed a commendable way of breaking down barriers and reducing the fear and ignorance, but became increasingly a further source of stress for the person living with HIV.

SAFETY AT A DISTANCE

Considering it essential to continue with confrontation, but somehow achieve some distance, I turned to the area of arts therapeutic work and explored ways in which drama could be used in an educational and therapeutic way at the same time. Mindful that the experience for the students was to be primarily educational and not personal therapy, it seemed however that my training and experience in dramatherapy and integrative arts therapy might enable me to use play, role-reversal and other therapeutic approaches.

Reflecting on the emotional intensity generated by the discussions around sexuality, the role of education and the fear and prejudice, it occurred to me that a dramatic recreation of what had actually happened to people when their HIV status was revealed might be an effective way of distancing the issues and yet at the same time drawing them closer. Sternberg and Garcia (1988) provide a useful source of reference in the practice of sociodrama, a group learning process focused on providing practice in the solving of problems in human relationships. The group is the subject and the focus is theme- and situation-oriented, as opposed to the in-depth personal work of the protagonist in psychodrama. Sternberg and Garcia suggest that sociodrama is a non-threatening, non-judgemental method of exploring and experiencing problem-solving.

Gradually the material for a piece of work which has become known as 'The Great Debate' has unfolded. Within the context of a short course for caregivers of people affected by HIV and AIDS, a dramatic representation of the challenges offered to people with HIV is acted out. Three groups are formed with the group role of Prejudice, Education and Sexuality. Only the prejudice group has a specifically protagonist role, and within that group members play the many voices of prejudice and ignorance; loud and accusing, homophobic, racist, quietly scathing, and fundamentalist bigots. All are equally powerful and often group members find themselves playing against their own true inclinations and feelings. The director offers a challenging statement to open up the debate which is responded to by each of the groups in turn. As this statement, 'People with AIDS have only got themselves to blame', is written up, there is a chill in the room, even though it is clear that it is intended to be deliberately provocative. The safe environment which has been created within the group during previous group activity and the early days of the course enables risks to be taken, and challenges to be offered in a dramatic way. Over and over again the very words which have been, and are, spoken in reality towards people with AIDS in wider society are hurled across the space.

There is certainly some role confusion. People who have brought strong anti-gay or anti-drug-user attitudes to the course find themselves appalled at the attacks on them in the drama and leap to their defence. Others who have considered themselves well able to defend themselves against attack in intellectual discussion find themselves disarmed again and again as the debate proceeds and their firmly held beliefs are seriously challenged. This is also true for the facilitators who have to work very hard to maintain the essential distance needed, but become increasingly aware of those issues which impact on themselves. The time spent in group processing is as long as the debate itself, and often group members seem dazed and confused by the experience. Although grounding is important, all group members are constantly reminded of the reality of this experience for many people in the wider community, and any attempts to dismiss it as 'just a role-play' are challenged with references to real-life experience. Neither is there any attempt to derole using 'silly games' as the work is grounded in reality.

This piece of work has been in use for six years now and has been able to respond to the changing key themes in the field: Government expenditure on HIV prevention and care of people with AIDS at the expense of other conditions; increasing spread into the heterosexual population; the 'innocence' of children and people with haemophilia versus the 'guilt' of gay men and intravenous drug users.

Heavy stuff to handle but, within the drama, these are issues which we can pick up and run with, reflect on later and integrate into our experience and practice.

ATTACHMENT, LOSS AND AUTONOMY

Other work has developed using a similar approach, and a style of facilitation which combines socio-dramatic direction with Boal Forum theatre is used to illustrate the support needs of people living with HIV and AIDS in the community. Here again assumptions are challenged, this time by the professionals themselves who are responsible for providing the care.

Taking the theme of self-empowerment of the individual, and referring to a key text in the much-maligned Community Care legislation which says 'The service should focus on the needs of the service user, not the service' (Audit Commission 1990), the support needs of the person with AIDS gradually unfold. Commencing with a simple sculpt in which the caregivers place themselves where they believe they are in order of importance, the protagonist then moves them to where he or she really wants them. This may include their banishment altogether, or a new position of intimacy. This can lead on to interviews with the characters in role as caregiver, and finally letting go and saying goodbye to those with whom there may be unfinished business. It is a constant challenge to keep this in the educational arena and yet it is clear that it is a very helpful and often cathartic piece of work, not only for those in role but also for the audience, so aptly described by Augusto Boal as 'spect-actors'.

The relationship between the protagonist and those in personal roles is always fascinating, particularly when the issue of same-sex relationships is addressed. The mother's possible rejection of the lover or even her own son or daughter, the brother or wife who cannot accept or believe that AIDS has touched their lives, the lover who may feel blamed for the infection and fearful about his or her own HIV status, are scenarios which appear again and again. Ambivalence towards the professional caregiver and the disempowerment of the client by paternalistic professional approaches illustrate very well the problems which hinder true autonomy and self-determination.

The theme of loss runs like a thread throughout the work in the area of HIV. Loss of life expectancy, loss of relationships, loss of self-esteem, loss of dignity, loss of material and practical support. This multiple loss presents a challenge to all who come into contact with the person living with HIV, as it may be dealt with in many ways. Anger and denial together make a vicious cocktail, and to be truly alongside someone in this situation may need very special skills. At times, however, the professional counsellor may be less effective than the home help or buddy, who provide a closeness and support which may not be inhibited by the professional distance of others. At the same time the intensity of this relationship can result in an overwhelming burden if adequate support is not provided for the caregiver. The central role of some of these less obvious caregivers is enhanced by the dramatic representation and leads to a new insight for many members of the group.

To draw these themes of loss together I have introduced a further piece of creative work which enables personal issues to be addressed through the safety of metaphor. Group members are invited to create an image of a loss experience, using an approach based on sandplay technique. Many objects which represent the world in miniature are provided together with paints and other creative materials, and each group member creates an image quietly in their own space and time. This is then shared with a partner, but not with the whole group, and a final group process takes place to ensure grounding at the end of the workshop. Although in the preparation group members are invited to choose an experience of loss which may or may not be the result of a death, often deeply hurting experiences are chosen and worked with openly with the partner. The powerful influence of the use of objects is evident, and although this may seem 'old hat' to most arts therapists, to introduce such a style of working to an often resistant educational group of professional caregivers without experience of the therapeutic milieu is a challenge indeed. In terms of outcome, however, the results are worth the risk, and over and over again important personal work is done which is therapeutic for individuals in the group.

Because of the borderline between education and therapy in this work, there are always two facilitators working together in a humanistic, non-interpretative way, and peer and external supervision is essential. Group members are also cautioned that they should not take away and use these techniques without appropriate training, although they are encouraged to think about more creative ways of working with their patients/clients in the future.

UNMASKING THE SELF

I have also introduced work with masks into a number of programmes, not only with therapeutic groups but as an extension of role-playing in educational settings. This is a very different experience from working with populations familiar with the concept of 'therapy' who, although perhaps anxious, bring a certain willingness to the group initially. The potential of the mask as a transitional object is very largely unexplored and the literature is scarce. However, convinced of the logic of 'masking to unmask' I have gradually introduced mask work into groups to explore the many faces of abandonment and in searching for a definable 'self'.

The earliest reference to the use of masks as an adjunct to role-playing is in the work of Pollaczek (1954). She suggested that in working with children, the child might explore the variety of roles which it is possible to play, and might even change roles. For the child or adult with a negative self-image this is a tempting possibility. In her work with children with speech impediment, Pollaczek observed that the stammerer might have the block to speech removed while wearing the mask, only for it to return immediately on its removal. She also noted the remarkable change which occurred in bodily movements and cites an example of a child who leaped up and down with excitement, banging his fists while wearing the mask, in a way which he had never been seen to do without it.

In the early 1980s experimental work with masks was carried out in France by De Panafieu (1982) and Saigre (1989). De Panafieu was convinced of the therapeutic potential of the mask, emphasising that the physical, emotional and intellectual aspects of the human personality are all brought together through it in a meaningful way. Jennings has pioneered work with masks in her dramatherapy practice in the UK and elsewhere since the 1970s, and through my professional association with her at the Institute of Dramatherapy I felt confident to develop this work further in my own groups.

In addition to creating faces of abandonment on death studies courses, I have used the mask in groups of health-care professionals, with therapy students in training and with others with an interest in self-development. Its value in helping with role definition in people otherwise uncertain of their identity has been valuable, and although it is yet an early piece of research I am personally convinced that it is a powerful tool for growth and transformation.

Although working with men and women, I have been particularly impressed with the power of the mask when working with men who have been trapped in strong 'male' identities and who want to explore their gentler, more feminine, selves. This is not always articulated prior to the workshop, but during the process of working with a variety of masks and then creating their own masks the subtle move from male assertion to a softness and tenderness is felt as well as seen. Taking photographs of this work has contributed to the process, as the images themselves emphasise many of the qualities which the mask-wearers cannot otherwise see for themselves. During the process stage of the work, I invite the mask-wearers to interview their own masks and comment on what they see. The questions are framed in a way which keeps the metaphor intact as they always refer to the mask and not the person. It is clear, however, that it is often many parts of their own personality which are being referred to in their responses and comments. Feedback from the 'spect-actors' is also important in emphasising the qualities which the creators/wearers may be striving for, but cannot see for themselves. Invited to comment on his own mask in a recent group, the creator of the mask said that he had been wanting to show beauty, tenderness and sensitivity, but couldn't get to it. Other members of the group described the mask as 'beautiful', 'gentle', 'feminine', 'tender', and hearing this added greatly to the experience. Another group member intended to make a playful, happy squirrel and keep away from all this sad therapy stuff, but found that her squirrel became spiteful, pursuing her as a monster of her own creation. Again in the processing, the expectation of how the mask would be and how it became were quite different, and the observations of the other group members enabled her to see parts of herself which were otherwise hidden away.

I have many questions which I am currently exploring (Ives 1995), as my work with masks continues. I am convinced of the potential of the mask as a transitional object, and intend to investigate further ways in which object-relations theory as well as the integration of arts therapies can inform and enhance this aspect of my practice.

NOT THE CONCLUSION BUT THE BEGINNING

The impact of this creative work on students in a very specialised educational setting is yet to be fully evaluated, but it is clear that the experience is educational and therapeutic for many students. Initial resistance to creative group activity soon gives way to cautious risk-taking, and by the end of most courses the group presentations provide a stimulating conclusion to the group life. The coursework submitted for assessment is also often of a creative nature, rather than a formal essay. These pieces of work have included wonderful photography albums, videos, books of poetry and sculpture in a variety of materials. The stimulation of the environment, the drama and the creative experience lead in turn to a new awareness of the individual's creative potential, and credit is given for this work on a level with intellectual and academic achievement.

The impetus for this creative approach to education came from the impact of HIV and AIDS on the lives of a specific community of people who were dynamised into action as the result of multiple losses. It is now extending further into the field of higher education, and issues which are difficult to address on a purely intellectual level are taking on a new existential dimension through the creative power and magic of the arts.

Millions of pounds have been invested by the British government in education about HIV and AIDS since 1988, and the messages have come a long way since the early tombstones and shock tactics. However, almost daily the media portray people with AIDS as 'victims', 'the innocent' and 'the guilty' continuing to perpetrate the myths of infection, generating further prejudice and raising the level of fear. The increasing incidence of new infections in the heterosexual population is of little interest compared to the latest 'gay with AIDS' story, and discrimination in employment, education and other aspects of life continues quietly unnoticed. Except, that is, for those living with HIV who cannot escape the everyday reality that at present there is no cure and the future is uncertain.

If the voices of the people with HIV and AIDS themselves go largely unheeded, it must become the responsibility of caring professionals to take on the role of advocate and, through creative and innovative forms of education, put them firmly centre stage where they cannot be ignored and overlooked. In doing so, however, we must be careful not to patronise and lose our sense of reality – a thought so well expressed by Derek Jarman shortly before his own death of an AIDS-related illness:

> We have to live with AIDS while they spread the quilt for the moths of Ithaca across the wine-dark sea. Awareness is heightened by this, but something else is lost, a sense of reality drowned in theatre. Thinking blind, becoming blind.

> (*Guardian* Arts, 15 September 1993, p. 4)

The shining lamp of knowledge is the only certain way to destroy the darkness born of ignorance.

REFERENCES

Akinsanya, J. (1989) 'Attitudes of nurses towards people with AIDS', Chelmsford, UK: Anglia Polytechnic.

Audit Commission (1990) *Care in the Community*, London: Department of Health.

De Panafieu, B. (1982) 'A journey with masks', *Psychologie-Medicale* 14(2): 289–293 (translated from French).

Frankl, V. (1963) 'Self transcendence as a human phenomenon', *Journal of Humanistic Psychology* 6(97): 61–76.

Hume, D. (1888) *A Treatise on Human Nature*, ed. S. Biggs, 2nd edn, Oxford: Oxford University Press.

Ives, C. (1995) 'The therapeutic and educational application of the arts', unpublished dissertation, University of Exeter.

Jarman, D. (1993) *Blue*, London: Basilisk Communications.

Pollaczek, P. (1954) 'Use of masks as an adjunct to role-playing', *Mental Hygiene* 38: 299–304.

Saigre, M. (1989) 'Mask therapy: a post-Reichian psychotherapy', *L'Information Psychiatrique* 10 (December): 1018–23.

Sternberg, P. and Garcia, A. (1989) *Sociodrama: Who's in Your Shoes?* New York: Praeger.

FURTHER READING

Bohmann P. and Fraser, M. (1991) 'Training home health AIDS to work with persons with AIDS', *Journal of Home Health Care Practice* 3(2): 68–75.

Breault, A. and Polifroni, E. (1992) 'Caring for people with AIDS: nurses' attitudes and feelings', *Journal of Advanced Nursing* 17: 21–27.

Coward, D. and Lewis, A. (1993) 'Lived experience of self transcendence in gay men with AIDS', *Oncology Nurses Forum* 20(9): 1363–1368.

Jennings, S. (1990) *Dramatherapy with Families, Groups and Individuals*, London: Jessica Kingsley.

Marshall, P. (1992) 'AIDS dilemma: risk versus responsibility in nursing care', *Kansas Nurse* 67(5): 3–5.

Moore, E. (1992) 'Courage to care: AIDS caregiving dilemmas', *Pennsylvania Nurse* 47(9): 20.

Pederson, C. (1993) 'Structured controversy versus lecture on nursing students' beliefs about and attitude toward providing care for persons with AIDS', *Journal of Continuing Education in Nursing* 245(2): 74–81.

Schultz, M., Macdonald, K., Heckert, K. *et al.* (1988) 'The Minnesota AIDS physician survey', *Minnesota Medicine* 71: 277–283.

Thurlow, P. (1992) 'Not in front of the students: nursing and sexuality', *Nursing Standard* 6(48): 54.

Wallman, S. (1988) 'Sex and death: AIDS crisis social and cultural context', *Journal Acquired Immune Deficiency Syndrome* 1(6): 571–573.

Web, A. and Bunting, S. (1992) 'Ethical decision-making by nurses in HIV/AIDS situations', *Journal of Nurses in AIDS Care* 3(2): 915–918.

Part II

Applied dramatherapy with individuals and groups

Chapter 7

Masking and unmasking

Dramatherapy with offender patients

Sue Jennings, John D. McGinley and Margaret Orr

Because the human face is the primary means of our recognizing, and thus identifying, one another, it deserves special attention in a study of appearance and their ambiguities. And because a mask is itself not merely the most direct but the most widespread form of disguise, the function of illusion in change may be most directly explored through an analysis of masks and masking conventions.

A.D. Napier

INTRODUCTION

This chapter is concerned with an innovatory dramatherapy project at Broadmoor Hospital which used Shakespeare's *A Midsummer Night's Dream* as a focal point for dramatherapy exploration. An intensive programme was introduced to staff and patients on Folkestone Ward, Kent House. At the time, dramatherapy was not practised at Broadmoor but the hospital had supported various artistic initiatives including performances by the Royal Shakespeare and Royal National Theatres, described at length in *Shakespeare Comes to Broadmoor* (Cox 1992). Broadmoor has its own drama group which stages performances, as well as a Creative Department which provides classes and workshops in art, music and drama. More recently a dramatherapist has been appointed for one day a week and, importantly, two nurses who took part in the project have been seconded by Broadmoor to undertake full professional dramatherapy training. This landmark will be discussed later when the results of the project are addressed.

The project took place over six months (August–February) at, on average, three-weekly intervals. Each session lasted three hours and was attended by patients and a core group of staff. Other staff joined when they were able. Staff joined in a debriefing session after each meeting as well as receiving a dramatherapy tutorial.

Attendance at the sessions was voluntary, but after the first session patients had to make a commitment to the whole of the project. All patients were given several standard psychological tests before and after the project as well as completing a questionaire at the end of the six months. This chapter describes the actual sessions as well as the context and evaluation of the work. The work of the group as a whole is described, with two patients being selected for greater detailed appraisal. They were selected because they present contrasting responses to the project; the remaining case histories are discussed elsewhere (Belton *et al.* in preparation).

THE BROADMOOR CONTEXT

Broadmoor is one of three maximum secure hospitals in Britain for the care and treatment of offender patients. It houses some five hundred patients suffering from a range of mental health problems and personality disorders. One-fifth of the admissions are women. The hospital has changed radically in recent years with a massive rebuilding programme which provides light and airy accommodation for staff as well as patients. Broadmoor's mission statement emphasises the importance of the secure environment not only for the safeguard of the general public but also for the well-being of the patient, thus providing a holding environment for appropriate care and treatment. A range of psychodynamic, cognitive, and supportive therapies are available for individuals and groups. Broadmoor has had a commitment to artistic and creative programmes as described in detail in Cox (1992).

OBJECTIVES AND FRAMEWORK (DRAMATHERAPY EPR PARADIGM)

The primary objective was to test the preliminary hypothesis that participation in dramatherapy workshops would improve the patients' self-image. Three-hour workshops would be run monthly over a six-month period. Through the use of dramatherapeutic methods (Jennings EPR paradigm) the patients would be directed through a process of growing self-awareness.

The dramatherapy paradigm (EPR)

The workshops were based on dramatic stages which parallel normal human development. The three stages of EPR (embodiment–projection–role) have proved a safe and useful paradigm as a basis for dramatherapeutic intervention.

Embodiment (E)

This stage involves dramatic action that is embodied in movement and gesture, a physicalisation, which develops alongside the normal infant stage in which body, exploration of body parts and sensory play are vital components.

Projection (P)

The experiences are projected into images through sculpting, drawing, painting, masks and other objects outside of the self. Masks are able to express and contain 'danger' inherent in, for example, light/dark, change/ standing still. This process can be compared to the projective play of infants. Much projective play has a sensory component.

Role enactment (R)

These images form the basis of drama games and role-play improvisations, ritualisation, and masked dramas, similar to the dramatic play of infants. Opposites need to be brought into the dialogue. All myths and drama build on polarities such as good/bad, light/dark.

A secondary objective of the project was the improvement of communication and trust between staff and patients, resulting from both the joint 'risk-taking' and the intensity of the interactions, in the workshops. It was hoped that this would also raise morale on the ward, and furthermore that the staff would obtain dramatherapeutic skills which they could integrate into their own working practice and dramatherapy studies.

RATIONALE FOR CHOICE OF PSYCHOLOGICAL INSTRUMENTS

Art and dramatherapy, which both work at a primary feeling level, are very potent forms of intervention with individuals and groups who have a variety of 'body problems'. The body is the starting point in all art and arts therapies and, indeed, in human development. The body and its experiences are intrinsic to drama and dramatherapy (Jennings 1992). If the body is the starting point in dramatherapy, this does not mean that we progress in a unilinear way from movement to role. What happens is that the movement dimension is carried forward in a multidimensional way and is part of the multifaceted human being. Much of what is done in art therapies is to assist people to reconnect with their bodies and to discover the hidden self – the body that is not seen. The choice of the instruments was dictated by the availability of reliable tests to suit the purpose of measuring self-image and matching the objectives of the dramatherapy paradigm which guided the therapist's approach.

Haward Body Barrier Test

The Haward Body Barrier Test (HBBT) was developed by Haward (1959) as a standard measure designed to measure the definiteness and penetrability of one's body boundaries. It is based on Fisher and Cleveland's (1958) concept that an individual's feelings about his or her own body are projected into fantasy images in response to test items. They hypothesised that the body represents a 'base of operations' as a segment of the world that is specially the persons's own. The body is hypothesised to incorporate a person's private site of past integrated experiences. It would represent a construct which the person has developed in order to make life satisfying for himself or herself. The body boundaries serve as points of contact with the external world and are often seen as a defence line.

Freud (1927) showed great interest in body-boundary phenomena, especially patient attitudes towards body openings (mouth and anus). The infant's first experiences are linked directly to body-boundary and self/other concept. Reich (1949) considered this concept and examined its implications by means of the concept of 'body armour'.

The HBBT consists of ten sets of three items. Each item reflects a different degree of protectiveness and definition of the object's periphery. Items are scored according to the greater degree of protection endorsed by the subject. The test has many advantages. Its scoring is objective and the protocols can be scored using a key. It has high face validity in relation to Fisher and Cleveland's theory, and high concurrent validity with Rorschach and has proved to have high reliability scores in terms of Cronbach's alpha, split-half ($r = .92$; $p < .001$) and test-retest ($r = .87$; $p p < .001$) (Rattigan 1976). Other investigators using this test have also proved its reliable psychometric properties (Mouratoglou 1984; Georgakis 1983).

Body cathexis scale

This scale consists of fifty-one parts of the body which are rated according to a five-point Likert scale ranging from strong positive to strong negative feelings towards the particular aspect. The original body cathexis scale from which this is adapted was developed by Jourard and Secord (1953). It is objectively quantifiable and psychometrically it has proven to be a consistent measure with high internal structure.

Repertory grids

Repertory grids can be used to measure change, as Shorts (1985) and Houston and Adshead (1993) have demonstrated with mentally disordered offenders in secure settings. The psychology of personal constructs suggest that we understand ourselves and others in psychological terms; and that we can study those personal constructs that we have each developed to predict events in our personal world. Thus if we can discover each individual's personal construct system, we are better able to understand their reactions to life events and re-construct 'index offences'. If the person's constructs, hypotheses or predictions are continually invalidated by experience, then they may well construct themselves by saying 'I have a problem' or they may try and 'make things work out in such a way that their predictions are validated' (Kelly 1955).

One of Kelly's basic tenets is that a person is fully functioning when they are able to construe the world in such a way that their predictions are validated. We have theories about events and why things occur, we make hypotheses about what will happen and we put these predictions to the test to see whether our thoughts are validated or not. Viewing behaviour 'as if' it were an experiment is one of Kelly's unique contributions to our understanding of the person (Fransella 1990).

In the present study, we were interested in using the grids to examine changes in patients' ways of thinking about themselves and how they perceived others: can any shift be identified towards acceptance of self as measured by positive change in the direction of 'ideal self' away from perception of self at 'index offence'?

In particular, we were interested in change in the following areas:

1 the ratings of self, ideal self, self at time of index offence, and how others perceived them
2 which significant others were associated with ideal self (idealised models)
3 what attributes and feelings are associated with self at index offence, ideal self and self now.

An experimental Rorschach

The Rorschach projective technique has been used systematically in male admissions assessments at Broadmoor Special Hospital since 1990 by psychologist Dr Mary Hill, following a full and conventional system of administration. However, the scoring system has been generally more circumscribed than would be usual. The original intention was to make an evaluation of the technique in a population of this type, and to this end a number of research scales were chosen from the published literature which offered some existing normative and reliability data, but which were thought also to have a particular potential relevance to the behavioural difficulties with which patients presented. All are concerned with the 'content' of the protocol, and have a generally psychodynamic orientation.

Two of the chosen scales are concerned with the amount of affect associated with different percepts, and taken from the Anxiety and Hostility Scales of Elizur (Elizur 1949), while a third scale which purports to measure 'suspiciousness' has been adapted from the first scale of the same name developed originally for the Holtzman Inkblot Test (Endicott 1972). There are also two scales which consider difficulties in the expression of sexuality, and these have been taken from Wheeler's list of 'Homosexual Signs' (Wheeler 1949 and Goldfried et al. 1971), and from Schafer's Scale entitled 'Fear of and rejecting attitude toward masculine identity, and feminine identification in men' (Schafer 1954). The latter scale has been developed within a more explicitly Freudian framework, and is a part of a much larger interpretative system developed by the same author.

RATIONALE FOR CHOICE OF DRAMATHERAPY PARADIGMS

As mentioned above, the *EPR dramatherapy paradigm* was chosen because of its safety and familiarity to clinician and patient alike. The drama-therapeutic process moving along an EPR continuum means that one can plot various interventions appropriate to the stages. Furthermore, the participants themselves can contribute ideas that are stage appropriate and thus assist in the democratisation of the dramatherapeutic content. For example, when working on Embodiment, patients came up with their own ideas for drama games and physical playing. It is important to recognise that the E stage is not just a warm-up: it is a developmental stage involving physicality which leads to the development of a body self and then a body image, i.e. the separation of my own body from other bodies and from the environment around me. Through the P and R stages, the client is enabled to separate out the two realities: dramatic reality and everyday reality (Jennings 1994a). One problem with offender patients is that these two worlds often merge, and extremely violent dramas can be played out within everyday life, rather than within a Greek tragedy.

The *preventative–curative dramatherapy paradigm* has emerged from the observation of healing rituals in non-Western societies (Jennings 1995) and the relationship between rituals which maintain health and those which cure ill health. When Shakespearean performances went into Broadmoor, patients were not doing dramatherapy (Cox 1992); they were witnessing great theatre as indeed most people have the opportunity to do. In dramatherapeutic terms this would be called 'preventative', insomuch as all theatre experience for audiences has a normalising factor and has links with artistic rituals which make statements or challenge behaviour through dramatised aesthetic scenes. The Theatre of Healing model of dramatherapy builds on the aesthetic experience and makes use of theatrical device and structure in order for participants to find themselves within the larger frame. The programme designed for Broadmoor through the EPR moved towards an exploration of *A Midsummer Night's Dream*, chosen beacause of its dramatherapeutic structure, which allows for the darker issues to be explored within the forest before a resolution takes place. Reaction by some to using this play – 'men won't want to play fairies' – completely misses the themes of dysfuntional families, cruelty and seduction that are dominant in the play (these themes are explored in depth in *Shakespeare's Theatre of Healing*, Jennings in preparation).

The closeness–distance paradigm: Landy (1993) discusses the concept of distancing in dramatherapy, and most dramatherapists will decide in their practice where they work in relation to the closeness–distance paradigm. Those who work in psychodynamic dramatherapy work closer to the client's reported experiences than those who work in para-theatre (Mitchell 1994) or Theatre of Healing (Jennings 1992), where clients find their experience within the distanced material. Working with distance could be seen to have at least three functions with offender patients. First, with new offenders when people are already too near to what has happened for any exploration, we could say that the stage is already overloaded. However, it is possible for exploration to take place with distanced material which will enable some separation out. Second, working with distance is effective with people who are unable to verbalise their experience in traditional forms and who respond to the use of metaphor, symbol and story. Third, working with distance is applicable with those who have already confronted the major areas concerning their offence, and rather than reworking the experiences yet again are able to work through the distanced material in order to gain new understanding and also to be able to move on. This happens when the material is put into an aesthetic form.

DESIGN

Eight patients agreed to take part but two dropped out. It was originally planned to have two control groups in an attempt to control for confounding effects of additional variables affecting the potential change in the patients on the workshops, for example the general ward milieu, other treatment, pharmacological and psychological factors, life events, etc. A control group was identified on the ward but it became immediately clear that patient discharges and movement between wards would negate the effort. Realistically, it would be impossible to control all potential intervening variables which might be considered implicated in any observed changes by a group comparison design. It was decided that the most relevant approach would be to use a series of single case studies to measure change in the patients who would participate in the workshops. If improvement in the self-image of patients on the workshops were observed, one could argue that the introduction of dramatherapy to the ward at least contributed to the improvements.

AIMS OF THE DRAMATHERAPY

The aims of the dramatherapy were as follows:

- To develop trust and communication in the group between patients, between staff and between patients and staff.
- To make use of a 'great' story within which the patients would find their own story, i.e. to enable them to work with their own material with the 'dramatic distance' of the text.

- To use masks in order to express images and feelings in a distanced form which otherwise would remain hidden.
- To use masks to enable the transformation of feelings and perception.
- To encourage dramatic play and the development of aesthetic experience.

ADMINISTRATION OF TESTS

Two psychologists (LR and JMcG) shared the task of administering the four tests, and four shared the task of scoring (LR, JMcG, SH and MH). The fourth psychologist had originally chosen the particular Rorschach scales used, and had developed an experience of scoring these on a larger number of Broadmoor patients.

Haward Body Barrier Test and body cathexis tests were completed by the patients.

The administration of the repertory grids was preceded at an earlier stage by the identification of the elements and constructs. A standardised format was chosen to allow for some comparisons to be made regarding individual responses. Broadmoor normative data was available to make the interpretation of results more meaningful.

Elements chosen were

- mother
- father
- person liked (past)
- person disliked (past)
- person liked (present)
- person disliked (present)
- girlfriend/wife/partner
- self now
- ideal self
- how others see me
- me when I committed my index offence
- responsible medical officer
- primary nurse
- most men
- most women.

Constructs chosen were:

- happy
- scared
- angry
- sad
- bad
- powerful

- anxious
- satisfied with physical appearance
- confident in friendships
- confident in sexual relationships
- two additional constructs freely chosen.

Rorschach test

The ten Rorschach cards were presented in standard order, and patients were given simple conventional instructions. They were told to look at each blot in turn, and to say what it could be – or what it reminded them of. There were no right or wrong answers, and they were allowed to take as long as they wished. A single response to card 1 was followed by the prompt 'Anything else?', but no other comments were made during the administration phase, itself followed by a brief enquiry designed to clarify or elaborate upon initial responding.

Protocols were then analysed by Dr Mary Hill to produce empirical summaries which contained three types of information:

1 Measures of projected affect were derived from the anxiety and hostility scales of Elizur (1949), and from the adapted suspiciousness scale of Endicott (1972).
2 Measures of sexual disturbance were obtained from Wheeler's list of 'homosexual' signs, and from the gender identification scale of Schafer (1954).
3 It was also possible to obtain a measure of general 'expressive fluency' based upon simple parameters such as the total number of main responses in a protocol, the number of cards which failed to elicit a percept, and the initial reaction time to each card.

THE SESSION CONTENT

Introduction: open session for staff and patients. What is dramatherapy? Where is it applied? How are people trained? Differences/similarities to dramatherapy and psychodrama. Explanation of the research project. Dramatherapy intensive workshop contrasted with dramatherapy group. Questions and answers. Dramatherapy books available for staff and patients.

Session 1

- Identity: similarities and differences, 'uniforms', hair, clothes; trust in ourselves and others. Continuum lines: length of stay in hospital, age, trusting/not trusting other people, trusting/not trusting self, flexibility/rigidity.

- Completing the four tasks in twos/fours/eights/whole group at exactly the same time (march on spot ten times, touch floor, complete the sentence 'drama is . . .', sing first verse of 'All things bright and beautiful').
- Working with/against the partner – rolling/pushing – I/we – resistance/cooperation; trust walks and falls in twos; crossing the minefield.
- The Great Escape: improvisation and scene-sharing.
- Feedback/discussion: themes – us/them, rejection, anger, signals, role-modelling, seeing myself as others see me.
- 'How many people have actually played?' 'Creativity is so important'.

Session 2

- Feedback: gap too long, importance of playing, 'let's do trust', mental v. physical cruelty, endings, 'not-knowing'.
- Dramatised fighting: shoulder-to-shoulder, pushing/pulling.
- Physical games: chain-tag, British bulldog.
- In threes discuss positive and negative incidents from childhood and choose one to dramatise/share.
- Each group chooses another's scene to develop and find resolution.
- Discussion: childhood and expectations; mother, father and teachers, school.
- Early event when there was an 'accident': enact and share.
- Early toy that was special/gave comfort (cf. Linus blanket): draw and share.
- Write a story which starts 'Teddy went on a journey. . . .' and ends 'and that's what Teddy learnt on the journey'. Share pictures and stories.
- Feedback and discussion: good memories as well as bad; what is drama-therapy? seeding in idea of *A Midsummer Night's Dream* (*MND*).

Session 3

- Further sharing of pictures and stories; introduction of new staff to group.
- Discussion on lies parents told us and that it mattered.
- Physical struggle in pairs; shoulder push; back massage; trust fall in pairs/groups; trust walk.
- Fairy stories: mime a character and others guess who it is; groups choose story and enact; create a new final scene and enact to group. 'Cinderella finally rejects the ring and therefore the prince', 'Three Billy goats decide that the grass isn't greener and return home'.
- 'There Was an Old Woman Who Lived in a Shoe': write a new ending and tell what happened to all those children, illustrated with a picture.
- Share work in progress.
- Feedback/discussion: siblings and parents; emphasis on workshop and not therapy group; workshop meant drama training as an actor would undertake

in voice and movement; discussion of monthly gap and could it be changed?

(SJ's subsequent illness meant the gap was bigger.)

Session 4

- Feedback: queries re nature of the group – training/therapy; 'credits' for attending, gap unavoidably too big, 'feels like starting from the beginning', limits and remits of the group.
- Physical shake-out: hands, feet, whole body, breathing; walking quickly/ slowly/slow motion on leaves, in water, in mud, on sand, on ice.
- Repeat trust continuum from Session 1 and compare (trust had increased); repeat for more confident/less confident.
- Brief guided imagery about a tree – one that you like/identify with (actual or imagined); draw tree – how old is it? name? where is it? share trees – ages 5–100 years.
- Create the landscape of the group by placing the trees: an island, seashore, desert, forest, field, garden, park. Look at spaces – closeness/distance.
- Feedback/discussion: feelings about trees especially from childhood; the actual trees remembered were in significant place. Discussion on *MND* – and the forest.

Session 5

- Watched cartoon version of *MND* and told story/discussion.
- Feedback/discussion: trees very significant; some changes – 'I don't want to be blown by gales'; 'Is it a hurricane or is it a breeze?' 'A breeze now – the sun has come out.'
- Breathing: rib-cage expansion, humming vowels, throwing consonants.
- Group chooses warm-ups and drama games (including British bulldog).
- Two groups: agree a phrase and say it in different moods (happy, sad, secret, proud, etc.); first group to guess all moods.
- Like with like: dolphin, whale, shark – wolf, fox, alsation – move round room and find others the same as yourself.
- Discussion and choice of character from *MND*.
- Staff and patients to create masks of character for next time from scrap paper, string, newspaper, etc. (paint and brushes available for next session).
- *MND*: SJ to leave video/text/Lambs' *Tales*, voice books for staff and patients.

Session 6

- Painting masks and sharing: 3 Aegeus, 3 Oberon, 1 Puck, 1 Titania, 1 Hermia, 1 Helena, 2 Lion, sharing of the process of mask-making.
- Designer's role: what costume would go with this mask? Design and paint.

- What setting would this mask/costume be in? Paint stage set for this character.
- Share masks, costumes and sets.
- Place sets in a 'landscape' to create the 'map' of *MND* with features of stage set: study of Aegeus, the courtyard, entrance to wood, different parts of wood.
- Focus on Hermia's family: what was family like when H was 10 years old? Three groups – create the family (remember who? what? when? where? why?) and share.

  (a) Strong Mr Aegeus very protective towards favourite daughter Hermia; mother very weak in the kitchen; Hermia's friend tries to get attention from mother.
  (b) Mrs Aegeus's suicide because she had been having an affair with Lysander's father and Aegeus had found out. Hermia brought up by her grandmother.
  (c) A very bitter and powerful Aegeus whose wife had died in childbirth.

- Discussion on Hermia's family and choices of friends.
- Explore masks: move round the room and interact with other masks; find sound and movement to go with mask; small groups and improvise; discovered: (a) Aegeus and lions (all the angry people); (b) Oberons and Puck (all the magical people); (c) Hermia, Helena and Titania (all the jealous people).
- Feedback/discussion: masks enable freeing of feelings – in improvisations 'things came from nowhere'; *MND* map similar to previous tree map – and some trees same in both maps; different roles that contribute to the theatre – director, designer, technician, etc; importance of designers.
- Agreement of second mask for next session – if mask 1 was from court then 2 must be from forest and vice versa.

Session 7

- Sharing new masks: 1 wall, 1 lion, 1 sunflower, 1 page, 2 fairies, 1 Hermia, 1 Aegeus, 1 Oberon, 1 ass's head of Bottom.
- Mask 1: write character analysis of mask in first person which starts: 'My name is. . .' and share with partner.
- Wear mask 2 and introduce yourself to the group.
- Discussion about the forest: 'place where unexpected things can happen', 'not what you thought', 'nasty surprises', 'Puck and others can be spiteful', 'meanness', 'pain'.
- In small group include the following when creating a scene: (x) lion, sunflower, Oberon and wall; (y) two fairies and page (requested fourth character); (z) Oberon, Puck and Hermia.
- Discussion: all groups struggling with being 'nasty' and presenting resolu-

tions. What happened before the resolution? x) very angry; (y) rivalry and spite; (z) practical jokes.

- 'That bloody woman – she really goes to the ends of the earth'; 'The spell will disappear when the rain comes'; 'I hate you roaming round all the time'; 'Build the wall – maybe we need it'; 'Happy sunflower headbutting a lion'; 'I am the chief fairy and I want to be Titania'; 'Can I really stay in the forest?'
- Feedback/discussion: the experiences of the deep forest; some people knew the forest of *other* people; focus on closure process for next session.

Session 8

- Share masks and pictures from previous session.
- Individual time to process journey through the eight sessions (all particip- ants had folder with all pictorial and written work and photographs).
- Which mask came out of the forest? Improvise in small group.
- Write and share 'my journey through the dramatherapy workshops'.
- Where do we go from here? Ward staff to continue a group.
- Final questionaire, feedback and grounding.

(Most of the techniques described above are in *Creative Drama in Groupwork* (Jennings 1986) and *Drama for People with Special Needs* (Cattanach 1992), which the patients also read to help plan their contributions; the remainder are in *Shakespeare's Theatre of Healing*, Jennings in preparation.)

RESULTS OF THE TESTS

Experimental Rorschach

Initially, there were considerable differences in the kind of protocols pro- duced by the six patients before their experience of dramatherapy. Quite high levels of affect were projected into the percepts of three of six patients, while two group members expressed very little emotion. In a similar way, signs considered indicative of a disturbance of gender identification were also present in exactly half of the sample, but largely absent in the others, and fuller details of these distinctions are given in individual patient vignettes. However, all but one member of the group provided a relatively impoverished record, containing no more than thirteen main responses, and such low levels of responding have been found to be more generally typical of male patients at this special hospital.

If one were to summarise the differences in Rorschach responding after dramatherapy, the main differences for five out of six patients lie in a greater fluency of expression. There are fewer cards rejected, protocols contain more main responses, and reaction times are usually brisker. However, the kind of

content provided, its associated affect and general orientation seem unchanged. The apparent shift on retesting has been to make existing attributes
and tendencies more readily accessible, and although there are recognised
limitations in the particular methods of scoring chosen, it is unlikely that
the use of a more comprehensive system would have altered this broad
conclusion.

Repertory grid results summary

After six months of the dramatherapy workshops, changes were observed for
each of the patients. Correspondence analyses of the results indicated that
there was one underlying dimension which was significant for all patients
($p = < .001$: $\chi2 = 105.26$). This could be described as a continuum between
the poles of 'ideal self' and 'self at index offence'. Change could be gauged
in each case by measuring the movement of 'self now' in a positive direction
(towards 'ideal self'), or in a negative direction (towards 'self at index
offence'), or no change at all (the position of 'self now' would remain static
in relation to each polarity). This unidimensional scale is represented thus:

ideal self ———— self now 2 ———— self now 1 ———— index offence
positive change

ideal self ———————— self now 1 ———————— index offence
no change   self now 2

ideal self ———— self now 1 ———— self now 2 ———— index offence
negative change

In every case, 'ideal self' and 'self at index offence' remained at the extremes
of the coordinates before and after the workshops. In all cases, change took
place in the positive direction. All other elements and constructs varied
according to their perceived relationship with the patient on these three
levels. For example, in most cases, the RMO and primary nurse were closely
identified with the 'ideal self'. Results in this test alone would appear to
support the initial hypothesis that the introduction of the EPR dramatherapy
paradigm through workshop participation did lead to significant movement
in the self-image of the participants. This could encourage the patients and
clinical team to pursue the real-life issues dealt with 'metaphorically' at a
safe distance in dramatherapy.

HBBT

The results indicated that all the patients were moderately defended before
and after the workshops. However, there was a significant shift towards
further defensiveness in two cases. This could be interpreted to suggest that
as a result of their experience in the dramatherapy they allowed themselves

to be more vulnerable to inner feelings and reacted quite defensively to protect themselves.

Body cathexis scale

The results were mixed, indicating that most tended to feel moderately positive about themselves in relation to their body, showing a positive trend in the second test. However, some indicated strong negative feelings on more than nine items which remained unchanged after the workshops. There was a suggestion of denial of any negatives, which could indicate a very threatened position. Some highly endorsed items on individual profiles were indicative of severe pathology, especially in sexual identity issues. There appeared to be some modulation of these scores post-workshops.

General

The fact that there was no consistency of scoring between the tests, particularly between the repertory grids and the body tests, could indicate differences in how the patients actually experienced conflict in their lives: physiologically (body awareness), cognitively (repertory grids) and unconsciously (Rorschach). This emphasises the multidimensional nature of assessing and treating the dynamics of any individual case.

CASE HISTORY 1

Two patients have been selected for discussion in greater detail. They both present contrasting responses to the dramatherapeutic work but share some similarities of diagnosis. Whereas with the psychological measurements used, patient A showed little significant movement in terms of change, the artistic material he created confirmed many diagnostic findings as well as indicating current areas of preoccupation that should be addressed. Patient B, however, showed significant movement on the repertory grid testing as well as reported change from various staff in terms of self-confidence, life management, maturity and relationships.

Patient A was admitted to Broadmoor in his late thirties having killed the drug-dealer boyfriend of his sister and then decapitated him. He had led a nomadic life from the age of 15 when thrown out by his stepfather, and had developed skilled Oriental crafts. Two serious but failed relationships made him angry and despondent, and a further trip to Asia had left him disillusioned so he returned to the UK to live with his sister. He had been in Broadmoor for five years and had participated in individual supportive psychotherapy, and also in self-esteem building with his primary nurse. There had been several incidents when he 'misread' movements and gestures by female staff.

Dramatherapy

Patient A joined the dramatherapy group willingly but 'languidly'. He was one of the philosophers of the group and started lengthy discussions to try and connect the drama work with his own spiritual understanding and Indian mysticism. He found much of the work difficult, especially when it came to improvisation, but he joined in willingly. At the end of the session on the 'Escape' improvisation he said, 'Sue, it is very hard to be in Siberia when you know you are in the recreation room.'

He found the idea of remembering a special toy difficult, and spent a long time deliberating. He then created a picture of his mother (Figure 7.1) and wrote the following story:

> Once upon a time. Mum had to go to work. While she was away, me and my friends went down the woods looking for nature. We found many wonderful things – mice, rabbits, birds, bears, snakes and trees. And lots

Figure 7.1 Patient A's picture of his mother

of wonderful things. We went back home to see mum and she would have some nice food to eat and a wonderful smile. And that's why I love my mum. So I learned that I love Mum always and forever.

In the feedback he said that the most important thing in his childhood was his mother and implied that that was how it should be and that it could not be a toy.

Patient A chose Oberon as his first character from *A Midsummer Night's Dream* (Figure 7.2) and wrote the following about him in the first person:

I am Oberon. I am the King of the fairies in the forest My magic powers are unequaled even my Queen can only dream of magic I look after all the mortels from the city and cast spells so that they Have Happy endings and I guied them to there true Destiny Im kind powerful. And I love the forest. And I creat Dreams and make them come true for everyone.

Figure 7.2 Patient A as Oberon

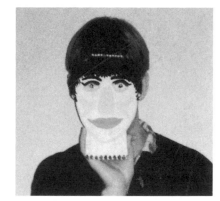

Figure 7.3 Patient A's mask of Hermia

His design for the costume and the set for Oberon were like camouflage with no differentiation between character and background. His instructions for the actor playing this character were: 'Kind Wise Loving charatable amusing Green colour'.

However, in the dramatisations he was much more interested in playing the part of Hermia and helped to create a scene about a strong Mr Aegeus who had a favourite daughter called Hermia. Mrs Aegeus was very weak and spent most of her time in the kitchen where Hermia's friend (Helena?) tried to get some attention. This scene was extremely powerful, and initial laughter at A playing the part of a little girl sitting on dad's knee – particularly since A is very tall and lanky – died down and the whole group became very absorbed in this dynamic.

His second mask was of Hermia (Figure 7.3) which like his first picture bears a strong resemblance to his mother. The mask has been created like a head into which he combed his own hair. He used this mask in improvisation with a very commanding Oberon (patient B) and whimsical Puck (staff member) to explore a scene of Hermia having magical dust sprinkled in her eyes in order for her to see her lover.

He wrote in the first person about his second mask:

> My name is Hermea I am a young Beautiful Woman I am deeply in love with my man + we have eloped to the forest Because my father wants me to marry another But as always I'll have my own way and I'll only Be happy an content to marry my true love and make him my Husband and have a large family lots of love and Harmony forever. . .?

His mask (Figure 7.4) of coming out of the forest, although the hair is standing on end, nevertheless had a strong resemblance to the previous two faces, though this time the mouth has teeth.

Figure 7.4 Patient A's mask of coming out of the forest

His final picture (Figure 7.5) with which to end the project was of himself as a ball floating down the river and not touching the banks which are identically painted. The turbulent river seems to get calmer as it bends. His 'journey throught the sessions' is as follows:

> In the beginning then Drama Drama Drama Fun Fun More Drama. Learning some things on the way then the end. Going down the river. And begin again.

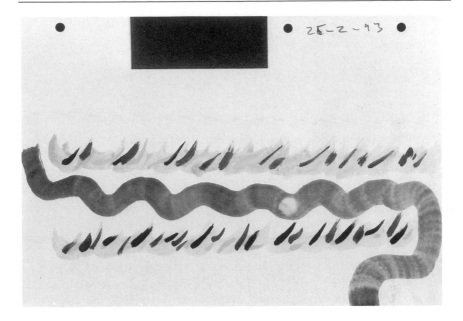

Figure 7.5 Patient A's picture of himself as a ball floating down a river

Psychological test results

Rorschach

These before and after records seem very similar: the main difference on retest is a slightly improved response time (RT) and an ability to handle all ten cards, providing a response to each.

There are two main differences: (a) These are relatively restricted records, with some suspiciousness in human interactions denoted both by the rejection of three cards on first testing, and then by the appearance of 'faces' in both sessions. It is important that these faces came as first responses to card 1 initially (task attitude), and then reappeared at a later stage on retest on cards hitherto rejected (7 and 9), and after the presentation of card 6. (b) There are also what could be considered oblique sexual references in both records, and in the second retesting session the perception of 'snouts' as rare detail on male card 4 is noteworthy. The inferences are largely those of poor gender identification, with an ambivalent sexual orientation.

There is some restriction and suspiciousness in human relationships, with a probable sexual focus, and this shifts largely in the direction of fluency of expression after dramatherapy.

HBBT

The test results indicate a moderately defensive position in regard to the patient's relationships with others. There is a trend, statistically not significant, towards more openness in the second testing.

Body cathexis scale

The results would indicate a strong suggestion that the patient tends to deny the existence of negative feelings altogether. All items before and after the workshops were endorsed at level 1 (strong positive feelings) and level 2 (moderate positive feelings). He would not acknowledge the possibility of a neutral or negative stance.

Repertory grids

The results of the grid analysis are consistent with the patient's tendency to intellectualise and deny negatives. His profile conforms to a unidimensional scale but there is little distance between 'ideal self' and 'self now' before the workshops. He is living very much in the present, but the past has not been resolved and is associated with his strongest negative feelings of scared, sad, bad, angry and anxious. He cannot admit to this cognitively. There appears to be a serious identity confusion as his current identity ('self now 2') is completely shrouded from view in the multidimensional statistical plot around 'ideal self'. It appears that this possible computer artefact, given that a plot is a two-dimensional representation of a multidimensional solution, is very consistent with the patient's clinical presentation.

Ideal self ————————— self now 1 ————————— index offence
self now 2

Appraisal

Patient A appeared to struggle with the significant themes that had been echoing throughout his life. In dramatherapeutic terms, his inability to create an imagined 'other' such as a toy or special possession demonstrates that he was lodged firmly in the Embodiment stage where self and other blend physically both with the dominant carer and also with the environment. It is only through the capacity to project outside of self into the world around that the person is able to separate or individuate. Furthermore this process enables the person to symbolise through imagined creation. We see that A had tremendous difficulty imagining Siberia in the early escape exercise and his special toy was his mother rather than a projective toy. His description of childhood was completely idealised and bore no relation to his actual history. He attempted to be daddy's favourite girl as Hermia in the improvisation with a non-idealised mother. He then developed Hermia's character through creating a mask which again looked like mother. The mask looked like a decapitated head, which he explored through improvisation and attempted to 'mend', and which he created as an extension of his own body. His mask of leaving the forest had similarities with the previous masks apart from the hair standing on end, which perhaps connects with his saying how much had been learnt in the forest. His closing picture of himself as the ball floating down the river illustrates his diffculty of 'anchoring' on the one hand but also shows the impossibility of escape from the confines of the river bank, whether of mother or the institution.

His dramatherapeutic work had either been reality-based and concretised as in improvisations and the faces of his mother or had been magical as in the Oberon mask, costume and setting. There was no process from everyday reality into dramatic reality and back again. Indeed everyday reality became confused in the dramatic reality. In dramatherapeutic terms this illustrates the indicators for psychoses (being stuck in dramatic reality) and for personality disorder (being trapped in everyday reality (Jennings 1994a) and the chaotic experience of self and the world without the dramatic imagination to move freely from one state to the other and back again. However, perhaps the fact that his final mask could be seen as quite frightening, with teeth and upstanding hair, is an indicator of his recognising another aspect of the strong, dominant, female image.

Patient A's dramatherapy can be seen as bearing out other diagnostic views, in particular highlighting both his struggle with his own unintegrated body-self and his swing of solutions between idealised memories and magical cures.

The clinical view (MO) is that Patient A had never been able to separate from his mother and that his two relationships were attempts to recreate the dynamic but failed. These issues were to the fore in his dramatherapy work when he also struggled with the nebulous father and dragon stepfather. He was able to externalise the mother/mask isues and had the opportunity, perhaps for the first time in his life, to play as a child and also to be a child. Interestingly water seems to be a recurrent theme in his images and in his relationships, which could benefit from further exploration.

The psychologist (JMcG) suggested that the test results indicate a very defensive patient who is having great difficulty in resolving his past experiences. He appears to be genuinely confused and ambivalent about his inner feelins and uses denial to resolve the conflict. Differences in his test results suggest a willingness to address the issues coupled with a state of helplessness in knowing how. Perhaps some directive therapy would be indicated to assist him towards their resolution.

His own feedback in the workshop questionaire stated that he had no preconceived idea of what might happen in the workshop and that he had joined out of curiosity; he thought he had learned about 'togetherness' for himself, others in the group and others in his life, as well as 'much much more' about himself. Perhaps that very word togetherness is the significant theme for A as he struggles to bring various aspects of his life experience and identity into an integrated whole.

CASE HISTORY 2

Patient B was admitted to Broadmoor in his early thirties after killing his mother. He was diagnosed as suffering from paranoid schizophrenia. Although defying his father and going to a secondary modern school, he developed asthma; he was unable to sleep alone and continued to headbang well into his teens, when both his parents left for lengthy periods of time. He travelled in Africa and then worked in Scandinavia before his paranoid hallucinations commenced. However, he settled into working with children with learning difficulties, where he met his first serious girlfriend. The trigger

Figure 7.6 Patient B's special toy

for his index offence appears to be his wish to stay in the same bedroom with the girlfriend in the family home. He has been in Broadmoor for four years and has been receiving anti-psychotic medication and individual psycho-therapy. For three years he has been in a psychodynamic self-awareness group.

Patient B joined the dramatherapy group with great enthusiasm. Although anxious physically about drama games and more boisterous activity, he nevertheless joined in everything. He was very ready to improvise and created dramatised fictionalised scenes from his own life, such as a serious road accident that the whole family had been involved in.

He created Pinkie, a rabbit (Figure 7.6) as his early special toy and wrote the following:

> Once upon a time, Pinky (7 years old) went on a journey to a magical pink land where everything shone and twinkled. He ate candyfloss that melted on his tongue and yet his hands and mouth never got sticky. In the soft breezes the noise would be of gently clinking little chandeliers that sparkled as the night drew in.
>
> In the morning the mist took away the precise shine and twinkling of everything. It was time to get back to the mum and dad where things didn't shine for very long. But Pinky always was left with a sour taste his mouth as the rowing boat rocked, the rollocks banging on the journey home.
>
> He learned when he got home, the Sunday dinner was there and it was always wholesome. So he learnt at home things, although boring, were real and didn't leave one feeling empty. And thats what Pinky learnt on the journey.

He chose to be Aegeus in *A Midsummer Night's Dream* (Figure 7.7) and wrote the following:

> I am Hermia's father – as you can see I am an angry man I have a permanent scowl. I busy myself with my trading business I am a merchant. My nose has the blood vessels showing as I am rather fond of my own merchandise. I want to build a business that will last long after I am dead. I would like Hermia to find a suitable partner so I could gain a son for my business. It was a devastating blow to lose Hermia's mother in childbirth, although nobody knows – I have never told anybody. My friends are strictly associates no one is close except for my accountant.

In the improvisation he played a very bitter and powerful Mr Aegeus whose wife had died in childbirth and was in the mask group with all the angry people. His instructions for people playing the character of Aegeus were: 'children must be obediant, thinks he knows best, loving but distant, authoritarian'.

He designed gaters and breeches with a tunic for his character, 'mostly in grey with red piping', and the stage set was a single tree, with a mountain, sky and grass (the tree a less defined version of his final tree picture).

Figure 7.7 Patient B as Aegeus

Figure 7.8 Patient B as Oberon

As Oberon (Figure 7.8) he was again an angry and powerful figure, upset at being left out of Titania's party. He said how important it was to have real leaves on this mask. He wrote as the character of Oberon:

My name is Oberon. I am King of the Fairies, I move about the forest unseen. From time to time I speak to the forest, that is the trees, birds, and animals. They *all* obey my will. I am most happy when strangers come into the Forest. Do we have games with them, he he he, it is best when they get lost and all my fairies frighten them.

What I really want though is to get rid of Titania she is an absolute horror she has changed so much since the first days I knew her. She promised to honour and obey and now look at her. She has her own fairies and they are creating trouble with my lot only last month they met and had a wild party at which I was not invited.

His mask when he came out of the forest seemed a self-portrait (Figure 7.9) with a final scene of several trees (Figure 7.10) as contrasted with the isolated tree in earlier pictures.

His journey through the sessions is as follows:

We began with Pinkie my stuffed rabbit that I took everywhere with me and how he went on a journey to a magical and mysterious land where he ate candyfloss but left.

Next there was the old woman who lived in a shoe – she had to call in the Social Services.

What kind of tree are you? I am an apple tree in a garden in Surbiton but unfortunately my fruit is not harvested.

In January we made masks. Mine was of Egeus from 'A Midsummer Night's Dream'. Then I drew his costume and a scene of trees, mountain and sky.

Figure 7.9 Patient B's mask of coming out of the forest

Figure 7.10 Patient B's final picture

In the penultimate week we playacted a scene with Hermia and her family. Then wrote a couple of accounts of how we saw our roles we were in.

Final week – looked at the work we had done, noted down names from the continuum of self-trust, trust of others, etc.

Psychological test results

Rorschach results

There is a very high expression of affect in fluent and rapid responding on B1 and B2, but B2 is relatively less constrained with the introduction of much more sexually explicit material, inferred from a more symbolised form in B1. The reasons for this change are not clear: it may be the effect of a greater licence to express after the dramatherapy, or the gender of the tester may have influenced responding (female–male), or there may have been a deterioration in mental state and a lowering of thresholds.

However, whatever these reasons may be the essence of the record remains unchanged, with a very overt expression of inner turbulence on both occasions, and gross difficulties in human relationships suggested by a low or absent H per cent, and the 'distancing' of percepts which are seen (e.g. man from space, ballet dancer). It would be surprising if sexuality was not a focus of these problems. Apart from the florid sexual disinhibition of B2, there are also many 'Wheeler' signs, thought to be indicative of a primarily homosexual orientation, and in addition there is the more sophisticated symbolism of the phoenix rising from the ashes repeated on (sex) card 6, and the eloquent crabs and crab shell response to the two female cards. The impression is thus one of a very barren experience of women, and a subsequent turning away.

Body cathexis scale

Patient B's profiles moved in a positive direction after the workshops, with markedly more positive feelings towards his sexuality.

HBBT

In this test, there was no perceived change from a moderately defended position, indicating some willingness to accept his vulnerability.

Repertory grids

The results indicate a very positive move in the direction of ideal self. This would be represented on the unidimensional scale thus:

ideal self ——————— self 2 ——————— self 1 ——————— index offence

All his negative feelings are closely associated with his index offence while his positive feelings are associated with ideal self. This suggests that he is experiencing an emotional flatness in relation to his 'self now' – his current position. Cognitively he has moved towards an ideal goal, while emotionally he remains in the past indicating the need for further resolution of the conflict in therapy. The results indicate a more positive note of acceptance and regard for his mother and father and a less idealised and therefore more realistic regard for his responsible medical officer and primary nurse.

Appraisal

Patient B illustrates a dramatherapeutic process through the stages of embodiment, projection and role. Whereas he struggled with physical prowess, nevertheless he gradually took more physical risks. He clearly identified with the disillusion as told in the story of Pinkie, and Pinkie too went on journeys as he had attempted to do as a young man. However, his journey had ended in frustration and eventual breakdown. It would seem that through the two characters of Aegeus and Oberon he was able to address his violent rage, and importantly was able to be his angry father looking for a son to live up to his expectations. In addition, as Oberon he was able to express his frustration and sadness, as well as outrage at not being invited to Titania's party. As with Patient A there is a recurring theme of water, with Patient B there is a recurring theme of leaves, on and off the trees and on his mask. Leaves had taken on a diabolical significance during his offence, and it would seem that there was some normalisation of the leaves within the dramatised story and pictures.

The clinical view (MO) is that the dramatherapy enabled him to accept inwardly the anger of his own father by putting himself in his father's place, i.e. by being father both as Aegeus and as Oberon. He was also able to explore and accept his own anger, something which had always been difficult. This process allowed him to find the inner strength to deal with his father's marriage to another woman.

The psychologist (JMcG) says that the results reflect the work of a very honest and compliant patient who is working seriously on his rehabilitation. Perhaps he is tending to intellectualise his condition while retaining an emotional defensiveness with regard to his inner feelings and possible sexual identity conflict.

Patient B in his feedback stressed how important it had been to work with women in the group and its usefulness in helping him work in integrated settings. In another communciation he thought the whole process was rather tame, but subsequently he thought it of benefit to the whole group. Patient B went on to the second dramatherapy project on the story of Odysseus.

CONCLUSION

This project served as a pilot scheme for discussion on the development of dramatherapy with offender patients. Patients and staff alike expressed overall satisfaction and a definite 'feelgood' factor after the sessions closed. All wanted to continue into another project, even the member of staff who initially expressed doubts about the classical material. It was a clear example of a 'collaborative' approach between staff and patients which can function alongside other individual and group therapies and artistic activities. This supports the notion of 'diversity' in contemporary programmes for offender patients (Reed 1994).

As a result of this project, two nurses from the group were seconded and supported to train as dramatherapists at the Roehampton Institute. This process reaches out and generates yet more dramatherapy resources for the hospital but is also a public statement that the institution supports drama-therapy.

Landy's Role Taxonomy (1993) was unavailable when this project took place. However it is interesting to note the diversity in the second mask/role choices compared with the first mask/role choices. The patients' first masks were all male and were vehicles for exploring and expressing anger and rage. Most of the second masks enabled playfulness and experimentation with gender, the child, the trickster and the fool.

The clinicians involved were in no doubt that the dramatherapy was able to reach parts that were inaccessible by other means, in particular through the use of distancing.

Although some of the test results were inconclusive, nevertheless there was no doubt from all concerned that there had been an improvement in self-image both individually and collectively for staff and patients on this particular ward.

The interwoven themes of the individuals and the group bring to mind the Temiar healing rituals which are said to strengthen the head souls of the individuals in the village as well as the village community as a whole.

I felt very happy when I went to make my second mask and wanted to make a mask of a daffodil because its Spring; I know there isn't a daffodil in A Midsummer Night's Dream so I made a mask of a Sunflower.

ACKNOWLEDGEMENTS

We would like to thank Dr Mary Hill, Dr Lona Roberts and Dr Sean Hammond for their help in administering the tests and analysing data, and Dr Murray Cox for advice and support, as well as Peter Belton, Jenny France and the staff and patients of Folkestone Ward for making this project possible.

REFERENCES

Belton, P. Jennings, S., McGinley, J. and Orr, M. (in preparation) 'Marks and metaphors: dramatherapy process and product'.

Cattanach, A. (1992) *Drama for People with Special Needs*, London: A. & C. Black.

Cox, M. (ed.) (1992) *Shakespeare Comes to Broadmoor*, London: Jessica Kingsley.

Cronbach, L.J. (1951) 'Coefficient alpha and the internal structure of tests', *Psychometrika* 16: 297–334

Elizur, A. (1949) 'Content analysis of the Rorschach with regard to anxiety and hostility', *Rorschach Research Exchange Journal of Projective Techniques* 13: 247–284.

Endicott, N.A. (1969) 'Objective measures of suspiciousness', *Journal of Abnormal Social Psychology* 74: 26–32

—— (1972) 'The Holtzman inkblot technique: content measures of depression and suspiciousness', *Journal of Personality Assessment* 36: 424–426.

Fisher, S. and Cleveland, S.E. (1968) *Body Image and Personality*, New York: Dover Publications.

Fransella, F. (1990) 'Personal construct therapy', in W. Dryden (ed.) *Individual Therapy: A Handbook*, Milton Keynes, UK: Open University Press.

Fransella, F. and Bannister, D. (1977) *A Manual for Repertory Grid Technique*, London: Academic Press.

Freud, S. (1927) *The Ego and the Id*, London: Hogarth Press.

Georgakis, E. (1983) 'Superficial and deep-seated cancers in relation to body image', unpublished dissertation, University of Surrey, UK.

Goldfried, M.R.B., Stricker, G. and Weiner, I.B. (1971) *Rorschach Handbook of Clinical Research Applications*, Englewood Cliffs, NJ: Prentice-Hall.

Haward, L. (1959) 'Haward Body Barrier Test', unpublished research paper, University of Surrey, UK.

Houston, J. and Adshead, G. (1993) 'The use of repertory grids to assess change: application to a sex offenders group', *Issues in Criminological and Legal Psychology* 19: 43–51.

Jennings, S. (1986) *Creative Drama in Groupwork*, Bicester, UK: Winslow Press.

—— (1992) 'The nature and scope of dramatherapy: theatre of healing', in M. Cox (ed.) *Shakespeare Comes to Broadmoor*, London: Jessica Kingsley.

—— (1994a) 'The theatre of healing: metaphor and metaphysics in the healing process', in S. Jennings, A. Cattanach, S. Mitchell, A. Chesner and B. Meldrum, *The Handbook of Dramatherapy*, London: Routledge.

—— (1994b) 'Unravelling dramatherapy', *Context* (Winter):

—— (1995) 'Forensic dramatherapy', in C. Cordess and M. Cox (eds) *Forensic Psychotherapy: Crime, Psychodynamics and the Offender Patient*, London: Jessica Kingsley.

—— (in preparation) *Shakespeare's Theatre of Healing*, London: Jessica Kingsley.

Jourard, S.M. and Secord, P.F. (1955) 'Body cathexis and the ideal female figure', *Journal of Abnormal Social Psychology* 50: 243–246.

Kelly, G. (1955) *The Psychology of Personal Constructs*, vols 1–11, New York: Norton.

Landy, R. (1993) *Persona and Performance: The Meaning of Role in Drama, Therapy, and Everyday Life*, London: Jessica Kingsley.

Mitchell, S. (1994) 'The theatre of self-expression: a therapeutic model of dramatherapy', in S. Jennings, A. Cattanach, S. Mitchell, A. Chesner and B. Meldrum (eds) *The Handbook of Dramatherapy*, London: Routledge.

Mouratoglou, V. (1984) 'A study of the body boundary and control concepts', unpublished research dissertation, University of Surrey, UK.

Rattigan, N.Y. (1976) 'Body image boundary and contraceptive choice: a partial validation study of the HBBT', unpublished research dissertation, University of Surrey, UK.

Reed, J. (1994) 'Report of the working group on high security and related psychiatric provision', London: Department of Health.

Reich, W. (1949) *Character Analysis*, New York: Orgone Institute Press.

Schafer, R. (1954) *Psychoanalytical Interpretation in Rorschach Testing*, New York: Grune and Stratton.

Shorts, I. (1985) 'The treatment of sex offenders in a maximum security forensic hospital: detecting changes in personality and interpersonal construing', *International Journal of Offender Therapy and Comparative Criminology* 29(3): 237–250.

Wheeler, W.M. (1949) 'An analysis of Rorschach indices of male homosexuality', *Rorschach Research Exchange Journal of Projective Techniques* 13: 97–126.

Chapter 8

"To feel absent from one's voice"

Trial therapy with a young immigrant woman

Alida Gersie

In this chapter I outline brief work with a woman who experienced anxiety states as a result of "feeling absent from her voice." I describe how I elicited relevant information so that we could decide together what kind of relief or treatment might be necessary. I discuss the principles which guided our search for pertinent issues, and I close the chapter by drawing some core themes to the fore.

INTRODUCTION

Whenever we are very nervous or self-conscious we may have the unusual sensation of hearing ourselves speak or sing. A careful listener hears the vocal tightness that ensues, the over-articulation and underlying hesitancy in all that is said or sung. These vocal signs convey, virtually in spite of us, the struggle with the desire to please as well as the longing for a more centered authenticity. The fear of being unable to meet internal or external expectation painfully circumscribes the freedom for which the person also yearns. This distance from one's voice is frightening, for it signals cleavage from a felt coherency of self. Such episodes of hyper self-consciousness are often short lived. They disappear as soon as some relaxation sets in. However, the persistent, conscious evaluation of the sound of one's own voice is worrying. The fear of fear often develops into a dreaded inner experience, made worse by emotional stress or physical illness. Then panic may ensue.

The experience of intensely felt vocal absence is healed when the speaker or the singer learns to relax or to attend to the pattern of distress which is entailed in the speaking or the singing and its accompanying commentary. In the course of growing up all of us need to learn to tolerate the fright of fear, and to calm ourselves in the face of dread. But attending to panic with dread in one's heart is hard to do: we want to fight or to take flight. Such is the way of things. It feels counter-instinctive quietly to witness something painful when we are on the run from knowing too much about ourselves. Yet, particularly when we are in the throes of terror, we somehow need to create a bridging capacity that will allow for new buoyancy of self to be generated.

Without this bridging capacity the crucial confidence in our self and environment remains out of reach. This experience of vocal absence and the resultant panic was the complaint of a woman whom I will call Naomi.

CASE DESCRIPTION

Naomi was in her early thirties, with that good-looking perkiness which covers the pain that dwells within. She had requested a therapeutic assessment session because she suffered anxiety states, during which she felt disoriented, and virtually unable to continue speaking, as if caught in a no-woman's land where language became noise. Her choice of words to describe what the panic felt like reminded me of Grinberg and Grinberg, who suggest that language serves as a tool which helps us to create and to assimilate our image of the surrounding world (Grinberg and Grinberg 1984). For whatever reason, Naomi's capacity to assimilate her surrounding world might have reached its limits. Though her tools to be in the world seemed to be intact, in the grip of anxiety her capacity to handle them appeared to be momentarily impaired. I felt that she was an unbelievably tired woman, who, however, did not look tired. This seemed a distinct disadvantage to her.

A glimpse of the immigrant's tale

When I first heard Naomi's voice on my answerphone, I was struck by its timbre of cheerful pain. It was an uncomfortable combination. The hint of a foreign accent suggested that she might be a stranger to this country, though her name sounded local. Her accent evoked echoes of the wearied version of the immigrant's tale, a tale which is saturated with yearning for the shores of other people's understanding and so often fails to lament what was also lost.

She was indeed a comparatively recent immigrant. I wondered aloud what it might be like for her to live with two countries and two languages. With some sadness she recounted how once she had moved here, three years earlier, she had immediately stopped speaking her native tongue. She had decided that it would be better that way. It had also coincided with advice she had received: "Steep yourself in the new language. Sleep it, dream it, love it . . . and you'll adjust more easily." As indeed she apparently had. She had rarely felt homesick, and had, to all intents and purposes settled in well, making through sheer effort and dedication a success of work, study and home. I noticed how she did not mention her more private and intimate life, but waited to see what would happen. I wanted to discover how she structured this story of her life.

Recently she had begun hearing the sound of her voice in a frighteningly different way, as if there was a large space between herself and what she said. Sometimes she had realized in terror that she was not to be found in any of the words; she was completely absent from her voice. For a brief moment she would with great clarity hear how her voice uttered familiar yet alien sounds. Then panic would strike. She added: "I hear my voice; it's a stranger's voice. I can still say what I want and I know what every word means, but the words don't mean anything. Do you understand?" I heard the fluctuating dynamics of her speech. Her accent had become much more pronounced, whilst sorrow softened the tightness of her voice.

To cry foreign

The feelings connected with language unease dated back a couple of months. The fierce anxiety attacks had only begun some weeks earlier when pressures at work (she had a part-time office job) combined with the requirement to meet a deadline for the submission of her academic thesis. She had been working night and day to find the precise, the right, and hopefully the successful, language. She added: "Writing in English is hard for me."

Mindful not to be led astray too quickly into a discussion of the problematics of English as a second language, I asked her to describe what being so anxious felt like. Hesitantly she recounted how it sometimes felt as if she involuntarily entered a inner acoustic space filled with words, which did not make sense any more. She described the pounding of her heart, and the dryness of her tongue in her mouth. Each panic state had begun during a meeting at the university. She would then excuse herself and hurry home. There, huddled up and thoroughly exhausted, she would fall asleep. When, after such a sleep, she awakened, it would be as if she had briefly visited a peculiar, foreign country. She added: "Then all I want to do is to curl back into my corner again and weep." She hesitated: "But I don't." When I inquired what stopped her, she answered: "Nobody would understand what I would be crying for. I would just cry foreign."

At this point she began to cry, at first quietly, then with deeper breaths, as if finally in search of the relief deep crying brings. Her cries did not sound abandoned, just eager to be wept, as if they had been held in a long while. She calmed down in her own time and re-established eye-contact. She looked refreshed.

To adopt a foreign language

I felt for Naomi, knowing from personal and professional experience the extraordinary pattern of loss and gain involved in the process of adopting a foreign language as a new primary vehicle for verbal expression. (Bauxbaum 1987). Surprisingly she had not asked me about my accent, but I am sure she knew that English was not my first tongue. Maybe she therefore trusted that I might understand something about the complexities of speaking in an adopted mother tongue. I certainly recognized her challenge to develop emotional access to early memories in the new language, to songs and to a sense of humor in ways that bind the felt past with meaningful expression in the new context. In these situations the actual deficit of accessible words so easily coincides with a felt deficit of self, which is only too often linked with having left one's country of origin in the first place. When this happens the real complexities of expressing oneself in a foreign tongue are only too readily attributed to the complexities of language, whilst it may be the case that the felt confusion emerges from other vulnerabilities. These may well be profoundly reminiscent of the pain of earlier days when we may have felt like a stranger in that other strange land: the place we once called home.

In my meeting with Naomi, I was again struck by the need we all have to discover and to describe the meaning we create out of our being in the world. Though I realized only too well that I had learned but a minute aspect of her life's story, it seemed apparent that the increase of external pressures had brought other needs for inner growth to the fore. Her anxiety appeared to be knocking at her heart to tell her that the longing for some kind of other development could no longer be denied. I wondered in which terrain of life it belonged. The thesis-completion simply seemed too easy an option.

Whilst I pondered these thoughts Naomi spoke about her longing to stop work on the thesis, to let it all go, before the hurdles were passed. Once more her voice had grown tight and dull: she was becoming absent again. I reminded myself of the earlier aliveness when she had spoken about "crying foreign." I sensed that Naomi had a lot to say that wasn't coming out just yet.

Why did you leave your country of origin?

I therefore asked her to tell me something about the reasons for leaving her homeland. The picture that emerged was one of a young woman who was offered a scholarship to continue study abroad, and who upon completion of one degree had decided to top it up with further studies. However, by then the scholarship had run out. She had been unable to get new financial support. Therefore she had taken up part-time work. She added that she loved her studies, felt settled here and planned to stay for ever. Then, as if between nose and lips, she noted that she had married six months earlier. I had certainly wondered which change she had not yet described, for it had been as if some big pieces of her inner jigsaw had been missing. Here was at least one piece. The other was probably linked with events related to her departure. I asked whether her new husband spoke her language of origin. She said "no". Did she feel somewhat at sea in her new marriage? I put it to her that mixed-language marriages may take extra work, particularly because in our most intimate world words matter so very much. She added: "That's not all. We have been trying to buy a flat, but everything keeps going wrong. So, we're still stuck in a room in the shared house where I lived before we got married." Naomi certainly experienced a range of stresses. Her capacity to cope was at straining point.

TO KNOW THE WORST AND THE BEST

Naomi talked more about her marital relationship. She had not told her husband much about her recent panic states. She quickly picked up that this might not be helpful to the building of intimacy. I interpreted the possible similarities between her way of coping now with this distress and habits she might have formed a long time ago in her relationships with her parents. I also wondered whether in our relationship too she might not be protecting me from knowing the worst. She shook her head: "It always takes me a while to talk with my parents, but in the end I talk. I'll go home and talk with my husband. I will. I have given up a lot to live here with him. I just didn't realize how much until now."

We sat quietly a while. The caution about a client's hidden problems with dependency needs came to mind: was Naomi appearing to cope too soon in her old familiar ways? Gustafson translates these cautions into principles for practice. In any pre-therapy interview the therapist needs to know the worst, the best (what means/has meant a lot to the patient), and to discover whether there is a buoyant feeling. This readily emerges when a client is asked to describe whether they ever gave up something for another person they loved. For such a sacrifice demands self-protectiveness, buoyancy and a level of calm security (Gustafson 1984).

Naomi's current worst scene seemed to be the state in which she felt beyond the reach of comfort or consolation when weeping all by herself. She described the best as being with her husband. The sacrifice concerned the fact that she had basically given up speaking her native tongue.

Having clarified the situation so far she now had to be helped to integrate the experience of fear and change into some kind of meaningful framework – meanings which might help her to link past and present. I was reminded of Dr Ludwig's words:

> The people who come to see us bring us their stories. They hope they tell them well enough so that we understand the truth of their lives. They hope we know how to interpret their stories correctly. We have to remember that what we hear is their story.

Naomi's story spoke of change at many different levels, and of the losses entailed in these processes. There were various possible explanations for Naomi's panic states. On the basis of the available evidence I concluded that they were probably stress- and exhaustion-related, and linked with the need to learn how better to manage intimacy in her recent marriage, amongst other ways by talking with her husband about his present inability to speak her language of origin. The fact that I would have liked her to be a bit more open and/or curious about the circumstances which accompanied her journey away from home three years earlier, when she was in her late twenties, was acknowledged between us, but Naomi noted that nothing special had happened. I accepted her preferred explanation of her life's events.

At this stage in the session Naomi needed more from me than clarity of orientation: she also wanted relief from her fear of the fear, a little bit of healing. Any stories or dramas we would develop in the space between us would have to strengthen Naomi's confidence and trust in processes of continuity, of links between places and people with full acknowledgment of the consequences of physical distance upon relationships.

Just to make sure that she did indeed prioritize the present over the past at this stage of her life, I asked again if she would tell me a little more about her family and friends in her country of origin. There was no evidence of any current trauma or even upheaval in any of these relationships. However, she did not dwell on details. For whatever reason, speaking about these relationships was not high on her inner list of priorities, so I had better adjust mine. Her overwhelming present demanded our attention. Having pondered the collage of facts and feelings Naomi presented, and those she evoked in me, I decided to tell her tale. I choose this story because it succinctly encapsulates the multiple themes which Naomi had brought to our work, and yet was sufficiently oblique to be able to function as a teaching tale. This is the story:

Some time ago there was a man, who was really busy. He had his own company and he worked very hard to keep the business together. It grew and it grew. One day he received a message that his grandfather was seriously ill and that he wanted to see his grandson before he died. Well, our man immediately settled his affairs for a few days and went to visit his grandfather. This grandfather was an immigrant, who had left his country when he was a young man. As far as his grandson knew he had arrived with nothing but his clothes and a pair of willing hands. That afternoon they met, those two people, the sick old man and his grandson. The grandfather said that he had a gift for him. It was a gift from the land back home. He had waited till this moment to give it to him, to his daughter's child. Now this moment had come. The old man struggled to put his hand in his trouser-pocket. Out came a smudged little bag. Giving it to his grandson and with a broken voice, the old man encouraged: "Look. Please look. Open it." When the young man untied the colourful string that had tied the bag for so long, and looked, he saw a few dark seeds. He heard his grandfather's voice: "I took them with me when I came. I harvested them all my life. They are our best seeds. Take care of them." This is what the grandfather said: "They are our best seeds." His voice lingered: "When you are ready, plant them". Soon after the grandfather died. When the time was right the grandson planted the seeds just as his grandfather had told him. They sprouted. In this way new gardens and new orchards grew.

Naomi listened quietly. Whilst I told the story, she had moved her hands as if shaping and holding a little bag. She looked at me: "Did I tell you that there was an orchard near my house when I was a child? I used to love that orchard." Without waiting for an answer, she added: "I can just see that little bag. I can just see it and hold it." We looked at each other and did not say much. I queried: "Do you have a lot of stories to tell?" She nodded affirmatively. "Are there other people as well as your husband whom you could tell them to?" A broad grin hastened to her cheeks: "Oh yes! Yes!" Once more I asked: "People you could speak to in both tongues?" They were near her, too. It was just that she had adopted the habit of speaking English with them.

Who might be the best listeners?

We sat together for a while longer and spoke about what Naomi really needed at this stage. Therapy? Counseling? More talks with good friends? Spiritual guidance? Ultimately it rested with her to explore the meaning of the feelings that played behind and between her words. She referred once more to the imaginary little bag of seeds. Shaping her hands in a suggestive manner she said: "There's a lot I brought with me. I had forgotten."

She was deeply thoughtful as a result of the realization that she had treated the story of her unfolding life as a series of recent anecdotes without history or tradition. Her wandering eyes suggested that she moved from dusty memory corner to brightly lit recollections. There was probably a lot of talking to be done. However, her best listeners might well be her husband and her friends. She decided that for now she wanted to do the talking back home, in her intimate life-circle. I felt peaceful about her decision, but asked that we might meet again six or nine months later. I also requested that she contact me immediately if the panic was to intensify a great deal, warning her too that the panic states might well continue unabated or even become more frequent, until some time after she submitted her thesis. I suggested that this might be the case because the panic was probably also her body's way of telling her that she needed to rest and sleep. After all, she worked extremely hard and little else had been able to get through to her to help her to take a break. As she had indicated that she intended to meet the thesis deadline, she was likely to stay exhausted for a while and therefore likely to panic again. With her symptom thus prescribed, she visibly relaxed. I asked to see her again both to extend the post-therapy efficacy and to see where she had traveled too. She agreed to this proposal.

SOME SPECIFIC REFLECTIONS ON THIS STAGE OF THE WORK

In this session we were able to achieve two things.

First, Naomi's experience of the panic had been contextualized and thereby normalized. There was nothing necessarily and inherently disconcerting about her fear of feeling quite so disconnected. In fact it was reassuring that feeling disconnected from language frightened her. She had not given herself due credit for how tired she really was, how little sleep she had and how harsh her self-regime had been in order to achieve the deadline for thesis submission. We had needed to establish whether her panic was primarily the result of sheer physical exhaustion, and/or connected with an underlying much deeper pathology. The latter did not seem to be the case.

In order to enhance her ability to cope I told her the story. Towards the end of the meeting Naomi said: "When I came here, I felt very tired and frightened. Now I'm a bit sad and just a little tired and there's a small bag of seeds." Then she added: "Something has changed, and I don't know what. It's like a gap was filled. It feels good, but it's a little odd." She provided ample evidence that her words weren't quite so meaningless anymore. She had regained language-instrumentality.

We had also clearly succeeded in the second task, namely deliberately to re-establish her access to some purposeful bridge with the past, as was contained in the story. As such, a renewed capacity to communicate meaningfully, within her terms and conditions had been generated. She realized that she needed to work towards further satisfactory solutions to her predicament. The story strengthened this resolve.

Naomi's preconceived notion of what mattered was that fear was at the heart of the problem. Her developing account suggested that her way of dealing with two countries, and therefore two cultures, left much to be desired. Once the past as "broken past" had been invited into the present through the imagery of the seed-story, she visibly shifted her internal position, from being overwhelmed by unnamable dreads, to that of storyteller with many untold stories. Whether and how she would make use of the possibilities this entailed were enfolded in time.

My encounter with Naomi evoked Anthony Storr's words: "the human mind seems so constructed that a new balance or restoration within the subjective, imaginative world is felt as if it were a change for the better in the external world and vice versa. This is the secret of creative adaptation" (Storr 1990, p. 124). Little did I know then that Naomi would shortly be reading these very same lines.

To comprehend intentional states

In my therapeutic practice I attempt to comprehend how intentional states, such as desiring, intending, believing, longing, grasping a meaning, manifest themselves in a troubled person's life. In the search for even a modicum of understanding of what, for example, "longing" might mean to another person, I rely on the concept of agency. Agency implies that actions occur under the influence of intention. I presume that, however torn-to-pieces a person might be, they will have something to say to themselves about their choices that is pertinent both to themselves and to others (Nisbett and Ross 1980). In each therapeutic encounter I try to work together with the client to re-establish a purposeful link between language, intention and action, and the everyday interpretation of this relationship. Meanwhile I try to remain conscious of the fact that intention, action and language are always situated in terms of time, our cultural setting and in the mutually interacting states of the participants in an interaction (Bruner 1990, p. 19). As such I could say that each new meeting with a client means learning their language – the way they articulate their world – and finding a meeting place where we can develop a new shared language, which facilitates change. Well or unwell, all of us are inevitably involved in a world of images, meanings and social bonds (Rosaldo 1984, p. 139).

A pragmatist's practice

Naomi had invited me to trace with her implied beliefs about the support that certain modes of life deserve or merit. Thereby I became more aware of her perspectives upon the life that is worth living. The "how" of her life was consequently greatly privileged over the search for answers to the question "why?" As such this therapeutic work is best described as a pragmatist's practice in which issues related to the praxis of living are given priority.

The story I told Naomi had relied for its survival in the oral tradition on comparative brevity, perspicuity, relevance and truthfulness. Additionally it depended on my efficacious use of these characteristics in the process of bringing the story to life between us.

These fundamentals of oral stories and storytelling are particularly important in the therapeutic context, where a client's ability to describe concisely or to embellish life's stories at will has frequently been lost to a torrential onslaught of contradictory feelings which submerge the felt craving for purposeful telling. In the midst of despair the willingness to tell withers. The restoration of the ability to recount within the possibilities offered by the four constraints can help a distressed person to begin to think of themselves again as an able storyteller. This is often experienced as profoundly reassuring. We should not underestimate the extent to which the very engagement with the act of storied communication enables both teller and listener to negotiate uncertainty by learning to manage anew the internal process of selecting information for the purpose of communication.

In search of good enough storying

Told stories exist between people. They are mediators between our private, personal and public worlds, or more accurately between those domains of life where we negotiate desires and beliefs. As such the act of telling and listening to a story also expresses the various ways in which our life is constituted

but that this demanded recognition, awareness, commitment and work. These themes were encapsulated in the story about the gift of seeds which I told her during our first session (Gordon 1978; Wells 1987).

I was struck by the development that had taken place. Now she was reading me a little story, taken from a book she had first seen here. I had purposefully constructed my story around a male protagonist, a woman's child. She emphasized a story with a man as the actor and had laughed with pleasure and relief when woman's rightful place was accorded to her too. Being about to feel self-congratulatory on how I had offered Naomi such a well-matched story, I caught myself. After all, what did I really know about the meaning it had acquired for her? In my mind's eye flashed the words "cheese and eggs." Below is the story those words refer to.

To establish just one meaning?

In a certain village, not so far away but not so very near, the lord of the manor ruled like a tyrant. He could not tolerate disagreement of whatever kind and demanded that his people gave total compliance to his rules, ideas and other strictures. One day, this man let it be known that he wanted to test his people's understanding of his decrees, and intended to do this through a dispute in sign. If one of the villagers understood him correctly, all would be well, if not, there would be trouble. Great fear lamed the people's will to step forward. Who would be the one who would dare to have a dispute in sign with the man, they all knew to be wicked?

Then the poultry farmer said that he was willing to meet the lord. The appointed day arrived. In full view of the villagers, of all those people who dared not be present and who yet dared not stay away, the lord said to the farmer: "You have to understand my signs and answer them in the same way." He then pointed one finger at him. Without a moment's hesitation the farmer pointed two in return. Then the lord took a piece of white cheese out of his pocket. The farmer rummaged through his trouser pocket. When he opened his hand, he showed the lord an egg. Finally the lord took a few seeds of grain and scattered them on the floor. Whereupon the farmer let go of a hen he had been carrying in a basket, and encouraged it to eat the grain. Then the lord exclaimed in amazement that his people truly understood him. The villagers were greatly relieved.

Not long after, a neighbor asked the farmer what had actually been discussed that day during the dispute in sign. "Ah," said the farmer, "It was easy. He pointed one finger at me, so as to say: 'I'll take out your eyes if you don't get it right.' So I pointed two fingers at him, suggesting that he had better not try. Then he showed me that piece of cheese which he took out of his pocket as if to say: 'Look how much food I've got, I don't even have to eat it all.' So I took out one of my eggs, telling him that I don't need his food. When he scattered the seeds on the floor, so as to say

'Look what I can afford to waste,' I just set my hen upon it to let him know: 'By your waste I will profit.'" The neighbour was rather impressed with the farmer's ability to understand the signs.

Well, it so happened that around that same time the lord hosted some visitors. He boasted to them about the villagers' understanding and how much they enjoyed living in his village. One of the guests became curious and asked how he knew all this. The lord then spoke about the challenge he had set. Then he described the dispute: I pointed one finger to the farmer so as to say there is only one master. The farmer then pointed two fingers at me which meant: "There is a lord in heaven and a lord on earth, and you are the one on earth." I then took out the cheese so as to ask: "Is this cheese from a white or a black goat?" He simply took out an egg, so as to say: "Is this egg from a white or a brown hen?" I then scattered some seeds to indicate there are people everywhere. After briefly looking at the scattered seeds, the farmer set his hen free, meaning that though we people are scattered, we also need to gather in one place. I then knew that my villagers understand me.[1]

The primacy of the given moment

Thus informed by one of my associations, I attended more fully to Naomi's voiced understanding of her process, rather than to my interpretation of the understanding I presumed her to have had. I was aware too that the old stories we tell attach themselves to the meaning that is most pertinent to us at a given moment in time. As such, any attempt to determine, without reference to the individual's authority, what meaning a story has for another person bears some similarity to what happened in the story about the dispute in sign between the lord of the manor and the poultry farmer.

I witnessed a quietly energetic Naomi, who had successfully completed a major task. She worked and loved and lived with a renewed sense of inner purpose. She said, with some surprise in her voice, that the anxiety attacks had not returned, but that she had continued to feel tired for some months. She said:

I nearly missed the attacks. You had suggested that they might be like an alarm-clock, telling me to wake up to something, like waking up to knowing how tired I was. For a while I worried that without them I would just be half asleep. Then I realized what I was doing to myself and laughed. If ever they come back, I'll first be frightened and then I'm also sure I will remember the alarm-clock.

She then continued: "Oh, we did something else. We're about to move house. We decided that we definitely wanted to live in a house with a garden. We just found one. There's an apple tree in the garden.

Can you believe that?" Whilst I saw in my mind's eye a house with the apple tree in the garden, and reflected on some of what this might mean to her, her voice said nearly pleadingly: "Alida, you do remember the story you told me, don't you?" Indeed I did. We then talked a little more about the story, its links to her life as she now anticipated it, about the difficulties and strengths of her current way of being, and reflected on the impact of our long-spread-out work together, finally to say good-bye carefully and attentively.

Thus Naomi entered and left my life. It had been a very brief therapy. When I later reflected upon our encounter a number of thoughts came to mind.

The state Naomi had experienced when we first met reminded me that from time to time in our life, and particularly just before major completions, all of us are likely to discover that in order to jump better we step back a little. When such emotional stepping-back occurs, we probably don't realize that our further emotional development depends on our capacity successfully to integrate those temporary regressions. Not to over-determine the outcome of periods of time when, owing to the stress and possibility of imminent change, we feel rather vulnerable, more than a little naked, haggard and inexperienced. During those hold-back and turn-about periods it is as if we had only just arrived in life, without good tools or an exercised awareness of how to negotiate some of life's more treacherous domains. Our passage through these somewhat dark nights of the soul then grants us the opportunity to learn, once again, that psychological change also involves letting go of over-valued ideas, to exchange them for others which, later rather than sooner, also become over-valued. Thus we move along.

In my experience many people who live with emotional unwell-being desperately try to hold a life of kinds together, defending themselves at great cost against the healing partial regression described in Naomi's case, precisely because such regression is so reminiscent of "losing it." Whenever someone's desperate attempt to cling to their former sense of coherency has to be surrendered to momentary profound emotional unwell-being, the person mostly knows and expresses two feelings: fear and shame. These feelings arise not merely because too frequently speech fails the client but also because too many listeners fail to hear their speech, which contains its attempt at well-being in its very unwell-being, seeking merely the means to lead its life. I use stories because they are potent stuff: denizens of the in-between world. They teach us about bridges. I hope to have demonstrated that Naomi needed such a bridge to reconnect with safer, inner shores. Our encounter probably contributed to her recovery of a generalized sense of well-being, but it was her basic vitality that enabled her above all to achieve this.

NOTE

1 Versions of this story have been found in Israel, Britain and Turkey. It is a favorite amongst many storytellers because it casts a fine light on the complexities associated with interpreting body language.

REFERENCES

Bruner, J. (1990) *Acts of Meaning*, Cambridge, Mass.: Harvard University Press.

Buxbaum, E. (1987) "The role of a second language in the formation of ego and superego", *Psychoanalytic Quarterly* 18: 279–289.

Coles, R. (1981) "Stories and psychoanalysis", *Storytelling* (Summer): 17.

Einstein, A. (1935) *The World as I See It*, London: John Lane.

Gordon, D. (1978) *Therapeutic Metaphors*, Cupertino, Calif.: META Publications.

Grinberg, L. and Grinberg, R. (1984) "A psychoanalytic study of migration: its normal and pathological aspects", *Journal of the American Psychoanalytic Association* 32: 13–38.

Gustafson, J.P. (1984) "An integration of brief dynamic psychotherapy", *American Journal of Psychiatry* 141(8) (August): 935–943.

Nisbett, R.E. and Ross, L. (1980) *Human Inference: Strategies and Shortcomings of Social Judgment*, Englewood Cliffs, NJ: Prentice-Hall.

Rosaldo, M. (1984) "Toward an anthropology of self and feeling", in R.A. Schweder and R.A. Levine (eds) *Culture Theory: Essays on Mind, Self, and Emotion*, Cambridge: Cambridge University Press.

Storr, A. (1990) *Solitude*, London: Collins.

Wells, G. (1987) *The Meaning Makers*, London: Hodder & Stoughton.

Chapter 9

The case of Sam

Application of the taxonomy of roles to assessment, treatment and evaluation

Robert J. Landy

INTRODUCTION

The taxonomy of roles is a systematic way to view personality in dramatic terms, that is, in terms of personae. I conceptualize personae as roles. I have defined role not only as a character in a drama, but also as

> the container of all the thoughts and feelings we have about ourselves and others in our social and imaginary worlds.
>
> (Landy 1990, p. 230)

and later as

> a basic unit of personality containing specific qualities that provide uniqueness and coherence to that unit.
>
> (Landy 1993, p. 7)

In devising the taxonomy, I first reviewed many of the most widely produced and anthologized plays in the repertory of Western literature since the beginning of Greek drama. My concern was to extract types of characters or role types, for example, heroes and fools, cowards and lovers, that reappear throughout theatre history and genre. The taxonomy is organized according to six domains, which I believe correspond to six prominent aspects of human existence: somatic, cognitive, affective, social, spiritual, and aesthetic. Each entry in the taxonomy contains the name of the role type, a description of its qualities, and a discussion of its function and style within the drama.

The taxonomy is used in drama therapy in conjunction with the role method of treatment (see Landy 1993), wherein clients are led through a process of invoking and working through roles, reflecting upon their role enactments, and learning to live in the ambivalence within and among their roles. The taxonomy is also part of a wider framework of role theory (see Landy 1993).

Underlying the taxonomy are several basic assumptions:

1 That human existence is dramatic and that such dramatic concepts as role and script can help elucidate the reality of action and being in everyday life.

2 That dramatic literature is a reflection of everyday life, not only in a social and cultural sense, but also in a psychological one. That is, the stage reflects the world and the people in it. Psychologically speaking, it mirrors not only the types of roles played out by ordinary people, but also the qualities, motivations, and styles of their role enactments. In understanding these aspects of theatrical characters, one can better understand similar aspects of ordinary people whose lives are inherently dramatic.

3 That it is possible and even desirable to schematize and categorize roles for the purpose of understanding human behavior and motivation as reflected in dramatic literature.

4 That each role type which appears to have some archetypal significance exemplifies one part of human existence. And that human existence is infinitely complex and greater than any one type or even the sum of its types.

5 And finally, that roles exist in complex interrelationships. Many roles coexist with their counterparts, and to be well enacted require the role-player to live within the ambivalence of two seemingly contradictory roles. For example, to play the wise person implies a struggle with one's ignorance.

As a drama therapist, I have used the taxonomy in a number of ways: in assessment, in guiding the treatment of clients, and in evaluation. In discussing each point, I will make reference to work with a single client, whom I shall name Sam. I treated Sam through drama therapy for a period of three years, meeting him approximately once a week for fifty minutes during that time span. He was referred to me at the age of 37 with little means of making sense of his rather complex existence.

ASSESSMENT

In practicing drama therapy within the framework of role theory, the drama therapist first needs to know which roles appear to be most problematic within the client's life. Many clients enter therapy because they feel bad or powerless or shut down or out of control or self-destructive. These feelings can be concretized in terms of roles found in the taxonomy, for example immoralist, victim, lost one, madman, suicide. Often, clients will say that they feel poorly but have trouble articulating the source of the feeling or a sense of its direction.

The assessment provides a way to focus upon the present feeling of imbalance or discomfort and even allows the therapist and client a glimpse of future goals. The initial assessment task is for the therapist to help the client invoke one role or a series of related roles. There are many expressive ways to begin. The drama therapist can proceed through the following: storytelling (a story made up by the client spontaneously); sandplay; drawing;

became clearer. He was the son of a prominent lawyer and law professor who abandoned the family when Sam was eight. The father's professional aspirations faded as he became mentally and physically ill. Sam visited his father often, even during his rather frequent hospitalizations for bipolar disorder. He died when Sam was in his early twenties, having never realized his potential as a brilliant advocate for the dispossessed and as a loving father.

Sam's mother was a promising and gifted painter, who abandoned her dreams of success when she got married. She became embittered when her husband left and took on various unconventional jobs related to the arts to support the family. When separated from her husband, she expected Sam to stand in for his father. Sam tried to live up to her expectations, but couldn't really play the role of husband as she wished. The mother, a highly moralistic person, believed in a fundamentalist version of Christianity and was regarded as generous and selfless by her neighbors. To Sam, she was a highly judgmental perfectionist.

Sam was a promising jazz musician who demonstrated great skill and even played with some of the outstanding younger jazz artists. But around the time of his father's severe illness and death, he stopped. He found temporary solace when brought into a moralistic, fundamentalist Christian church by a beautiful young woman whom he later married in the church. They soon had a son. Sam supported the family by working part time as a plumbing contractor, organizing building repairs. He managed to make a living but had difficulty collecting on his debts and keeping up with the competition.

The church group folded when the pastor left for another town. Sam was devastated and confused. Sam's wife, whom I shall call Bonnie, worked only sporadically. She had been a sexually abused child and, suffering the effects of an abusive childhood, had trouble living up to her responsibilities as wife and mother. She was immature and narcissistic, frequently taking on the role of needy child in relationship to her son and her husband. The marriage was going poorly and Bonnie and Sam fought constantly. Toward the end, Bonnie had affairs, the knowledge of which she imposed upon Sam, even as she berated him for his sexual inadequacy. Sam was unable to find a way to make peace with Bonnie, but out of a mixed sense of Christian fellowship, guilt, and fear, he was incapable of separating from her. He loved his son and tried to be a good father, even though he was under a heavy emotional burden.

Stages of treatment

There were several stages in our work together.

Stage 1

The first stage involved a further exploration of Sam's role system. Sam played out many versions of heroes and villains, and saints and sinners, and bad fathers who tried to be good, and beautiful women who turned out to be beastly. A recurring image was that of the double, the disguise, the face beneath the mask. Sam created the sinning saint, based upon the pastor who abandoned the church and maybe even based upon his father who abandoned him at the age of eight. He created an image of a flower with a long stem that was attached to a box containing an explosive charge. A detonator stuck out of the box, ready to discharge its explosive contents. He created, in a story, one of his most powerful characters, Rupert Stosh, the good man who liked to do bad. Stosh, a demonic Nazi-type, appeared to be a wealthy, kindly philanthropist, but actually operated an underground slave labor nuclear plant. During this early stage, Sam and I became familiar with those role types that would dominate his psyche.

Stage 2

During the second stage, Sam desperately needed to extricate himself from his marriage. He felt alternatively humiliated and enraged by his wife, whom he experienced as changing from needy, helpless child, to sexual, desirable woman, to castrating, destructive demon. Even so, Sam was still incapable of separating. During this stage, he redefined the image of the farmer. No longer like Farmer Sam who, though bad, tried to be good, this type was all good. He created a version of a fundamentalist Christian farmer who had a sense of hope and purpose. This farmer was loyal, rooted in tradition, free and clear of depression, anxiety, and shame.

At the same time, Sam revised another of his earlier roles, the gatekeeper. Whereas the first version was a small man who kept things safe and within bounds, the new one was an irascible old man, coughing, farting, and judging, an utterly obnoxious creature who was out of control, untamable. Sam's former sense of the warrior, as a fighter for a just cause, was also transformed. The new version began as a "worrier," one who experienced intense anxiety yet repressed the anger associated with the worry. Whenever the anger was expressed it appeared to be out-of-control. This version of the warrior looked like an out-of-control gatekeeper.

As Sam was working on these issues in therapy, he acted out his repressed rage in reality by striking his wife in the street with the back of his hand. This temporary transformation led him from weak husband to brutal husband, a role he could not accept, but that would haunt him for the next two years of his life. Although he would never again play out that role in real life, he would take it on in therapy as he moved into the next stage of treatment.

Stage 3

In going back to the sandbox, Sam again invoked the camel, whom he named "Hm," the heroic searcher. Sam spoke of Hm as the sound for self-healing, for proof of being, for good things and for battle. This time the figure of Farmer Sam was asleep or buried in the sand and Hm felt free of his power.

In the sandplay, Hm ended up with his head buried in the sand and his genitals up in the air, exposed. Sam remarked: "This feels good for him. He wants his head to be in the womb of earth. His balls are up in the air but he's trusting that no one will hurt him."

I was concerned that Sam felt too vulnerable and wasn't able to go through with his separation by himself. Not only did he need to find an appropriate way to express his anger, but he also needed some kind of internal regulator in the form of a kindly gatekeeper, a mediator, a friend and helper. As Hm lay buried in the sand, another figure appeared in the sandbox. It was a tree that is eaten by Hm and then rematerializes. The tree told him: "Take more of me . . . Don't worry. I'm giving you food and rest. You won't need me all the time because you will remember me and thus remember yourself."

Sam recognized this role as friend and helper. Checking with the taxonomy (Landy 1993, p. 197), I noticed that the function of helper was "to move the hero further along his path or to rescue another from difficult circumstances, remaining loyal throughout the many twists and turns of the journey." The tree was an important object representing, in many ways, the qualities that I exemplified for Sam. However, he needed someone with more power in the world to help him separate from a loveless, destructive marriage and move on with his journey. He needed, in fact, a lawyer, a role more difficult to depend on for that was the role played out, ultimately in failure, by his father.

Eventually, with the help of the lawyer, Sam was able to separate from Bonnie and retain custody of their son. It was such a traumatic step, however, that it demanded nothing less than a biblical ritual of violence and revenge, devised and enacted in minute detail by Sam.

While the lawyer in Sam's real world negotiated the terms of separation, Sam and I spoke of ways to discover an inner capacity to separate. We agreed upon a ritual that Sam would construct. We also agreed to meet for two hours at a time to enact the ritual. This was to mark the next stage of our work.

Stage 4

Sam created a fictional persona named Richard to proceed through the steps of the ritual. Richard was not only the offended, vengeful husband, but also a kind of priest, practiced in sometimes dangerous spiritual arts. Yet this role did not hold enough moral weight, at least not in a secular sense. In order to obtain further support for his right to carry on the dreaded ritual, Sam allowed the priest role to transform into that of a lawyer. The lawyer provided the moral and legal justification that Bonnie deserved the punishment she would receive. At times, Richard would shift to the role of plaintiff, the one sinned against. Sam also included the figure of a judge who would render a verdict against Bonnie.

Sam incorporated all the roles of priest and plaintiff, lawyer and judge into his ritual. It took on the structure of a trial with Richard also becoming the prosecutor out to prove Bonnie's guilt and justify the judge's sentence: "Death by execution!" Sam referred to the ritual as "The Trial, Execution, and Burial of Bonnie." Following the trial, Bonnie would be executed, then buried.

The ritual began as Richard told me a story from the Bible, Judges 19, that provided a motivation for the trial and subsequent sentence:

> A concubine runs away from her man and sleeps around with other men. She returns to her father's house, where her man is waiting. The father talks the man into staying overnight. The man leaves late the next day with his wife. They wander about and are finally taken in by a kind farmer. The townsmen, suspicious of the strangers, set out to rape and kill the man, but the farmer persuades them to take the woman instead. The townsmen rape the woman all night long. She makes her way back to the farmer's house, then dies. The man returns home, cuts the woman up into twelve pieces and distributes the pieces to all the tribes of Israel.

I noted the following roles: the seductress or immoral woman who becomes a victim, the father, the victimized or cuckolded man who becomes a victimizer, the kindly farmer, and the brutal killers.

In role of lawyer, prosecutor, and judge, Sam tried Bonnie and found her guilty of adultery, theft ("stealing breath from Richard and goodness from herself"), murder (of love), lying, demon possession ("having to do with her illness"), and arson ("for burning down her relationship with her son"; this reminded me of Farmer Sam's burning of his children).

Sam then proceeded with the execution, which was a grisly and frightening ritual. He lit a candle and began to torture and dismember a female doll, cutting it up with a real, very sharp knife, and carefully wrapping each piece in napkins that were originally used for his wedding. He then took on the roles of the funeral guests, speaking for each, trying to justify his separation.

It was very difficult for me to witness this enactment and to remain fully in my helper/guide role. Sam's actions frightened and at times repulsed me, and at some dark level, they even fascinated me. I feared a loss of control, not only in Sam, but in myself. Was I witness to a dark satanic ritual? And by silently witnessing, was I condoning Sam's behavior? In taking on the powerful roles of wronged husband, lawyer, prosecutor, judge, and executioner, Sam wielded an enormous power. Would I succumb and need to stop it, or could I contain it within my shaky presence? At times, I questioned my competence to deal with such deep material. Shouldn't there be an expert present, one skilled in containing primal feelings of rage and violence? I was but a mere drama therapist.

As fundamentalists call for their Bibles when in mortal danger, I needed my taxonomy for reassurance that this performance was indeed simply a drama. Just at the edge of turning on the lights and putting a stop to the grisly scene, I caught myself. This was, after all, an enactment of roles, my primary field of expertise as a drama therapist. Out of fear for my safety, I had slipped into the role of judge myself. I suddenly realized that if I judged him as an *actual* perpetrator, that is, if I was unable to realize that Sam was in an imaginative dramatic mode, I would lose him. My credibility was on the line and I was being tested. In many ways Sam had finally trusted me enough to allow me into a dark part of his psyche. I had to be there for him, impartially, or risk the loss of our bond.

Later, consulting the taxonomy (Landy 1993, p. 217), I discovered that the judge's function was not only to "punish criminal acts," but also to "maintain order." That was what I needed to do in that moment, to maintain a sense of containment in the face of chaos, of acceptance and kindness in the face of enacted cruelty. I needed to hold clear in my mind and consequently to remind Sam that there is safety and balance in the drama, that on the other side of the Dionysian, ecstatic figure, is the Apollonian god whose function is to maintain a sense of form and order. I played Apollo to Sam's Dionysus. Or, in another sense, Sam played the ecstatic Dionysus, performing forbidden acts, even as he maintained the rational Apollonian controls offered by his creations: Richard, the lawyer, and the judge. By living in this ambivalence, that is, by setting up his murderous act as a ritual, with built-in controls, Sam was able to finally release an enormous well of pain and anger.

However, the release did not have an immediate effect. Sam walked around for days with the dismembered pieces of the doll, unable to dispose of them, to bury his relationship and complete the separation. When he finally did, he felt completely lost, like a worshipper without an object of worship.

Stage 5

The next stage of therapy continued for many months as Sam worked with and through his three images of women. This was a cloudy period where the clarity of the roles presented in the assessment was lost. Both fathers and mothers could be emasculating and violent. Farmer figures showed up with contradictory moral qualities, sometimes either good or bad, sometimes both good and bad.

Sam and Bonnie were divorced. Temporarily, their son lived with Sam, as Bonnie was unable to assume the role of mother. Sam was a devoted father but clearly needed time for himself. Bonnie remarried within a very short time. Sam's experiences with other women were failures at best, humiliations at worst, as he continued to choose those who exemplified qualities of the child, beauty, or castrator. None were able to fill the void left by his loss of parent, lover and god.

The legal roles enacted in his ritual took on even greater significance as

Bonnie not only demanded custody of their son, but also accused Sam in court of physically abusing their son and of abusing drugs.

There would be a trial and Sam needed to prove that he was a fit father, an abuser neither of his son nor of himself. Feeling guilty as charged, Sam wondered: Could it be true that he wounded his son and wife and everyone else in his circle of intimates? Could it be that he was even responsible for his father's desertion and death and his mother's unhappiness? In the role of defendant, desperate to prove his innocence, Sam began to spin out of control. One night, a week before the court date, Sam stepped over the edge, and reeling from a disturbing manic episode he admitted himself to the psychiatric unit of a large city hospital.

It seemed that Sam had hit bottom. His hero's journey appeared to come to an abrupt halt. No longer father/farmer, gatekeeper, monk, warrior, or saint, he retreated into the role of the mentally ill person, who exists to "reveal the dark, shadowy sides of human nature and challenge the conventional notion of sanity" (Landy 1993, p. 178). All the control manifest in his ritual execution finally came crashing down upon himself. Because he was incapable of killing and burying Bonnie, she symbolically rose from the dead to kill him.

A psychiatrist became his helper in the hospital and prescribed medication to stabilize his intense mood swings. Sam was diagnosed as having bipolar disorder, manifested in a severe manic episode. Within two weeks, he was back home and returned to drama therapy for the next stage of our journey together.

Stage 6

It was hard for Sam to get back on the path. He was in denial of his newly enacted role, that of the mentally ill one. He found the most beautiful, sexual woman he could and gave her money for one blissful night of pleasure. The beauty was a seductress, "using beauty as a means to satisfy her material needs" (Landy 1993, p. 176). She had very little satisfaction to give back.

Sam fell into a deep depression, exacerbated by his refusal to take the prescribed medication. During one session he said: "I'm pushing the limits of madness and death."

In therapy he said he felt like a holocaust victim, just like his father. In recognizing the connection, Sam began to look at the father role in all its fearful contradictions. The father was supposed to be strong and protective and "provide a positive masculine role model" (Landy 1993, p. 208) to his son. But, in fact, Sam's father was weak, suffering from severe mood swings, clinically diagnosed as bipolar (see Madman in the taxonomy, Landy 1993), with severe physical disabilities which eventually led to his premature death.

I needed to find a clear direction myself. It seemed that my task was to help Sam accept his current position as victim to his madness, as son to a father who, in part, left a legacy of madness.

Shortly after returning from the hospital, Sam made up this story:

A guy was 100 per cent disabled. He has worms in his brain. He's been a victim all his life. The doctors stick instruments up his butt and find worms. They shine a light in his mouth. They see the worms inside. He's in pain. The doctor gives him medicine and says: "You are 100 per cent disabled. You must go right away to the sanatorium." He runs home for car fare. His throat closes up and he can't talk. He closes his door, but the cops are waiting for him. He goes to the fire escape. The born-again Christians tell him to jump. He does and falls in the snow. His head crashes open and the worms escape and vanish. The snow soothes his head. He feels relief.

Reflecting upon the story, Sam said: "The worms were his gift of knowledge. My father didn't want to give up his illness because he thought it was his intelligence."

Over several months, Sam and I explored this thought. Does wisdom only issue from sickness? Could one be wise and healthy at the same time? And what would that mean? The story became important on many levels. For one, it was Sam's first acknowledgement of his disability, of the fact that, like his father, he had bipolar disorder. But unlike his father, he had help in the form of medication and drama therapy, which would not erase his illness, but rather provide support for the healthier sides of his personality, represented by roles that could survive the inner holocaust. The story led him into an understanding that his father, refusing help and with little ability to take on heroic, survivor roles, held on to his madness as it represented, perversely, knowledge. Going deeper, Sam became aware that his father's role of madman protected him from intimacy, from becoming a loving father to his son and a loving husband to his wife.

Stage 7

The final stage of treatment concerned a discovery of how to be another kind of father, the kind specified in the taxonomy, one who could love his son, even as he came to live with Bonnie and her new husband. During our final months together, Sam was able to understand that Farmer Sam and Rupert Stosh, the secretly brutal men, though based upon his confusing parents, were fearful and shameful parts of himself. No longer in denial of his illness, fear, and shame, Sam was able to proclaim: "My disability is my ability."

The actual trial, for which Sam was well prepared, exonerated him of both violence toward his son and drug abuse. During the pre-trial period of accusation, Sam was only allowed to visit his son while supervised. After the trial, he could see him freely and resume the role of father. It was a difficult role to maintain, but Sam persisted, even as he allowed the demonic, anti-paternal voices to speak.

EVALUATION

Applying the taxonomy to the case of Sam, I found that at the end of treatment Sam had discovered a way to integrate his many confusions and reconstruct a viable role system. For one, he returned to playing and composing music, reclaiming the artist role with commitment and confidence. He approached his ability as artist with a healthy respect for his disability, accepting the possibilities of slipping into manic and depressive phases. The full re-discovery of the artist role led Sam "to assert the creative principle, envisioning new forms and transforming old ones" (Landy 1993, p. 241). This principle would guide his recovery from not only an aesthetic crisis, but also a moral and spiritual one.

Within a short period of time, Sam took himself off psychotropic medica-tion, relying on therapy as the bridge to a self-sufficient existence. He began to reconnect with a community of musicians and artists whom he now saw as his "church."

In one of our final sessions, Sam stated that he had been living a double life. In examining this thought, he was ready to accept a number of role ambivalences. A major one was that of child/father. Through therapy, Sam came to mourn the loss of his denied childhood and of his own father who was unable to provide adult guidance. In doing so, he was better able to be a father to his son, in spite of his humiliating hospitalization, trial, and divorce. Further, he was ready to father himself, that is, to direct his own journey. Part of this fathering concerned accepting the loss of the dependent client role in relation to me as therapist who had helped him discover a new way to care for a man in need.

He was also ready to accept the role ambivalences of being both disabled and able-bodied, artist and plumber, moralist who sometimes harbored immoral feelings. Even his early roles became integrated. As mentioned above, the bad, murderous father had been transformed into a figure of moral complexity who was able to distinguish between feelings, such as "I feel angry," and actions, such as "therefore I will act out violently." In understanding this distinction, Sam recognized the importance of expressing feelings as an alternative to acting out in explosive, manic episodes or implosive depressive ones.

The gatekeeper as little guy was incorporated as a helper who modulates the stress caused by living the double life of fundamentalist farmer and brutal father, of immoral moralist, of warrior and worrier, of beauty and beast. He became a kind of transitional figure, a go-between, whom Sam conceptualized in biblical terms, citing a psalm of David: "The lines have fallen to me in pleasant places" (Psalm 16, verse 6). Sam recognized the lines as boundaries separating his contradictory tendencies to feel acceptable and unacceptable. As he was able to set boundaries, Sam acknowledged that he had an inner regulator, a metaphorical gatekeeper, who would help temper the highs and lows of his disabilities and abilities.

The heroic figures searching for meaning, whether in spiritual or aesthetic abodes, were still intact in Sam's psyche. However, at the end of his therapeutic journey, hero, god, and artist were present in a deeper sense as Sam bore the wounds and the badges of the passage. His was a journey of fire.

And finally, Sam came face to face with at least an understanding of how he had split the complex figure of She, the woman, into three: innocent, whore, and castrator. At the end of our work together, Sam was no longer frantically looking for the perfect beauty, the innocent virgin, or the castrating shrike. In fact, he recognized the importance of viewing a love object as a human being.

One of our final sessions involved a reflection upon the disposal of the parts of the executed doll. Sam reflected upon the ritual that had occurred two years earlier:

It did not eradicate things. I wanted it to be an end-all. It opened me up to understand my relationship with Bonnie. But it was incomplete. I never knew what to do with the body parts. I went to Con Ed (the electric company). I met this worker and told him that I was breaking up with my wife and cut up this doll because it was so painful. I told him I had to get rid of it before I signed the divorce papers. I wanted it to burn in the city incinerator. He was very sympathetic but told me it would be a violation of some code. There are toxins in plastic dolls. I finally recycled each part. Recycling meant it would come back in a new form. It did – the court case – but something good came out of it. The court case led to my hospitalization and an acceptance of my disability. The case wasn't about me being violent or abusing cocaine but being mentally incompetent to take care of my son. My dignity was stripped away. I felt humiliated and raped. The worst part was being attacked as a good father.

I asked him to take on the role of the Con Ed worker, whom he named Joe, and speak about this incident. Sam chose to speak to a fictional wife at the dinner table. As Joe, he said:

A funny thing happened at work today. A guy came in and wanted me to burn up something in the incinerator – his wife. It was a doll, you see. He didn't seem crazy. He wanted me to take up this cut-up Barbie doll and burn it. I understand what would drive a guy to do this. You don't want to take out the violence on a real person. The anger builds up. I turned him away. It sends polycarbons in the air. I felt compassion for him. It seemed he had everything in control. I think he got rid of it. Makes me think of all the shit I've put up with. Maybe I should cut up a couple of dolls. Maybe cutting up the doll saved him. Maybe he cut up himself and got cut up by others. I feel compassion for him.

The odd thing was that this character, a plain worker, an everyman, little guy, gatekeeper type, embodied the very qualities that Sam was searching for all along: understanding, acceptance of pain, and compassion. In many ways this character embodied the saintly aspects of Christ. I turned to the taxonomy (Landy 1993, p. 238) and noticed that "through assuming the role [of Christ], one asserts a moral power and transcends one's spiritual vulnerabilities, participating in the unconditional love and grace of the gods."

Sam's search came full circle from abandonment by father and priest, by mother and wife, and by his own judgment of his somatic, aesthetic, and moral imperfections. The grail he had been searching for, the epiphany, appeared in the form of a worker talking to his wife at the dinner table. The message that this blue-collar Christ delivered was simple: be compassionate. When he took on this role, Sam said that he wanted so very much to forgive his father. He told me that the ritual was complete, that he had finally buried the pieces.

CONCLUSION

Sam's therapeutic journey was an arduous one that tested my abilities and led me to question my disabilities. In some ways we were engaged in a parallel process, searching for ways to contain the passions and the roles unleashed through the rituals of storytelling and enactment. The process was successful to the extent that we could find safe ways to visit and revisit very unsafe inner territory. I was reminded throughout of the reason why drama becomes such a safe craft for many therapeutic voyages: it proffers an alternative reality, that of images and reflections, through its imaginary walls of distance shaped by fictional characters and stylized actions. Because Sam could mutilate a doll, he spared those represented by the doll the consequences of violent action in the world. And, twice removed, because Sam had a fictional priest/lawyer named Richard as his stand-in, he was spared the overwhelming guilt and shame that might have otherwise precluded the enactment of his powerful ritual drama.

Sam's case is emblematic of a classical heroic search for meaning. As we have seen, Sam was able to integrate holy and demonic impulses and even carve out an effective moral referee, a worker standing at the gate who knew when to protect the environment from the toxic wastes of human suffering, and when to allow genuine feelings of human compassion to be released.

The taxonomy guided my own exacting journey with Sam. It was my lode star, my book. It led the way not only into Sam's mind but also to my own issues as a man in search of a father, lover, and god.

NOTE

1 For a full description of each role type, please refer to the taxonomy in Landy 1993.

REFERENCES

Landy, R.J. (1990) "The Concept of Role in Drama Therapy," *The Arts in Psychotherapy* 17:223–230.
—— (1993) *Persona and Performance: The Meaning of Role in Drama, Therapy, and Everyday Life*, London: Jessica Kingsley.

Chapter 10

'The tethered goat and the poppy field'

Dominant symbols in dramatherapy

Katerina Couroucli-Robertson

INTRODUCTION

My work in dramatherapy has been mostly in long-term therapy groups or with individual clients. Through the years I have developed a personal mode of working which I try to adapt to different clients in order to meet their own individual needs.

Patients are often attracted to dramatherapy as it sounds less threatening than other forms of therapy. They might imagine that more acting is involved than therapy and that this will be their chance to try their hand out as actors. Others might feel that their problems could be disguised through the drama and they will not be asked to pour out all their intimate feelings with words. Elsewhere (Robertson 1995), I have talked about ways of working with symbols. In this chapter I would like to investigate more closely ways of finding the metaphors and symbols and the art of deciphering them so as to put them to work dramatherapeutically.

During every dramatherapy session the main theme is actualised through some form of action. Like an alchemist's experiment, different ingredients are used and through these a new element evolves, a metamorphosis takes place analogous with the holy sacraments. As Elizabeth Rees has said: 'Theologians explain sacraments as outer signs of inner realities, and that is a fair definition of symbol. . . . Symbolism is a language not of abstractions but of feelings and images' (Rees 1992:14).

Similarly, during a dramatherapy session small rituals take place which represent both the individual and the group. The symbolism in the rituals is seen and felt, but not interpreted or verbalised. Actions take place which have specific symbolic meaning, after which a new reality is established.

In this chapter I will be referring to some of my work experiences which show how metaphor and symbolism work in dramatherapy. Different names have been substituted, and small changes made to events, in order to protect confidentiality. I am deeply grateful to my clients for allowing me to publish this work and I believe that my growth has evolved through them and will continue to do so.

THE USE OF IMAGE AND METAPHOR IN DRAMATHERAPY

Spring has come. The grass is full of yellow daisies and scarlet poppies. The swallows are back. I lift my head and see Beethoven chords in the sky. The birds are sitting in the five strands of the telegraph wire. As I watch they change their positions on the musical score as if not only singing but composing the opening bars of the day.

The above picture doesn't bring to light some cosmic symbol, but as a metaphor its meaning can be recognised even by a child. These visual symbols gave me the opportunity to see the musical score out of its own context. The birds took on a double role, both as a note of music and also as the inspiration of music coming from the skies.

This for me is an everyday example of dramatherapy in practice. The role of the dramatherapist is to help her[1] clients see their situation on a metaphorical level, so they have the opportunity to investigate their predicament from a different perspective. During a dramatherapy session certain themes may be brought up by the members. Depending on these the dramatherapist needs to find ways of putting to work the symbols which represent them.

To symbolise, according to Rosemary Gordon, is

To be able to experience the existence of links between objects which are also recognised to be separate and distinct: thus without sacrificing uniqueness to wholeness, or wholeness to uniqueness one succeeds in experiencing both what is individual and what is universal in any particular object or situation.

(Gordon 1975, p. 17)

A patient of mine once said to the group: 'I feel like a goat who has been tethered to the same tree for years and is suddenly released, the cutting of the cord has made me feel stunned and my feet are stuck in the earth.' (This person had been married for seventeen years and lost her husband in an accident about five years ago.) The stunned period of her life had lasted for five years, a time she needed for mourning her great loss. It took five years and a dramatherapy group to help her in her search for personal development so she that could venture further away from the length of cord which had kept her tethered to the same tree for so long.

In her group we were able to play with that metaphor, and it was interesting how it was discovered that the age for exploring the world around us is not a fixed one. It is certainly not a privilege only for the young.

One member in the same group felt that she wasn't tied to her tree by a cord, but she had certainly not ventured very far beyond it. Another member, while working with this picture, related how he had chewed the cord until he was freed. For several years following that action he had gone far beyond his tree, but now he had returned within its vicinity. Yet another member felt that she had two cords holding her tightly to her tree and that if she were ever set free she would run away for miles.

Later, during another session, we worked on the idea of the cord. Who was responsible for putting it round their neck, and how complacent had they been in accepting it? How much can financial support from a parent keep one tethered, and for how long?

THE GROUP AS A METAPHOR

Our clients may not always come out with images or applicable metaphors in the initial sharing; however, the metaphor may be in the situation itself presented by the group.

In the following section I would like to demonstrate how the predicament of some group members brought the following story to my mind.

Monday's group

This group consisted of six female members in their twenties, some of whom were training as play therapists and one female dramatherapist. The group was running for a second year with one new member.

This was the fourth meeting of the group in the new academic year, and the session during which the group would close. No new members would be accepted for five months. The theme from the previous session was a feeling of doom and stagnation as five out of the six members were without a job and all in need of financial support.

The members were Mary, Efy, Jane, Pauline, Margaret and Natalie.

Natalie had left a message that she wouldn't be coming; she said she had to visit her parents who lived outside Athens. Her absence could have been due to the previous session during which three members were missing. In the previous year, when a member was missing without a good enough reason, she would then miss the following session herself. Efy was late.

The group started with the four members present.

MARGARET   We (*referring to herself and Mary*) had a serious reason for missing last time. The opening date of this new training we want to do coincided with our group. We couldn't miss the first meeting. My life is a mess, I have so many commitments I have no time to think.

MARY   I really didn't want to miss the group but this course is so important to me. They have promised us all jobs when we finish in December.

DRAMATHERAPIST   We had a message from Natalie, she won't be coming. Perhaps she is cross about the absences of last time.

MARY   Oh no, she had practical reasons for not coming.

DRAMATHERAPIST   When does something stop being practical and become intentional?

MARY   You mean like our situation, but you don't know what we will have to go through. We will have to kill ourselves for three months because this course also coincides with our play therapy training. Of course the play therapy training is more important to this other course, it is just the opportunities this will provide us with. I feel that I am married to play therapy.

DRAMATHERAPIST   So this other course is a lover?

PAULINE   Do you think your husband will wait for you?

MARY   Oh yes he will, I have him well trained.

JANE   I am pleased because a friend of mine telephoned me to invite me to her wedding. We had a fight a year ago and haven't spoken since. I was really glad she called and I will go to the wedding even though usually I never go to weddings, I don't believe in them.

MARY   This new course won't last for ever but I am certainly not getting the support I would have expected, neither from my friends nor from my boyfriend. I feel very disappointed, no one understands what I am going through.

(*Possibly she was referring to other members in the group who could have also taken the course but opted out.*)

MARGARET   I didn't expect any support, I am just not sure whether I will be able to cope.

(*Efy came in twenty minutes late.*)

EFY   (*she seemed totally unaware that she had arrived in the middle of something*) I am sorry I am late, the traffic was terrible . . . . Last time would you believe it, I didn't come because my car broke down and I had to wait half an hour for the service to come . . .

DRAMATHERAPIST   Today the group is closing for five months, so you will have a chance to really get to know each other.

Warm-up

After a short physical warm-up the group played a game of musical chairs, which allowed them to play with no inhibitions.

I chose this warm-up as, on the one hand, it was a well-known game but, on the other hand, it was a game of competition where the members were asked to fight for their own space, disregarding the others and often intentionally tying to trick them out of their space. On a metaphorical and unconscious level this was happening in the group. During the game of musical chairs such behaviour is encouraged as it is part of the rules.

Action

DRAMATHERAPIST   Sit somewhere comfortably and I will read you a story.

Chicken Little

Once upon a time there was a little chicken whom everyone called Chicken Little. One day, while she was out in the garden (where she had no right to be), a rose leaf fell on her tail. Away she ran in great fright, for she thought the sky was falling.

As she ran along she met Henny Penny.

'Oh, Henny Penny,' cried Chicken Little, 'the sky is falling!'

'How do you know that?' asked Henny Penny.

'Oh, I saw it with my eyes; I heard it with my ears; and part of it fell on my tail,' said Chicken Little.

'Let us run and tell the King,' said Henny Penny.

So they ran along together till they met Ducky Lucky.

'Oh, Ducky Lucky,' cried Chicken little, 'the sky is falling!'. . .

In abbreviation they then met Goosy Loosy, Turkey Lurkey and finally Foxy Loxy who led them to his den from which they never, never came out again!

After hearing the story the five members were each invited to take parts: Efy, Henny Penny; Margaret, Ducky Lucky; Pauline, Turkey Lurkey; Mary, Goosy Loosy; and Jane, Foxy Loxy. They dressed up for their parts and enacted them and did it with a lot of laughter. When they got to Foxy Loxy he made them hold the sky up so it wouldn't fall down, and sing a song simultaneously. This was the song they sang:

We didn't see it with our eyes
we didn't hear it with our ears
the sky was never able
to fall on to our wings.

there is not one nor two
there are not three ducks
there are many who fell
into the fox's traps.

Feedback

MARGARET   Do you think the sky has fallen on our tails?

EFY   I chose to do the part of Henny Penny because I believe I am a scatterbrain. I used to be much worse.

JANE   I chose to be the fox, so I can see how it is to be really nasty.

MARY   I don't feel any better.

PAULINE   I just wanted to follow the crowd.

MARGARET   I chose Lucky Ducky because I feel that I need all the luck I can get.

Reflection

This was a new beginning for the group and I felt that they were having some teething problems. Perhaps the subtext was a feeling of uneasiness. They did not feel secure, and also there was some underground resistance to the new member who reacted by appearing not to notice. Natalie's way of coping with the absentees by being absent herself was a way of acting out, a way which was familiar to the others and represented the group's way of dealing with situations. The story of Chicken Little came to mind because of the similarity of their situations and the dangers they were putting themselves into. One person may feel overweight at seven stone and another might feel the same problem when twelve stone. Both feel very strongly about their problem and may have difficulties dealing with it. However, the truth is that the second person has a more serious problem than the first. If one therefore allows an unimportant problem to take on such dimensions there is a danger of falling into a more serious trap prepared by someone wanting to take advantage of the situation. That situation, I felt, was part of the group's experience at that time. Being the beginning of the year some of the members were getting all worked up over their timetable. Perhaps the anxiety was of a more serious nature and had to do with identity and purpose in life. However, the way in which they presented their predicament brought to my mind the story of Chicken Little. Acting out the story of Chicken Little turned out well, as the fox chose to give them a task which involved group cooperation. Moreover the fox (another group member) was not a threatening figure towards them but just mischievous. Through the story, they had a chance to reflect whether the sky was really falling on their tails and connect it with their own predicament.

There is general agreement that myths and fairy tales speak to us in the language of symbols representing unconscious content. Their appeal is simultaneously to our conscious and unconscious mind, to all three of its aspects – id, ego and superego – and also to our need for ego–ideals. This makes it very effective; and in the tale's content, inner psychological phenomena are given body in symbolic form (see Bettelhelm 1976, p. 36).

SCHEMATIC REPRESENTATIONS OF RELATIONSHIPS

The following three sections each discribe a way of working dramatherapeutically with geometric shapes, each depicting a visual image of the interactions between persons and situations.

Looking at relationships from a different perspective gives our clients the opportunity to see their life situation represented in a schematic design which may help to clarify certain aspects of it for them. This can be applied to the developmental dramatherapy model, first with projection, then with embodiment and finally with role-play.

The linear representation of life

This is a brief description of session 6 of a new dramatherapy group. The group met once a week for one and a half hours, and each member remained for as long as they felt they were gaining something out of the group. This group consisted of four members, Louisa, Susan, John and Helen, and one dramatherapist. Their ages ranged from 24 to 42.

The theme from the previous session was: How easy is it to be a member in a group and how much can I share with the other members?

The group began with the three members as Helen was late. Louisa was quite anxious about something and was not certain whether her problem was something she could bring to the group.

LOUISA   I have a problem but I don't think I can share it with you as it involves my family.

SUSAN   I think that it is something you can share with us and I would be interested.

LOUISA   The problem is that my mother is putting pressure on me to go to another group at some other centre where she could also attend and then we could have the same therapist. She always interferes with my life to the extent that I dare not make any intimate friends any longer because she would interfere and make me feel exposed.

SUSAN   I have a similar problem with my relationship with my daughter. It was very close when she was younger but now she wants more of a distance. I understand her but it isn't easy to let go.

JOHN   I also have a problem in that area. I feel emotionally tied to my parents and I would rather not be.

(At this point Helen arrived in a state of anxiety because she had got lost.)

HELEN   I don't know why I got lost this time, I have been here before, mind you my father had driven part of the way with me the last few times.

Warm-up

During the warm-up the group members were asked to became couples, with one partner leading the way and the other following, at first very gently, the one who was led being blindfolded. Next the partner being led had his eyes open, and this was followed by one leading the other against her will. The group members all had turns in taking different parts. They followed my instructions and gave the impression that they felt they were playing games. Some were freer with their movement and contact with others while some were more restricted.

This exercise was designed to give them a bodily feeling, of what they had talked about at the initial sharing. They had referred to relationships of dependency and how these were affecting them. The warm-up took place so that they could embody the feeling of being guided, either blindly, or willingly or, lastly, unwillingly.

Action

The members were each asked to draw on a large piece of paper themselves on one end and their mothers on the other, and to join the two with arrows, showing where the two arrows met.

On Louisa's paper her mother's arrow covered three-quarters of her paper. Her comment was: 'Not only she interferes with my life but she also loads her life on to me by telling me all her problems.'

Helen's arrows met in the middle of the page and she said that she and her mother had an ideal relationship. She also added that her mother had a better relationship with her sister, even though she wasn't asked to give that information.

Susan's paper had her mother's arrow also covering three-quarters of the page, and her comment was: 'I can't leave her behind, she needs me.'

John's showed his mother's arrow taking three-fifths of the paper, and he repeated what he had said earlier: 'We both depend on each other emotionally and I would like the dependence to be much less from both sides.'

After making the drawings and commenting on them they were each asked to choose a group member to represent one person in the drawing, and, together with themselves and the aid of a cord, to sculpt their drawing in the flesh. After they had both taken on the role of one person in their drawing they made a statement to each other from that position.

Next a brief deroling took place, followed by feedback during which the group members talked about relationships and ties to their original family and how free they were to get away from those in order to make new relationships.

Reflection

All members were experiencing strong ties with their parents or children and had become aware that they needed some breathing space. Possibly the subtheme was: How close am I becoming to this group? How much can I rely on it? and even a fear of becoming dependent on it.

This exercise was a simple way of representing a relationship, and one which could have been drawn by any member, thus enabling them to share with the group some intimate information without having to put it into words. Once they had seen their relationships depicted on paper, these became clearer to each member. After this experience they could decide if they wanted to change the meeting place of the two arrows.

The following is another example of the same linear representation used for punctuality, done by an individual client, Anastasia.

She arrived twenty-three minutes late, something which happens quite frequently.

ANASTASIA   I am sorry I am late, I had some wine.

DRAMATHERAPIST   Are you trying to tell me that you are being naughty?

ANATASIA   I always have wine with my lunch, it is just that I can't seem to manage my time well. I am always late for everything. I am always late with my deadlines at work and if I didn't have them I wouldn't hand in any work at all. . .

DRAMATHERAPIST   Make me a drawing of yourself and your lateness on a large piece of paper. Draw yourself on one end and at the other the place or person you are going to.

A. ———————————— therapy
A. ———————————— work
A. ————— friends or her animals in need
A. ——————————————————————————— lover
A. ————————————————————————— her own needs

After making this representation of her punctuality Anastasia saw very clearly how much she was neglecting her self and by extension her own body. She told me that she was drinking and smoking hash more heavily than usual and that she wanted to give her body a break. She wanted to start gymnastics and eat healthy food.

During this representation didn't make her into a changed person, but it helped her to visualise how she was treating her life and those around her. Her lateness wasn't a matter of incapability, but it expressed lack of motivation and perhaps a not very high opinion of herself.

The pyramid of life

Another example of what I call schematic representation in dramatherapy is the pyramid of life, an idea I got from a picture on the wall of an old coffee shop in a faraway village. This picture depicts the circle of life, beginning with the baby on the first step, a boy going to school on the second, an adolescent, etc., until old age, which is represented by an old man with a walking stick.

This group consisted of five female members, all in training either for dramatherapy or play therapy, and one female therapist. The ages of the group members ranged from 24 to 30. The group met once a week for an hour and a half, and this was the second year. All the five members had been in the same group during the previous year. There had been other members in the group originally.

The group members were Regina, Tessa, Lisa, Penny and Sonia. The described session was the fifty-seventh.The group theme from the previous session was the question whether the development of their lives was in balance with their ages.

The session began with everyone present except Penny. There was a ten-minute silence.

TESSA   Every time I have supervision of my play therapy work, I develop a fever. Today I woke up crying but I don't know the reason.

REGINA   I also wake up crying without knowing the reason.

TESSA   They tell me at my supervision group that I have a problem with authority. I consider all authority bad yet not when it comes to therapy. Will I ever be able to become a therapist? Do I have what it takes? Perhaps play therapy is easier.

DRAMATHERAPIST   It is a mistake to think that children are easier to deal with than adults.

REGINA   I would hate to have a group of adults because they can answer back.

(*Penny comes in. She doesn't give an explanation for being late.*)

DRAMATHERAPIST   What is the matter with you this year Penny? You are often late.

PENNY   I don't know, I am late everywhere, at work, at my classes, here, and there doesn't seem to be a reason.

LISA   On the contrary, I am always early for everything. In the morning I have to take two buses to get to work but I am always twenty minutes early. Then I go on to my classes and I am the first one there. Next I come here, which takes three buses and I am still early.

DRAMATHERAPIST   Do you feel as though you do things mechanically?

LISA   Yes.

Warm-up

During the warm-up the members were asked to walk in their usual manner, then to get into one pair and one threesome and adopt a common step. Finally, they were asked to walk in line as a group with the same step. After they had mastered this, they were asked to change their step all together, with one person always walking out of line.

This warm-up was designed for them to experience how it felt in their bodies firstly to be in line with the others and second to be out of line. In fact they discovered that it was easier to walk in line even though it might appear to be easier the other way round. During this warm-up, they were able to experience physically the theme which was occupying them both logically and emotionally.

Action

For this stage the group members were each given a piece of paper on which a pyramid with indentations had been drawn, with four steps on either side and a central step in the middle.

One of the members guessed that it was the pyramid of life. She had also seen a similar picture.

They were asked to imagine that each step represented a highlight in their lives and to make a drawing of it, starting from the first side where they would have been babies and going on progressively until their old age. The gap between each step had to represent a fixed number of years, so they needed to work out how long they believed their lifespan would be.

They found this exercise very difficult, and found it almost impossible to imagine themselves in old age.

- Regina: She had divided her pyramid in units of ten, thus the end of her life would be at 80. She placed children and marriage between 30 and 40 but wasn't sure if she really wanted them or whether it was something she was expected to do. On each step she made the symbol of what would be expected at that age and it was all fairly vague.
- Tessa: Her units were every five years so her pyramid ended at 40. She explained that she just couldn't imagine life after 40 and that was why her pyramid ended there. It didn't necessarily indicate that she would die early. She was more specific with her symbols, drawing the important events in her life during the first steps, leading to education and four children, which were placed between the ages of 30 and 40. Somewhere in the picture was the father of her children, but no marriage.
- Lisa: She also had units of ten. Her symbols were fairly general, with children at 30 and a career at 40.
- Sonia: Her units were every ten years with marriage and children at 30. No career was represented anywhere. She just had family life continuing until she became a grandmother and finally at 80 she was alone with her husband.
- Penny: Her units were every seven years, giving her a life expectancy of 56. She also had marriage and children around 30 but she wasn't sure whether that was what she wanted. The other symbols were again fairly vague.

At the end of this session we discussed the meaning of life in general and whether the ultimate aim of each woman should be to get married and have children. The session had demanded a lot of concentration and lacked magic, but it certainly got the members thinking more clearly about what they wanted out of life . During the following session we were able to follow up this work in more dramatic ways, making the pyramids come alive.

Reflection

It would appear that these women were not clear about their identities and what they wanted them to be. On the one hand, they were fighting conventionality in the form of marriage, but on the other they were not quite sure what it should be replaced by. It was interesting how little their careers featured in the drawings, and also there was very little talk about it. The subject did come up in the initial sharing. Perhaps the subtext in this group was to do with confronting authority, an authority which took on a wider meaning as though it represented conventionality.

The pyramid of life was an exercise given to them so that they could both visualise how their life was shaping out and what their aims were. They were also asked to compare it with what they would have considered the norm for a woman today. Did they feel the need to follow the norm owing to pressures from society or their own family? Or was this something which came from their own inner feelings? What is the norm today, and how different is it from their mothers' age?

Triangles and triangular relationships

Archetypes

- God the Son, God the Father, Holy Spirit
- Persephone, Demeter, Hecate
- Client, therapist, supervisor
- Id, ego, superego

The triangle is a very ancient symbol which represented life in primitive art. In its highest sense it concerns the Trinity. In its normal position with the apex uppermost it also symbolises fire and the aspiration of all things towards a higher unity – the means to escape from extension (signified by the base) into non-extension (the apex), or towards the origin or the irradiating point. Nicholas of Cusa said of the triangle that truncated (without its apex) it served the alchemists as a symbol of air; inverted (with apex pointing downwards) it symbolises water; and inverted but with the tip cut off, it symbolises the earth (Cirlot 1962, p. 350).

In therapeutic work using the image of a triangle all the above symbolisations may emerge and new ones may also develop. This could occur during the physical warm-up, during which a client may feel these images bodily, or at a later stage when using projective means.

For me the triangle represents strength and stability and can be used schematically to represent relationships.

The idea of a triangular relationship first brings to mind a negative connotation. An individual in a triad is preserving two relationships simultaneously, usually one with the husband or wife, and the other an illicit and often secret relationship. However, this is only one version of what I would call a triangular relationship.

Basically by triangular relationship I mean any relationship where three different persons are interacting and influencing the relationship within the triad. The first and most basic triangular relationship is that between mother, father and child. After this several others follow, which to a large extent we have all experienced. For example:

- parents, child and grandparents
- brother, sister and mother
- husband, wife and husband's work.

There are a large number of such examples, each applying to a different situation.

Three stands for the relations within the nuclear family, and efforts to ascertain where one fits in there. Thus, three symbolises the search for one's personal and social identity. From his visible sex characteristics and through his relations to his parents and siblings, the child must learn with whom he ought to identify as he grows up, and who is suitable to become his life's companion, and at the same time his sexual partner (see Bettlelhelm 1976, p. 220).

Unless we were all orphans and childless it would be very difficult for a couple not to have other persons influencing their relationship. Therefore a triangular relationship, far from being a negative symbol, represents the norm in its different forms.

In a triangular relationship there is no hierarchy as such. A triangle can have three different bases. The sides and angles may be different, but there is no dominant feature. In a triangle, relationships are contained and kept safe. If one of the triad were missing the dynamics would change and a new situation would develop.

Working dramatherapeutically with the triangle as an image has endless possibilities. To begin with, during simple embodiment exercises, the shape itself can be explored. This can be achieved by one client alone (making triangular shapes with her body walking in triangles, designing triangles in the air, etc.), or by three, six, and so on making a triangle or triangles amongst themselves and interspersing them. The approach can be in one, two or three dimensions. After the physical exploration of the triangle the next step can be projective work, done through a drawing or design. On the first level this can be purely artistic and on a second level the schema can be used as a container of a triangular relationship. Finally, the work can be developed so that the triad (the three persons) is acted out in a play or story which has such a relationship as its focus.

Example of session on triangular relationships: Wednesday's group

This group consisted of eight women from the ages of 22 to 42 and one female dramatherapist. The group had been running for five years with one of the original members still present. The members, four of whom were new in this fifth cycle, were Elisabeth, Allison, Sue, Maria, Vicki, Martha, Brenda and Jenny.

This was the nineteenth session of the new academic year and the theme from the previous session was love, romance and sex in women. All members were on time.

MARIA   I saw my mother in a dream. She was ill and my father wasn't looking after her. The truth is that she wasn't happy in her marriage, her parents arranged it for her. My father was older and he never really inspired her romantically. In fact she left him several times but he always managed to get her by the bus stop before she set off for the big city and bring her back by force. That is one of the reasons I don't like men. Also she had always wanted to become educated but wasn't allowed to, so I am doing it instead.

DRAMATHERAPIST   Your mother was a strong woman.

MARTHA   Had she been strong she would have done what she wanted.

SUE   The truth is one doesn't have any choices in life.

JENNY   I left early last time because I had an appointment with my X lover and I wanted to be prepared. I couldn't tell you at the time because I was worried that the meeting wouldn't be a success. In fact it went well because I feel now that I am really cured of him.

DRAMATHERAPIST   How is that connected to the group?

JENNY   I am not sure.

MARTHA   When I was having trouble with my boyfriend last year, I used to be late for the group. It comes down to putting him before yourself. I am still involved with him even though he has another girlfriend. I want to get out of this triangular relationship.

ALLISON   I have had an awful week and have let off steam on my boyfriend when really I am cross with my father. He spends a fortune on my brother and begrudges me the pennies.

Warm-up

With three large pieces of cord, the ends tied together, members were asked to become different forms of triangles. With the dramatherapist also participating there were three triangles formed. The group worked with those three triangles, discovering all the different forms they could take and how they could relate to each other.

Action

The members were asked to draw three large triangles, one of the past, one of the future and one of the present. They had to think of themselves in connection with two other members of their family, and according to the relationships with each to choose in which corner to place each individual taking into consideration the lengths of the sides of the triangles.

This exercise absorbed them deeply. When they had finished they were asked to imagine placing one triangle on top of the other, so that they could rest on parallel relationships. This was when they really made some connections and discoveries about themselves, as in the following examples:

Example 1

1st triangle	(past)	mother	father	child (Brenda)
2nd triangle	(present)	violence	husband	Brenda
3rd triangle	(future)	boyfriend's mother	boyfriend	Brenda

In this example the client remains in the same corner of every triangle. Her mother is seen in connection to violence and there is a negative mother-in-law figure. All her relationships with males are represented on the same corner.

Example 2

1st triangle	(past)	child (Sue)	mother	father
2nd triangle	(present)	Sue	parents	husband
3rd triangle	(future)	child (John)	Sue	husband

In this example the client stays in the same corner in the past and present triangles while in the future triangle her child takes her place and she that of her mother. The men stay in the same position.

Feedback

ELISABETH   I have made some serious discoveries and I would like to work with them next time.

SUE   I discovered for one more time how much I hate my mother. (*She has placed herself in the same position as her mother: does she also hate herself?*)

ALLISON   I feel very bitter about my father.

VICKI   I just realised that I haven't referred to my parents at all, only X lovers.

Reflection

In this group there was a feeling of security and a wish for members to really work with their difficulties using the help of the other members. During the above session, very intense work had been done by them all and they wanted to share this with each other. Perhaps the subtext was the integration of group–members–dramatherapist, another triangular relationship.

The reason for wanting to work with triangular relationships was obvious from the first sharing of the group members. However, working with a triad was something left over from the previous session. Some of the group members saw women as fulfilling three different functions which could not be connected. These were: women as mothers, women as lovers, and women as daughters. By working with the image of the triagle, these three factions could be connected to from one whole person.

During the following sessions we worked in different ways with the triangles that members wanted to address. One of these ways resembled psychodrama. The work with the triangles finished with the myth of Demeter, Persephone and Hades, which we worked on over several sessions covering five scenes of the story done by two separate groups. Working from the safety of the distance provided by Persephone's story, or any other myth, is perhaps the final dramatherapeutic stage for working on triangular relationships.

By working with the image of the triangle, I wanted to convey the idea that basically all dyadic relationships are influenced by one or more third parties, and that this is not a misfortune, but a fact of life.

CONCLUSION

The use of the dominant symbol gives the dramatherapist the opportunity to work with her client on a metaphorical level.

Learning to find the symbol is like young children learning how to read. They put sounds together and when they recognise these as a word which is meaningful to them they are enchanted. For a child to be able to read a written message and act on it without any verbal instructions is like the opening of a new word. So it is with a dramatherapist recognising the symbol her client or clients are giving her. This symbol may be direct or indirect, and may have many different interpretations; however, by recognising it the therapist has gained insight on another level.

Every group or individual goes through stages, using certain symbolisms. It is not something which is worked out logically; it just happens spontaneously. The symbol is kept for as long as it is needed and then discarded for a new one to take its place. An example of this comes from the story of 'The Poppies':

> Once upon a time there was on old lady who used to send her daughter to pick herbs. One day in May when the fields were full of flowers and all the trees were opening their leaves, her daughter entered a field but instead of picking herbs she picked poppies and, with a needle that she happened to have on her, she sewed them to her dress. . .
>
> (Mela 1979, p. 131)

'Wearing her poppies' came to mean, to the group which was working with the story, the time a young girl reaches puberty and becomes interested in appearing beautiful. This meaning does not need to be analysed, it is understood.

'Each fairy tale is a magic mirror which reflects some aspects of our inner world, and of the steps required by our evolution from immaturity to maturity' (Bettelhelm 1976, p. 309). Seeing reality through a metaphor makes it easier to talk about. It is less painful to share with the group that you feel like 'a tethered goat' that has been released, than to say that your husband had been old-fashioned, believed women should work in the home with the children, had been a bit tight with the household allowance, etc., and that after his violent accidental death there was terrible pain but also a feeling of release.

'Dramatherapy is a group process which explores, at many levels of metaphor, dramatic engagement between members of a group' (Jennings 1987, p. 1). Working schematically opens up new vistas and gives one's clients the opportunity to see a third dimension. It is like rediscovering that the earth is round. They are able to make sense of a situation which is contained in a schema.

When I was talking to a Portuguese theatre director whose actors have cerebral palsy, he told me of his way of presenting a performance to the audience. He believes that the wheelchair his actors usually use for moving about restricts their natural movement, and therefore he designed a new way for them to perform. His actors took their position on the ground without artificial help, while the audience had to look down on them from a height. He reversed the tables, so to speak, in order to suit his actors and also to allow his audience to appreciate art from a different perspective.

'The great German astronomer Johannes Kepler asserted that there are no more and no less than three dimensions of space on account of the Trinity' (Jung 1964, p. 381). If one was to equate those dimensions of the Trinity to everyday life one could see what he meant. Reacting as the Holy Trinity to a crisis, one would have every quality necessary for coping: the humanity, the knowledge and the wisdom.

I believe that as dramatherapists we can offer our clients the opportunity of working with the three dimensions. This can be actualised in real forms, by working schematically or through the magic of symbols which are both universal but also individual.

DEDICATION

I would like to dedicate this chapter to Smargda Papoulia, the first drama-therapist to be trained by the Greek Association for Dramatherapists and Play Therapists' 'Theatre and Therapy', whose loss has left a feeling of emptiness in every person who came to know and love her.

NOTE

1 For the sake of convenience I alternate feminine and masculine forms in this chapter.

REFERENCES

Bettlehelm, B. (1976) *The Uses of Enchantment*, Harmondsworth, UK: Penguin.

Cirlot, J.E. (1962) *A Dictionary of Symbols*, London: Routledge & Kegan Paul.

Gordon, R. (1975) 'Dramatherapy with individuals', in S. Jennings (ed.) *Creative Therapy*, Banbury, UK: Kemble Press.

Jennings, S. (1987) *Dramatherapy Theory and Practice for Teachers and Clinicians*, London: Routledge.

Jung, C. (1964) *Man and His Symbols*, London: Picador.

Mela, G.A. (1979) *Green Folk Tales*, Athens: I.D. Kolaros.

Rees, E. (1992) *Christian Symbols, Ancient Roots*, London: Jessica Kingsley.

Robertson, K.C.- (1995) 'Cues to the dramatherapist from the group', in S. Mitchell (ed.) *Dramatherapy: Clinical Studies*, London: Jessica Kingsley.

Chapter 11

The drum, the mouse and the boy in the glass palace

Brief dramatherapy with a client with chronic catatonic schizophrenia

Elektra Tselikas and Jörg Burmeister

INTRODUCTION

This chapter is an account of a brief dramatherapeutic intervention (ten hours) with a client with chronic catatonic schizophrenia. It shows how ritual, storytelling, music and different objects were used to create containers and a context within which the client could discover the transitional space of play, and thus transform 'passive withdrawal' into 'creative distance'. This distance enabled him to take the risk of entering into an active communicative relationship with the therapist and subsequently with the staff and his parents. In that sense it shows in an exemplary way how the paradox of dramatic distance as well as metaphors can work in short-erm treatment to generate healing communicative responses.

THE SETTING

Once upon a time . . . there was a young man in a rehabilitation ward in a psychiatric clinic near Zurich, Switzerland. His name was Peter.[1]

Peter was 31 years old. In his file he was diagnosed as having a catatonic exacerbation of a chronic-paranoid schizophrenia. He was admitted to the clinic in October 1991 and showed a progressive mutistic/autistic picture, with affective rigidity and psychomotoric restraint. My[2] suggestion to try dramatherapy was accepted at the case conference with relief. The dramatherapeutic intervention took place from February to April 1994.

The consultant psychiatrist (Jörg Burmeister) and I defined the aim of the therapy as to create some kind of contact with Peter which could be later taken over by other persons (caring staff and/or parents) in order to maintain and develop the therapeutic results. We also agreed that I should see him in short sessions with intensive frequency, morning and afternoon for fifteen to twenty minutes each, three times a week. This is an innovatory model of brief dramatherapy which needs careful clinical and dramatherapeutic supervision.

THE CHALLENGE

The challenge was: How to do dramatherapy in a one-to-one situation within a limited period of time (ten hours for the whole intervention) and with a person who does not speak or move? How to manage the dimensions of depth and mutuality (Cox 1988) within that timeframe with a person who would not speak?

THE THEORETICAL CONSIDERATIONS

In our theoretical considerations we adopted an interdisciplinary approach, making fruitful use of dramatherapeutic, psychodramatic and psychoanalytic concepts.

For the dramatherapeutic part we drew mainly on the embodiment/ projection/role (EPR) model of dramatherapy (Jennings 1994), the story-making approach of dramatherapy (Gersie and King 1990), and the role model of dramatherapy (Landy 1993). We were further inspired by Grainger's hypotheses on dramatherapy and schizophrenia (1992) as well as Landy's work on distancing and individual dramatherapy (1986 and 1992).

Furthermore, we drew on some hypotheses from object-relations theory and psychodramatic concepts (Leutz 1986).

Benedetti (1983) inspired us by his detailed and differentiated description of schizophrenia from a psychiatric point of view.

Finally, Cox's and Theilgaard's work on metaphors (1987) as well as Cox's work on the therapeutic process (1988) helped us structure the process within this short dramatherapeutic intervention.

THE TRANSFORMATION PROCESS

Phase 1

Peter and I had thrity-eight sessions of fifteen to twenty minutes altogether, which totalled ten hours of dramatherapeutic intervention. In the first ten sessions I did some kind of scanning. Scanning of the room, the possibilities for me to be in the room (where to sit, what to sit on, etc.), scanning of his actions and reactions or non-actions and non-reactions, feeling his rhythm, scanning of our interaction. The first time I came in he was in bed. I sat on what I subsequently found out was his chair[3] and introduced myself; I also talked about what I was going to do with him.

Before leaving I said that it would be nice if he stood up when I came back in the afternoon, but if he liked to lie down for a little longer that would be all right.

While I speak he looks at me from time to time. When I come in the afternoon he is up and sitting on his chair, hands in his pockets, facing the window, but with his head leaning on one side and his eyes looking down. This is his position; he sits like this practically all the time and is immobile. I say something about the sky, and he looks out at the sky. Then I hum. I take on his rhythm; I become very slow and try to 'double'[4] him, do what he does. What he does is very little; it is almost imperceptible, practically nothing. Still, I am observing all the details of his expression: if and when he moves his eyes and looks at me or elsewhere; his body 'movements' (there is no movement in his body except belly convulsions and the differences in the rhythm of his breathing or in the movements of his mouth). I am in the mist, I don't know how to interpret all this, but I observe.

On the third day I introduced a little drum and played with it. The agenda then was: greeting, 'the sky is blue' (or cloudy, accordingly), humming and drumming, saying goodbye and stating when I would come again. I repeated this for five days, increasing the action by inviting him to play on the drum as well. Peter did not react to my invitation. He just looked at me more and more intensively as our meetings progressed. On the fifth day (tenth session) he seemed quite excited. He looked at the drum that I had put at his feet near to him which I invited him to touch. He bent forward with his upper body towards the drum and said in a commanding, rejective way: 'Take this drum away.' I immediately removed the drum and kept very quiet. I had mixed feelings: I felt frightened by his reaction and was at the same time very happy about his speaking to me. Jörg, the consultant psychiatrist, was flabbergasted and encouraged me to continue with the same intervention.

Theoretical considerations

Benedetti (1983) describes the psychopathology and psychodynamics of schizophrenia in an impressive way. His description of the autistic tendencies of persons suffering from schizophrenia is especially interesting for the present discussion. According to him the schizophrenic client controls his[5] split world through an autistic arrangement with the split. The schizophrenic person often feels omnipotent, whereas the feelings of omnipotence are paired with those of powerlessness. Loosing the autistic shell would mean being confronted with the whole of powerlessness. And this is the paradox: autism saves individuality into a psychosis that is the destroyer par excellence of individuality (Benedetti 1983, p. 23). So, leaving the autistic/mutistic position must have been a terrible challenge and stress for Peter. This shell had to be defended.

The drum, however, appears in mythology as the vehicle with which the shaman travels into other worlds or states of consciousness. The sound of the drum can remind us of the mother's heartbeat that we feel in the mother's body as the first ordering of the world (Timmermann 1989, p. 82). So, one could say that the drum puts the schizophrenic person in contact with his soul and in contact with the world; this is threatening because of the danger of splitting and/or engulfment. This would mean, in our context, that the autistic 'order' established by the schizophrenic client is in danger of being over-thrown. Still, according to Benedetti, the need for communication is a basic characteristic of the human soul. Despite the autism, this need finds a way of expressing itself, however distorted the form might be (Benedetti 1983, p. 46).

Communication takes place even though the responses might be negatively connotated, fearful, rejecting and mistrusting. The schizophrenic person feels a contact ambivalence; and at the same time, while making contact, his auto-destructive aggressivity is orientated away from the self as it is directed towards the therapist. Therefore contact takes the form of distrust, scepticism or negative transference (ibid.). In our sessions, it looked as if the drum had created some openings for the chaos to express itself. The challenge for me was now to stay with it, to partially sink into what was happening with Peter, to partially take his position in order to accompany him at this point of 'almost imperceptible movement, which . . . is seen to be the moment when feelings of great dynamic force are changing direction' (Cox 1988, p. 273).

Jörg encouraged me to continue in the same way, despite Peter's negative reactions. We decided to create a ritual that could contain the chaos that was being touched; a secure setting that would allow his personal dynamic defences to be slowly relinquished. Dramatherapy builds on the ritual/risk principle of theatre: I decided to use the drum to create an opening and ending ritual to mark the stage, the time and space of our being together, so as to allow for Peter the risk of leaving the autistic shell within this framework.

Phase 2

On the sixth day, after what I had felt was a 'violent' incident with the drum as described above, I decided to leave out the drum for the next two sessions. I do the usual sequence: 'greeting, sky, humming, saying goodbye'; I talk a bit more about the sky. His body is more lively, there is more tension; he has taken his hands out of his pockets, he holds them and cracks his fingers once.

On the seventh day I go in with a folding chair and a black bag with the drum, a mouse and a fabric ball with chimes in it. I have put everything in the bag so I can take it out and let it disappear again in case it feels too threatening. Peter looks at me with astonishment and curiosity. I explain that I have this bag here, tell him what I intend to do with it and ask him if he agrees. No answer. Then I take the drum out and play a little. I introduce a rhythm that from now on will be our opening and closing ritual for all sessions. I then let the drum disappear in the bag. Next I take the mouse out of the bag. Peter looks very interested and intrigued. After I play with it and he has looked at it for a while, he lowers his eyes again and drifts off. His belly is convulsing. I close the session with the drum and the rhythm I introduced at the beginning.

When I call his name in the goodbye sentence he suddenly moves his whole upper body, takes his hand out of his pocket, looks at me and says: 'Isn't that chair broken?' I am very astonished; the chair is broken, indeed, but I say: 'Where is it broken?' Peter: 'There!' he stretches his arm and shows me. I look: 'Oh, yes, it is broken, but it doesn't matter, it holds, it won't break down, it really holds!' When I say this he lowers his eyes and doesn't respond any more. Then I say I'll be back in the afternoon, and leave. I am wondering if this is a metaphor and what it means. Intuitively I feel that I ought to reassure him, that there will be no 'breakdown' and that I am here to hold the chaos.

In the subsequent two sessions he embodies the rhythm with his head when I play the drum. For the rest he is rather detached; he seems intrigued only by the mouse but does nothing more than look at it, sometimes intensively. I demonstratively show to him that I have mended the chair and reassure him again that it will certainly hold.

I feel I should allow the situation to open more, I should develop the interaction instead of acting immediately to secure things. Indeed, it seems more appropriate to 'secure things' by structuring the situations and possibly reframing them, rather than by doing something concrete, like mending the chair. One could say that this might be colluding with the client's fears . . . We decide that I should take off the mending tape and invite Peter to do it with me; then remove it in an obvious way.

In fact, in the next sessions I tell Peter that I will take the mending tape off, and ask him what he thinks about it. No answer. I then demonstratively take the tape away while he looks very astonished, with big eyes. An intensive looking interaction develops. I then try to leave with him a piece of the tape I've taken off. When I go out he asks me to take the chair and the piece of tape with me. I'm still wondering if the chair is a metaphor and what this communication around the chair means.

Theoretical considerations

Cox and Theilgaard (1987) discuss the transformational power of metaphors. Grainger, on the other hand, connects the faculty of doing 'as if' with the capacity for social interaction (1992, p. 166). The 'as if' faculty enables us to share experiences and meanings by moving backwards and forwards between ourselves and the person we are thinking about. Furthermore, social life and interaction build on differences and similarities. Both these capacities (expressing oneself through metaphors and doing as if) are lacking in the schizophrenic person. Metaphors are taken literally; the absence of distance between self and other obviates the need for real personal communication. In schizophrenic terms: 'If I know exactly what I mean, why should I struggle to make things clear for others?' Now, how can dramatherapy/drama and metaphorical expressions be beneficial to the schizophrenic client?

> Dramatherapy, like drama itself, is an arrangement of forms – roles, conventions, contrasts, similarities, modes of understanding, ideas and feelings – which encourages us to discriminate between, and choose among, a range of different kinds of perception or ways of perceiving.
>
> (Grainger 1992, p. 167)

In life, the processes whereby this shaping is carried out are often overlooked or concealed. In drama these relationships are clearly revealed. They are clearly marked, and hence the structure allows us to distinguish (confusion as opposed to order, love as opposed to hatred, and so on). Thus dramatic structure permits us 'to relate to' by allowing us 'to distinguish from' (ibid.).

Furthermore, the distancing created by the fact that we are in role and that it is happening in a stage world detached from the 'real' world enables us to concern ourselves with it in a way that is more immediate than our everyday preoccupations allow. These characteristics of drama are found again in dramatherapy. Drama and dramatherapy can support and promote the ego-building process of identification and differentiation (ibid.).

Bearing these considerations in mind, there are some hypotheses that could be formulated with regard to the development of phase 2 in Peter's transformational process. Peter starts embodying the ritualistic rhythm that gives boundaries and looks intensively at the mouse. Still, he drifts away and comes back at the end, or 'just before the end' (Cox 1988, p. 157) to enter an active communication sequence with the therapist. Peter was coming out of his shell. There was an obvious effort to get in contact with the therapist, and the chair seemed to be a good mediator. Maybe the chair offered a transitional space (or object), as the other objects were too actively handled by the therapist? Paired with this communicative effort, there was paradoxically also a greater retirement. In his description of the psychodynamics of schizophrenia Benedetti mentions the importance of the existence of the therapist within the 'non-existence'[6] of the client: in the person of the therapist the client can find himself again, through the participation of his unconscious with the therapist's presence and her unconscious attitudes, which melt with his (Benedetti 1983, p. 47). Perhaps the merging point with the therapist was being reached. In fact, what had to be dealt with now was the structuring of this phase in the relationship, in order to allow for Peter not to lose himself in the person of the therapist; in order also to help him explore the role(s) he will choose to play (Landy 1992, p. 102) while entering into social interaction. Peter had been playing the role of the catatonic by now. Through the interaction around the chair he seemed willing to leave that role behind and to become an active player, one who surprises

> through a kind of dramatic transcendence – unrehearsed, unconscious. This occurs when the client transcends his everyday role . . . and accepts

the challenge of the therapeutic stage – the permission to play. To play
what? The many complexities (of the chosen dramatic role(s)).

(ibid.)

Working with dramatic distance seemed appropriate here. I had already
introduced the mouse as a transitional object that would help Peter in the
process of relating and differentiating. A story could now function as a
container for the relationship between client and therapist and could provide
for the necessary distance in the identification and ego-building process. The
storytelling approach offers excellent possibilities in dealing with a para-
doxical situation as described above.

Gersie and King point out that tales possess inherent reality which we
somehow recognise. Besides, tales connect with our longings, dreams and
need for hope. They also link the individual and the collective, and function
as a connection between our inner and outer worlds. The words of the stories
are collective but the imagery individual: 'Whenever we listen to a tale we
prepare ourselves to be introduced to the process of creating structure and we
open ourselves up to be inspired' (Gersie and King 1990, p. 31). Thereby, an
interaction between teller and listener is created and the tale is like a journey
remembered. In that sense a tale introduced at that phase would offer the
container necessary for the interaction between client and therapist, a
container that could further help to touch the chaos and structure the process
of identification and differentiation.

According to Gersie and King stories are gatekeepers between our inner
and outer worlds. The story is like a guide that takes us from a known place
to adventure (Gersie and King 1990, p. 35). In the case of schizophrenia it
could help connect the black hole of negative identity and nothingness, the
landscapes of death, with the world of social communication. While we listen
to the story, we create, through the imagination, a separation between our
actual situation and one that we imagine as an alternative. A distance is thus
created that allows for reflection and eventually actualises the alternative.

This movement between inner and outer world or conscious and unconscious material can be compared with a trespassing of thresholds. Ritual
becomes relevant here and it is the reason that tales always begin to a
ritualised sentence and end in the same manner. This reflects the structuring
of the dramatherapeutic process whereby the building up of dramatic reality
and the coming out of it are of primordial importance (Jennings 1994, p. 102),
in order to set the boundaries within which the client can feel safe to risk
social contact. The drum had already been introduced as an opening and
closing, a boundary-marking ritual. The mouse functioned as a transitional
object. A story would now offer a container and allow for the emergence of
an intermediary or transitional space in which experimentation with alternative role possibilities, nearness and distance, and the risk of activating latent
potentials and the longing for communication, would be possible.

Phase 3

On the tenth day (nineteenth session) I introduced the story of the boy in the glass palace, which I created especially for Peter, incorporating the catatonic role he had been playing and integrating the different elements that made up our relationship by then:

> Once upon a time there was a boy living in a glass palace. When he looked outside he saw the sky; the sky was sometimes cloudy and sometimes the sun came through. When the sun came through, it sent its rays down to the glass palace, through the glass, and the light would come through to the boy and look like a rainbow in a thousand colours. The boy was delighted but also frightened at the same time, because he didn't really know what to do with all those colours. So he looked for a friend in the glass palace. He looked and found a little mouse. The mouse was very small but very clever. It wanted to help the boy so it began digging a deep hole. When the boy looked into the hole, he found a lot of music instruments and a drum. He took the drum and began to play with it. And then he put the drum away.

At the end of the session I ask if I should leave the drum there. Peter says 'Take it away.' Then I ask if I can leave the chair there. He says: 'Take the chair away.' I take everything and leave.

On the eleventh day I repeat exactly the same thing with the same questions and answers at the end. In the staff meeting the staff report that according to their observations he is deteriorating. In fact he has been rejecting since last week, which coincides with the behaviour he showed in the sessions and which was theoretically interpreted and discussed above. We nevertheless decide to continue.

In the next two sessions there is a remarkable evolution, first of all in Peter's body posture. He sits in a twisted position with his lower body looking away from me and his upper body looking towards me. When I tell the story and arrive to the point where the mouse digs a big hole he bends forward with his upper body and looks down in front of him as if he was looking into a big hole. For the first time he looks at me when I say the goodbye sentence. His bodily expression is very lively this time. In a meeting with his key person I hear surprising things. He has been extremely lively while bathing; he has shaken hands with the key person; he has laughed heartily several times in his bath; he has told the key person which trousers he wants to put on and at what time he would like to take his bath; he has gone around the wing for a while and eaten a salad in the dining room; and finally he has expressed the wish to go into his room and make himself a cup of tea.

In the subsequent four sessions I repeat the story and try to leave the mouse with him, which he repeatedly refuses saying 'I want no mouse' or 'Take the mouse away.' On the fifteenth day (twenty-ninth and thirtieth sessions) I introduce a new element in the story, which is that 'out of the hole with the drum and the instruments there came wonderful music from the instruments'. Out of a portable cassette player that I take out of my dramatherapy bag I play Mozart, Concerto for Piano No. 21, second movement. He looks astonished and interested and listens to the music. When I finish and want to leave he looks at the chair and says: 'You should cover this chair!' (he means the bit that is broken). I ask 'Where do you mean?' Peter: 'There!' and indicates with his head. He perfectly distinguishes left and right. Then I say: 'Well, I'll see what I can do, maybe we can mend it together.' For the first time he says goodbye to me when I leave.

The subsequent sessions are extremely lively: Peter asks me to take the chair to the carpenter's, and when I ask him to repeat what he said because I didn't hear it he repeats it in 'good'[7] German. In one of the sessions I leave the chair folded behind his back and he turns his upper body 180 degrees in order to look for it. In the next session he is standing arranging his flowers when I come in. Again a discussion develops around the chairs. He tells me I wouldn't need to leave my chair there as there are enough chairs in the room. His body becomes ever more lively. The staff tell me that when they took him to hospital for his leg to be looked after[8] he descended the stairs by his own without any problems; back from hospital he took care of his leg by himself, binding and unbinding it. Both things were unseen so far.

Theoretical considerations

We are all impressed about what is happening. On the other hand, it seems difficult to interpret his expressions. Though interpretation doesn't seem to be the main point. As Benedetti puts it:

> In the case of a psychotic ego that is being dissolved the primary therapeutic task does not lie in the interpretation of symptoms. What is primordial is to be *with* the client and *with* his symptom. In order to understand this, one should consider that the psychotic symptom hides a double aspect. It has two functions, two interpersonal aspects, namely communication on the one hand and defence on the other.
>
> (Benedetti 1983, p. 189, our translation, original emphasis)

There is a special challenge for the therapist here: how to be in and out of the relationship, 'sink into', double, take over the rhythm of the client and at the same time stay in control of her 'regression' in the service of her client's regression (Cox 1988, p. 265), and hence keep the distance and the sovereignty to reverse this relationship. Landy (1992, p. 99) mentions the principle of aesthetic distance as a means of handling several degrees of closeness and separation. He defines the ideal state of aesthetic distance as one where the emotional and rational parts of the self are in balance, as an 'intelligence of feeling' (ibid.). This is all the more important in the one-to-one therapeutic situation as the therapist is part of what is being played, takes on roles and so on. Precisely these elements that seem to be delicate in the relationship give the resources with which to handle the situation: 'Dramatherapists have "dramatic" ways of demonstrating separation and boundary setting. Their primary media are the stage, the story and the role' (ibid., p. 100). Indeed, the stage had been marked by the drum and its rhythm in opening and closing the sessions; the story created distance by framing experience in another time and another place; the roles were implicitly defined: Peter was client and playing the 'madman', while I was therapist and playing the 'helper'. In the process of our being together our roles began to shift. Peter was leaving the catatonic role behind. Through his transformation my role was changing also; this needed to be made explicit in the dramatic play, as 'the roles that each chooses to play create a boundary from the other' (ibid. p. 101).

I now introduced the role of 'storyteller' for myself. This would also create the frame for the separation work that had to be started. The peak had been reached (in terms of time, depth and mutuality (Cox 1988)) and now we had to prepare for closure and separation. Peter was entering social interaction, thus taking the risk of leaving the autistic shell and letting go of the catatonic role as it no longer served him. He was finding a new balance discovering new roles, taking the 'helper' into himself. The 'storyteller' could now go further, to other places, to tell her stories to as many people as possible, so that as many people as possible could enjoy them.

Phase 4

In fact, in the thirty-third session (seventeenth day) I introduce a sentence saying that the story teller would go further and that maybe another storyteller will come by and tell another story, so the story will survive the ages and there will be many stories in the world and people telling them and listening to them. After I finish the dramatic part I refer to what I had told Peter at the beginning, namely that we would work together for a certain amount of time. Now we are approaching the end. While I speak he looks at me. In the afternoon, he looks depressed. His body posture and tone lack the energy that was there in the last few sessions. I do the whole programme, but there is very little energy from his part. In the subsequent sessions, which are structured in the same way, there is a strong eye-contact interaction while I speak. There seems to be a mourning phase, with stereotyped movements that stop every time he looks at me. The drum seems to give containment and to soothe; his belly convulsions are calmed when I play the drum and he then seems more concentrated and willing to get into contact. In the final session he is remarkably lively and engaged again. I repeat the whole sequence and when I get to the point where the instruments begin to play I notice that I hadn't rewound the cassette. Staying in the dramatic reality I say 'the instruments must get ready' and push the rewind button. Peter starts laughing like an accomplice and looks at me in a very warm, charming, loving, communicative way. I double this. I then continue with the story which I have reframed after he said he would not keep the mouse.

After I finish the story and say that it is the last time I am coming, I take the mouse and say I would like to give it to him as a present. In the same rejecting, almost ritualistic way Peter says in Swiss German: 'I want no mouse.' I continue looking at him holding the mouse and start saying something; he repeats 'I want no mouse', first in Swiss German and then in a mixture of Swiss German and 'good' German. I take the mouse, say goodbye and ask if he would like to give me his hand. No reaction. I then offer him my hand. No reaction. I then say goodbye and walk out.

CONCLUSION

The ambivalence between the need for communication on the one hand and rejection or defence on the other was present until the end. The interesting result of this brief intervention was that transformation began through the process of distancing and following the steps postulated by the developmental model of dramatherapy (Jennings 1994, p. 97; Cattanah 1994, p. 28). The need for communication could be expressed first through the body by embodying the rhythm of the drum, and by using the body to address the receiver of the communicative act. Transformation was further promoted through the use of the story, which again created distance and allowed for an imaginative projective play and an experimentation with alternative role possibilities.

The objectives, defined as 'establishing contact', were undoubtedly met. Peter not only reacted to the stimuli he was exposed to, he also talked to the therapist, even in 'good' German in order to make himself understood. He became more lively and moving, communicating also more intensively with the caring staff, and even taking care of himself.

> One of the most rewarding moments at sea is when the auxiliary engine, however necessary it was for earlier progress to be made, is relinquished. Slow but 'autonomous' movement begins as the sails fill; though this depends upon a facilitating environment. If this fails, the engine may need to be started again.
>
> (Cox 1988, p. 275)

Dramatherapy was not yet institutionalised in the clinic. A serious effort was made to continue, with Peter's key person, the contact-establishing process that had begun. This person was to use the structure established through dramathcrapy and described above in regular sessions in order to maintain the contact with Peter and his interest in the outside world.

Indeed, in the follow-up period the ritual and the contact process were further differentiated. Peter's parents were actively involved in that process, too. Then, nine months after starting the treatment and nearly three years after admission to the clinic, Peter went home to live with his parents.

NOTES

1 In order to keep anonymity the name and surname have been changed.
2 This account will be in the 'I' form as far as the dramatherapist's actions are described, as these have been carried out by one of us alone (Elektra Tselikas), whereas the background work of planning and reflection has been a joint venture.
3 It is an open question whether the whole interaction that developed later around the chair could have something to do with this detail at the beginning.
4 'Doubling' is a psychodramatic concept meaning that someone (e.g. the therapist) takes over the client's body posture, movements, etc., tries to 'immerse' herself into the client's feelings and situation and eventually speaks what the client would not be able to say. The 'double' resembles the mother in the very early stages of life when, in the baby's perception, baby and mother merge; the mother's help and care is then felt as an extension of the baby's self (Leutz 1986, p. 46).
5 For the sake of convenience I alternate masculine and feminine forms.
6 'Non-existence' because his ego does not exist or is disintegrating. According to Benedetti the schizophrenic emptiness can only be contained through the therapist's attitude and it is through communication that the client's unconscious can be structured (Benedetti 1983, p. 49).
7 'Good' German is the German language spoken in Germany as opposed to the Swiss German dialect spoken in the German part of Switzerland. The fact that Peter spoke to me in 'good' German is remarkable because it shows that he was making a real and conscious effort to make himself understood and communicate with me, whom he obviously and very correctly identified as someone who didn't speak the Swiss dialect.
8 Peter had a problem with his leg and was taken to hospital from time to time for a check-up.

REFERENCES

Benedetti, G. (1983) 'Todeslandschaften der Seele' (The soul's death landscapes), Göttingen: Verlag für Medizinische Psychologie.
Cattanah, A. (1994) 'The developmental model of dramatherapy', in S. Jennings, A. Cattanach, S. Mitchell, A. Chesner and B. Meldrum, *The Handbook of Dramatherapy*, London: Routledge.
Cox, M. (1988) *Structuring the Therapeutic Process*, London: Jessica Kingsley.
Cox, M. and Theilgaard, A. (1987) *Mutative Metaphors in Psychotherapy: The Aeolian Mode*, London: Tavistock Publications.
Gersie, A. and King, N. (1990) *Storymaking in Education and Therapy*, London: Jessica Kingsley.
Grainger, R. (1992) 'Dramatherapy and thought disorder', in S. Jennings (ed.) *Dramatherapy: Theory and Practice 2*, London: Routledge.
Jennings, S. (1994) 'The theatre of healing: metaphor and metaphysics in the healing process', in S. Jennings, A. Cattanach, S. Mitchell, A. Chesner and B. Meldrum, *The Handbook of Dramatherapy*, London: Routledge.
Landy, R. (1986) *Drama Therapy: Concepts and Practices*, Springfield, Ill.: Charles Thomas.

—— (1992) 'One-on-one: the role of the dramatherapist working with individuals', in S. Jennings (ed.) *Dramatherapy: Theory and Practice 2*, London: Routledge.

—— (1993) *Persona and Performance: The Meaning of Role in Drama, Therapy, and Everyday Life*, London: Jessica Kingsley.

Leutz, G. (1986) *Das klassische Psychodrama nach J.L. Moreno* (J.L. Moreno's Classical Psychodrama), Berlin: Springer Verlag.

Timmermann, T. (1989) *Die Musen der Musik* (The Muses of Music), Zurich: Kreuz.

Chapter 12

'Sharing my story'

Dramatherapy for survival

Clare Woolhouse

INTRODUCTION

In this chapter I describe my work, as a dramatherapist, with a young boy in a primary school. I shall call him Adam. I shall put the work into its context of dramatherapeutic intervention within an education authority, briefly outlining referral and assessment procedure. I shall explain my decisions about the model and style of the work, and describe in detail the dramatherapy process which spanned a year and a half, highlighting significant themes and threads.

BACKGROUND: REFERRAL AND ASSESSMENT

I am employed by an education authority as a member of a team of teachers and ancillaries who work with children and young people with emotional and/or behavioural difficulties (EBD). My job is to support pupils in mainstream schools and to help them maintain their places there and to achieve their full educational potential. I do this mostly by facilitating individual or group dramatherapy sessions with the children referred to me. Work can be short-term (a ten- to twelve-session programme) or long-term (a year or more).

When children are causing concern over their behaviour in school, staff refer them to our service. An initial assessment is carried out by the head of the service, who in turn refers each child to a member of the team, each of whom has specialised skills in working with children with EBD.

This referral was unusual in that Adam's brother, not Adam, was causing concern over his behaviour in school. However, as both boys had been heard causing disturbances outside school hours, I was asked to assess them both.

In a school context, I assess by discussing the child with staff, through observation in class, paying particular attention to behaviours such as interaction with peers and adults, motivation and the ability to engage with tasks. I also use a simple individual assessment activity. At this stage, I am assessing the child's need for support intervention within the brief of my team. This could be for individual or group therapy, for counselling, for a behaviour management programme or for supporting the child in the class-room with academic work.

I observed Adam in class. His academic achievement was age-appropriate and he conformed to all classroom expectations of behaviour. At the time I thought he looked a little 'lost' or bewildered and was somewhat overanxious to please adults. Although other children were friendly to him, he did not seem to have any special relationships. However, there was very little to suggest an emotional or behavioural difficulty like that of his brother.

I then assessed Adam individually. For this I used a very simple task in which I invited Adam to draw a picture of himself, to write his name, and to draw his house and his family. This was to give me some information about his self-image, his developmental level, his ability to engage in a task, and his way of expressing himself creatively. I was also able to assess his response to me in a one-to-one situation.

Adam was delighted to come to his assessment and to receive some individual attention. His self-portrait was a drawing of a head divided from the rest of his body, with prominent hair and a smiling face. In the stomach area was a box shape in which he drew what he called the 'magic button'. He spoke of 'poison in my belly'. For his name he wrote his brother's in jumbled writing (his class work showed him very capable of writing simple sentences including his name and address), and his house was a scribble. He did not draw his family.

I had a strong gut reaction after working with Adam. I felt that something was badly wrong. His self-portrait indicated a poor self-image and a negative relationship with his body (it was separated from the head, the thinking, feeling part). His powerful image of poison and the 'magic button' were disturbing elements for a five-year-old to include in a picture of himself, and seemed at odds with the cheery model pupil role he played in class. I wondered if the image he had created could be about sexual abuse.

I took the pictures to supervision where I was able to reflect carefully on my own reactions to them and receive objective guidance on where to go from here. This was the beginning of a three-way process in which I as the therapist, the client and the supervisor embarked on a journey together. Supervision was intrinsic to the work and essential for it to progress. One important aspect of this was the need for me to be clear about my brief. Whatever my initial hunches, I was not doing disclosure work. My aim was to provide support for Adam by helping him to explore what I believed were significant emotional difficulties. These were indicated by the assessment, but they were not yet revealing themselves through his behaviour in school and were therefore largely invisible to the outside world.

This was the beginning of Adam's story. Although his therapy is now finished, his story has no happy ending: indeed it has no ending at all. During the course of the therapeutic process, his story ebbed and flowed, became clearer and cloudier, as Adam explored and experimented with ways of coping with his life; of surviving.

As I describe Adam's process. there are certain themes and threads which I think are significant. These are:

- clusters and innovations in the images Adam used
- the shifts he made from unconscious expression of feeling to conscious references to everyday life, i.e. moving from his interior to his exterior world
- the changing persona or role he adopted in the sessions
- the way in which my role as the therapist changed from a reactive to an active one
- the transference and counter-transference and introjection which occurred
- the reflection process and the importance of supervision
- the client's changing behaviour outside the dramatherapy sessions
- dealing with closure.

It seemed appropriate for a child of his age to use the EPR model of dramatherapy. A revisiting of earlier developmental stages (described above) would provide him with security and the opportunity to engage with safe, self-affirming activities as well as to explore troubled areas.

EARLY DAYS

In laying the foundations of our work together, I was careful to set up a safe space with clear boundaries. I felt this was particularly important for Adam, as I guessed adults could be, for him, potentially threatening, frightening or demanding. Within this structure, I decided that he should take as much control as possible over the content and course of the sessions. This could well be in contrast to a lack of control experienced in other areas of his life. In early sessions I was there to support and contain a creative experience for Adam who I sensed was in a fragile and very needy state. I was ready to move with the flow rather than attempt to channel it. Rather like a play therapist, I provided a variety of materials for drawing and modelling, and accepted his choices as valid.

In the first session he chose to use plasticine. He started to experiment with making shapes. I made no suggestions or attempts to direct his activities. I simply acknowledged and accepted what he did. He made two sausage shapes, one long and thin, one much fatter. He commented on the fat one: 'He gets bigger, doesn't he?'

He enjoyed the *Where's Wally?* book and looking for the cartoon character hidden amongst crowds of other people. He drew a picture of Wally. It was a tiny, precisely drawn figure with hair made from string stuck on with Sellotape. It had a face with no mouth and big hands. Next to it he copied a piece from his class reading book which he had brought to show me: '"Stop,

stop," said the milkman, but the truck went on.' At the very end of the session he did a quick pencil drawing at the side of the paper. It was the 'nasty man who hides, and puts his foot out to trip you up'. I thought the picture looked like a penis with semen coming out of it.

Adam had brought up a great deal of material at this session while I remained in the 'witness' role as the therapist. Landy (1986) describes the therapist in this mode:

> She becomes not only the follower, but also the witness, one who is there to see and affirm. At her best she is a brave and compassionate witness who can remain intact, yet caring, as demonstrations of darkness are re-enacted.
>
> (p. 107)

Adam checked out my willingness and ability to do this by making regular eye contact to ensure he had my 'permission' to express himself freely, and that I would accept what he presented to me. He was relaxed and seemed to be enjoying the creative process despite the disturbing images which emerged. He was simply letting me know what it was like to be him.

As a therapist, I believed that Adam needed time, space and the opportunity to build up his trust in me. However, I was obliged to report my concerns about possible interpretations of his images to other colleagues. Whilst there was agreement that the images were disturbing, this was not the type of evidence which warranted further investigation at this stage. I was to continue to work with Adam within my support brief and report regularly to the other professionals involved.

For the next few sessions he worked in a tactile way using Playdo, finger paints and felt pens. Images of pigs emerged regularly. He began to make occasional references to his family.

I had an unplanned absence due to illness and the school did not pass on my message to Adam explaining that I was away and why. When I asked him what he thought when I did not come, he said: 'I thought the man would come and get me.' I asked him if this was a real man or a man in his head. He said it was a man in his head and that he thought the man was going to fly away out of his head. I asked him how he felt about the man, whether it was a nice or a nasty feeling. He said 'nice' and became very giggly. He said that the man had his knickers on his head. He was still giggly and uncomfortable. I acknowledged this. 'It makes you feel very giggly.' 'Yes.'

Adam needed help with these overwhelming feelings. I suggested he draw the man. He became calmer and drew a tiny, precise figure which had a 'big eye' and a 'little eye', and which he named. He squeezed correction fluid on to the picture using a Tippex pen. He put Tippex on his own head and the palms of his hands. He became very uncomfortable and needed to wash. He put a blob of Tippex on the paper and said this was a picture of himself.

In the session he also interspersed his activities with 'magic' and played guessing games; for example, he asked me to guess which colour he was going to use or if the crayon box he covered with his hand would be big or small when he took his hand away. He covered up his man's name and made it go away with a magic spell. It did not feel right to join in with these games and I said that I would not make guesses, but would wait until he was ready to show me or tell me about what he was doing.

He was very much more tense than he had been in previous sessions and he made far less eye contact. After the break, there was obviously a great deal of unexpressed feeling which he felt might overwhelm him: the man would fly away out of his head. The man image was a bringing to consciousness of part of that feeling. Other elements in the session seemed to be unconscious representations of conscious, everyday reality. Reflecting on the session afterwards and in supervision, it seemed to me that Adam's material could be indicative of an abusive situation. The use of the Tippex, for example, could well have been dramatic play about touching or receiving semen. Apparently male abusers sometimes like to ejaculate in the hair of their victims. (Hair was prominent in many of Adam's images.) The games and spells he made up might be his own versions of those used by his abuser(s) when encouraging him to participate in the abuse by making it seem 'fun'.

Again, I needed to remind myself of the purpose of the therapy. As a dramatherapist, my function is to follow through the image and explore its meanings creatively. Yet when play emerges that seems to be a reflection of an actual experience, rather than a symbolic expression of feeling (with the Tippex, for example), should one not work with that outer reality with a view to gaining information, if not evidence? It was all very well moving gently and carefully in the client's own time, but if I strongly suspect that a five-year-old is being sexually abused, should I not be pursuing a line which could lead to specific disclosure, and fast? As far as the law goes, a few drawings of Wally and some phallic plasticine models do not constitute evidence.

However, it was my job to contain myself and my feelings, as well as those of my client. Just because I wanted it to be over and sorted out did not mean that this was best for the client. He was crowded with unconscious, semi-conscious and conscious feelings which he had to be able to explore safely. His need was to stay with the metaphor and I had to follow that through. In order to remain 'intact yet caring' I used the structure and support of my supervision sessions to examine my feelings about sexual abuse, and explore the counter-transference I experienced of a fiercely protective mother towards a hurt child. I also needed to gain information about victims and perpetrators of abuse, and most of all to be guided towards creative ways of helping my client to 're-enact' his 'demonstrations of darkness', whatever the source of that darkness might be.

Jennings (1990) identifies four internal states of the therapist, all of which may be present and influential on his or her work and which must be acknowledged during the reflection process. These are:

- the internal patient
- the internal therapist
- the internal supervisor
- the internal creative artist.

(pp. 47–50)

I needed to be very aware of these states and to use them positively for the purpose of the therapy, which was to help and support the client. Otherwise it would have been very easy to be overwhelmed, as my client was.

Adam needed an experience which would be creative, yet contained and safe. My supervisor introduced me to sandplay. I filled a tray with sand and gathered together a collection of models of people, animals, vehicles and scenery, and natural objects such as shells and fir cones. I was prepared to embark on a phase of projective work.

SHARING THE STORY: PROJECTIVE PLAY, STORYMAKING AND ROLE-PLAY

In the next session I presented Adam with the sand and objects. He was instantly taken with them and began to play. I invited him to use them to make a picture and maybe to tell a story. I sat and witnessed his playing, sometimes making comments which were intended to support and affirm what he did, or sometimes to deepen or move on the unfolding story.

During the sessions in which I used sandplay with Adam, various images and themes recurred. Pigs were often protagonists, as were 'baddies' (pirates or men with guns) who were aggressive and swore, saying things like 'you're a little bugger'. A yellow breakdown truck came to represent a 'dirty/clean' theme. The sand would become dirty in the story and the truck (sometimes several) would have to be brought in to make it clean. The dirty sand would then have to be put in the dirty hole or bin which Adam once said was 'someone's bed'. Other themes emerged about hiding or burying. Sometimes a single animal would be left buried deep in the sand at the end. Gradually a theme of being found or rescued was expressed by the breakdown truck retrieving hidden animals by 'thinking where they were'. A strain of vulnerability was often present, expressed through Adam's use of baby animals. Sadness was a prevalent feeling, sometimes represented by the animals who were hiding when the 'baddies' were punished or taken away. Almost always if I asked how a character was feeling, the reply would be 'sad'.

After a while Adam started to create his own models. In one session he found some Blu-tack and spontaneously made a model figure which he called Billy. He said that Billy was a naughty man because he said rude things and that he was falling to pieces. He was very distracted and unsettled in the session, and seemed, like his model, to be in a very fragile state.

He needed some grounding and safety. We returned to the embodiment phase and he spent a couple of sessions playing with Playdo and finger paints in a tactile way. In one session, while he painted a pig, he spoke of family arguments and how he was slapped by his brother and father.

Since he had spoken of his family, next session I invited him to make Playdo models of a family. I deliberately did not specifically suggest *his* family in order to allow him to keep a safe distance from his experience. He made a little girl, a teddy, a snake, birds and fishes. He made a dad with no body and a jumper on 'so no one can see his body' and a mum with an eye patch. (His mother had recently injured her eye.) Then he told a story about the family in which a little girl sneaked downstairs in the night, ate lots of food, took beer from the fridge and got drunk. When her parents came down they thought she was dead and called an ambulance.

I decided to be more proactive, and offer a 'reframing' of his story. I asked him if I could tell the next part. He was delighted. I said:

> The little girl had a very special friend called Teddy. [He had made a model of a teddy.] Teddy was very special because he could talk, but even better than that he was especially good at listening. When the little girl felt sad, she would remember about Teddy and even if she wasn't actually with him she could make a picture of Teddy in her mind and she could tell him whatever she wanted to, whatever it was.

I then asked Adam what happened at the end of his story and he said: 'And then the daddy got on the motorbike and then he drove away. The little girl said to Teddy, "Where's my daddy gone? I feel sad." Teddy said, "Daddy's gone away on his motorbike."'

In this story there seemed to be a mixture of symbolic and everyday reality. It was possible that Adam could have been retelling something that had really happened to him or one of his siblings. My response was to introduce a positive image as a way of suggesting the possibility of positive change. I was taking an active part in the creative process. I encouraged him to take control over his feelings by finding his own way of bringing the story to a close.

In the next session, Adam wanted to draw. I thought we should continue with the family theme and asked if he would like to draw a family. He drew a mummy with big hands, and a spider in a web with a tail which 'wags and strangles you if you get caught up in it'. He gave it three names including his own. Again there was a confusion between everyday and symbolic reality. This time I decided we needed to clarify the everyday and we spent time discussing who were his family members and which lived in his house.

In supervision, I reflected on the spider/web picture as a powerful image of being caught up or trapped. Next session I suggested he made up a story about it. He drew a spider, a fish and a web. The fish did not like being wet and needed Sellotape to keep it warm. It was frightened of a dragon which had one eye and would come and eat them. They knew he would come and eat them because his mouth was open. Adam was creating an image which was frightening to him. To leave him grounded for the end of the session some reframing was necessary. I asked him to think of a friend for the animals. Eventually he came up with a dragonfly. I told him a story about how the dragonfly could zoom around very quickly and see very far and could warn the animals when the dragon was coming. He thought of some more friends for the fish. I asked him how the story ended and he said it ended with everyone saying 'nothing'.

After an extended holiday break during which Adam spent time away from home with relations, we resumed our work. His class teacher mentioned he had been 'telling tales' a lot in class. In this next phase, Adam began to explore the tension between the real and ideal elements in his life. He made a Playdo model called Peter and then he drew Peter's house. The house had bars on the windows and a door which had many paths to it. The door was colourful on the outside but Adam said that when the door was locked it had no colour: 'It looked like that, but it wasn't.'

We wrote a story about Peter. Adam invented a schoolboy character who did everyday things, had a family and lots of animals, had a simple, ordinary life.

After a while I changed my approach. I took in a variety of hand puppets. As well as providing a new medium, I thought it would allow me to intervene more directly and dramatically with his stories.

After experimenting for a while with the various puppets, Adam chose a young male puppet for himself, which he named Jim, and a soldier one for me to use. He set up a table as a stage. Jim chatted to the soldier puppet, telling him what he had been doing in school. Jim had a friend, a Robin Hood puppet. Jim and Robin Hood kept disappearing under the table where the soldier puppet could not see them. They rubbed their faces together and whispered. 'They said they were going to eat their dinner but they weren't really,' he told me.

I decided to change puppets to a friendly dog rather than the authoritarian (judgemental?) soldier. Every so often I would make the dog woof or tap the table with his nose, but kept him above the table. Adam made the other two puppets tap in reply. He wanted to know what the dog was doing and I said that the dog was listening and waiting in case the puppets wanted him to hear the whispers. The Jim puppet said: 'I'm not really Jim and Robin Hood's not really my friend. He used to be but he's not any more.' Then Adam said that it would be better if the puppets were above the table where I could see them.

Adam's puppet play seemed to be a vivid enactment of a dilemma. It depicted two worlds, one above and one below the surface, represented by the puppet stage he set up with the table. In one world he played the part of a boy participating in ordinary school life, while in the other he was engaged with secret things, unseen by others. This was an intensely powerful session.

My supervisor's input made me realise that Adam's role-play was under-distanced: too close to his actual life to leave much room for imaginative exploration or to provide a great deal of safety. Adam himself let me know that this was so. Although I tried to continue using the puppets in subsequent sessions, he did not want to play with them again.

In the following weeks I became increasingly aware of a new strand of behaviour in Adam. He was pushing boundaries: he made demands, asking to keep pieces of equipment or for me to bring particular things next session. He seemed more detached, older, possibly more knowing. I felt that he was experimenting with his own power, seeing how much he could manipulate me. I responded by clarifying the boundaries and the previously negotiated rules about what things he could keep and what were for the session only. There was an issue about power and control making itself felt. The counter-transference I experienced was about irritation and rejection. I felt that he was devaluing our work and therefore me, that he wanted only to take material things from me and had no other investment in our relationship. I felt somewhat used, as indeed he had seemed to feel in earlier sessions.

In another session he chose to use Playdo and made a model of a man with a moustache (which he did not name). He once again used the Tippex pen and put blobs on the legs and belly of the model. We talked a little about the 'white stuff'. He told me it went on the belly and on the arms and that it made him feel sick. He did not wish to say anything to his model so we talked about what we should do with it. He wanted to put it in the bin, so we made this into a little drama.

The model was fried in a pan, tossed like a pancake, broken up, wrapped in newspaper and ceremoniously deposited in the 'smelly bin'. He was very satisfied with this outcome. I had encouraged him to be active and take control over the monster he had created. I had also adopted a more active role and had made specific suggestions about how we could deal with the monster together.

There was a week's break for half-term. The school informed me they strongly suspected that Adam and his brother had been responsible for vandalising the church next door to the school during the week. Neighbours had reported seeing the two boys breaking windows.

We began a new phase of the work, using a variety of materials to make three-dimensional images. During this time Adam was mostly in his more detached, imperious persona. The frequency of his eye contact was very much reduced from earlier in the therapeutic process. He still pushed boundaries, yet became angry when things were not the same as usual, for example having to use a different table. He was obviously feeling very insecure and needed me to remain calm, clear and consistent. This felt like hard work at times. The images he created were concerned with layers and covering up. They seemed to reflect his changed attitude to me, which was less open and trusting, even cynical.

As we drew near to a long summer break, I decided to introduce a semi-closure activity with the aim of helping him to process and contain some of his experience of the sessions. I invited him to spend the last few sessions making a 'special box' which he could keep and into which he could put whatever he wanted, possibly including some pictures or stories to remind him of things we had done together. Like the three-dimensional images, the box was made multilayered, coloured and recoloured and labelled on the outside with the names of his family members. He rejected any suggestions I made about putting 'memories' of things which were important to him from our work and could only think of keeping money in the box. I felt he was making his allegiance with his family and his own priorities clear to me. This was understandable in view of the weeks he would have to manage without the structure of school and weekly dramatherapy. Nevertheless, the 'internal patient' in me felt rejected at the lack of confirmation of the importance of the therapy to my client.

Before in the last session of term, staff told me Adam had tried to strangle a girl and had seemed serious about it. His teachers were very shocked as they had never seen behaviour like it from him. I am afraid I was not at all surprised. Adam brought up the subject of my seeing him the following term. I said I planned to continue the sessions and asked him what he thought. He thought that it would be 'good'.

ENDINGS

We met again after the six-week summer break; in the meantime I had become pregnant, and was planning to leave work in a few months. I had twelve weeks remaining to work with Adam which I decided should be used to prepare for closure. The structure would be based on a return to the EPR model we had used throughout the therapeutic process.

The first few sessions were spent re-establishing links after the long break, talking about things done in the past, returning to familiar activities and books, and looking towards the future. In one early session, I explained to Adam that I was leaving and why, and discussed with him the number of sessions we had left to work together. I could not predict how this would affect him.

I provided Playdo for him so he could express his feelings safely. He said nothing, but tore off chunks of Playdo and pummelled and kneaded them. He began muttering the rhyme 'pinch, punch, first of the month'. I suggested he made a 'Pinchpunch' model so that he could focus what were clearly angry feelings. The model he made consisted of a collection of disconnected parts rather than one figure. There was pink hair and a pink face, a tiny body, feet, no arms, and 'squirty bits'. Pinchpunch had to be slapped and kicked 'to stop him messing about'. Adam frequently told him to 'keep that out [nose], and that shut [mouth]'.

He spent three sessions working with this model. For the first two I adopted the supporting-witness role, encouraging him to express his angry feelings in connection with the model, but interjecting with comments where those feelings seemed likely to overwhelm him. In the third I actively joined his drama. Pinchpunch seemed to need punishing and Adam frequently knocked him down with balls, as if he were a skittle.

During this period of work I was aware that Adam had some difficulty distinguishing between himself and his role, and I had to focus on helping with this. This was the beginning of a change in him. In the following weeks I noticed he began imitating me, for example by adopting certain words and phrases I frequently use, and even copying my tone of voice. It felt strange and was certainly very different from his recent demanding, pushy persona. I was reassured by my supervisor that this was a useful change. He was introjecting a positive role model. In this way he may have been preparing himself for the end of the dramatherapy process. He was taking strength where he could.

Together, we began the last part of this story: finding a way to leave each other and to end the work. We moved on from the embodiment and projective work of the Playdo models to some role-play using masks of Pinchpunch and another character, Jupiter. Adam spent several sessions working on a happy, sad and angry mask for each character and then together we role-played with them. It evolved that Jupiter was a four-year-old boy and Pinchpunch was seven (representing Adam and his brother?). Jupiter was sad because he was always being hit. He was only happy when he had cakes to eat.

I encouraged the Jupiter character to find ways of outwitting Pinchpunch, such as using speed and stealth. We worked on Jupiter asserting himself by using a strong voice and saying clearly what he felt. We reversed roles to see what it was like to be Pinchpunch. Adam developed Jupiter's character to that of a clown who was happy when he was surrounded by children.

He made up a story, which he dictated to me, about Jupiter performing tricks to children, and choosing a girl to help with the tricks (because she was nice). He 'magicked' himself up into the air. Then Pinchpunch kicked the girl into the air where she bumped into Jupiter. Adam continued: '"Who are you?" said Jupiter. "I am the girl who was with you," she said. The story is beginning with the end.' I asked if anything else happened. He went on: 'There was a balloon and Jupiter said to the girl, "You hold on to my shoes. I will get on the string of the balloon and take you to Scotland."' He stopped again here. I felt that it was important not to leave the story literally 'hanging in the air' so I suggested he find a way of ending it. He dictated:

They walked into the woods and saw a mouse and the mouse saw a man with a gun in his hand and said to him 'Shoot them two' and the man did. The girl and the boy fell to the ground. They was dead. The story is finished now.

For the final sessions I needed to help Adam reflect on the whole of the therapeutic process. I did this by photographing all the pictures which he had drawn, and we used them to make a book which, as it were, told the story of the therapy. He found this a very pleasing and calming experience, and, as we talked through all the things we had done together in the sessions, we gently arrived at a point where we could say goodbye to each other, and off he went with his story.

The ending process seemed to be a positive experience for Adam. He had appeared to accept the fact we had to finish our work together, and the reason for it, without a struggle. Maybe he had used the therapy effectively enough to feel able to do without it. He had taken what he needed to help him explore some of his difficult feelings, even if the source of those feelings never became explicit. Perhaps the difficult situation, whatever it was, had altered, and he was not as disturbed and unhappy as he had appeared to me when we first met.

It is interesting to reflect on the different roles Adam adopted during the latter stages of the therapeutic process. He changed from the demanding, manipulative, angry persona, to the needy 'sick' child. He introjected a role model of the therapist. In the final stages, he showed himself as a child able to look at his own creations with pleasure and pride, and take on board with reasonable equanimity what could have been a difficult, even painful closure. He had explored all of these roles within the therapy.

I also had to work on my own reactions to ending this piece of work. I will probably never know what was actually going on in Adam's life during the eighteen months I worked with him, or what had happened during the five years before that. I do not know whether or not I left him in a world still haunted by fear and sadness. However, I believe I helped him find some strength with which to cope with his life. As a dramatherapist, this is one of the difficulties I find I have to accept: that endings are not necessarily conclusive or tidy, and that it is not necessarily my role to 'know' in fact or detail what is 'wrong' with a client.

Working with Adam was an illuminating, painful and creative experience. As time went by I became increasingly aware of the dramatherapist's need to be guided not only by instinct, training and supervision, but also by the client. As Adam's needs shifted, and he experimented with different roles, I realised that I too had to find the strength to adapt and change. Client, therapist and supervisor together sought a way for Adam to share his story; to find a way for him to survive.

REFERENCES AND FURTHER READING

Jennings, S. (1990) *Dramatherapy with Families, Groups and Individuals*, London: Jessica Kingsley.
—— (1993) *Playtherapy with Children: A Practitioner's Guide*, Oxford: Blackwell Scientific.

—— (1995) *Dramatherapy with Children and Adolescents*, London: Routledge.
Landy, R. (1986) *Drama Therapy: Concepts and Practice, Volume 2*, Springfield, Ill.: Charles Thomas.
Menuhin, J. R. (1992) *Jungian Sandplay: The Wonderful Therapy*, London: Routledge.
Oaklander, V. (1978) *Windows to our Children*, Moab, Utah: Real People Press.

Part III

Gender issues in supervision and practice

Chapter 13

Gender issues in supervision

Marina Jenkyns

THE SETTING

When Virginia Woolf was asked to talk about fiction she entitled her lecture *A Room of One's Own* (1928). I unashamedly steal this title, adapting it to apply to the space we call supervision. Supervision implies a looking over, a sense of a wider vision. A room is connected with other rooms, part of a house, therefore part of a greater whole. The room of supervision likewise has interconnecting doors and adjacent rooms. It is like the study where the therapist can retreat to read and think and write, a room to reflect in and learn from. It is also like the playroom where she can be in Winnicott's 'potential space' and engage in a creative encounter with another, teasing out an understanding of the work with clients which lies below consciousness. It can be a laundry-room where washing out the 'stuff' (literally material) of the interaction between client and therapist can be done, ironing out the client's projections, the therapist's counter-transference, sorting and gaining a sense of order in the chaos of the work.

When I was a child trains used to be divided into compartments with a mirror on each of the opposite walls. I used to enjoy trying to get into a position where I could see the mirrors reflecting each other backwards and forwards into infinity. The room of supervision is also like that compartment. In one mirror there is a reflection of both the world 'out there' which is the dramatherapy experience of the clients, which in turn reflects further back into their lives and the realities of their inner and outer worlds – what they bring with them to the therapy. In the other mirror is the therapist with her world. The supervisor is there trying to keep both mirrors in view, sometimes getting caught up in the picture and seeing herself reflected backwards and forwards in the image as well.

In this chapter I want to take one part of the many, many themes which it would be possible to explore under its title 'Gender issues in supervision'. It is that of the mother–daughter relationship.The exploration of this rela-tionship from a feminist perspective has added greatly to our understanding of the issues which women bring to therapy (Chodorow 1978, 1989; Orbach and Eichenbaum 1982, 1992; Ernst and Maguire 1987). The claims for this relationship as it impacts on the inner world of the woman and on the outer world of the society in which she lives, are well documented by clinical experience. Some understanding of these issues needs, I believe, to be part of the furniture which the supervisor has in any of the rooms I have mentioned. It has become an essential ingredient of what is now known as feminist psychotherapy. All I can do in this short chapter is draw out some of the issues as they relate to the therapy and supervision processes and urge the reader who might be unfamiliar with the ideas to read further; suggestions for such reading are made at the end.

Briefly the position I adopt here is that gender is a social construct. The concepts of sex and gender are frequently confused. Males and females are biologically determined and their sex role is, except in cases of hermaphrodism, clearly defined; no negotiation is possible. (The issue of transsexualism is beyond the brief of this chapter, though clearly connections with the theme exist.) However, how men and women live out their lives is profoundly influenced by those sets of experiences and expectations which society places upon them through the phenomenon known as 'gender'. It is determined by cultural attitudes and behaviours (Money and Erhardt, 1972; Orbach and Eichenbaum 1982).

Chodorow (1989) refers to Karen Horney's assertion that men have to continually prove their manhood, their identity. This is because a man knows that he is biologically different from his mother and therefore cannot identify with her. She refers to Margaret Mead's (1949) assertion from a cultural perspective that, 'Maleness is not absolutely defined but has to be kept and re-earned every day' (Chodorow 1989, p. 33). Chodorow then goes on to compare the girl's experience and its implications in a gendered world. 'A girl's conflicts, rather, are about whether she wants this [feminine] identity, an identity reliant upon her ability to inhibit herself and to respond to the demands of others' (p. 42). We need to take up this assertion that women inhibit themselves and that their role is to respond to the demands of others. I find it still common to have conversations with men whom I think have thought through many of these issues and find myself being shocked to hear comments like: 'But surely women have got equality now', or, even more worrying by its subtext, '*Surely women have got what they want now*'.

What these men, and indeed many women, appear not to understand is that the necessity to inhibit oneself and to respond to the demands of others is written on the psyches of women because of what is written on their bodies. Men with the best will in the world cannot suckle a child. The woman is therefore put in the role of primary carer at the very time when the infant is most vulnerable. Her responsibility is great. Failure to take up this responsibility could result in the death of her child. The effect of this role on the way a woman experiences and sees herself is profound. She must, in the light of this responsibility, put the infant first, and herself second (or third or fourth or fifth if she has several children and a husband to nurture as well). What does this mean in practical terms?

It means that the woman must be dependable because she is depended upon. She must react to the demands made on her, she must be there for her baby's needs, she must anticipate them, she must contain her infant's fears and panic at the strangeness of life outside the womb, she must soothe and comfort; she must. . . must. . . must. If she does not comply then society says punitively, self-righteously, 'She ought to have', or 'She's inadequate'. She cannot have a will of her own because she is dominated by her baby's needs; she must have less sleep, less time to do things that might nurture her, less. . . less. . . less. And if someone lives with the word 'less' for long enough she is 'diminished'. This is exemplified by a woman in a group I worked with who had lived for so long with this situation and with society's condemnation as well, that she said of the experience of reaching out into the air in a simple warm-up exercise: 'It was so wonderful to feel all that space around me. I'd forgotten it was there.'

Mothers do not spring into the world fully formed with no past behind them. Every mother has been some other woman's daughter. And every daughter has had a mother who was a mother's daughter too. There is an issue of inheritance here. And not just the inheritance of the genes but also that of the pyschological impact of the gendering of society. Susie Orbach puts it like this:

> The mother will identify with the daughter because of their shared gender, for when a woman gives birth to a daughter she is in a sense reproducing herself. When she looks at her daughter she sees herself. . . . she not only identifies with her daughter but also projects onto her some of the feelings she has about herself . . . . In this projection she is seeing her daughter not as another person but as an extension of herself . . . she sees a vulnerable, undefended, expressive, eager little girl. This in turn re-awakens – still at an unconscious level – the part of her that feels needy and wants to be nurtured, responded to, encouraged.
>
> (Orbach and Eichenbaum 1992, p. 40)

The fact that in her relationship with men the emotional caretaking is not reciprocal means that she unconsciously passes this message on to her little girl, treating her in ways that clearly give the message that she must not expect too much, must learn to curb her expression, her needs, her self. The other aspect of this is that where her daughter expresses need the mother must suppress it, just as she has repressed this 'little girl' part of herself. But the reawakening of her own deeply repressed unmet needs in relation to the child of the same sex with whom she feels this strong identification means that, at an unconscious level, she looks to her daughter to fulfil the needs her own mother never met. This ties the daughter to the mother; she learns to take care of her mother's needs. Nancy Friday tells us that, a girl's first child is in fact her own mother (Friday 1979). The little girl learns not to cry, or at least, not too much, not to ask for more, not to be adventurous, not to worry mother, not to do what mother couldn't have the chance to do, not to compete, not to become a separate individual in the world. Not . . . not . . . not. So the little girl, like her mother before her, becomes diminished.

Because her role is to continually deny her needs and her own creative self-expression of who she is in the world in any other way except as a mother, she is 'objectified' in society. She is not a subject but an object, there to provide and minister to the needs of others, not to assert her own. This being an object rather than a subject has grave consequences, for how can the daughter achieve a strong sense of her own subjectivity if she is modelling herself – and through such a complex relationship – on someone who is not a subject? (See Chodorow 1989, ch. 5.)

Within the therapy situation the results of this cycle can be seen again and again. The fear that the woman might become 'too much' for the therapist or might take up too much space in the group is a common phenomenon. There is often a need to look after the therapist, a need to excuse the therapist for what she cannot give her. As I write I think of a woman in a group in a clinical setting who responded to my forthcoming absence with: 'You've given to us, and now you're going to give to someone else and I think that's really nice.' Her underlying feelings could only be expressed through an acting-out – her absenting herself from the session when the group resumed.

So what happens to all the anger, the rage, the disappointment, the envy? Just as with mother they go underground. To try to let these have the light of day is a risky business. We have only to witness the ubiquitousness of women's assertiveness being perceived as aggression to see this. This perception is disturbing on two counts. First it implies that if a woman states her needs and the fact that she has rights – if, in other words, she claims her subjectivity rather than her objectivity – this is synonymous with an attacking form of anger. It also implies that women have no right to anger. The anger is turned inwards and takes the form of illness or depression or both. And then the message is repeated; it is evident in the number of women who go to the doctor suffering from depression and are met with the message that they must suppress it. I know of a woman who discovered her mother in advanced stages of cancer. The old lady had not told anyone because she 'didn't want to make a fuss'. The depression which set in after her mother's death took the daughter to the doctor who prescribed tranquillisers. Fifteen years later she was still on them, unable to manage without, leading a half-life of dependency. Her own daughter began to have problems, but not until these somatic symptoms were suceeeded in her young adulthood several years later by more so-called 'nervous symptoms' was the granddaughter given any help, and then only in terms of drugs.

Lest we should be in danger of attributing these attitudes only to men I end this scene-setting with a tale which points, I think, to the theories I have introduced being institutionalised. I wrote to all the women doctors in one wide catchment area suggesting that I run a dramatherapy group for women. Naively I thought I would be doing them a favour, that they might welcome the opportunity to offer such a space to women to whom, I imagined, they might be prescribing the usual tranquillisers, at a loss to know what else to do. Out of the twenty doctors not one replied. Overwork? Probably. Budget problems? No, this was before the days of NHS Trusts and GPs managing their own budgets. Too much bumph through the letter box? Yes, I can concede that too. But might it be just possible that these women, giving out day after day after day, at a level of which they were quite unaware could not bear to give to those 'little girls', their patients, what their 'little girl inside' had never had? A place for them to be heard, to allow their feelings expression, to be able to be angry and rageful and grief-stricken, to be able to grow by means of trying out new things, being creative, and having fun with 'mother'. To have a room of their own.

Having set the scene, let's explore some of the ways in which this relationship manifests itself in the female client–therapist–supervisor triad. In what follows the supervisor's internalised model is that of the six modes of supervision as defined by Hawkins and Shoet (1989). Although the client here is a wife and mother the same dynamics apply to women whose lives are not framed by those relationships. Feminist psychotherapy shows these dynamics at work in the lives of many women whose lifestyles and sexual orientation are different from that of this client.

THERAPY SESSION 1

MRS H. I shouldn't be bothering you, really, I don't know why I'm here. No, that's stupid, of course I know why I'm here. It's just that – well I hardly know how to begin. You see, I hardly know who I am. I know that sounds ridiculous, a comfortably off middle-class woman, what worries can I possibly have? There'll be people who are much more deserving of your time than me, I'm sure. (*Long pause*). And yet . . . Oh, God, I can't even tell you what I've done, it's so dreadful, so terrible. Whatever I thought I wanted for myself, I must have been mad . . . I sounded so sure when I left (*Breaks down, crying*). . .

THERAPIST Would you like to tell me what's happened? (*Thinks to herself*: that's not a very helpful thing to say – it's clearly not that simple. Somehow I feel I need to pull away from her.)

MRS H. I can't I feel so . . . you wouldn't understand. How could you possibly understand? You've probably got a husband and children of your own . . . (*Stops and looks up with a kind of longing at the therapist*). . . Have you?

THERAPIST Perhaps you feel very guilty about something. You're afraid I will judge you.

MRS H.   Yes, of course you will judge me. What else can you possibly do? (*Pause followed by a prolonged burst of crying*) Don't send me back, please don't send me back.

THERAPIST   (*gently*) Can you talk to me about what the thought of going back feels like? (*Thinks to herself*: I'm feeling this overwhelming sense of anger and I'm also starting to feel irritated with her. What's hers and what's mine?)

MRS H.   I'm sorry, I've got to go. I'm sorry to have taken your time. Please. I know I must owe you some money. I've got it here for you. I'm all right really. Please don't worry about me. I'm so sorry.

THERAPIST   (*Feeling a rush of despair from Mrs H. and the anger draining away*) But we have a lot of time left. Do you feel you could stay? You don't have to tell me anything you don't want to. You don't even have to say anything at all. But you might find it helpful just to stay here with me . . . quietly.

MRS H.   *looks at her for a moment and then looks away, gathers up her things, holds out some money in cash, looks around as if looking for somewhere to put it, eventually gives it awkwardly to the therapist and moves towards the door. She looks absently round at the therapist's room but appears not to be taking in whatever it is that she's seeking, for it feels to the therapist as though she is looking for something.*)

THERAPIST   Perhaps you would like to telephone me to make another appointment, perhaps you need time to think about if you would like to come back.

MRS H.   (*Quite distant now*) Yes, thank you. Goodbye.

SUPERVISION SESSION 1

THERAPIST   I want to talk to you today about a woman I saw last week. (*Pause*) I'm not sure that I'll see her again – she only stayed for twenty minutes.

SUPERVISOR   Well, perhaps you'd like to tell me about her.

(*The therapist is looking vaguely in the direction of the box where the supervisor's toys and objects are kept and at the pile of cushions.*)

SUPERVISOR   Would you like to work symbolically or through talking?

THERAPIST   It's funny, I feel it's really difficult to get started. I've got this awful dread that you're going to judge me. And I couldn't possibly bring myself to work with the toys today, I can't think why because I often do. (*Pause*) This woman's really getting to me in some way that I just can't work out.

SUPERVISOR   She seems to be stirring up a lot of feelings in you which you can't quite grasp. I suggest we go back to the beginning and you just talk me through the sessions. I'm sure we'll get a sense of what's going on as we go.

THERAPIST   Oh! When you said 'go back to the beginning' I realised that I don't want to go back, I don't want to go back to working with her and I'm afraid you'll send me back . . . of course, that's what she said, 'Don't send me back, please don't send me back.' Yes, she really is getting to me isn't she?

SUPERVISOR   (*Smiles encouragingly*) Yes, well that's probably a good sign that you're going to be able to help her but we need to spend some time freeing you up a bit. (*Thinks to herself*: That sounded a bit patronising, I wonder why I said that – a bit parentish.)

THERAPIST   I'll try and tell you what happened. The first time she came she started by telling me that she didn't really know why she'd come, that she didn't know why she was here – which she said in the same breath as feeling she didn't know who she was – almost as though they had equal importance. Then she said that what she had done was so terrible; what she actually said was, 'Whatever I thought I wanted for myself, I must have been mad . . . I sounded so sure when I left.' And then she broke down and cried. And then I said 'Would you like to tell me what happened?' and, as I said it, it felt like a formula, not helpful at all, and I realised I was distancing myself in some way from her. As though she might pull me into something and I needed to pull away. It was clear that she was finding it terribly difficult to tell me, so just asking her wasn't much use, was it? I mean, well it wasn't was it?

SUPERVISOR   You seem to want me to judge you; it may have something to do with Mrs H.

THERAPIST   Well, yes, that's true. Because then she said that she felt I wouldn't understand; that I probably had a husband and children of my own. And I said to her that perhaps she felt very guilty about something, in fact I remember saying to her, 'You're afraid I will judge you.'

SUPERVISOR   And what did she say?

THERAPIST   She said, 'Yes, of course you will judge me, what else could you possibly do?' (*Long pause*) I realise why I feel you will judge me. It's because I couldn't manage to do any sort of assessment with her, I couldn't find a way in. And she left.

SUPERVISOR   As though you couldn't be a separate adult with her.

THERAPIST   Yes, yes, that's it exactly. I couldn't do my adult job as a therapist, I just felt I was getting sucked in to something powerful and, and . . . in fact I've just realised that she took care of the session in a sense. She left, she took charge of the money, I mean she could have just walked out, or simply left without referring to paying me and let me sort it out. But she did all that. Yes, and it was funny the way she did it. Almost as though she was used to handing over money and then felt wrong footed and didn't know how to give it to me.

SUPERVISOR   (*Who has been monitoring her own feelings*) I can't help feeling that Mrs H. was terribly angry about something.

THERAPIST   It's funny you should say that just now, because in fact I actually started to feel terribly angry. I'd forgotten that. I suppose that's significant. It was after Mrs H. said 'Please don't send me back.' I said to her something like 'could she tell me about what going back felt like' – I didn't even know what she was so afraid of going back to, but I assumed she'd left her husband and children from the allusion she'd made to them earlier. Suddenly I felt this overwhelming sense of anger which I felt she was projecting into me. But immediately after I felt irritated with her and those feelings seemed to be mine. I didn't say anything, but it was after that she said she was going.

SUPERVISOR   What do make of these feelings now?

THERAPIST   I'm not sure. I just can't work out what's her and what's me.

(At this point the supervisor suggests that they work with two chairs, one to represent the therapist and the other to represent Mrs H. Using the two chairs the therapist re-enacts the session from the point at which Mrs H. has said 'Please don't send me back.' In the reconstruction the therapist suddenly realises why Mrs H. might have terminated the session. She deroles the chairs and resumes her conversation with her supervisor.)

THERAPIST   On Mrs H.'s chair I suddenly felt this fury against this man, this husband. I felt I could have become out of control. It felt so threatening, I suppose all she could do was go, if she felt like that. But then I suggested she stay. I still can't undestand that – and why I felt so irritated after the anger. OK so the anger's hers, but I'm pretty sure the irritation is mine. And I'm beginning to feel it now, beginning to be fed up with all this. It sounds awful to say it but in a way I hope she doesn't come back. What do you make of it all?

SUPERVISOR   I think that Mrs H. has powerfully let you know about the anger she feels towards her husband, but that she covers that with guilt. I don't know whether you feel that this is right, but I think she was testing you to see if you could take the anger, to see if you'd get swamped by it as well. I wonder if something happened to give her the message that you couldn't . . .

THERAPIST   Yes, you're right, something did happen. I said to her that she could stay, there was plenty of time left, etc., but I remember that I said, 'You might like to stay with me here. . . quietly.' As I said the first bit she looked up at me, and then, when I said the word 'quietly', she looked away and started getting her coat and bag together. And even before I spoke at all I felt this sense of despair coming from her.

SUPERVISOR   What do you make of it now, as you reflect on it?

THERAPIST   I don't know, perhaps that she thought that she wouldn't be allowed to be angry; she'd have to be with me 'quietly'.

SUPERVISOR   *(Who has now heard the 'despair' mentioned for the first time, which corroborates this feeling that has passed through her from time to time in the session*) I'm wondering if there is something here which is part of your material, maybe for you to explore in your own therapy?

THERAPIST   (*Suddenly feels incomprehensibly dismissed by the supervisor*) Yes. (*Pause. Decides to deal with having felt dismissed, but not by telling the supervisor directly.*) I think I need to say something about that here, now, though yes, it needs to go further I agree. When I was little I was always having to 'be good', not make too much noise, especially when my father was working. I used to feel so angry about that but I could never say. That must be why I used the word 'quietly'. And that's where the anger came from which I recognised was different from the anger I could identify as her projection. That's why I felt irritable. She reminded me of something I didn't want to be reminded of, and it was something about which I've got a lot of anger. Little girls should be seen and not heard, especially in relation to fathers. Hmm, (*she adds quietly*) and husbands in some respects.

SUPERVISOR   (*Who has been processing why she suggested so promptly that the therapist take her own issue to therapy before even knowing what it was, contrary to her usual practice of identifying the counter-transference issues openly in the session*) If she does come back, my sense is that it isn't just the anger she's afraid you don't want. It's the degree of the despair.

After a little more discussion the supervision session ends. A couple of weeks later Mrs H. contacts the therapist again and they arrange a time to meet. This time the therapist is able to conduct her assessment; the details she discovers about Mrs H. are briefly paraphrased below.

Mrs H.'s new client has recently left her husband and three small children. This was an unplanned move but she had had some disagreement with her husband. He had disappointed her in a way she had never dreamed would happen; 'he just didn't let the miracle happen' as Mrs H. put it, returning to this phrase often. Mrs H.'s mother had died when she was an infant. She had been brought up by her father who always described her as 'the apple of his eye', and by her nanny. The old lady was still with the household and Mrs H., in great distress, said that the nanny would be a better mother to her children than she could ever have been. She had married straight from home and had three children early and in fairly rapid succession. Then her father, now quite elderly, began to fail. Shortly after this her husband became seriously ill. After various consultations with the medical profession she was advised to take her husband away for an extended holiday for him to regain his health and strength. Their financial situation was not good, though her husband worked hard, Mrs H. asserted. However, she had managed to obtain the money, and her husband's condition improved. They returned home. Recently her husband had been given promotion. But something had happened which Mrs H. had said she could not speak of yet, she felt too confused. She said she would like to continue coming to see the therapist for a few weeks. 'Just till I get myself sorted out.' She said that she didn't want to lose sight of her mission to find out who she was. She brushed aside her own words that at times things feel really awful, saying she realised that what she needed was to find work and be independent, but she confessed that she found the prospect frightening. Maybe the therapist could help her with this. Well, yes, when things were really bad the thought of doing away with herself had crossed her mind. It wasn't serious, however, and anyway she'd be too frightened. She blamed herself for being a coward. On being asked about her relationship with her husband she said that she really had no idea about it. This was one of the things that confused her most. Sexually she supposed it was all right; her husband had seemed to think so.

On being invited to ask questions about the therapy, Mrs H. seemed to have nothing to say. The therapist explained how dramatherapy worked. The only reaction came when the therapist explained the use of toys and objects. She found herself pointing out the dolls' house to Mrs H., who had reacted very oddly. 'Doll husband, doll wife, doll children,' she had said to herself. The therapist had found it difficult to address this and had felt as though she was being let in on a half-secret. It was agreed that Mrs H. should come for six weeks once a week, at the end of which they would review her needs. Mrs H. was adamant that she would not need more than this. Times were agreed and practical details attended to. Mrs H. was clearly very keen to pay as she went along; she appeared surprisingly assertive on this point.

THERAPY SESSION 3

THERAPIST   Hello, do come in.

(*Mrs H. looks over at the pile of cushions and then away again, confused, almost guilty, and then goes towards the chair she has sat in on her two previous visits.*)

THERAPIST   (*Wondering whether to take up this look and deciding to*) Well as this is dramatherapy you might like to make yourself comfortable on the cushions or the sofa. Please feel free to use the room how you would like.

(*Mrs H. seems to be watching her closely and yet is completely absorbed in herself at the same time. The therapist finds it distracting and wonders why. A long pause during which the therapist decides to say nothing but wait and listen with her antennae.*)

MRS H.   (*Suddenly*) I came back because of the squirrel. (*Her hands are clenched tightly around a handkerchief which she now starts folding and unfolding absently but with great tension.*) I mean, it wasn't because of you, that sounds awfully rude, I mean well, oh dear there you are, I am a scatterbrain you see, I can't even explain myself. I mean, well what I want to tell you is that after I left the first time I saw you, a squirrel suddenly ran out from under the fence. Then it stopped and looked at me, you know how they do, they're such pretty little things. It was holding something in its paws and I tried to see what it was, you know, I just expected it to be a nut or something, but it ran off. And I suddenly felt so terribly disappointed. I tried to shrug it off but somehow I couldn't. I kept thinking of it and thinking of it. And in the end I decided I'd better come and tell you about it. And the last time when you asked me things I just replied and the squirrel went right out of my head . . . (*She tails off, almost sheepishly, and looks uncertainly down at the handkerchief which is now lying in her lap, crumpled; she plucks at it but doesn't pick it up again. In the silence which follows she looks up quickly at the therapist as if to see her reaction, and then down again.*)

THERAPIST   (*Who has observed the hand movements, gently*) I'm glad you came back to tell me about it. (*Pauses to see Mrs H.'s reaction to her words and then adds*:) Would you like to show me how the squirrel was holding its paws?

(*Mrs H. slowly adopts a bowed position, raises her hands and holds them out to the therapist, cupped, and looks up at her. Suddenly she starts to cry, quietly at first, then with fuller sobs, gradually she puts her hands down; they lie limply at her side.*

As the crying increases the therapist feels a wave of anger inside her. Again she has the feeling, as in the first session, that she wants Mrs H. to stop it, though she isn't even aware of what the 'it' is.)

MRS H.   I feel so awful, crying all the time. When I left I felt so strong and now I just don't know what to do.

THERAPIST   Perhaps the time for deciding what to do isn't quite right yet. Could we stay with the squirrel?

MRS H.   Very well. What would you like me to do?

THERAPIST   (*Suddenly feels stuck. Feels she's made a mistake but can't quite fathom what.*) You told me you would like to tell me about the squirrel and that was why you came back.

MRS H.   I don't know what to say about it. I don't know what to say about anything. I need a job, then I'll know who I am. (*Long pause. Sudddenly she gets up and walks over to the dolls' house.*) Why do you have this here?

THERAPIST   Would you like to explore it?

MRS H.   No. No, it's all right. Thank you.

THERAPIST   (*Suddenly has a picture of Mrs H.'s children in her mind. Decides to go with it.*) I find myself wondering about your children. Perhaps you'd like to tell me about them.

MRS H.   I'm terribly sorry. I must go. Please forgive me. (*She picks up her bag and takes out a brown envelope with the therapist's name on it and gives it to her.*) Goodbye and thank you very much.

SUPERVISION SESSION 2

The therapist has now met Mrs H. twice since she spoke to her supervisor last. She outlines Mrs H.'s situation as far as she understood it from session 2, then continues.

THERAPIST   I'd like to focus on the last session because she left early again. And I felt absolutely furious. I just felt so impotent. I know I felt in a muddle; she seems to wrong-foot me and I end up feeling totally inadequate.

SUPERVISOR   Do you think Mrs H. feels totally inadequate?

THERAPIST   I don't know, maybe she does.

SUPERVISOR   Let's hear the whole session. (*Thinks to herself*: I feel I want to get a handle on this client. I wonder why I want to 'get a handle on her'? It's almost as though she's my client not the therapist's. Are we fighting for ownership of Mrs H.? This reminds me of her father and her husband; she seemed owned by them the way it came across. Perhaps Mrs H. is fighting for ownership of herself . . .)

THERAPIST   When she came in she looked at the cushions but she wasn't able to respond to my invitation to sit on them. Then suddenly she said, 'I came back because of the squirrel.' Apparently after she left me the first time she'd seen a squirrel come out from under the fence. She said she wanted to tell me about it but the awful thing is I never really managed to help her to do that. She spoke of it being a pretty little thing and wanting to see what it was holding in its paws. Then I asked her to show me with her hands. She cupped them and bowed down, she seemed to shrink in her chair somehow, and held them out to me. Then she cried.

SUPERVISOR   Yet you think you didn't help her to tell you about the squirrel? I think she told you a lot and it sounded as though she needed to release something very painful which she associates with the squirrel.

THERAPIST   As you say that, it makes me think that perhaps the thing that the squirrel is holding in its paws is herself. The squirrel ran off and she was disappointed.

SUPERVISOR   Yes, I'm sure you're right and time will tell. I was wondering if it was perhaps the therapy session. She didn't know what was in it, maybe you were the squirrel too, holding something for her to eat, in store for her in the therapy but she didn't know what it was and was disappointed she might not have the chance to know; after all, she'd not given herself the chance.

THERAPIST   Yes, that makes sense – how will I feed her, and what sort of food will it be? I've just thought, she called the squirrel a 'pretty little thing'. She's very pretty. I wonder if she's been called a 'pretty little thing'. I suddenly wonder if her father or her husband called her a squirrel. (*Pause*) I suddenly feel terribly sad.

SUPERVISOR   Stay with the sadness. Let's see where it leads.

THERAPIST   (*After a fairly long pause*) I know exactly where it leads. It leads to a kind of emptiness. It leads to the point in the session where I tried to encourage her to return to the squirrel after she'd cried and then said she felt awful for crying and that when she'd left home she had felt so strong. I suggested she return to the squirrel, and she said 'What would you like me to do?' and I suddenly felt completely stuck. I didn't recognise it at the time but I realise now it was an awful sense of emptiness. And soon after that she said it would all be all right if she got a job. 'And then I'll know who I am.'

SUPERVISOR   Defending against the inner emptiness by wanting a role 'in the world'. I find myself wondering about her role as mother. Has she spoken much about it yet?

THERAPIST   No. Still, I feel I've got something to think about now. And there's another piece of work I'd like to talk about.

(*The supervisor is a bit taken aback by the speed of this but doesn't stop the therapist; she decides to hold on to her feelings and the process while continuing to listen to the therapist. To herself she thinks:* Hold on a minute. There's something that doesn't feel quite right here. I have a feeling we're re-enacting something that is part of her work with Mrs H. It's as though she's leaving early, like the client did.)

THERAPIST   And I really am worried about this group of children. We've had six sessions now and I really feel we need a lot more than the ten which the Children's Home has agreed. I'd like to talk through this and the ideas I've got.

SUPERVISOR   I think what you're talking about is connected to Mrs H. somehow. I don't want to stop you talking about the children's group, but I wonder if we might miss something important if we stop so abruptly here with our conversation about Mrs H.

THERAPIST   I've just realised that you said you found yourself wondering about her role as mother. In the session I found myself wondering about her children. And do you know when that happened? She looked at the doll's house and suddenly I had this picture of her children in my mind and I asked her about them. I suppose I took the attention away from her.

SUPERVISOR   Do you have any idea why you might have done that?

THERAPIST   Well it might have something to do with her role as mother but it might also be that that somehow denied her the child in herself at that point. Perhaps I wanted her to be an adult, responsible, looking after her children. I automatically related the doll's house to her children; I thought perhaps seeing it there, in my room, might have made her think of her children . . . surely she must be missing her children . . .

SUPERVISOR   Perhaps you are seeing her mother role as more important than who she is – or her struggle to become who she is.

THERAPIST   Yes. I think you're right. No wonder she left early. Maybe

I need to look again at some of my issues here, especially about what I still expect of women. She mentioned doll daughter, doll wife, doll children in the second session.

SUPERVISOR   Well, your thinking that the children's group needs longer has some relevance here, I think. Perhaps the 'little girl' in Mrs H. needs longer than six sessions. Let's hope that if she wants to she can find a way to let herself stay.

CONCLUSION

Whilst I shall comment briefly on just some of the implications raised by the dialogues, the conclusion really belongs to you, the reader, for in any therapy or supervision it is our own process which we must continually monitor and rigorously analyse. I invite you to chart your own way through these sessions, and by reading between the lines to monitor your own reactions and think about what you might have done in the circumstances.

You will have realised, if you are familiar with the play, that our client is none other than Nora Helmer, from Ibsen's play *The Doll's House*. Over a hundred years later she is alive in therapy rooms all over the country – or more likely, not in therapy rooms, but struggling to cope and understand what being her own person really means and the price which has to paid for this.

In the therapy and supervision sessions we saw the client's need and her immediate bonding with the therapist, which was so frightening that it had to be defended against. Issues of merger and separation were already strongly in evidence even in session 1. The push/pull of the mother–daughter relationship was evident, in the relationship between client and therapist, and in the difficulty of allowing Mrs H. free access to her child within without her feeling put down and treated like a child. One of the supervisor's tasks will be to help the therapist to refrain from compensating for her own unconscious envy of the client's needs being met by over-protection of Mrs H. and treating her like a doll just as Mrs H.'s father and husband did. Thus she has to support Mrs H. in her own wish for independence while at the same time supporting her unmet infant-dependency needs. This will be one of the central tasks of the supervisor, to 'hold' the therapist enough to help her 'hold' the client, to help Mrs H. be the child she needs to be in order to become the adult she wants to be.

We saw how the therapist fed into Mrs H.'s unconscious conviction that she would not be able to bear her, that she would be 'too much'. We saw how she looked after the therapist by leaving early, not being able to take the time that was hers, being meticulous about payment. Whilst the leaving early could have been construed as aggressive, which it undoubtedly was at one level, the supervisor managed to get underneath the anger to the despair and feed this back to the therapist, for it is this that the 'diminished' Mrs H. will need the most support with. Her fear of becoming dependent on the therapist, with all that will evoke in her of the early mother–daughter relationship, especially for Mrs H. whose mother died when she was an infant, is evident. It manifests itself in her wish to get a job and have only six weeks' therapy.

The supervisor's difficulty is that being a woman herself, however much she will have worked on her own issues related to her gender, let alone if she hasn't, they will always resurface as long as all three women are living in a gendered society. She has to be rigorous in monitoring her own process, particularly as it happens within the supervision session where the dynamics of the therapy session are often replayed as we saw in these dialogues. In this situation, as time goes on, the supervisor herself, at a deeply unconscious level, might become envious of the care and attention Mrs H. is receiving. Or she might feel that 'her daughter' the therapist is doing better than her and might unconsciously give out these messages so that the therapist has to guard against envious attack. She will become diminished again, and Mrs H. will receive less than 'good-enough ' mothering as a result. The ramifications are many; readers who have found this chapter interesting will, I hope, go back to their own study, or laundry, or playroom, or whatever room they are now moved to enter, and continue the dialogue for themselves.

REFERENCES

Chodorow, N. (1978) *The Reproduction of Mothering*, Berkeley, Calif.: University of California Press.
—— (1989) *Feminism and Psychoanalytic Theory*, Oxford and Cambridge: Polity Press.
Ernst, S. and Maguire, M. (eds) (1987) *Living with the Sphinx*, London: Women's Press.
Friday, N. (1979) *My Mother/My Self: The Daughter's Search for Identity*, London: Fontana.
Hawkins, P. and Shoet, R. (1989) *Supervision in the Helping Professions*, Milton Keynes, UK: Open University Press.
Ibsen, H. (1980) *Plays Two* (translated by M. Meyer) London: Methuen.
Mead, M. (1949) *Male and Female*, New York: William Morrow.
Money, J. and Erhardt, A. (1972) *Man and Woman, Boy and Girl: The Differentiation and Dimorphism of Gender Identity from Conception to Maturity*, Baltimore, Md.:
Orbach, S. and Eichenbaum, L. (1982) *Outside In and Inside Out*, London: Pelican.
—— (1992) *Understanding Women*, London: Penguin.
Woolf, V. (1928) *A Room of One's Own*, London: Penguin.

FURTHER READING

As well as titles listed in the reference section the following books might be of interest.

Churchill, C. (1992) *Plays Two*, London: Methuen.
Dokter, D. (ed.) (1994) *Arts Therapies and Clients with Eating Disorders*, London: Jessica Kingsley.
Houston, G. (1990) *Supervision and Counselling*, London: Rochester Foundation.

O'Connor, N. and Ryan, J. (1988) *Wild Desires and Mistaken Identities: Lesbianism and Psychoanalysis*, London: Virago.

Ussher, J.M. and Nicholson, P. (1992) *Gender Issues in Clinical Psychology*, London: Routledge.

Welldon, E. (1988) *Mother, Madonna, Whore*, London: Free Association Books.

Chapter 14

Playing with the perpetrator

Gender dynamics in developmental drama therapy

Cecilia Dintino and David Read Johnson

PERPETRATOR AND VICTIM

It is common in psychotherapy for the client to be a victim: of society's stigma, of family rejection, of economic or social injustice, of childhood or sexual abuse, or of psychiatric illness. Our clients suffer. However, some clients have committed horrible crimes against society, their families, or innocent victims: incarcerated prisoners, combat veterans, or psychotic patients who have become violent (e.g. who have killed their children). It is usual practice in developmental drama therapy for the perpetrator figure, whether super-ego, internalized critic, or real person, to be portrayed and worked with. However, what happens when the client is a perpetrator? What happens when the crimes have been against women and the therapist is a woman? Is therapy possible or even indicated in circumstances like these?

One complication is that often underneath the perpetrator is a victim, of racism, childhood abuse, or poverty. In our setting, this is exquisitely true, because the Vietnam combat veteran is surely a victim of society's rejection and a witness to horrible death in Vietnam, but he is also often a participant, or silent witness, to atrocities against innocent men, women, and children during war. He is a perpetrator underneath a victim. Many times his "traumas" are having killed innocent children. Sometimes the trauma is having raped an innocent woman. Does his searing guilt need expiation, or punishment?

Sarah Haley (1974), in a remarkable article entitled "When the patient reports atrocities," describes the tremendous strain on the therapist who treats perpetrators. Maintaining one's balance, clinically and ethically, is extremely difficult, though

> psychotherapy is not of use until the therapist is perceived as someone who can hear horrifying realities, tolerate natural feelings of revulsion, yet resist an equally natural tendency to punish .... The therapist must be with and tolerate the existential reality of the patient's overt or covert view of himself as a murderer.
>
> (p. 191)

Such toleration takes place in the context of the therapist's own self-confrontation: "The first task of treatment is for the therapist to confront his/her own sadistic feelings, not only in response to the patient, but in terms of his/her potential as well" (p. 194). However, this condition of tolerance should be differentiated from supporting the immoral behavior: "the therapist must align himself with that part of the patient's ego that now views his actions as ego-alien, and explore with the patient those factors that occurred when his usual sense of right and wrong gave way" (p. 195).

These highly charged processes challenge the therapeutic alliance in traditional verbal therapy settings. We will examine them in the free-play environment of drama therapy with its greater complexity of patient–therapist interaction.

PLAY

Play is a method of freedom (Johnson 1991). Play allows unconscious, suppressed, or nondominant aspects of the self to emerge without censure from the super-ego, internal critic, or social mores. The emergence of buried aspects of self allows individuals to resume their personal growth through the integration and transformation of these parts with the rest of their developing self or identity. This quality of play, often referred to as "sublimation" or "regression in the service of the ego," is one of the essential foundations of the therapeutic action of drama therapy (Kris 1953).

In the developmental method within which we work (Johnson 1982, 1986, 1991, 1992), the condition of free play and improvisation is central. The therapist attempts to create and sustain a "playspace" within the session, being an imaginal form of interaction in which both clients and therapist understand that what goes on is pretend, and is more than real (Johnson 1992). Through this mechanism, the inner worlds of the clients are revealed, as the therapist nonjudgmentally responds and enters into them. As in client-centered therapies, the therapist puts aside his or her own perspective and attempts to experience the world from the frame of the client (Rogers 1951).

What if this world, however, is not a sad and victimized one, stimulating the usual caring sympathy of the therapist, but one filled with violence, denigration of women, unbound sexuality, or hate? How can one be empathic with evil? What if one's clients are not neurotically oppressed by their overly strict super-egos, but having weakened or absent super-egos, are filled with heinous impulses uncontained by conscience or a sense of morality? What if in the course of our developmental method we come face to face with a revelation of evil? Does the basic principle of providing a nonjudgmental, playful arena of freedom still apply? Or should limits be set? Does the therapeutic use of play and improvisation have a limit? And if so, where is that limit located?

MORAL DIMENSIONS OF THE PLAYSPACE

We propose that the limit lies at the differentiation between evil and the *representation* of evil; between acting out by projecting unwanted aspects of the self onto other people in a harmful manner, and pretending to do so. This is similar to the principle of *sublimation*, in which sexual and aggressive drives are channeled in nondestructive ways (Kris 1953). This is also the concept of *aesthetic distance* (Landy 1983; Scheff 1979), in which aspects of experience are balanced between arousal and engagement, on the one hand, and evaluation and distance on the other. This is also the principle of *humor* (Freud 1927) in which the person takes on the perspective of their super-ego and consoles the ego that it is not really in danger. The playspace is therefore an interpersonal encounter characterized by sublimation, aesthetic distance, and humor, maintenance of the playspace is the fundamental duty of the drama therapist, and is equivalent to saying that conditions of safety and moral limits are in place. In order to maintain the playspace, the overt dramatic images must shift as the feelings and thoughts of the participants evolve, so that inner and outer expressions maintain their correspondence. This process of shifting we term *transformation*.

This theory is sorely tested, however, when extreme conditions are confronted, such as in the clinical setting where we work. Veterans can playfully, with distance, conduct scenes in which body parts are passed around, women are raped, or children eaten. Their playspace in a sense extends beyond ours. We react with a countertransferential gasp, in which our own spontaneity dies, and our anger is aroused. Our own moral outrage is evoked, and closes us down. Perhaps this is a natural process and we should trust our own moral standards to tell us when to place limits on the play. On the other hand, perhaps this countertransferential reaction indicates unnecessary inhibitions still existing within us, which limit our ability to enter the playspaces of our clients. When we stop the play or divert it, we prevent clients from completing a natural process of the transformation of the images, from horror into pity and grief, from crime into moral guilt.

What is the basis of our assertion that the process of transformation of imagery is a naturally healing one? Essentially, states of race or sex hatred involve a profound state of projection, in which undesirable internal states are experienced within external objects or persons, justifying their hostility or denigration. While all people engage to some degree in this naturally defensive process, perpetrators are particularly engaged in it. To the extent to which unacknowledged, suppressed, or rejected aspects of self are projected externally, the self is depleted, and thus experiences a deficit of gratification. The instinctual desires therefore are intensified in direct relation to their disavowal. Erwin Staub, in *The Roots of Evil* (1989) points out:

> It is very important for people to be willing to acknowledge in themselves impulses or feelings regarded by society and thus by their parents as undesirable: anger, hostility, sexual desire. People who do not acknow-

ledge these feelings in themselves tend to project them onto others and experience hostility or moral outrage.

(p. 74)

Thus racism, sexism, ethnic hatreds, and stigmatization of the mentally ill or homosexuals find their roots in this defensive process. The targeted external objects become a stimulus for the release of sexual or aggressive drives. Freud laments in his 'Civilization and its discontents' (1930) that civilization's attempts to suppress the instincts will only serve to strengthen them, leading to an even more frightening outbreak. "Civilization is built up upon a renunciation of instinct," leading to a "cultural frustration that dominates social relationships among human beings," causing "the very hostility against which all civilizations have to struggle" (p. 144).

In our drama therapy sessions, this process of projection is initially directed at the therapist herself, or at the drama therapy, and is experienced as overt resistance. This corresponds to the *rage* stage as identified by James and Johnson (in press). Soon, however, if the therapist can engage the members in the free associational process, the objects of projection will become imaginary ones. roles and images created within the playspace. True, they will be identical to the original external objects: denigrated, hated, feared objects imbued with the clients' sadism, sexism, or racism. However, unlike the real external objects who resist these projections or retaliate, the imaginary objects do not, and in fact are flexibly manipulated and transformed according to the clients' will. They become immanently more interesting and gratifying. It is here that the therapist will struggle with strong countertransference feelings about "playing" at hurting women or children. Nevertheless, these imaginary objects are not identical to real objects; in fact they are *both external and internal at the same time*, since they are projections into an imaginative space. We are now in the *shame stage* of group process (James and Johnson, in press).

As the play proceeds, the delight and lack of resistance from these imaginary containers of projected hate, who are beaten into submission to the clients' delight, create feelings of familiarity and safety. The impulse to play not only the sadistic punisher but the masochistic victim strengthens. The attraction comes from the covert recognition that the victimized role is the lost part of the self. As clients begin to play out these previously projected parts of themselves, they are given the opportunity to experience these shamed, hurt roles as internal objects.

Thus, the effect of the drama therapy process is one of *reinternalization*, of reconnection with disowned parts of self, and of reclaiming lost gratifications. This corresponds to the *empathy stage* (James and Johnson, in press).

Paradoxically, when the clients have achieved some degree of reinternalization, the dramatic process feels less threatening to the therapist exactly because the feared and frightening material is now owned by the clients, rather than forcefully projected into the therapist. Thus, even though the dramatic imagery may be deeply personal, regressive, or instinctual, the therapist will experience the session with greater safety. In other words, the feeling of safety is due to the internalization achieved by the clients.

Interestingly, as Peller (1964), Bruner *et al.* (1976), and others have noted, play serves the function of turning passive into active, for example, when the child comes home from the dentist and plays doctor. However, the considerations above also suggest that for perpetrator/clients, play can turn active into passive, that is, transform abusive and sadistic experiences into those of the frightened victims of aggression or disfavor. The underlying principle appears to be that a fragmented self has a natural tendency toward reintegration, and that once engaged in a process of free play, it will tend to balance itself by seeking out what has been split off or set aside.

WORKING WITH VIETNAM VETERANS

As the female drama therapist working on the inpatient unit of the National Center for Post-Traumatic Stress Disorder, I (C.D.) ran several drama therapy groups and led the play rehearsal group. The veterans are admitted in cohorts for a four-month intensive program including review of their traumatic memories, creative arts therapies, medication, education about their illness, and rehabilitation. The work allows staff to get to know the veterans intimately, and in general the unit functions smoothly.

Unlike many of the therapeutic modalities used on the unit, which are highly structured and closely tied to reality, drama therapy allows the patients to reveal aspects of their inner worlds and imaginations. In addition, these images are acted out physically in a dramatic form, though a patient would never be allowed to actually hurt or sexually entice anyone. However, the reality of the veterans' previous lives, combat experiences, and the depths of evil that they have encountered make the work challenging.

Initially I found working with these men extremely difficult and evocative of extremely strong countertransference responses. Particularly challenging moments occurred when disturbing imagery emerged from group members. They often asked me to play the role of a seductive female, a whore, or an innocent "Donut Dolly" offering sweets amongst combat hell. These roles often proved inaccessible to me in the playspace as they instantly evoked my shame and guilt. Members occasionally pulled sexual objects from the "Magic Box" (Johnson 1986) such as vibrators and soiled undergarments, causing a hesitation in my spontaneous direction of the session, and soon to a caving-in of dramatic structures and an impasse. Sometimes I overheard sexual comments being whispered among the men, evoking my self-consciousness and anger. At these times, however, the only way I could conceive of addressing the behavior was to stop the play and "get real." At other times I found myself unintentionally enacting behaviors suggestive of sexual acts, such as moving my hips, jumping, or swallowing objects. When I realized what I was doing, I became frozen and rigid with guilt and shame.

As I became more comfortable in the setting and knowledgeable about the veterans, I began to trust the dramatic container of the playspace to hold the play of images that were emerging. As long as a feeling of playfulness, distance, and pretend existed, I began to allow myself to become immersed in the scenes, whatever their content. Material of sexual or aggressive nature, especially if indirectly expressed, was engaged with and externalized exuberantly in the play. This playful exuberance may have communicated to the veterans that their imaginations were not to be feared or judged in this setting. Increasingly I noticed transformations of the disturbing imagery into images of vulnerability, shame or humiliation, as James and Johnson (in press) have reported. Sexually threatening material gave way to fear, sadness, betrayal or loss. For example, I was transformed from a whore to a humiliating older woman who witnessed their first act of impotence, or a rejecting date. After these roles were played out, I was enrolled more often in male roles: father, president, dead buddy; or idealized female roles: loving girlfriend, comforting mother. The atmosphere of toughness changed into that of a playground of children, laughing and crying. The sexual threat diminished as their transference to me shifted to one of seeking guidance and protection. In addition, once I had fully engaged in their play and accepted the heinous imagery unconditionally, the occasional acting out after sessions (usually by joking with me in the hall or making sexual comments in public) ended. My role with the veterans appeared to decrease their acting out of fantasies. I was no longer a threat to their fragile sense of themselves. I had witnessed their violence and their impotence and expressed my reactions. Our relationship was no longer one of attack and defense, pretense and alarm. Paradoxically, once I let myself play with them, I became an authority, even a respected one.

When the playspace is successfully created, a sense of increased flow, timelessness, and unbound energy exists. Players feel uninhibited; metaphors come forth. Their bodies are less constricted and more integrated with their affect. Laughter comes easily as does the ability to play out roles, characters and thoughts with a full commitment of the voice, body, and senses. When the playspace is weakened, shame-filled self-consciousness emerges, energy drops, and safety becomes an issue.

We believe that it is our goal to find a way to continue to *play* with the horrendous images that are emerging. Only in this case is the therapy enhanced. This requires training and a prior exploration of one's own internal world, with its demons and commandments. The therapist should ideally experience this terrain with a sense of comfort and familiarity. The following case example illustrates how during the fifth session the therapist initially avoided an image of a huge woman's vagina or rectum descending on the group. In the sixth session, she was able to open herself to the play with this image, with the result that deeper feelings of despair and longing were expressed by group members. The group consisted of eight men, all Vietnam veterans with post-traumatic stress disorder.

CASE EXAMPLE: BUBBLES

(Note: In the following case report, comments in italics are the thoughts of the therapist as they occurred during the session. Comments labeled *Reflections* are the thoughts of the therapist and the supervisor as we reviewed the group in supervision.)

Session 5

The group begins with much energy and flow. All members except for Carl are engaged in the playspace. Carl has difficulty connecting with his body. He often appears disassociated and has difficulty paying attention. He is a small man and functioned as a tunnel rat during his tour of Vietnam. He is often the group's scapegoat and target of ridicule. All of the seven other men commit their entire bodies, voices and energy to the sound and movement phase of the warm-up. The sounds and movements consist of ripping, cracking, pulling, pushing, chopping, kicking, grunts, strains, exertions. Phrases that emerge are "take that," "oh no," "not me."

Eventually an image of pushing something very heavy into the center is initiated by Howard. This heavy image is passed around the room with much exertion and strain. When the image is passed to me, I strain to lift it towards the ceiling. Group members transform the image into something that is now falling from above. The group offers associations about what it is. Larry comments that it is leaking. Rick suggests that it is leaking from the upstairs bathroom. Howard screams with much energy and laughter that it is all the "shit" from past weeks' groups. Chris steps forward to help me but the group's vocal cues and increased energy let us know that we are unable to hold it up. "It's dropping!" "Too late!" Howard yells, laughing very loudly. There is an overwhelming sense of release and energy in the playspace. Everyone moves backwards as if there had been an explosion. I announce that there's crap all over the room. Howard immediately jumps in and rubs it all over himself. Ned pretends to be casually walking and slides in it, falling to the ground. The drama therapy intern jumps in it. Carl cautiously steps into the center and eats a small piece, putting another small piece into his pocket – the group moans. Jeremy dances in it. I ask if anyone else would like to roll in the shit one more time. Ned says he really only slipped in and needs to actually jump in. The group agrees that I should roll in it also. *(This offer feels somewhat like a dare: can I really stand their mess? or am I being seduced?)* With the encouragement of the group, Ned and I simultaneously dive into the middle of the circle and roll around next to each other. The group claps and cheers us on. *(I have the image of mud wrestling and begin to feel shame and guilt. I clutch and feel this interrupt the flow of the play. The rest of the group seems to respond to my cringe and an impasse brushes over us like a cool draught.)* We awkwardly stand up and re-establish our circle.

Therapist's reflections

I am unable to play with this feeling of being humiliated. I am filled with a sense of shame that blocks my imagery, and I feel responsible for the constant breaks in flow. I feel like a whore. I see them as failed warriors, tainted killers . . . impotent heroes . . . Is this my shame or theirs? If it is mine, I shouldn't let it intrude on their play. If it is theirs, then why should I have to be burdened with it? I hesitate to play with the projection and transference. These sexual, erotic references are connected to the team of women who run the unit – women in real authority, their competent wives, their own emasculation. Perhaps I am afraid of castrating them, again.

Supervisor's reflections

From what you are saying, they seem to be letting you into their cave of horrors. Why should anyone want to go there? Do you want to go there? It's really a fairly sizable mess. How can one differentiate every detail and assign it to them or to you? The question is, do you want to be there or not? If you do (because you are interested in helping them), there's no way to avoid the muddy floors, the darkened tunnels, the decaying remains.

As I stand up, I look upward, as do other group members. Howard says, "What is that?" Daryl says that it is very big. Jeremy says that it covers us all and is very large, like an umbrella. The group becomes energized by this group creation and everyone speaks in mysterious tones, bodies swaying in a rocking motion. Larry says that it is hot and stifling in here. Carl says that he is having trouble breathing because there is little air underneath. Jeremy says that it smells. Howard says it's sweaty. We are all getting hot and feel stifled by the developing image. I feel a shortness of breath and a sense of dread. Ned comments that it is very colorful. I mention that it is oppressive. There is a sense of anticipation and suspense in the room. Chris cries out: "It's descending on us!" Daryl suddenly screams: "IT'S BUBBLES THE EXOTIC DANCER!" Suddenly there is a gush of energy and Jeremy notices a sequin falling from above which he reaches and jumps to grab. The group members all join him scrambling for BUBBLES' sequins, some catching them on their tongues like snowflakes.

(I stand frozen, clutched inside, as the unmistakable representation of a large vagina descending on the group materializes. I am filled with conflicting urges such as: to stop the play and punish the group, to join the flow and letting myself go. I imagine yelling "PINNATE!" and puncturing open the descending, engulfing plaything.)

The group members do not notice my paralysis as they are truly engaged in their own spontaneous play. Finally, Daryl asks if this is bothering me. Claiming that I am not bothered but unable to hide my disgust, I recommend that we put Bubbles and everything else back into the ceiling until next week. Ned says, "Don't blame me, I thought it was a flower." We end the group.

It does not feel like a good ending. I feel guilty and confused, as if I am Bubbles the exotic dancer and had just entertained the men in the group.

During the next week, Jeremy made a sexually inappropriate comment about a female staff member in a public setting. This was possibly an indication that the playspace container may not have been sufficient and that whatever motivates the desire to humiliate had not been successfully unearthed in the session.

Therapist's reflections

The feeling of guilt remained with me after the group, which suggests that I wasn't able to protect the containing function of the playspace. I wondered what the men were left with. Who is Bubbles? Had I encouraged them to open up to their inner world and then told them it is bad and unacceptable? But it *is* bad and unacceptable! Perhaps if I was able to tolerate their urges to humiliate and annihilate me (which is their projected desire to annihilate themselves) by allowing more play with the Bubbles image, they could then reclaim their destructive instincts and not act out their self-loathing.

Supervisor's reflections

You seem to be blaming yourself for not going further, yet you didn't want to go further. You ask who is Bubbles as if you are supposed to know. There is only one way to find out more about Bubbles and you avoid it. Why not? The answer is surely not going to be pretty. You are filled up with thoughts and feelings and you believe they are all unjustified, personal, distorted. Yet they are more likely connected to the core of the issue. Why cannot you give them a voice within the play? Your moral outrage? Your fear and warnings? Why cannot you say what is on your mind? Perhaps you believe that what is on your mind will harm the group? or is too transparently a measure of your own deficient personality? Frankly, my guess is that what is most on your mind is Bubbles.

Session 6

Listening carefully to the pre-session comments I pick up on a theme: women, authority, lovability. Jeremy speaks of his fiancé. Others speak of the female unit chief and the scandalous comment made by Jeremy. We begin our group with the usual ritual of bringing down the theatre curtain. Immediately upon entering the curtain (denoting the playspace), Ned looks up at the ceiling and says, "Yep, Bubbles is still with us, she is sitting up there on her trapeze swing." I look up and yell in a humorous fashion: "Bubbles, stay away from here, you are a sexist image and you make everyone feel uncomfortable. Don't come down here. Keep your sequins to yourself. We are not interested in what you have to say." I then ask the group if they think it is safe to enter the playspace. They all agree that Bubbles is too much to handle and we should proceed without her. Jeremy (the one who had made the comment), does not want to address Bubbles at all: "Bubbles we do not want to deal with you. You cause us much trouble."

The group warms up with sounds and movements and again evokes many scatological images such as farts, snots, wetting oneself, and picking noses. Eventually Jeremy yells, "Enough, I can't take it." I comment that I am glad Jeremy is here to warn us when we are getting out of hand. The group starts to play with things being out of control, laughing and begging for Jeremy to stop us. Rick once again pulls his shirt up and does a belly-dance in the center of the room. I announce in a circus ringleader's style: "Ladies and Gentlemen it's Rick and his magic belly!" Howard immediately steps forward and begins to rub his belly as if it is a crystal ball. "Look into my eye," Rick says, indicating his belly button. He goes to various members and they ooh and aah as they look into his stomach although no one will say what they see, even with my prompting. I say, "Hmm, I see something." Larry steps forward and begins to pull something from Rick's belly button. Rick gyrates his stomach and says WOAAHH as Larry continues to pull it from his stomach. Larry says that it is a long cord. Howard steps forward and cuts the cord. Daryl takes it and coils it up, miming how long it is. Jeremy steps forward and then mimes throwing it out the window. I point out that Jeremy just got rid of our image again. He responds: "Oh I am terribly sorry, let's replace it with another." He hands a tiny object to Daryl, which is passed around, shoved up noses, chewed, spit, smelt, smeared . . . Finally Daryl swallows it and then shits it out. He exerts much energy when he is shitting in the middle of the room, acting as if he is constipated. I yell, "Yipes, someone get the bucket!" We scramble to hold the bucket, yelling PUSH Daryl, PUSH Daryl . . . He finishes and he looks in the bucket, saying "looks like a lot of hot water to me." I ask if anyone else would like to contribute. Larry comes in the middle as we all yell PUSH PUSH PUSH, and he dumps. A few more people dump. Then Rick comes forward again pushing from his belly. He yells "I'M PUSHING, PUSH PUSH." Then someone yells, "THE BABY IS COMING!" "Get the hot water." Rick pushes and pushes and Howard and Larry deliver his baby. Larry calls it a PTSD baby and, as the doctor slaps it a number of times, says, "Yep, it has no feelings, totally numb, PTSD all right."

The baby proceeds to get slapped, kicked, and stepped on. Chris then changes it into a basketball and dribbles it. Ned takes the ball and throws it up to the ceiling. He looks up: "Oh no Bubbles has the baby." He pleads with Bubbles: "Please, drop the baby." They decide it is Bubbles' baby all along. Ned looks up toward the ceiling continuing to plead. Suddenly he reaches his arms up, screaming that Bubbles is falling from her trapeze. He falls on to the floor from the weight of her. The group screams and laughs as Ned pretends to crawl out from under her. Daryl screams: "Make her get back up there!" The group begin accusing each other of bringing her here.

"You're the one who invited her here." "Not me." "I want nothing to do with her." I say, "It couldn't have been me that invited her here." Carl asks if I was jealous of Bubbles. Jeremy asserts emphatically: "I DON'T EVEN KNOW BUBBLES!" The rest of the group protest, saying that Jeremy is holding back and that in fact he does know her. He smiles. The group then passes around accusations: "You know her more than I do." I ask the group what they know about her. Ned: She's a 500-pound dancer. Rick: She weighs 120 lbs and was abused as a child. Chris: She actually means well, I feel kind of badly picking on her. The group gives him a mocking OOOHHH, but a feeling of sadness arises in the group. Howard: "All I can say is she has huge tits and ass." "And what else?" I ask. "That's it," he replies, "Huge tits and ass." I say, in an exaggerated manner, "But Howard, you're objectifying her, what else do you know about her besides her body parts?" He laughs: "I don't know anything else about her." *(He is very energized by this and responds with recognition when I mention objectification. I assume he's heard this before.)* I say, "Boy, Howard you have a lot to learn about women." He very energetically responds and points his finger at me indicating that I hit the bullseye: "There you go, you're right, I do have a lot to learn, I always have this problem." Larry says, "I notice that she has a heart as big as her other body parts." I ask if Bubbles has anything to do with me but they ignore this comment. *(They seem more focused on Bubbles than on me.)* Then Rick responds by saying that she actually does work with veterans. Larry laughs and says that she works with each one of us veterans. Daryl says that she was locked in a closet for a weekend. Chris says that she has too many tattoos. Carl comments that she hasn't had any action in a long time. Silence. Impasse. *(Was he referring to a thought that I wanted some action, or to his own impotence?)*

After the uncomfortable pause we decide to get rid of Bubbles by sending her back up to wherever she came from. We stand underneath and send her up gently. Some of the men make a pleasing ooohh sound as they push her up to the sky. Immediately after sending her up Ned mentions that "the damned PTSD tree is still in our way" (an image from a previous session).

Therapist's reflections

I was encouraged when the men actually took on the role of the woman by giving birth. They gave birth to a numbed-out PTSD baby, that is, themselves. The objectified woman moved from myself, to an imagined character Bubbles, and then to themselves as a vulnerable baby. Is this internalization? Then they gave the baby to Bubbles: Mother Bubbles, with ass, tits, and vagina? I felt resistant enrolling as Bubbles. Wasn't she still an object for humiliation and rape? Was I missing her connection to their mothers who have rejected them? Would my enrolling as her bring the men closer to their issues and feelings of impotency and vulnerability? Am I afraid to look at their personal despair? And now that Bubbles is out of the way, what will we find in the PTSD tree?

Supervisor's reflections

You imply that they may be connecting with their feminine side. How often do these warriors get to be pregnant and have babies? How often do they belly-dance or are crushed by a falling vagina? I find myself thinking about climbing back into the womb: what better way to avoid the draft and Vietnam and adulthood and PTSD? Or death. What are you going to find on the PTSD tree? I think death.

The group then decides to chop down the PTSD tree. We chop and yell "Timber!" as it falls with a crash. After we run for cover we turn to look at the tree. We walk around it in a circle commenting on what we see. Eventually Chris looks closely and notices some deep roots. We imagine that each root extends to each person. "What should we do?" I ask. Someone suggests we can pull them up and look at them. I ask who dares to go first? Jeremy volunteers. "Okay, we are going to reach down and pull up Jeremy's root," I announce. Suddenly the group begins to laugh and giggle. I hear someone say, "We're going to pull on your root Jeremy."

I slump, realizing the intention of my dramatic structure has been changed and is once again eroticized. Partly because of my exhaustion from trying to keep the group away from this imagery and partly because I am curious, I say, "It seems I can't keep this group off one subject." The next moment is filled with an undefinable feeling. Then I quickly yell, "Let's pull!" We pull with much energy until we pull up Jeremy's root. Howard says, "It's very small." Larry says that he needs a magnifying glass in order to see it. Jeremy laughs aloud and seems to go along with the group's estimation of the size of his root. Next we pull up Howard's root. The group agrees that Howard's root is huge and very heavy. Daryl notices a wart. Howard laughs, showing some embarrassment at the recognition of his status as the biggest man in the group. Larry volunteers to go next: his root is described by the group as being long, skinny, broken and old. Larry becomes sad and agrees that his roots are indeed broken. *(The group seems comfortable and aware of the double meanings: both sexual and familial roots.)* They continue to pull up each other's roots. When they reach Chris' turn, his roots keep coming up. "We just can't reach him," Howard says. *(I feel this is another here-and-now reference to the fact that Chris remains outside of the group and refuses to let others in.)*

Next it is Carl's turn and he seems frightened and pale. The group begins to chant "Carl! Carl!" clapping their hands. He seems defensive, pretending not to care. "I already know what they're going to do," he says to me. "Go for it guys." *(I feel protective of him and worry that the group is going to make fun of his small stature.)* The group pulls and gets nothing. Ned says: "He's not connected. No roots." Howard notices that it looks like Carl stands on loose dirt. I begin to think he is going to faint or lose his balance. "Carl, it must be very difficult not to feel connected." He seems sad and agrees. I ask the group to help him back to his place in the circle. They all hold him and walk him back. He just stands there staring at us. There is a sadness in the room.

Next it is Ned's turn. He becomes very animated and stands in the middle of the circle holding his genitalia, screaming, "NO NO PLEASE DON'T TAKE MY ROOT, I NEED MY ROOT PLEASE NO." The group attacks him and we pull as Ned screams, gradually raising the pitch of his voice until finally we pull up his root. Screaming in a very high pitched voice, he holds his genitalia, indicating castration. The group shows great interest in his root. Members mention that it is very smelly, old, and mysterious. One member suggests that the way to analyze roots is to cut them open and look inside at their inner circles; this will tell us more about the history and the age of the tree. The group becomes very invested in this idea. Ned screams, "NO DON'T CUT MY ROOT!" Howard holds the root and tells the group to chop on the count of three. This they do, with Ned still screaming and holding his genitalia. Larry passes around a piece of Ned's root for everyone to analyze. The group describes their pieces as stagnant, not rooted in many places, old, going way back to past lives, lots of deprivations, centuries old. Ned seems sad. He nods his head in recognition of these observations. He sadly notes: "Not sure if it's any good. It appears rotten." There ensues a pause and a silence. More sadness.

I ask the group to put everything back into our box and send it up to the ceiling until next week. This closing ritual is done with a quiet, meditative, accepting tone and atmosphere.

Therapist's reflections

The sadness that I feel replaces any feeling of threat or eroticized energy. Could it be that their defenses have dropped? They have acknowledged their own inadequacies and vulnerability. I was in a room with men whose roots are old, dysfunctional, and decrepit.

Supervisor's reflections

There it is. Closeness among the ruins. Who would have thought that your journey would lead you here? The fearful imagery at the gates was there to scare you off. How much more grief awaits you as you go further? You have been a witness to what they have done to themselves. So yes, in a way you have destroyed them as they were. Who are they now?

Discussion

Gender dynamics are the container for much projection. Issues of power, authority, exploitation, desire, and insecurity find a welcoming arena for display within the gender interplay. In our experience this interplay takes place on several levels. The first level consists of overt projection into gender power struggles. As a female leader, Cecilia's authority was initially directly challenged by the male patients. This type of challenging consisted of refusal to participate, denigrating sexual comments, and gestures made directly to the leader that interfered with movement into the playspace. These behaviors elicited anger, frustration, and insecurity from the leader, thereby preventing her from helping the group to move on. This level of gender struggle requires the leader to establish her role as authority and guide. This is accomplished first by communicating her authentic and sincere desire to help the men overcome their suffering, in part by demonstrating her awareness of their suffering. Second, she establishes highly bounded task, space, and role structures in the session, utilizing well-defined entry and closure rituals that demarcate the arena of play and pretend. It is very likely that the men feel threatened, unsafe, and frightened of the impulses within their inner world. By defining the structure of the session, the leader enables the male members to gain trust and assurance of her capacity to keep them in control. This is very important as it sets the foundation for the playspace. The playspace cannot be uncertain, as it is crucial in providing a space for examining and stretching rigid definitions of self and other. Many perpetrators are trauma victims with feelings of profound mistrust. Most traumas involve intrusions across personal, spatial, or body boundaries. One cannot ask the perpetrator to visit his crimes and meet his injured self without setting up perimeters of safety.

Countertransferential desires to reject the men are helpful signals that a playspace is not fully in place and that the men feel unsafe and therefore will be unwilling to engage in the journey. There is a danger in acting out on these countertransferential feelings by humiliating the men, canceling groups, showing up late or pushing into play without establishing the playspace. Each of these choices can constitute a replaying of the abusive process the men understand. It is as if they seek to evoke a humiliating response from the therapist. We wonder if it is here, in this repetitive dance of patient noncompliance and therapist's rejection that many leaders give up on the perpetrator, deeming him incurable or undeserving of treatment.

The next level of gender dynamics occurs within the playspace. This level involves projections that are gender-based but less directly related to the leader. For example, the play with Bubbles contained imagery related to sex, domination, and violence, but now directed toward an imaginary object or person within the playspace, not the actual leader. Cecilia still felt intense guilt, embarrassment, and anger which led her and the group to an impasse in the play. However, she found that because these images were not directly related to her, she had some room to bring her feelings into the playspace and allow the men to play with them. This indicates that Cecilia's counter-transferential feelings were truly evoked by conflicts inside the men. The men were subsequently able to play out these gender polarities, including playing out female roles: for example, the men gave birth, belly-danced and held hands with each other. Playing with these projected representations of shame, self-loathing, annihilation, and longing allowed the men to reinternalize these feelings and feel less threatened by their existence. Simultaneously Cecilia found it less threatening to voice her own genuine feelings within the play.

The gender dynamic finally plays out on a deep level. The therapist is challenged to stay in contact with the perpetrator/victim while he feels the painful, vulnerable, long-defended-against feelings that he has hidden from himself and others. In this stage of the play Cecilia was able to tolerate the playing out of feelings of vulnerability and impotence, thereby possibly helping the men to tolerate their own range of feelings, from weakness and fear to rage and destruction.

However, as the men take back their own projections, the therapist concomitantly feels pressure to do the same, and so may become aware of her own personal conflicts. As a woman, Cecilia found it difficult to be with a man who is feeling impotent, childlike and needy. Her desire to protect his manliness, to prevent him from feeling small in her presence, reflects her own gender-based assumptions and dynamics in her family of origin. All of these reactions and feelings can find an expression in the playspace, coexisting simultaneously at different levels of meaning within each client and therapist. The therapist's capacity for empathy at this time is enhanced by her awareness of these diverse meanings, and appreciation, both humble and ironic, of the complexity of the human project.

CONCLUSION

This group demonstrates the process of reinternalization discussed above. The veterans initially targeted the therapist as an external object in the environment on which to project their fear and hatred of women in authority. As the playspace was developed, the veterans created imaginary objects of their projections such as Bubbles and the PTSD tree. They began to experiment more flexibly with female roles themselves, and finally were able to acknowledge their vulnerable shamed parts. The therapist simultaneously experienced a reduction in her countertransferential rage and found herself comfortable with the intimate nature of the play with these veterans.

This case also illustrates the importance of ongoing supervision to help the therapist achieve perspective on the material arising in the group. The supervisor can help the therapist identify emergent issues as well as to moderate the therapist's countertransferential rejection of the clients and withdrawal from the playspace.

We believe that the drama therapist can facilitate a therapeutic process of great power by trusting in the playspace as a healing arena. When treating perpetrators, whose use of projection is fundamental to their stability, tolerating heinous imagery is a necessary step in the therapeutic process. The recognition that the playspace is not reality helps the therapist to maintain her equilibrium in the face of her important task: to heighten her clients' capacity to acknowledge their past actions and future potential for violent behavior, as they choose to behave differently. This choice can be brought to life within the drama therapy, for each moment in the playspace is a choice not to act in violence, is a restraint from violence against the therapist, and therefore against women.

REFERENCES

Bruner, J., Jolly, A., and Sylvia, K. (1976) *Play: Its Role in Development and Evolution*, London: Penguin.

Freud, S. (1927) "Humour," *Standard Edition of the Complete Psychological Works* 20: 161–166.

—— (1930) "Civilization and its discontents," *Standard Edition of the Complete Psychological Works* 21: 59–145.

Haley, S. (1974) "When the patient reports atrocities," *Archives of General Psychiatry* 30: 191–196.

James, M. and Johnson, D. (in press) "Drama therapy in the treatment of post-traumatic stress disorder," in E. Irwin (ed.) *Theoretical Approaches to Drama Therapy*, Springfield, Ill.: Charles Thomas.

Johnson, D. (1982) "Developmental approaches in drama therapy," *International Journal of Arts in Psychotherapy* 9: 183–190.

—— (1986) "The developmental method in drama therapy: group treatment with the elderly," *International Journal of Arts in Psychotherapy* 13: 17–34.

—— (1991) "The theory and technique of transformations in drama therapy," *International Journal of Arts in Psychotherapy*, 18: 285–300.

—— (1992) "The drama therapist in role," in S. Jennings (ed.) *Dramatherapy: Theory and Practice*, London: Routledge.

Johnson, D., Feldman, S., Southwick, S. and Charney, D. (1994) "The concept of the second generation program in the treatment of post-traumatic stress disorder among Vietnam veterans," *Journal of Traumatic Stress* 7: 217–236.

Kris, E. (1953) *Psychoanalytic Explorations in Art*, London: International Universities Press.

Landy, R. (1983) "The use of distancing in drama therapy," *International Journal of Arts in Psychotherapy* 10: 175–185.

Peller, L. (1964) "Developmental phases of play," in M. Haworth (ed.) *Child Psychotherapy*, New York: Basic Books.

Rogers, C. (1951) *Client-Centered Therapy*, Boston: Houghton Mifflin.

Scheff, T.J. (1979) *Catharsis in Healing, Ritual, and Drama*, Berkeley, Calif.: University of California Press.

Staub, E. (1989) *The Roots of Evil: The Origins of Genocide and Other Group Violence*, Cambridge: Cambridge University Press.

Chapter 15

Dramatherapy and violence against women

Susana Pendzik

INTRODUCTION

This chapter summarises eight years of my experience as a dramatherapist, working with violence against women in different settings, countries and cultures. Throughout this journey, I have learned that, just as violence against women is a cross-cultural occurrence, dramatherapy too is a cross-cultural tool that can help to raise awareness, combat, and heal the wounds of this problem.

The reasons for this are varied and may be clear to those who are familiar with dramatherapy. They have to do with dramatherapy's ability to provide a safe *distance* from events which are, by any standards, too close; they revolve around the opportunity that dramatherapy offers for exploring the *as if*, to women whose lives seem to follow a predetermined, unalterable course; they relate to the discipline's capacity to bring forth a variety of *roles*, so that those caught in the cycle of violence can break away from the known and destructive patterns of abused/abuser; they stem from the *social dimension* of theatre, which brings the problem out to the community, thus shifting the focus from the personal to the social level. The *anthropological* basis of dramatherapy also plays a part by providing a flexibility in form and content that can be adjusted to particular cultures. From ritual to soap opera, choices can be made from a within range of dramatic forms, and material gathered from local folklore and myth, ensuring that the therapeutic component stays in touch with the client's roots. But above all, dramatherapy's secret ingredient that makes it a useful modality to help battered women, is its call to *action*.

According to Leonore Walker (1979), one of the psychological consequences of domestic violence is that it creates a chronic sense of powerlessness. In her view, many abused women feel they have no control over their lives: they are in a state of learned helplessness. Besides leading to depression, this feeling may evolve into an ingrained belief, a leading axiom in the abused woman's perception of reality, by which *nothing can be done* to change the situation.

The word 'drama' points the opposite way. As embodied by its Greek etymological root *dran*, drama means 'a thing done' (Landy 1986); and it is precisely in this respect that dramatherapy can be an invaluable tool to promote the unlearning of helplessness. By using an approach which by its own nature furthers women to *act*, dramatherapy accomplishes two things at once: it invokes those aspects of the self which are needed in order to move away from the violent relationship, and it sends a message that helps to consolidate a positive self-image in the woman – of being capable of action, and therefore of change (Pendzik 1992).

This is not to say that verbal therapy is inefficient. Indeed, as reported by support and self-help groups alike, sharing their experiences with other women has been for many the first step out of the violent situation (Harris 1980). Dramatherapy is not against words; after all, shared experiences in a circle is one of the oldest forms of storytelling. As they listen to other women's stories, some may be inspired to follow their heroines footsteps, or be moved to change their course of action.

I found that many approaches are employed around the world to help abused women carry the 'seed' of dramatherapy. Whether narrating personal stories, using role-play, or other action-oriented techniques, 'action' seems to be the key in the process of empowerment – for it is the ally of change. While words are not necessarily inefficient, they may be insufficient – particularly if they come in lieu of actions. When 'talking' takes the place of 'doing', words lose their power: they become reactionary – an instrument of the forces that oppose change. Dramatherapy does not allow words to stand in the way of actions, for it does not only invite active participation: by definition, dramatherapy cannot exist without 'action'.

The journey that this chapter embarks on is an illustration of the different ways in which dramatherapy can be used to deal with violence against women. It narrates the story of my own work as well as my observations of the 'seed' of dramatherapy in other people's therapeutic interventions.

STORIES OF BUENOS AIRES

'Lugar de Mujer' is an independent, non-governmental women's centre that began its formal functioning shortly after democracy was restored in Argentina, in 1983. It provides lectures, workshops and a variety of services for women. One of its projects is the Programme of Prevention of Domestic Violence, led by Lucrecia Oller, which includes self-help groups and legal advice to abused women, as well as a training programme for lay counsellors.

When battered women are hesitant to come, Lucrecia uses a metaphor to convince them to join the self-help groups. She says: 'It is as though you are terminally ill, and the medicine that would save your life is given to you at a certain place and time' (Oller, personal communication). She purposely resorts to a death-related image in order to stress the potential life-risk involved in domestic violence, and to shatter denial – one of the most common, and at times lethal, defence mechanisms used by abused women (Walker 1979). The metaphor may be shocking, but in her experience it prompts women to *do something*.

At Lugar de Mujer, self-help groups are 'open': women can come for as many sessions as they need, leave when they are ready, or stay long after they've resolved their personal situation. Each meeting is a mixture of women in different stages of the process. Some are struggling to get out of the abusive relationship; some have stayed with their partners, but learned that violence is not to be tolerated; others have left the batterers and are trying to get on with their lives. All of them are bonded by an invisible thread: they are survivors of violence.

A variety of action-techniques are employed in the self-help groups – including role-play and dramatisations. In addition, story work has been used for consciousness-raising purposes. However, my main focus in this section will be on the connection between storytelling and telling one's own story.

According to Oller (1988b), telling the personal story plays an important part in the restoration of the battered woman's *sense of personhood*. Although the experience might have been told before, it is the group's attentive ears and acceptance of its veracity that make a difference. Words take on another meaning when they are believed, treated with respect, listened to with the utmost care; testimonies are enriched by the glance of an encouraging audience. Lucrecia's account of this aspect of her work would strike a chord in anyone who is aware of the power of storytelling. It reveals that narrations are granted the status of a sacred text, told within a sacred time and space. Hence, when a woman first joins the group, her telling of the story has the cathartic flavour of an initiation. In Oller's words:

> She finds herself sitting in a circle with other women, who in a round, begin to speak about themselves, about how they have been or are trying to get out of the same violence she's suffering. . . . When her turn comes, the others listen attentively, respecting what she wants to tell . . . . She realizes that they all have been through similar situations, that every word she utters has a meaning shared by all, that every silence is a reflection.
>
> (1988b, p. 2; my translation)

Speaking about tales in general, Gersie and King (1990) point out that telling any story involves a risk on the teller's part, because 'in the process of telling we allow another person access to our knowledge and experience' (p. 40). Therefore, when we share a story we're choosing to make these contents 'accessible, public and available'. For a battered woman, the risk is great. To begin with, her story is painful and personal. The possibility of being rejected and/or misunderstood by her listeners fuels her feelings of shame and guilt. But more than that, she was told not to tell; she was given a script of silence that contradicts everything that the act of telling stands for. She was told that domestic violence should be kept a private matter to which others should have no access, and that her knowledge and experience are worthless. Telling one's story in front of an audience is a first step out of abuse not just because of the self-affirmative attitude it requires, but also, from a dramatherapy perspective, because it is an act of rebellion against the imposed role of the silent victim. It is a movement towards embracing a new and significant role, that of the teller. An encounter with this role is of particular value in the case of battered women, as it incarnates the part of us that 'enables each of us to know ourselves as someone who has a voice which is worth listening to, someone who can be heard and understood' (Gersie and King 1990, p. 32).

Advocates of group work with battered women refer to the advantages of narrating personal stories as a means of helping women to come out of the isolation in which many find themselves, and establish a framework of support where they feel accepted. In dramatherapy terms, however, exchanging stories not only creates bonds and furthers intimacy, but it also places each woman's experience of abuse in the context of a bigger story. Every narration is a retelling of one's story; each woman's experience is another version of *everywoman's story*. Once told, it transcends the personal boundaries. The story becomes a piece of the puzzle that makes violence against women a generic problem common to us all.

> Because she had some pairs of firm and friendly eyes to count on; because she had some ears that listened to the story of her life to count on; because she had two hours . . . in which she was a protagonist . . . and had to be the eyes and the ears for other battered women. That's how she came to understand that her case was not the worst of all – but rather like them all. That's how she saved her life.
>
> (Oller 1988a, p. 9; my translation)

SAN FRANCISCO'S DIRTY LAUNDRY

It had been a long day, a tiresome week, an intensive month, when the phone rang, and this woman at the other end of the line was crying for help. 'How did she get my home number?' As she unfolded in my ears the terrifying story of her life – rape, abuse, escaping, illegal alien . . . a daughter left behind . . . wants to bring her over . . . so that she doesn't suffer . . . maybe kill her . . . there's no other way . . . then kill herself . . . – my mind was moving painfully fast: I couldn't personally help her. Then the scene shifts to a slow motion: I hear myself referring her to a suitable agency; I see my hand sluggishly hanging up; an indefinite thought begins to take form in my mind, emerging as the woman's pain mixes with my feelings of impotence for being unable to help her. Suddenly, it rushes through my whole being like a thunderbolt: 'Perhaps the theatre group's next performance could be on women's abuse!'

'Teatro Mojado' was a bilingual, Latina theatre lab, based in San Francisco, that evolved out of a dramatherapy group I had led at New College of California. Its first play, *Papeles picados*, dealt with the members' experiences as Latinas living in the US. The group was envisioned both as a theatrical voice representing Latin women and as a therapeutic framework, where participants could explore personal issues. A further aim of Teatro Mojado was to reach out to the community, bringing theatre to segments of the population whose access to the arts is limited. In the autumn of 1986, when I received this woman's phone call, the group was looking for a topic for its next performance, and I had just gone through a training in domestic violence. I proposed the idea, and the group immediately and enthusiastically adopted it.

For over six months we explored domestic violence in various ways, from reading literature to interviewing abused women; from drama improvisation to a review of violence in our lives. Working towards the creation of the play was a fascinating – if, at times, painful – journey. As I have written (Pendzik 1988), the process that led to the performance of *You Don't Air Your Dirty Laundry* could be compared to a shamanistic descent to the underworld.

Theatre and drama exercises were used throughout the creative process, and the dramatherapy approach served the purpose of incorporating personal material. However, the fact that we were working towards a performance and not just sorting out personal contents through drama, instilled a focus that cannot be underestimated. *Most of the learning and therapeutic processes occurred through the struggle to give a theatrical shape to our perceptions.* It was in the constant dialogue between content and form, between feelings and aesthetics, that fruitful insights were conceived, as though the solving of 'technical' matters in fact involved finding solutions to the problem of abuse.

One instance will suffice. Using an improvisational technique of scene free-association, we embarked upon the creation of a dream that could have been dreamt by a battered woman. Soon the image of a labyrinth emerged, and with it, the Minotaur that was lurking inside. Finding a symbolic representation for the abuser was a major turning point in the creative process. It left us with a sense of accomplishment, of having found something to rely on, something with which to transcend the personal realm and move the problem to the collective. The Minotaur was also a powerful symbol that allowed us to express our anger, indignation, and total repudiation of violence, without turning the play into an 'anti-male' manifesto. The problem was not 'men' but the feral, inhuman, misuse of power and force perpetrated against women.

However, as soon as the exhilarating feeling of having found the image of the Minotaur was over, we were faced with having to find a theatrically convincing way to present it. Compared with the image's strength, any solution that the group came up with seemed either impossible to perform, inadequate, or parody-like. No mask, voice or technical device appeared to produce a believable picture of a woman defying and defeating a Minotaur.

When we had failed every attempt, a last-minute idea came to us. Invite the audience to participate! As an observer later noted, giving spectators the responsibility of lending their support to the heroine made them clearly aware of the situation (Olivarez 1987). Implicating the audience, then, was more than a technical recourse. The term 'public' has a double meaning, denoting both 'people watching a show' and 'representatives of the community'. In our performance they played both roles; and this helped to crystallise the notion that violence against women is a problem that can only be solved with the support of society at large.

Referring to the measure of success in a therapeutic piece, Renée Emunah (1994) points out that a dramatherapy production should not only concentrate on the personal achievement of the performers, but also aim at attaining theatrical excellence. In her words, 'works of art should be communicative, evocative, and engaging' (p. 290). Furthermore, she adds, 'a production that seems to serve the actor only is likely to also be limited in terms of therapeutic benefit' (p. 292). Though dramatherapy always encompasses an aesthetic principle, the process of developing a performance heightens the need to refine, transform, communicate and edit the contents. The invisible eyes of an audience push the search for aesthetic quality to new dimensions. Performers are brought into contact with the rough material over and over again. This exploration fuels self-discovery. Rehearsals lead people to acquire new coping strategies; they facilitate the elaboration of experiences because – as Schechner (1985) states – they are acts of 'restoration'. As opposed to commercial theatre, where rehearsals are made solely for the audience's eyes, therapeutic performance aims at maintaining the delicate balance between seeing and being seen. Performers are encouraged to develop inner as well as outer eyes. Rehearsals are a growth process whose purpose is to create as many bridges as possible between experience and communication. As Teatro Mojado learned, having a vision is one thing; finding a way of communicating it is an entirely different matter.

MEXICO: ANTS' NESTS NEED ALSO TO BE BIG AND CONSPICUOUS

In my stereotyped imagination, Mexico appeared as the 'cradle of *machismo*'. Shortly after moving there, I learned that Mexican women were neither better nor worse off than in other places, and found many groups working on domestic violence. As in most of the so-called 'third world', women's struggles in Mexico spring not so much from ideological concerns as from basic, day-to-day necessity. Feminism is not just a theory but a way of life and of survival. Lacking funds, and mostly without support from the state, women's thinking is by necessity more empirical and infinitely creative. The image was that of numerous ants' nests: women worked steadily and efficiently, each making her contribution. I found my nest in the Feminist

Collective of Xalapa – the capital of the state of Veracruz, in the Gulf of Mexico.

Though work on domestic violence was being done, I sensed that Xalapa's 'ants' were working rather in isolation, and that one way of multiplying their impact was to establish a training programme for lay counsellors. The *Programa de Capacitación para el Trabajo con Mujeres Maltratadas* was carried out from November 1989 to June 1990, coordinated by psychologist Laura Sotomayor and myself. Since details on the programme appear in previous publications (Pendzik and Sotomayor 1991; Pendzik 1992), my focus here will be on the aspects which were illuminated by the use of dramatherapy as the training's main modality.

People who begin to work with domestic violence soon realise they are dealing with a problem whose bottom line is *death*. The possibility that a woman might die colours the counselling relationship. Many factors exacerbate the impotence experienced by those who work with abused women. Violence has no logic: a woman might get killed because 'the soup was cold'. Nothing can be predicted. No profiles of batterers or of battered women are available. Violence crosses all boundaries: educational, social, religious or ethnic. A socialisation of guilt and shame prevents women from defending their rights, and the nature of the cycle of violence leads many to drop charges or go back to the abuser. Hence, it is easy for people working with abused women to lose perspective, become over-involved, develop strong feelings of anger and resentment, fall into the trap of abuse; or the opposite: become emotionally detached, treating women in the same manner as some surgeons, who come into an assiduous contact with death, and refer to their patients as 'lungs' or 'kidneys'.

Participants' attitudes towards the problem during the initial stages of the training oscillated between over-distance and over-involvement. Many felt they were coming to help battered women, emphasising the difference between *us* and *them*. Some assumed that they would learn about a population that had no connection to their lives – as if violence against women would only strike certain people, or as if one could be 'immune' to it. Those who had had previous contact with domestic violence at work exhibited strong emotional reactions towards the women – mostly anger and resentment for their unwillingness to change.

The training began with an intensive three-day workshop, aimed at making participants aware of the problem and its social etiology. On the second day, members were asked to write a short biography of a battered woman they knew. It was not our purpose to uncover assumptions and prejudices – which had been addressed the preceding day. We specifically requested, then, that she be a *real* woman rather than a fictional one. We wanted to bring trainees closer in touch with the abused woman's inner feelings, for which reason she had to be made of flesh and blood, then deconstructed, and finally reconstructed into a character.

The fact that it was about violence in someone else's life, as well as the writing mode, made this part of the exercise safe. Distance was drastically modified at the embodiment phase, when trainees were requested to read the biographies in front of half the group, altering the pronouns to the first person. As each read their piece, a change of atmosphere was effected: voices deepened, emotions flowed, silences spoke ... long pauses gave way to tears ... to recognition ... to insight ... to empathy ... to silence ... to new words.

One of the advantages of using dramatherapy with battered women's counsellors is the exquisite balance that it provides between experiencing and reflecting. Schechner (1985) states that drama has a way of deconstructing reality into 'not me' and 'not not me'. Empathy is a function of aesthetic distance. Entering a role means getting out of myself to meet someone else; exiting a role means returning to myself enriched from the meeting. Empathy lies in the breach between 'not me' and 'not not me', where I see, at the same time, how would it be if I was an abused woman, and that I am not her. The double negative operating in dramatic enactment has the effect of opening us to a role, while reminding us that we are not it. 'Getting into someone else's shoes' – the usual metaphor for 'getting into a role' – is a perfect example: someone else's shoes never fit completely nor feel as comfortable as ours. We are always aware they are not *our* shoes.

This is connected to the ambivalence that exists in role and role-taking. Landy (1993) mentions three ways in which role ambivalence is experienced: (1) as conflicting forces within the role; (2) as opposite and conflicting roles; (3) as an existential paradox. By taking on the battered woman's role, the conflicting sides within her are felt and acknowledged by the counsellor. This is the road to empathy. However, since ambivalence is hard to tolerate, some abused women turn to others to carry one side of the conflict for them; and often good-intentioned people fall into the trap. Questions like 'How can you stay with him after what he's done?' or 'How can you put up with it?' rob the woman of her anger, and thus of her courage to act. Through role-play one may sense the futility of these phrases, see the counter-effect they may have upon the woman, and learn not to take the conflict away from her. Landy's third point – the existential paradox – is the awareness that any role is both 'not me' and 'not not me'.

Role-taking is an exercise in developing empathy, learning to tolerate ambivalence, and being in touch with one's own and with someone else's process – all of which are indispensable skills for anybody who attempts to work with domestic violence. Role-taking played a major part during the training. It was essential in supervision – particularly in order to sort out conflicts with specific women, or to rehearse a variety of approaches. Playing the role of facilitator also helped trainees find, define and refine their personal style of facilitation.

The programme included work on five areas which I have found to affect most battered women: self-esteem, decision-making and autonomy, inter-personal relations, expression of emotions, and perception of the women's role (Pendzik 1992). Dramatherapy allowed trainees to explore personal material on these areas, while keeping the boundary between 'therapy' and 'training' distinctively clear. Dramatherapeutic thinking was encouraged by having participants design action-oriented exercises in each of these areas, which were first tried out and assessed within the group, then implemented with the women, and finally reassessed. Thus, the training functioned also as a dramatherapy lab.

SWITZERLAND: THE WOUNDS OF RACISM

Violence against women inevitably led me to the violence that we, women, inflict upon ourselves because of racial differences or any other expression of 'otherness'. It began in Germany, as the signs of racism became increas-ingly visible. I had been periodically invited by Agisra – a German organ-isation working against women's racial discrimination and sexual ex-ploitation – to give a series of four-day workshops to women working on violence against women with foreigners. The groups were ethnically mixed. In the first workshop, the growth of racism in Europe was the subject of our conversations at breaks. A year later, the topic became more central to our activities. By the third workshop, the racial and ethnic tensions among participants became intolerable: the women could not bring themselves to open up in front of one another. Racial discrimination in 'progressive' organisations became the most urgent issue to be addressed at the workshop. I decided to devote my next workshop to this problem. Two workshops, one in Spanish and one in English, were carried out in September 1994, sponsored by the Kinderdorff Pestalozzi, in collaboration with *Nosotras* – a group for Latin women living in Switzerland. The workshops were called 'The wounds of racism'.

Women from all over Europe were invited. The workshops took place near the town of Trogen – about an hour away from Zurich. The materials used were mostly left-overs or collected from the garbage. This was not just due to ecological reasons; it was also a statement about the scarcity of funds being allotted in Europe to fight against racism.

Structurally, the workshops moved from personal to collective. The first two days were devoted to personal 'wound' stories. Members began by making a box that depicted their ethnic identity. A modified form of play-back theatre that I have devised (which in addition to scene replay offers several dramatic elaborations of the story) was used to explore personal 'wounds'. The last two days were geared towards the symbolic and the collective. Huge, body-size masks of racism were made, and used to create a common piece. One group performed a theatre piece; the other a burning ritual. Though the process that led to these final works, and the performances themselves, were extremely powerful, the fragment I have chosen to share is a storymaking exercise I did with the Spanish-speaking group. The technique was simple: I provided the story's skeleton and allowed the group to fill in the rest. It went more or less as follows:

Once upon a time, there was a faraway planet inhabited by two kinds of beings: the Blues and the Oranges.

- Members had to decide on the spot to which group they belonged. They were instructed to get together, and, without words, to design a salutation performed by these beings when they met or parted.
- Salutations were presented, and subgroups formed, facing one another. Questions were formulated to establish the basic traits of each group. They were answered or shown by different members:
  The Blues were. . . . beings; the Oranges were. . . . beings. Here we see how Oranges express anger at each other. . . And how the Blues do it. . .
- On their own, each group elaborated a description of their society, as if it was a document for an anthropologist of the earth.
- Each group had to design a living picture – anything that could be videotaped by the anthropologist. Pictures were performed and documents read by each group in front of the other.
- Beings formed a line according to chronological age.
- The oldest beings of both Blues and Oranges were asked to join together and invent a 'myth' that explained: 'How did it happen that this planet became populated by two types of creatures?'
- Adult members of each group designed separately a 'legend' that ran among their people about their relations with the others.
- Young beings of both Blues and Oranges together were asked to create a 'vision' ('What will happen in this planet?').
- Pieces were dramatised, from 'myth' to 'Blue legend' to 'Orange legend' to 'vision'.

The result was so amazing that I took the bits and pieces and compiled a collective story which I reproduce below.

Bluorange (Zulnaranja)

Once upon a time, there was a faraway planet inhabited by two kinds of beings: the Blues and the Oranges. They were different people, both in colour and in character and customs. The Blues were soft and industrious. They lived in communes and worked the land, producing food and medicinal plants. They were meditative and quiet. Men took care of the household; women were expert in the elaboration of medicines. When a common conflict arose, they hung a flag in the middle of a square to call upon everybody and discuss it publicly. Their main problem was their enemies – the Oranges – by whom they were frequently looted, and whom they deeply feared. Often conflicts revolved around amorous encounters between Blues and Oranges. Strict prohibitions existed among the Blues on this matter – for they detested both the Orange colour and the vague brown that resulted from its mixture with Blue.

The Oranges were active and hot: they were warriors. For these passionate and courageous people, the main activities in life were love and war. They had built bedrooms all over the planet for love meetings between wars. Once a year they held a huge Feast, to which the Blues were invited, having to leave before dawn. A fighting spirit was essential for this society – whose number was far less than that of the Blues. Their conflicts were survival and reproduction. Orange warriors were trained to get war booty from the Blues. They believed in the Sun-God of the Oranges – in whose honour they danced every morning. When it was cloudy, they felt they were being punished, and lit fires.

An old Blue legend said the Oranges' precarious condition was a result of greed. There was a time when they had lived in harmony; but the Oranges wanted the Sun just for themselves. Then the Sun got angry, and made a storm that lasted days and nights. Plants refused to grow again in Orange lands, and the Oranges became dependent upon the Blues for survival, having to buy or steal their food. This was why they felt punished when the Sun did not come out.

The Oranges felt their right to steal was justified because of the cruelty with which Blues treated the mixed offspring – the outcome of love. Their legend told that they had lived together, until the Oranges found out that the Blues were killing brown children at birth because of their colour. For a minority group, such unjustified discrimination was a criminal act of violence – meriting war and enmity. Thus, in their annual Feast they made indiscriminate love to the Blues, and when the babies were about to be born they stole them to save their lives.

In spite of the differences, the same Creation Myth was told by the elders – who knew the story. It said that in the beginning, Bluoranges were one people and had one God: the Sun. Then one day, someone saw the Moon – and quarrels, rivalry, and antagonism began. They took positions; they fought; they became so divided, that life together was no longer possible. Thus they turned into the two distinct and hating enemies that inhabited the planet.

One clear morning, a group of young Blues and Oranges, worried about the future, got together. They had a common Vision: the restoration of the Bluorange society. They settled in a hidden corner of the planet, prepared to defend it from attacks by the Oranges and to survive the Blues' economic sanctions. They are there up to this date. Time will tell what became of them . . . And that will be another story.

Emotional involvement during the process was intense; dramatic reality was astonishingly deep. Group identity and belonging were established almost effortlessly. Although each group worked mostly on its own, the synchronicity was impressive. As I walked around the Blues' territory I heard a woman shouting 'Thieves! They steal from us!' while I had just heard an Orange proudly exclaiming 'We rob them!' The women seemed to know exactly what the story was before it was conceived.

Jennings (Jennings and Minde 1993) wrote that people can be broadly divided into 'settled cultivators' and 'hunter-gatherers' – an idea that fits perfectly well with the civilisation created by this group. Such expressions of shadow content would not have surfaced in non-symbolic interactions – at least not where they could be owned and transformed. When choosing the colours, I was not thinking of Sun–Moon symbology, but was just trying to avoid colours which have strong political, racial, or other connotations. The colours proved to touch an archetypal chord. Ancient aspects of social life emerged as aggression, anger, fear, discrimination; became incarnated in the symbols. The story was a mirror in which 'first world–third world' could look at themselves. I watched the face of anxiety of White Europe being robbed of its wealth by a flood of foreigners with a different colour; I saw its angry minorities becoming desperately violent. I glanced at the world reflected in the microcosm of the group, and suddenly realised that it was *us*: We were carrying out the Vision! We were in a hidden corner of the planet, like the Bluoranges, trying to restore harmony and communication!

ONE LAST WORD

Dramatherapy has the capacity to operate on multiple levels at the same time; and this is precisely what violence against women requires. A woman's personal story cannot be overlooked. Her own particular experience demands attention; but her story does not occur in a vacuum: it has a social dimension that concerns us all. Her story needs to be translated into legible symbols that speak to others. Through dramatic elaboration, personal stories become shared stories. Moreover, touching the archetypes is an integral part of healing from abuse; and dramatherapy does that naturally because of its openness to symbolic worlds. By bridging between levels, dramatherapy serves as a mediating vehicle that transforms personal into collective, symbolic into real, and vice versa – without neglecting any of them.

REFERENCES

Emunah R. (1994) *Acting for Real: Drama Therapy Process, Technique, and Performance*, New York: Bruner/Mazel.

Gersie, A. and King, N. (1990) *Storymaking in Education and Therapy*, London: Jessica Kingsley.

Harris, S. (1980) *Support Groups for Assaulted Women: A Working Model*, Toronto: Education Wife Assault.

Jennings, S. and Minde, A. (1993) *Art Therapy and Dramatherapy: Masks of the Soul*, London: Jessica Kingsley.

Landy, R. (1986) *Drama Therapy: Concepts and Practices*, Springfield, Ill.: Charles Thomas.

—— (1993) *Persona and Performance: The Meaning of Role in Drama, Therapy, and Everyday Life*, New York: Guilford Press.

Olivarez, A. (1987) 'Drama therapy and Chicano/Latino theatre: a mirror of expression and healing', unpublished manuscript, Senior Project for the Interdisciplinary Humanities Programme, New College of California.

Oller, L. (1988a) *Grupo de autoayuda: La experiencia de trabajo con mujeres golpeadas*, Annual Report, May 1988, Buenos Aires: Lugar de Mujer.

—— (1988b) *Autoayuda entre mujeres golpeadas*, paper presented at the International Congress on Mental Health Care for Women in Amsterdam, Buenos Aires: Lugar de Mujer.

Pendzik, S. (1988) 'Dramatherapy on abuse: a descent to the underworld', *Dramatherapy* 11(2): 21–28.

—— (1992) *Manual de técnicas de apoyo para el trabajo con mujeres maltratadas*, Xalapa, Mexico: Colectivo Feminista de Xalapa.

Pendzik, S. and Sotomayor, L. (1991) 'Training battered women's counsellors: a dramatherapy lab', *Dramatherapy* 13(2): 15–19.

Schechner, R. (1985) *Between Theater and Anthropology*, Philadelphia: University of Pennsylvania Press.

Walker, L. (1979) *The Battered Woman*, New York: Harper & Row.

Chapter 16

Jacques and His Master
Working with oppression and marginality

Andy Hickson

MASTER   . . . Jacques, what was she like? Describe her.
JACQUES . . . Lovely breasts.
MASTER   Bigger bum than breasts?
JACQUES (*Hesitating*) No. Breasts bigger.
MASTER   (*Sadly*) Shame.
JACQUES You like big bums?
MASTER   Yes . . .

Milan Kundera, *Jacques and His Master*

This chapter describes some of the processes gone through by a small-scale theatre company in putting on a production of the above play and providing workshops for a secondary-school audience. It was a new company with no public funding and a new pool of theatre workers. We had visions of an integrated mixed company trying to get away from national stereotypes and wanting to combat oppression with every encounter. We were confident and full of energy and a little confused.

PLANNING AND PREPARATION

The prospects were good. An advertisement was placed in the main theatrical job vacancy newspaper, the *Stage*, and with a Black Theatre Company, Double Edge. We were flooded with over four hundred applications from actors and actresses, black and white.

I needed to organise some auditions. I wrote to fifty applicants prewarning them that there would be a period of unpaid work where we would rehearse the second act of the play and then perform it with a theatre of the oppressed participative workshop. This we would present as a Showcase for potential funders and bookers (a Showcase is a special presentation of work where people who could either promise money or might want to book the show are invited to watch).

Thirty-five of the applicants replied and we auditioned them all. It was a hard choice but I got some good people: a strong, mixed cast. Jacques was played by Glenn Dallas, Master by Tony Cealy, Innkeeper by Sharon Hogan, Saint Ouen by Michael Bridgeland, Marquis by Naiambana, Old Bigre by Sarah Case, and Justine played by Juley McCann. The assistant stage managers were Lisa Stubbs and Hal Hickson, the stage manager was Helen Pringle, the designer was Penny Green and I was the director. Now the job really started! I was asking twelve people to work for nothing but expenses for two weeks in the hope of getting paid employment at the end of it.

Jacques and His Master is a play by Milan Kundera, translated into English by Simon Callow. The play is the story of Jacques and his Master who are travelling through life. As they travel they philosophise and recount stories of past love affairs, stories that come to life on stage. There are three main love stories, all of which are variations on each other. We get to look at relationships from different angles, and we also question why we might condone one person and not another for the same action. We are entertained throughout, while being weaved backwards and forwards in time. The past is relived for the characters and they relive the past. We are shown that each and every one of us can be oppressor and oppressed.

FORUM THEATRE AND THE THEATRE OF THE OPPRESSED

I wanted to mix the theatre of the oppressed with an established theatre piece. Most of the cast had no experience of Augusto Boal's work, and I was still trying to come to terms with the whole concept myself after two intensive workshops with Boal in London and several others with Gordon Wiseman in Manchester. As far as I could understand the theatre of the oppressed was based on the concept that theatre should be used for helping people to discover and tackle oppression in their lives, whatever that oppression might be. Forum theatre (explained in detail further on in this chapter) was one of the techniques of the theatre of the oppressed – a tool for spotting and combating oppression.

This was not a project for the faint-hearted. Was it possible that we could put on a play written by a white East European man, translated by a white Englishman, directed by a white Englishman, with a cast of two black Englishmen, one black African man, one white Irish woman, one white Englishwoman and one white Englishman. The stage manager was a white Englishwoman and her assistants were both English and white, one female and one male. Every one of the above was of strong convictions, high intelligence and complete integrity.

This play had to go through two main processes. The first was an unpaid Showcase and the second was a paid London tour. At the second attempt I had managed to get the rights to *Jacques and His Master*, a play I had wanted to put on for a long time.

We jumped straight in at the deep end. I had decided that the first week would be a rehearsal and blocking of the play mixed in with exploration games, voice and body warm-ups, talking and looking at what oppression meant to us. The second week we would concentrate on forum theatre and further rehearsal.

THE FIRST WEEK'S REHEARSAL

The first week's rehearsal began: everyone turned up on the first day! We shook away those initial cobwebs with a few 'getting to know you' games and a voice and physical warm-up. This was a start-of-the-day ritual which we continued every day – a different group member would lead the waking and warming-up session each day. Awake and finely tuned we then got to work on the script. Everyone had read the play and I wanted a common understanding. The first issue was its setting in history. I wanted it to be timeless and this caused problems. The general consensus of the group was that they need to know which era their characters were from. 'How can a black African man play the part of seventeenth-century Marquis and be true to his character?' My argument was one of integrated casting and that it did not matter whether we were black or white, we were all people and as people we were actors and we had the potential to characterise ourselves as any other person, black or white, man or woman. The group seemed to agree that there were not any black Marquis in the seventeenth century; although we didn't know, no one felt the urge to find out. I still wanted the setting to be timeless but was finding it hard to put across my vision. We reached a compromise after much discussion, to make it a play that was set a few hundred years ago telling stories that were timeless. We agreed that the black African actor would play the part of the Marquis as if he were white. One of the white actresses would play the part of Old Bigre as if she were a man. Jacques and his Master were played by black men. To me it was still timeless, I had this vision of two travellers, Jacques and his Master, journeying through time recounting to each other stories of past love affairs.

They were men and they were talking about women. The language used was often predictably male:

JACQUES   Right. Now, where was I?
MASTER   Your old dad bashed you over the head. You signed up, and eventually you found yourself in front of a shack where they looked after you and where there was this very pretty woman with a large bottom . . . (*interrupting himself*) Jacques . . . now Jacques, frankly, now, I mean *really* frankly . . . this woman – did she really have a big bottom, or are you just saying it to make me happy . . .?

(p. 68)

Was I in danger of setting up one of the very stereotypes I had tried to avoid – the stereotype of the *womanising black man*? It was too late to change and

I thought that if it was an issue then it could be worked out in the forum theatre session. The play itself was full of oppression:

- man against woman
- woman against man
- man against man
- woman against woman
- young against old
- old against young
- friends against friends
- and the oppression of language, to name but a few.

The play was brimming with oppressive examples to explore. We were ready to discuss any issue; everyone was allowed to have their say and nothing was brushed under the carpet. The atmosphere was fiery and this heat was channelled into the play.

We worked non-stop for the first week and as a group gelled together very well. Everyone had their turn in running warm-up sessions. We used a whole variety of creative action methods and games incorporated into the rehearsal process. For example: one game that Augusto Boal invented he called 'Change the President'. This is played in groups of five, one person being the president and the others the presidents's subjects. The others copy everything the president does: words, sounds, movements, expressions, and so on. They follow the president around the room mimicking everything until the facilitator shouts 'Change the president'. The president then becomes a subject and a subject becomes the president, and so on until everyone has had a chance of being the president. We used this game to explore power and lack of power. What did it feel like to be in control of your subjects? What was it like relinquishing that power? What similarities did they see between their character and the president? Was the president ever without power? And so on.

THE SECOND WEEK'S REHEARSAL

In the second week I introduced forum theatre to the rehearsal process. This is when the confusion started. After a few sessions everyone understood the mechanics of forum theatre: where a play or scene about someone being oppressed (for example, bullying) is performed to a group of people many times. The audience have to try and help the oppressed person (the protagonist) in the play or scene by suggesting paths that he or she can take to help relieve the oppression and by then coming on stage and demonstrating these suggestions. The difficulty lay in the fact that people could not quite get to grips with the idea that in the theatre of the oppressed we only look to actively change the protagonist who is being oppressed and not the oppressor. The reason for this is that the oppressors can look after themselves and, let's face it, the only people we can ultimately change in our own lives are ourselves. If we change our behaviour will other people change their behaviour towards us?

Forum theatre is not just about conquering our oppression; it is also about recognising it and trying to find ways around, under or over it. It is about sharing our ideas and trying them out in a safe space. It is about finding out about other people as much as finding out about ourselves.

The company were hooked although still slightly sceptical, one question being: 'How can forum theatre help a black man at the feet of a pack of violent racists?' I couldn't answer this and I still can't. For forum theatre to have any effect on any kind of institutional oppression it would have to be played in every village, town and city in the country every week of the year for years and years!

THREE DAYS TO GO

Three days to go and the nervous energy was at a peak. Everyone was scared stiff of the forum session. Forum theatre (see Boal 1992) is where the audience after watching a play are invited to watch it again, this time not as passive audience members but as active onlookers. Whenever they see someone being oppressed they should shout out 'Stop!' When someone shouts stop the actors freeze in their positions and the onlooker explains what oppression they have seen. They are then brought on to the stage where they take the role of the identified protagonist. The play then rewinds to just before the oppression and then starts as before. If the audience member had taken over the role of a child being bullied at school they would now try to find a way to stop the bullying by changing the way they behaved. It could be anything: for example, if the protagonist in the play had given in to the bully straight away and given over some money, the new protagonist might try something else, such as 'I haven't got any money today'; 'If you don't stop I'll tell the teachers'; or they might seek the assistance of some friends – strength in numbers. The possibilities are endless. The actors in the play would now have to improvise around this new plot but, very importantly, while staying true to their characters. A whole forum session can dwell on just one point in a play if you let it. The trick is to get the audience as much at ease with itself as possible, and at the same time to generate enough angst for them to want to do something about it. For professional actors who are used to staying within a set framework, coming out of this structure can be very frightening.

Our group's forum sessions took on all kinds of possibilities, some just for fun and some for reality. Would it work with an audience who had just watched part of a play? Would they be ready to come up on stage and show what they might do in a situation? If no one got up the workshop would fall flat on its face. What about violence? An audience member might get violent even though there was a rule of no *actual* violence. It might be a good time to bring in the facilitator of the workshop who is called the Joker. The Joker is in control of the forum, keeping it moving, bringing up the audience members, and so on. The Joker also states the rules. Each forum group sets its own rules, with the proviso of the fewer rules the better. One rule has just been mentioned, that of violence; another is that no *actual* sexual contact can be made. The only other rule we had concerned overtly prejudicial language. For example, we would not have allowed someone out of context to call one of the actors a 'black bastard' when 'bastard' would have been sufficient. In everyday life someone would not say 'you white bastard'!

TWO DAYS TO GO

The most exciting thing was that anything could happen. Two days to go and I took the day off to meet some of the people turning up to the Showcase. They were people who were promising money if they liked it! The actors had a day with outside facilitators, in the morning Sue Jennings and in the afternoon Gordon Wiseman. They had a day totally away from the play, playing with dramatherapy, telling stories and practising workshop techniques. The whole group found this day to be invaluable. Gordon was able to clarify certain concerns about forum theatre. Both he and Sue imbued the actors with a confidence in themselves that they had not had before, or to be more exact that they had not *seen* before.

ONE DAY TO GO

The penultimate day brought with it a technical rehearsal and a dress rehearsal. The Royal Court Theatre had loaned us the costumes. These final rehearsals are needed to make sure that everything works when it should, such as the lighting and sound cues, costume changes, and so on. We had all invited some friends over to watch and practise on. Only a couple of people turned up, but we did not let this stop us. To our delight it seemed to work very well. We were ready for the impending day.

THE SHOWCASE

The Showcase was due to start at 7.00 p.m. We did not meet up until the afternoon, when we held a group warm-up and energiser using techniques like group hums and a game called 'Salt and Pepper'. Everyone then went off to do their own personal pre-performance preparation, such as meditating, eating and walking in the park. I was a bag of nerves; I spent the time buying gifts and good-luck cards for the group. The tour rested on this one night: if we were liked we would get the money. Gordon had already agreed to play the part of the Joker (see above) in the workshop session; I had rehearsed the actors, and the play was up to them now. All that was left for me to do was to give a five-minute introduction at the beginning of the play and then be very nice at the end to everyone that had attended.

It started on time; the play was very well received and Gordon ran an excellent workshop. I was very nice to people afterwards and they were very nice to me. There were people interested in funding us and there were people interested in booking us. I was overjoyed.

FUNDING AND CONTRACTS

Now the real fun started. Chasing that elusive promised money. We obtained enough money to tour for six weeks or so, working on Equity contracts (people need Equity cards to work on Equity standard contracts). We now needed to re-rehearse the play and get the group back working together in a good atmosphere. We got off to a good start: I brought the whole group back (no one had dropped out) for a paid rehearsal period and a paid London tour. Half-way through the rehearsal was when things started to go wrong: people were taking days off and a friend of one of the cast knew someone who was trying to get funding for a similar project. They had not been successful and there seemed to be anxiety as to whether we would. People were getting irritated with each other. Looking back I feel there was a nervousness going into the unknown. The Showcase felt a long time in the past and the workshop session seemed a misty haze. The same question kept being asked: 'Will people really respond in the forum session?'

We were still missing a large four-figure sum from our pivotal borough. After much talking on the telephone I was promised the cheque by the next post. It arrived and was banked. No more money worries!

A new energy lifted us through the last days of rehearsal. We were ready. The day before the tour was due to start a letter was received from the bank. The borough had bounced their funding cheque and had advised all the schools in the borough that had booked to cancel their booking immediately. We were devastated. A sit-in at the council offices achieved nothing; they refused to meet us and refused to give an explanation. How was I going to pay all these actors and crew who had already worked so hard for no pay on the Showcase? I managed to secure a loan. All the places that had been cancelled in the borough were taken up by other institutions. The tour consisted of a variety of venues which included schools, colleges, youth clubs, theatres and a prison.

THE FIRST PERFORMANCE AND WORKSHOP

The first performance and workshop was at a school in Waltham Forest. We had a mixed audience of 100 people who were aged 14 and 15 years. They loved the play and they were really enthusiastic about the workshop. It was the largest forum theatre workshop I had run and I was terrified. Once it started it seemed to be over in seconds. One memorable moment came when a loud and seemingly violent young man made an intervention about the way Saint Ouen treated a lady friend. He came up on the stage and took the place of the lady friend (very surprising for a young man to take on a female role in front of his mates). He then proceeded to give Saint Ouen a verbal diatribe, the like of which you rarely see. He reduced Saint Ouen to a quivering wreck. There was no actual violence but it seemed as though it could explode at any moment. The intervention ended when it was obvious that Saint Ouen had no answers left, and the audience cheered and clapped as did the other actors. The actor who was playing Saint Ouen and the young man shook hands and they both talked about not taking it personally; they were both actors in a scene (the actor revealed to me after the workshop that he had never been so scared in all his life). I was told by the Head of Drama afterwards that students who often contributed nothing in class were the ones who were making the interventions. She wrote to me a week later that her classes had done some further work with some of our techniques and that the whole group had thoroughly enjoyed both performance and workshop and were enthralled at participating in the action.

This response was repeated in venue after venue. Each workshop tended to have different themes as each group of people would pick up on different things in the play, but each had the desired effect of showing the mechanics of forum theatre and getting people to think about issues in their lives.

THE RELUCTANT AUDIENCE

After about five days we performed in the early evening at a youth club. It had been billed as a big audience with people from other youth clubs in the area being shipped in by minibus. No one turned up. We had no audience. The youth leader ran around frantically making telephone calls to bring in the audience. We said we would wait. One hour later we still had no audience and the cast were getting very restless. A few young men had drifted in and were playing pool in the corner but they had no interest in watching a play let alone a workshop. We gave the youth leader another half an hour and said that we would perform the second act of the play with a condensed workshop. This seemed to satisfy him, and eventually, one and a half hours late with a reluctant audience of about twenty young black men and women, we started. The actors did extremely well despite the constant coughing and people getting up to go to the toilet or to play pool. They got through a good performance and now it was my turn. My nightmare was happening. No one was interested in joining in. I tried every trick I knew but to no avail. It got to the point where the audience was barracking me. 'Who do you think you are to try and get us to do this?' said a white woman at the back. I made the fatal mistake of engaging in an argument with her. I was on a road to nowhere, alone and no way out. I then apologised to the group for not getting this session to work, but asked if they would bear with me while I tried one last thing. I think the argument must have sparked some interest in them because they said yes.

I took the actors on a side and asked them what they thought about improvising some short scenes on topics that I would get the audience to suggest. They agreed and the audience also liked the idea. We started working on some issues of racism, such as scenes showing racial attacks. The interventions started coming thick and fast; everyone wanted to get up and have a go at the racist. I was so excited to have finally got the workshop moving that I forgot totally about direction. What was happening in that session? We were seeing person after person coming up and reacting violently to racism. We were seeing black people being angry. The youth leader pointed this out to us afterwards and said he had been unhappy with the whole affair, particularly the fact that people had only shown this violent energy: why couldn't we have steered it to show a more positive side of black people? I understood what he meant, though a part of me was still pleased that I had got any reaction at all . . . How easy it was for us to slip into a way of working that could sometimes lead us to oppress the very people we were trying to help.

The whole group was in very low spirits after this venue, and the next one threatened to follow a similar vein. We had borrowed three video cameras and planned to record the next show and workshop. We made one fatal error: we forgot to check with the school whether they minded about our recording. By the time the audience came in all the cameras were set up. The show went ahead and was watched with much delight. Then the workshop started. We played a lot of games with the young people, and were about to start on the forum when a strange atmosphere came over the place: no one would say a word. The drama teacher, quite irritated, asked about the cameras. It was at that point that I realised the school had not been asked and I was extremely embarrassed. I apologised profusely and offered to turn them off. She then said that she was just about to stop everything and ask us to go but she had changed her mind and if the students were happy to be filmed then we could carry on. The forum was excellent with some brilliant interventions. We were back saved from the brink and on the rails once again.

THE FINAL WEEK

With everything going well we had the last week of the tour left. The shows and workshops were getting really good responses. The pressures we were feeling were from each other. The group started becoming very irritated with each other. Some people refused to travel in the minibus and made their own way there, and others were late every day and thus made the others wait. People's habits or inconsistencies seemed to be made into big problems. This wrangling carried on till the end of the tour but nobody let it affect their work. In fact I am sure that some people used it to help their performances. Whatever they did each performance was electric.

One of the last performances was in a newly built high security prison. It was a frightening place to be in. We had to sign for security passes and go through locked door after locked door after locked door. One of the actors had signed himself in as Marlon Brando. He really thought he was going to be stopped coming out and put back inside for trying to escape! He wasn't. The prisoners, about fifty of them, watched the play two feet away from the edge of the acting area. No one had performed in a prison before but they gave the best performance of the tour. The audience joined in, shouting encouragement to the characters (as one would watching a football match) and telling them whether they should do this or that. The applause was explosive. Unfortunately we were not allowed to run a forum theatre workshop; we were told that it put us at too much risk. So we held a question and answer session instead and talked to the prisoners about oppression and what it meant to be oppressed. The discussion (naturally) centred around the oppression of captivity and prisoners in for sexual offences. They liked it and we were a success.

This way of working, which includes both performances and workshops where the outcome is usually unpredictable, can often cause a lot of stress as well as binding the actors together. At the end of the tour we were ready to separate and we celebrated with a bit of a party which no one seemed to stay at for long. People wanted to get out of each other's pockets. We had had a good run and now it was time for rest. Most people kept in some kind of contact and I have worked with two of the black actors again on many projects. One in particular was a forum theatre workshop tour of England. We came up against the same barriers as before: the establishment seem to be scared of the theatre of the oppressed, and funding therefore was very difficult to obtain. Our audiences, on the other hand, could not get enough. A black man and a white man were working together performing to multiracial groups, all white or all black groups, to mixed-gender groups and single-sex schools. We were getting positive responses all the time. It was as though people suddenly felt they had *permission* to be able to say or do what they thought and not what someone else had told them to do. People learned, too. They found a new way to explore concepts; they recognised that others also had their point of view. Everything that came out of these workshops seemed to be constructive and a pleasure to be involved in for all concerned.

CONCLUSION

In this chapter I have tried to give the reader an overview of how one group worked and coped together over several months. Our play was well received and the workshops were liked by most participants. Was it a success? Yes, zin many ways it was. We had fulfilled our aim of exploring oppression and had managed to pass on the concept of the theatre of the oppressed to quite a lot of people. Several obstacles (some of our own making) had been put in our way and we overcame them; nothing, it seemed, would let this project die. Various projects have since grown out of *Jacques and His Master*, in particular a national forum theatre tour, Invisible Theatre projects and a new play on bullying.

ACKNOWLEDGEMENTS

I would like to thank the following people for their hard work and support on this project: Michael Bridgeland, Simon Callow, Sarah Case, Tony Cealy, Tony Chapman, Glenn Dallas, Lorna DeSmitt, Norman Goodman, Penelope Green, Hal Hickson, Ros Hickson, Sharon Hogan, Sue Jennings, Juley McCann, Naiambana, Helen Pringle, Hilary Renwick, Lisa Stubbs and Gordon Wiseman.

REFERENCES AND FURTHER READING

Boal, A. (1992) *Games for Actors and Non-Actors*, London: Routledge.
Hickson, A. (1995) *Creative Action Methods in Groupwork*, Biscester, UK: Winslow Press.
Kundera, M. (1986) *Jacques and His Master* (translated by S. Callow), London: Faber.

Chapter 17

Different therefore equal?

Dramatherapy and frame analysis with a learning disabled man

Martin Gill

> We live in a system built on illusions and when we put forth our own perceptions, we're told we don't understand reality.
>
> Anne Wilson Schaef

INTRODUCTION

In this chapter I set out to explore some of the value systems that may be operating between therapist, client and social agency, in the context of a social services dramatherapy practice for people with learning difficulty-mental handicap ('people with learning differences' as I shall call them).

I describe how a combination of drawing, masks and role work were explored with a man who may have had communication problems in relation to his absent father I explain how erving Goffman's 'frame analysis' (1974) assisted my understanding of our experience together, and helped me to clarify its otherwise ambiguous meaning in relation to occupation and gender issues. I also refer to D.W. Winnicott and the importance of play in the facilitative relationship between adult client and therapist.

SETTING THE SCENE

Although I do not believe that dramatherapy sets out to be a political process, it must operate within a political system. [But see also Part IV – Ed.] The State, through its penal institutions and relief agencies – health and social services – is one of the main employers of arts therapists in this country. Within such a framework dramatherapy, like any specialism, can be used for good or ill. It can be used as a means to facilitate self-discovery and self-expression, or as a means to impose control or to prescribe 'correct' behaviour.

For the past eight years I have offered a community-based dramatherapy service to people with learning differences as part of a social services department. During this time I have learned many lessons about my self and my culture from the people with whom I work and play. In this chapter I want to share some of these experiences with you.

I believe it to be a great injustice that people who have so-called 'learning difficulties/mental handicap' have been deliberately separated from the rest of society; thus to participate in a process of change which seeks to reinstate such people to their 'valid' rather than 'invalid' status in society has been my main preoccupation over the past ten years. We live in a society where people of different abilities, ages and gender have at times been socialised into accepting limitations of their fullest expression and potential. Dramatherapy as an enabling, transformative medium counteracts this process, accepting communication for what it is in a non-repressive way.

Any understanding of an individual's behaviour in a socio-political or philosophical context is complex and always relative to the perspective of the observer. I therefore present Goffman's frame analysis as a multilayered map which allows us to interpret or experience the world of human interaction in a dynamic way. Such 'framing' and 'reframing' approaches are common to several forms of therapy including NLP (Neuro-Linguistic Programming) or Process-Oriented Psychology. It is not my intention in this chapter, however, to explore these disciplines. Nor am I primarily concerned here with Goffman's earlier dramaturgical approach to human behaviour. Drama-therapist Brenda Meldrum (1994) has already provided an excellent introduction to this approach in her chapter 'A role model of dramatherapy and its application with individuals and groups'.

FRAME ANALYSIS AND ERVING GOFFMAN

In his later work, Goffman himself played down earlier theatrical role metaphors, realising that life was far richer than a series of roles and parts played out by actors. He eventually sided with his critics who argued that life was not a metaphor for theatre 'all the world's a stage', but rather theatre was a metaphor for life.

Goffman sees the dramaturgical metaphor as a stepping-stone to a more complex analysis. He believes in his early work that as social beings we know and define ourselves and our roles in relation to our interactions with others (Goffman 1956). How we value ourselves is influenced to a large extent by how an 'audience' (others) values our performance of roles in life. In this early work Goffman indicates that many individuals seek to maintain a 'status quo' through an allegiance to power relations between individuals within a culture even when it is not in their own or other's best interest to do so. Opportunities to step outside of such a complex system to gain a new perspective or discover a new role are few and far between. It is in this context that I believe dramatherapy makes its contribution.

In his later work Goffman shows that complexities of social life can be understood when we place different 'frames' of reality around them. When we see someone act or behave in a certain way we cannot decipher its meaning until we install assumptions about what we have seen. For example, when we see an old person fall and hurt themselves in the street, we may be appalled. Another time someone may see the 'US President slip on the steps of the Whitehouse and find it hilariously funny' (Goffman 1974).

Goffman further defined 'frame analysis' as an examination of 'the organisation of experience', and a 'frame' as a principle of organisation that defines a situation (1974, p. 11). Social interaction is made meaningful by frames, the most fundamental of which Goffman calls 'primary frameworks'. There are two kinds of primary framework: a 'natural' and a 'social' framework. Natural frameworks define situations in terms of physical events that are unguided by human hands, such as cloud formations or tidal flow (p. 22). By contrast social frameworks make sense of events in terms of human intervention. Goffman simplified these interactions to five primary assumption 'frames' of social reality:

- *make-believe*: observers and participants are aware that this reality is short term and 'playful'
- *contests*: competitive and cooperative games
- *ceremonials*: customs made up of the officials and the officiated
- *technical redoing*: exhibitions and roles are practised and maintained in a pseudo reality
- *regrounding*: here an ambiguity of motives is accepted and serious frames can be turned into unserious ones; for examples, the dealer employed in a casino plays a pseudo role of a gambler to keep real gamblers motivated.

Goffman saw that, rather than operating independently of each other, these five frames are 'laminated' like glass sheets on to each other, making up complex layers or 'doorways' of human assumptions through which we see and understand, or rather misunderstand, each other. When we recognise these primary doors, says Goffman, we find 'keys' through which the whole mass of human activity can be observed and placed into context (1977).

Goffman states that we transcend any constraints of primary frameworks when our expectations about them are unhinged. This is particularly so in 'make-believe', where reality becomes pliable.

It is my belief that dramatherapy seen in the context of Goffman's 'make-believe' frame enables us to see how such an approach is an integral, yet overlooked, part of human interaction. Make-believe allows us to transcend over-identification with a narrow view of reality or with such limitations imposed on us by others. It is in the context of this idea that I wish to describe gender issues as part of my work with a man with a learning difference who, to ensure confidentiality, I shall call Thomas.

THOMAS

I first met Thomas in 1983 in a North Wales adult training centre. He was a large man, aged about 32 years, with a face like the actor Jack Nicolson. He was operating an industrial staple machine to produce paper plant pots for the market garden business. He looked up from his work, smiled and gestured to the pile of a hundred or so finished pots with a sweep of his open hand, and said, in a long-drawn-out, husky accent, 'See?' He then turned back to what he had been doing as if the visit of an interested, gawking stranger was a commonplace occurrence, which I later learned it was.

We next met in his local further education college where we had both been asked to take part in an innovative special needs course. I had been asked to set up a dramatherapy group which would encourage communication between the students. He, with the help of his social worker, had asked to be a student. Or rather he had said the word 'Yes' when asked if he wanted to go to college.

It was here that I realised that although Thomas satisfied the course demands by doing the written work, he was clearly isolated on a participation level from the other group members. When asked a question in front of the group he would stare into his eyebrows, poke out his tongue slightly making quiet guttural sounds, and take between five and ten minutes before he made a reply. When he did speak, it was usually an anecdote relating to some past event from his life in the city with his father. He clearly wanted to tell his story. However, the rest of the group placed him under pressure to hurry up. This would only increase his reluctance to respond.

There was no medical diagnosis or other evidence to suggest that Thomas had been brain damaged and so I assumed, rightly or wrongly, that there was either a conscious or an unconscious decision on his part to communicate in this way. His tutor suggested that with Thomas's agreement I might be able to offer him some one-to-one support in addition to the group work to improve his communication skills.

My own aim in offering this additional work was to provide a less pressurised environment, to move at Thomas's own pace so that he could be heard. I knew from my own experience of therapy that simply 'being heard' is in itself a facilitative and empowering experience.

I had seen that Thomas had an interest in painting and drawing, so I chose to ask him if we could use this medium as a meeting point. I explained to him that I was interested in offering him a space where we could explore his ideas about the world and that he would have the choice to opt out at any point. I made no suggestion that what we would do together would be a clinical treatment, but said that it would be rather an opportunity to be heard in a collaborative manner. I suggested that if any problems did surface we could face them together. He agreed to this contract.

Because the boundaries of time and place are an integral aspect of therapy I negotiated with the college for the regular use of a room for one and a half hours each week. As a community-based dramatherapist I go to great pains to ensure that spaces will be available each week and, as in this case, for at least one year and during summer and half-term breaks.

Thomas's case manager and GP supported the tutor's referral to offer Thomas six initial dramatherapy sessions with a view to continuing for up to a year.

The first thing we did together was to visit the local art shop where I encouraged him to buy an artist's folder to contain his finished work. Thomas and I then started our journey.

Our first explorations together were drawings of colours, shapes and textures. Thomas would sit with his face very close to the paper, move the paint with his fingers and scratch images with his pen and finger-nails. Much of his work was meticulous and carefully executed. He would often take the full hour to produce one picture. As I mirrored his pace this felt for me like a peaceful meditation.

During one session in the third month of our work together Thomas spontaneously poked two holes in one of his paintings and used it as a mask. I responded in kind. We produced a sequence of paper mask paintings with vivid patterns and colours, and started to use these in a series of sound dialogues. In all we explored around thirty different images and gave them different voices and movement qualities. Gradually, these patterns became more representative of people Thomas knew.

He made and wore a mask he called his 'father' and told me in role that he had decided to phone Thomas at the weekend. I was able to ask this mask lots of questions about how he saw his son. The answers were very positive, and always concluded that his intention was to visit soon.

During one meeting (around the eighth month of our work together) I discovered an aspect of Thomas that illuminated a whole new side of his personality .

In role as his father he had said that one day, when he was rich enough, he would come and take Thomas away to live in happiness for the rest of their lives together. He told me that he was soon to become a millionaire. To follow up this money theme I suggested that we made some pictures of bank notes.

Thomas's drawing was quite accurate. He then wrote some words on the bottom of the paper which read, 'The missing man'. He asked me to guess why he had written this. I suggested it might be to do with his father. He said 'No, try again.' After several attempts he eventually showed me the water-mark of the Duke of Wellington on the note and started to shake with laughter. I said to him that he was a magician!

I marvelled as he then took a wallet from his pocket and placed my five-pound note inside. It was one of those trick wallets you buy at a joke shop. He had kept it since his father had given it to him as a small boy. He opened it again and the five pounds had gone.

To follow up this session I asked Thomas if he would like to meet a friend of mine who was a magician on the local entertainment circuit. He agreed and over the next few weeks we met and rehearsed a half-hour show. After this rehearsal process, I went to see Thomas perform a magic act in his group home. He wore a full regalia of stage make-up with top hat and tails. As he told jokes, pulled a rabbit from a top hat and a silk scarf from a false thumb he appeared open, expressive, alive and happy.

Back in the mixed dramatherapy group Thomas was noticeably more communicative. His delayed speech manifested to a lesser degree. It was clear to see that he enjoyed contact with the other students. At the end of the course he moved into full-time work at a nature reserve information centre, where his drawings of birds and plant life and people who visit the centre are shown regularly.

His father did eventually visit, and Thomas, rather than discuss his need to be taken away, spent the time showing his father around his work project, congratulating himself for the achievements in his own life.

THOMAS'S 'DRAMA' SEEN IN THE CONTEXT OF FRAME ANALYSIS

Thomas' job as a plant-pot maker at the adult training centre was arguably an enactment of someone else's frame of reality as well as his own. In a sense he had to act out a pseudo role, a *technical redoing* from an industrial model of what men of low estate are supposed to do from nine until five: toil. I say 'men' because with the exception of the 'instructor' in a white coat he was part of a large room full of men in blue overalls similarly occupied, whilst in the next room the women in pink aprons made teddy bears and tea-cosies to sell to visitors.

Power relations between people find expression in the work setting more than in any other social activity. For most of us there is amicable sharing of skills and energy within our choice of career or occupation; for others the work ethic is imposed as a way to justify existence, to fill time or to confer status.

Goffman (1977) states that our illogical alignment to cultural definitions of sex differences is most explicit through the 'ceremonies' and 'rituals' wherein we show respect for others in conventionalised and perfunctory ways. The overalls in the adult training centre were arguably symbolic costumes of the various levels of ceremony and authority in regard to gender, power and conventions within the centre. The behaviour or 'performance' of those who wore them was governed by the expectations of the roles these costumes represented.

Thomas was quite aware of his role as a 'working man' showpiece for the benefit of visitors. In a sense there is a tacit agreement that such venues are work-exhibition centres where parents and other well-meaning visitors are given a good impression of the staff and management through the adult-like performances that people with learning differences give.

Seen through the 'frame' of competition, however, the job of operating an industrial staple machine within such an environment is of relatively high status, particularly amongst the other workers at the centre who would only be allowed to use blunt tools in case of possible injury. In the context of these other workers Thomas's role was highly enviable. Other men would no doubt compete for his job once he left to go to college. Paradoxically, the women's competence in the use of needles and scissors was not seen as a reason to suggest that they too might be able to use the industrial machinery alongside the men.

I believe that Thomas was aware that his job contained a certain ambiguous value. His request for me to 'see' was perhaps a genuine statement of achievement and self-esteem. On the other hand, there was a quality of irony in his presentation which was very similar to that of the magician who wished to create an illusion for the benefit of an audience. When given the option to retain his job or to attend college he had little hesitation in choosing the latter.

Many of the staff in Thomas's life at the 'adult' training centre acted within the conventions of authoritative and directive, rather than facultative, roles. This issue is understood more clearly once we understand the complex and perhaps confused position such people must occupy. At any one time these workers are expected to act as:

- group workers: towards twenty adult trainees, who at any one time may have been displaying role distance in the form of withdrawal or childish regression
- parental figures: unable to offer individual attention for more than a few hours per week
- technicians: caring for the health and safety of workers
- stage managers: trainees are kept in a state of readiness to be displayed to visitors to the centre.

This is further complicated by the fact that many staff members feel as if they must act in 'loco parentis' rather than adult to adult in their interactions with the trainees.

The frame analysis illustration in Figure 17.1 summarises some of the assumptions of reality that may have operated for Thomas at the adult training centre.

Once Thomas left the centre and moved to the further education college, his 'contact' with other people, free from constraints of ceremony and convention, increased tenfold. Because of the smaller group size, role relationships between tutor and students were not so confused or hierarchical and much more time could be spent to offer him one-to-one support.

As a student at college Thomas came into a culture where his own integrity would be recognised and valued much more. Specially trained tutors would try to bring out his talents and interests whilst developing their own educational goals. It was perhaps for the first time since he left school, for example, that his interest in painting and drawing had been recognised. As a result the group conferred upon him the role of the 'artist'.

Make-believe	Fantasies about wealth and escape shared with close friends
Contests/Cooperation	Sense of pride in high status of role as machine operator
Ceremonial/Ritual	Adherence to authority, gender roles Sense of place Timekeeping
Technical redoing	Display of pseudo 'working-man' roles for visitors
Regrounding	Awareness that the job was unpaid production-line work

Figure 17.1 Frame analysis: Thomas at the adult training centre

As a model of 'new services', however, Thomas was still on show. Visitors would call in to see his work, only this time he would also have the opportunity to display his own ideas and interests. There was also a legitimacy in his role as a student which, like that of other people in the college, would not be seen as role-play of something else. The only ambiguity in this process would be the omission of a recognised certificate at the end of the course. The teaching goals seem to have been the acquisition of tangible 'life skills' to enable graduates to live a more 'normal' life in the community.

Much of the college work was *cooperation* or *contest* in the form of tests and quizzes. It was during this time that Thomas's speech differences were highlighted. In a sense his role at the work centre had cloaked and perhaps reinforced these problems, as the men in his company were discouraged from talking whilst 'on the job'. The demands upon Thomas to communicate language at a pace that was acceptable to the rest of his college group raised another important issue: industrial culture puts a premium on speed and efficiency, yet the ability to speak eloquently or fluently is at odds with the cadence of life of most learning disabled people. As a result such people can often find themselves marginalised or ignored in meetings or in classes. This

Make-believe	Memories and fantasies about father shared in group
Contests/Cooperation	Inability to compete or cooperate in oral test. Withdrawal. Cooperation in written work
Ceremonial/Ritual	Teacher/student liberalism
Technical redoing	Displays for visitors
Regrounding	Awareness that the role of student would not lead to qualifications for paid work

Figure 17.2 Frame analysis: Thomas at the further education college

was obviously a concern for the tutors, who felt that efficient speech was a life skill and as a consequence referred Thomas for one-to-one therapy work.

The frame analysis in Figure 17.2 summarises some of the assumptions of reality that may have operated for Thomas at the further education college.

My decision to offer Thomas one-to-one work was, as I mentioned earlier, a chance to provide him with a less pressurised environment in which he could move at his own pace so that his story could be heard. Simply 'being' with Thomas, therefore, in a neutral space, following his lead, in a less authoritative or directive way, provided an environment where he could discover his own definition of convention and assert his own personal authority. At the same time, the boundaries of time and space, with the additional 'containment' function of the art folder, provided the *ceremonies* through which we could operate.

As a 'contest/cooperation' experience this was an opportunity to redefine the conventional expectations of our roles as males during 'work' hours. The expression of ideas and emotions through playful expressive activity has tended to be seen as inappropriate, childish, or something that should take place away from the work environment. Most dictionary definitions of the word 'work' seem to be based on the antonym of 'play'. Clinicians like Winnicott, however, consider the 'self-actualising' qualities of play vital for children, and, in my view, this applies to adults too: 'It is in playing and only in playing that the child [*individual*] is able to be creative and to use the whole personality. It is only in being creative that the child [*individual*] discovers the self' (Winnicott 1982, p. 63; my italics).

The interplay of mask creatures in our sessions was joyous and full of laughter. Its effect was to loosen the more rigid conventions and role expectations, which paved the way for the emergence of a new self-definition in the emergent role of Magician.

If we look back to the frame analysis of the adult training centre (Figure 17.1), it is possible to see that there is a repression of 'make-believe' as a shared experience. This perhaps led Thomas to repress or internalise this aspect of his personality and to develop fantasies of escape from the more rigid roles that the centre advocated. The process that Thomas and I shared, therefore, was much more likely to have been understood in relation to childish 'make-believe', and, therefore, as not 'work' and certainly not 'manly'. Such 'ageist' and sexist attitudes overlook the importance of play as a means to attain self-discovery.

To describe our work or play as equality between two men would be a distortion of the truth. I was still in role as therapist and Thomas's material was the focus of our work together. Our ability to disregard these differences and to continue in a flowing and natural way is a 'keying', perhaps, of the *regrounding* frame of reality in which such ambiguities do not hinder the experiences people share, even in the otherwise unequal therapist/client relationship.

Within frame analysis, too, there is often an ambiguous interplay between frames of reality, described by Manning (1992) as a 'keying of a keying' which is particularly evoked during make-believe activity. For example, the make-believe trick that Thomas played in the therapy session was supported and concretised by a *regrounding* experience. He then rehearsed for a performance (*technical redoing*) through which, in an ambiguous role (*regrounding*) he cooperated with an audience in a *ceremonial* way for the purpose of *make-believe*. Put crudely, in the context of frame analysis, Thomas's magic show gave him the opportunity to fire on all five cylinders. Table 17.1 shows a possible summary of the combination of frames as they progressed through the dramatherapy experience to the performance and on to Thomas's work placement and meeting with his father at the outdoor exhibition centre.

SUMMARY

Dramatherapy participants, through the construct of make-believe, are offered the possibility for 'reframing' experiences to take place. To open the doors of experiencing others is to redefine the status relation that exists between people: it is in this sense, too, that the 'tacit agreement' of any dominant culture is questioned and worked upon; it is through making such relative

Table 17.1 Aggregation of the dramatherapist's perception of Thomas's experiences

Frame	Dramatherapy	Magic show	Job and visit from father
Make-belive	Playful experiments with masks, voices, use of paints Interaction of imagined characters: millionaire father etc.	Laughter and playful qualities experienced through convention of 'magic' entertainment	Jokes, tricks and humour possibly expressed between staff, workers and visitors
Contests/ cooperation	Cooperative production of masks Interplay of therapist and client in improvisation	Challenging audience to not be tricked Cooperation as they participate in act and are willing to suspend belief	Self-validation to father
Ceremonial	Time and space Containment in folder	Conventions of magician act: costume, make-up and audience interaction	Taking his father on a tour of his work project Thomas experienced as a figure of status in his own right
Technical redoing	Rehearsal of magician role in preparation for performance	Exhibition of skills	Exhibition of paintings to general public
Regrounding	Accepted ambiguity of roles in client/therapist relationship and therapist as audience	Control given to Thomas by audience, staff and others	No apparent ambiguity of roles

mechanisms available that the key to past, present and future doors might be grasped, and validity through self-esteem, status and cultural terms might be achieved.

In the process that Thomas and I shared, I believe we removed the following barriers which had otherwise prevented any possibility of self-actualisation:

• the incongruous imposition of time and efficiency
• the demand to communicate effectively in groups
• conventionalised models of 'normality' and authority
• the imposition of a predetermined concept of maleness and adulthood.

In their place the following were brought into being:

- the time and space to project and create reality afresh at a pace which matched Thomas's own rhythms
- an acceptance of the communication for what it was
- a non-authoritative and playful relationship.

In Goffman's terms, by discovering the role of magician, Thomas had gained the key to a door which later allowed him to define himself through his interactions with others. From their willingness to act as an audience he knew that these others valued his contribution, as I had done by accepting the masks and the emergence of the magician role in the one-to-one work. The work with me, therefore, was perhaps only the vehicle for this discovery and not the discovery itself.

CONCLUSIONS

Within many local authorities there exists a very positive view towards the facilitative role of the arts therapies as an empowering process, as is indicated here by a Director of Social Services, Lucille Hughes, in a report to fellow directors in Wales:

> It should come as no surprise to us that the arts are a means for all human beings to find a way of finding happiness, discovering gifts, maturing their personality and promoting their spiritual growth. Since time began the arts have had an honoured place in most societies. What seems to have gone unnoticed in our society is the immense potential of the arts as a tool to help disadvantaged people.
>
> The challenge to local authorities is to harness the arts to their task of enabling handicapped people to realise their potential and live a fuller life in the community. It is fortunate that it is possible, under the guidance of a therapist, for other workers to use the arts as a means of helping clients. Even if there were a much more adequate supply of arts therapists, a significant part of their task would be to make their field accessible to other workers.

Such positive support has been one of the mainstays and, at times, survival mechanisms of the arts therapies services in their formative stages as a profession. However, with the more recent moves towards service procurer/ provider status and case-manager led services, it will be less possible for directors to advocate innovative approaches. Although the two are not mutually exclusive, service managers may have financial considerations at the forefront of their minds in relation to basic cost-efficient 'packages of care' as the guiding principle for any future service delivery for people with learning differences.

As I mentioned at the start of this chapter, the process of dramatherapy takes place within a political system, where 'work'-based ethics have still remained highly popular. This may be due in part to the fact that economics provide civil servants and reformers with a common or sympathetic language which enables these groups to ignore more difficult conceptual agreement about the nature of human reality and to focus instead upon the economic/industrial determinants of behaviour. Many civil servants employed to design community care services for people with learning differences still insist that such people are socially valued or 'valorised' (Wolfensberger *et al.* 1972) by their 'work' and 'leisure' activities. The agreed 'norms' of the dominant culture, they argue, form the basis for developing or maintaining roles for people with learning differences. Therefore offering people like Thomas any kind of work would be considered an enabling practice. Many feminist writers argue, however, that the economic principles themselves are an attempt to 'assimilate' these people into a largely male industrial self-concept or dominant culture. They argue that people with learning differences are an identifiable oppressed group who, like women, should be given the means to self-determination (Brown and Smith 1989).

The opportunity to have a job of work is arguably considerably significant to the self-esteem of a person with a learning difference. 'Work' alone, though, does not as Ruskin said 'maketh the man'. Such approaches must in my view honour the unique creative, expressive and spiritual qualities of a person as well.

Although the outcome for Thomas was an overall improvement in his communication and ability to work cooperatively with other students, I see that the value of our work was not in moving towards this simple goal but rather the opportunity for Thomas to move at his own speed to find his outer identity in relation to his emerging personal story, and, perhaps, a chance to construct his own version of manhood and fatherhood in relation to his absent father.

I believe that to work with someone of one's own gender does in some cases have special meaning both for the therapist and the client. By saying this I do not advocate that therapy should be a segregated experience. Admittedly the work I did with Thomas could easily have been equally well carried out by a female therapist. I believe, though, that the empathic response to the client's material is sometimes assisted by the similarity of experience between the client and the therapist.

In certain other circumstances I believe the gender of a therapist can be detrimental. As a male dramatherapist working with a mixed population of male and female clients with learning differences there are several gender issues I consider prior to a decision to begin a therapeutic journey. The checklist that follows serves as a guideline:

- Has the client requested to work with a male or female therapist?
- Does the nature of the issues involved call for a male or female therapist? For example, if the work is likely to be about disclosure relating to sexual

abuse would one-to-one contact with a male or female re-create the original pattern of abuse?

- What expectations is the gender of the therapist likely to give rise to in the group or individual? For example, would this reinforce notions that women are better carers or that men are unsafe?
- Will there be a co-worker available, and if so how will their gender affect the dynamics?
- Is there a medical/behavioural diagnosis or report which indicates that cognitive or physiological problems are likely to occur? For example, some clients can become confused about the meaning of physical contact in action therapies. If this is a problem then clients themselves need to be carefully informed about the nature of the work.
- Are all staff and parents aware of the nature of the work of the drama-therapist? People who are blind or who lack easily understood speech are often the most vulnerable to sexual or physical abuse as they are unable to explain such abuse to others. Because of this, male workers are rarely left alone with female clients in day-care settings and 'toileting' of female clients is only done by women. Male therapists are, therefore, particularly at risk of accusations of malpractice if similar clear boundaries and good work-practice methods are not adhered to. As a general rule, unless otherwise indicated, I choose to work with a female co-worker and avoid the use of settings which are isolated.

If there appears to be an obvious conflict of interests in relation to any of these questions then I defer the referral until a more suitable time or suggest alternative sources of help.

CONCLUSION

I hope that this chapter has shown that an understanding of a gender, learning difference and service provision is based primarily upon the value judgement of an observer, which can change in an illusive way once the observer's frame of reference changes. A wider picture offered by a theory does not mean the total picture has been seen. I believe we must approach theories in a playful way, taking from them any positive qualities they contain. Some theories are used to shape a world view in a detrimental way, while others can lead to insights though which human beings may aspire to their highest values and interests. Such changes of perspective have been taking place throughout human history.

The politicians, parents and ordinary people who have been instrumental in helping to dismantle the asylum system have achieved something on a remarkable humanitarian scale. In the rush to close the hospitals and adult training centres, however, there has been a tendency to pre-empt or overstate the next set of values that people with learning differences should aspire to, rather than discover new ways to listen to them.

Dramatherapy is a new way of listening. It gives permission for people to play; to be spontaneous; to explore; to invent; to have power; to change; to stand back and see their lives in a different light or from a different perspective. In general, people with learning differences embrace this opportunity wholeheartedly.

To answer the title of this chapter, 'Is different therefore equal?', I must admit that although this is a belief which I hold as a personal truth, it is unfortunately not yet reflected in the outside world. There is a harsh reality to the illusions that many people live under. It is still unsafe, for example, for women and members of ethnic and disabled groups to walk alone at night in many of our cities and towns . Many people still face barriers of discrimination on the grounds of gender, race, mobility, IQ, wealth, age or first language. I have a sense of hope, however, that dramatherapy can contribute towards a more egalitarian world through its commitment to empower individuals and to disentangle the illusions that can sometimes control or overwhelm authentic expression.

ACKNOWLEDGEMENT

I would like to acknowledge the kind help of the following people in the preparation of this chapter: John Casson, John Dickens, Pauline Down, Elizabeth Gall, Roger Grainger, Dr Gordon Grant, Lucille Hughes, Sally Hanson, Sue Jennings, Marcia Karp, Rachel Mathews, Paul Ramcharan, Ken Sprague. I would like to give special thanks to Thomas, for his kind permission to use the material of our sessions together as the subject of this chapter.

REFERENCES AND FURTHER READING

Blatner, A. and Blatner, A. (1988) *The Foundations of Psychodrama: History Theory and Practice*, New York: Springer.

Brown, H. and Smith, H. (1989) 'Whose "ordinary" life is it anyway? A feminist critique of the normalisation principle', *Disability, Handicap, and Society*, 4(2): 105–119.

—— (1992) 'Assertion, not assimilation: a feminist perspective on the normalisation principle', University of Kent, UK.

Goffman, E. (1956) *The Presentation of the Self in Everyday Life*, Cambridge, Mass.: Harvard University Press; Harmondsworth, UK: Penguin.

—— (1974) *Frame Analysis*, Cambridge, Mass.: Harvard University Press; New York: Harper & Row.

—— (1977) 'The arrangement between the sexes', *Theory and Society* 4(3): 301–302.

Manning, P (1992) *Erving Goffman and Modern Sociology*, Cambridge: Polity Press.

Meldrum, B. (1994) 'A role model of dramatherapy and its application with individuals and groups', in S. Jennings, A. Cattanach, S. Mitchell, A. Chesner and B. Meldrum, *The Handbook of Dramatherapy*, London and New York: Routledge.

Moreno, J. L. (1953) *Who Shall Survive? Foundations of Sociometry, Group Psychotherapy and Sociodrama*, Beacon, NY: Beacon House.
Schaef, A. W. (1990) *Meditations for Women Who Do Too Much*, New York: Harper Collins.
Winnicott, D. W. (1982) *Playing and Reality*, London: Routledge.
Wolfensberger, W. and Tullman, S. (1989) 'A brief outline of the principles of normalisation', in A. Brechin and J. Walmsley (eds) *Making Connections*, Milton Keynes, UK: Open University Press.
Wolfensberger, W., Nirje, B. *et al.* (1972) *Normalization: The Principle of Normalization in Human Services*, Toronto: National Institute on Mental Retardation.

Part IV

Dramatherapy, politics and culture

Chapter 18

The rainbow bridge and the divided space

Demys Kyriacou

Could one say that by finding a bit of the outside world, whether in chalk or paper ... that was willing temporarily to fit in with one's dreams, a moment of illusion was made possible, a moment in which inner and outer seemed to coincide? Was it also true to say that it was by these moments that one was able to re-establish the bridge ... and so be re-awakened at least to the possibility of creative life in a real world? ... that by these moments of achieved fusion between inner and outer one was at least restored potentially to a life in which one could seek to rebuild, restore, re-create what one loved, in actual achievement?

Marion Milner

INTRODUCTION

Over twenty-one years have passed since the invasion of Turkish military forces on the island of Cyprus, an independent country since 1961, situated in a politically crucial area at the far-eastern end of the Mediterrenean Sea. Because of its particular position on the map, Cyprus in its long history, with the exception of several years of independence, has been continually under the rule of a number of conquerors, beginning long before Christ. At the present time half of the island belongs to the Greek Cypriot authority whereas the other half is under Turkish occupation. Prior to the invasion Cyprus's population was mixed, the Turkish Cypriots being the minority.

Although, on a diplomatic level, a viable political solution satisfying both the Greek Cypriot and Turkish Cypriot sides has not yet been found, groups of individuals from both sides, some of them belonging to the worlds of art, science, drama and literature, have been trying for the last several years to find ways of bridging the gap that exists. This they are trying to do by putting aside political propaganda but without losing sight of the deeply political significance of the problem. They are trying to understand each other's demands and needs, focusing on the need for sharing and promoting civilisation and peace between the two communities. These groups – 'Conflict Resolution Groups' as they are called – are trying to find ways, first within the groups themselves, and then in a broader context, of understanding the need for a solution to the Cyprus problem, applying their ideas in practical terms to everyday life. Their endeavours have been included in the work of the Institute for Multi-Track Diplomacy (a non-profit, non-governmental organisation with a global scope, headquartered in the USA, and committed to the non-violent resolution of ethnic and regional conflict), as well as in that of the NTL Institute (an innovative group of select applied behavioural science experts who are dedicated to understanding and developing solutions for facilitating productive change in every facet of life). An example of this work was a ten-day intensive workshop, co-sponsored by the above institutes, that took place in Oxford in July–August 1993. The workshop consisted of a bicommunal training of trainers programme in conflict resolution and inter-group relations entitled 'Catalysts for Change in Cyprus'. In this workshop, under the coordination of a number of therapists, ways of healing the gap were examined and worked through.

WORKING DRAMATHERAPEUTICALLY

Late in 1994 I had the challenging idea of working with this large group dramatherapeutically, using *bridges* as the central metaphor. Discussing the matter with some of the members of the group I was encouraged to believe that a positive answer would be possible in the near future.

This short chapter is concerned with the thoughts, images, metaphors and possible ways of working them through that have emerged during the incubation period of this project over the past few months. This period has not been devoted to a structured planning of the proposed future workshop in the strict sense of the word. On the contrary, it has involved a 'letting go' of the necessity of preparation, and a 'letting in' of images and intuitive concepts around the central metaphor of 'bridges'. It resembles what C. Jung called 'directed association and amplification', a kind of pre-warming-up for the dramatherapist.

Generally speaking, bridges are used in connecting two or more seemingly separated spaces between which lies a kind of obstacle or hindrance that is difficult or dangerous to ignore or overcome in other ways. Bridges can be found or built on many levels. On a material, concrete level, they connect parts of cities, motorway junctions, separate spaces of various buildings, etc.; still on a concrete but more abstract level, bridges are created between countries by means of TV satellites, fax, mail, means of transportation, etc. On a symbolic level, bridges of communication exist between people; between the inner parts of ourselves, or what we sense as I and not-I in ourselves; between inner and outer realities; and also between what drama-therapy considers as dramatic reality and everyday reality.

Bridges also help to restore the lost continuum between two or more spaces, either on a concrete or on a symbolic level. This is the case with the

Cyprus problem, which is dramatically reflected on all levels, beginning with the concrete–topographic. On this level northern Cyprus (N-space) is occupied by Turkish Cypriots, and southern Cyprus (S-space) by Greek Cypriots, the two spaces separated by the so-called 'green line'. (The term 'space' is not used here in the sense of just a number of square kilometers, devoid of life, but has a multilevel dimension which includes inhabitants, language, tradition, etc.) These two separated spaces stand where once stood one single space with a mixed population from both nationalities.

The continuum was lost in 1974 and remains so. In this chapter I choose not to enter into a detailed political analysis of the Cyprus problem, although the matter itself has a deeply political nature, and if the proposed workshop becomes a reality the dramatherapist must have a clear pack of relevant information in his or her 'dramatherapy bag', amongst many other ideas and skills.

For more than two decades N-space has become a land of shadows for the residents of S-space, a kind of 'forbidden space', and vice versa; while the green line that cuts Cyprus into two has a ghostly quality stripped of life, role-playing an inaccessible high wall that cannot be surmounted. Strong feelings of anger, bitterness and guilt, as well as numerous fantasies, have been invested in the two spaces by both sides; spaces burdened with projective feelings that seem intolerable.

By moving 'N' and 'S' spaces into the *dramatic space*, with the *safety* a dramatherapy group can provide, the metaphor of bridges can act as a catalyst for the working through of all those feelings and fantasies that keep both sides isolated and far apart from each other:

> metaphor can serve as a container for feelings which are too overwhelming to be tolerated . . . it can prove to be a vehicle for carrying, mobilizing, expressing and integrating affect and cognition . . .
>
> (Cox and Theilgaard 1987, p. 99)

When the situation, as it was before and after the division of Cyprus and its population, is embodied, projected and role-played by the group within the context of a myth or fairy tale of the 'one space that became two', images, feelings and fantasies about the consequenses of such a shift will surely emerge, carrying the seeds of possible solutions and transformations. Members of the group can elaborate on the idea of the divided space, on the image of the green line and the metaphor of bridges, finding ways of expressing them with their bodies while interacting with each other.

As a group they write the 'Myth of the one space that became two', one member at a time writing a sentence or two, taking over the story where the previous member has left it, without reading or knowing in any way what has been written by the other members. They refer to an unknown mythical space, avoiding the use of proper nouns such as Cyprus, Turkish, Greek, etc. This is the first step into the dramatic space within which lie all possibilities and which provides one of dramatherapy's basic tools: that of *dramatic distancing*, the paradox of which helps the members of the group to explore possible traumatic areas within a context of safety, 'too far yet too close'. Thus they have the opportunity to write the story for the first time; because even though a story is well known, by touching upon it in this way we actually tell or write it for the first time.

> Each story is re-created in the interaction between teller and listener . . . no matter how often and how faithfully a teller tells a tale, it can never be told exactly the same way twice. The audience, situation, time, personal history and, above all, the moment, effect the communication and determine the bond which needs to grow. Each tale is told only once; once and for all. Thus although a tale may be old beyond memory, it is always new; the same, yet permanently different.
>
> (Gersie and King 1990, p. 32)

In a way, the metaphors of the 'one space that became two' and of bridges comprise two sides of the same coin, one side expressing the idea of *division* and the other that of *unison,* acting thus as a pair of opposites in terms of process.

Looking at it from another angle, one more pair of opposites appears: that of 'N' and 'S' spaces. In fact, in the language of archetypal psychology the one space is the *shadow* of the other! The metaphor of bridges is the uniting factor, or what C. Jung would call the 'Eros principle', which brings closer, binds and harmonically fuses together seemingly opposing elements. The 'shadow' incorporates all the unaccepted elements of a person or nation, and is usually projected on to a person or community for reasons satisfying psychic economy. Examples of this on a national level were the USA and Russia, or in World War II the Germans and Jews; more recent examples are Palestinians and Jews, Serbs and Muslims, Turks and Kurds.

The case of the Turkish and Greek Cypriots is similar, the one group incarnating for the other their shadow qualities. The topography of the divided space resembles much of what on a psychological level would be the I and the not-I, ego and shadow, conscious and unconscious; the green line being a symbol of the pre-conscious. But in the case of the Cyprus problem one could speak of a 'perverted' division, because until recently there was no healthy interplay between the two spaces. There is what appears to be 'a split of absolutes', each side stubbornly supporting what it considers to be right and just, and throwing or projecting on to the other whatever it considers to be unacceptable.

COLOURFUL MEANINGS

Strangely enough, calling the borderline 'green' has given an ambiguity to its symbolic significance, since green – in contrast to red – is a permitting colour. Green traffic lights signify that one is permitted to move on, to continue, to cross the junction, while red lights signify 'stop'. Green is also a spring colour, one of growth, abundance and optimism; it is the colour of vegetation and of trees, which in their turn are powerful metaphors of connection between what is above and what lies below. Evergreen trees are symbols of the everlasting side of life, all that endures. On the other hand there is also a negative symbolism, green being the colour of corpses (the Egyptian god Osiris was depicted as green).

The dramatherapy group works on the metaphor of the green line in trying to figure out the bridging process. Are the bridges going to be 'built' over the separating green line? Or could it be that part of the bridging process is the inhabiting of the separating line by residents of both spaces? Are the bridges going to have any particular colour or are they going to be multi-coloured *rainbow bridges* connecting, crossing and interpenetrating all levels of human life? What other changes and transformations could take place in respect to the separating line as part of the bridging process? And how could these changes be transferred from the dramatic reality the group would be working in and materialised in the everyday reality?

Let us start a fire
that will cremate those fences
along which we
skirt the edge of ourselves
aliens, not lifting except in
dreams the latch of our breast.
(Burkart 1963, translated by R. Cambridge and quoted in Cox and
Theilgaard, 1987, p. 91)

Finally, a second story is written at the closure of a long workshop such as this, a tale of *the divided space that became one* (or even a group drawing, or a group sculpt), depicting the possible changes that could have taken place in the group, and how these could mould everyday reality, promoting peaceful solutions to the problem of both communities as it has been shaped during the last twenty years.

REFERENCES AND FURTHER READING

Burkart, E. (1963) 'Das Zeichen' ('The Sign'), in *Deutsche Lyrik: Gedichte seit 1945*, Munich: Deutsche Taschenbuch Verlag.
Cox, M. and Theilgaard A. (1987) *Mutative Metaphors in Psychotherapy*, London: Tavistock Publications.
Gersie, A. and King, N. (1990) *Storymaking in Education and Therapy*, London: Jessica Kingsley.
Jennings, S. (1990) *Dramatherapy with Families, Groups and Individuals*, London: Jessica Kingsley.
Jennings S. (ed.) (1987) *Dramatherapy: Theory and Practice for Teachers and Clinicians*, London: Routledge.

Jung, C. (1953) *Two Essays on Analytical Psychology*, translated by R.F.C. Hull (*Complete Works* vol. 7), New York: Bollinger Foundation.

—— (1956) *Symbols of Transformation*, translated by R.F.C. Hull (*Complete Works* vol. 5), London: Routledge & Kegan Paul.

Milner, M. (1986) *On Not Being Able to Paint*, London: Heinemann Education Books.

Chapter 19

Dramatherapy

Radical intervention or counter-insurgency?

Dan Baron Cohen and James King

The Damned

This woman sat in her home every day
She wanted to go out
She wanted many things
But she was denied them
So she promised the world to her daughter
But she would never let her go out
because she was lonely

Night after night the mother cried in her bed
But every morning she came down the stairs
with her husband's smile on her face
One morning her daughter asked her why she smiled
I hear you crying in your sleep every night
The mother cracked and exploded like a dam
unable to bear the strain of her suffering
Her daughter got caught up in the flood
and thought she'd broken her mother
So she hid the tears under her bed
in case someone accused her

Now some years later
the mother found her crying in her room
Go to the priest, she said, and he'll build you a dam
And he did!
And the tears went away!
But every time the dam broke
she had to go back to him
And her daughters and their daughters did the same
And they all dreamed of the time
when they'd no longer need a dam

Until one day
one of her great great grandchildren
playing with tears she'd found under her bed
was scolded for crying without cause
So she went up to the priest
who was now very old and asked
Father, see these tears
who owns the river the dam's holding
The old priest was shocked at the question
Sure it's a mystery
All I have is the design

And she spat in his face
and tore up the design
and flowed away to be free

Threshold Derry, 1992

This chapter consists of reflections shared between Dan Baron Cohen, community theatre activist, and James King, community theatre lecturer. James worked with Dan on the 1992 Derry Frontline *Threshold* community theatre project, and Dan coordinated a project for James's community theatre Continuing Education Diploma at Magee College, Ulster University, in 1993. These reflections are based on dialogues recorded in the summer, and edited in the winter, of 1994. As such, they span the transition of the ceasefire of 31 August 1994, which lends them both a sudden sense of history and poignancy.

In January 1992, a few of us prepared a performance art-piece to mark the 20th anniversary of Bloody Sunday. It included a row of thirteen bottles of milk across the top of the city wall, facing the Guildhall Square, with a length of string hanging down to the ground from each one. The bottles of milk represented the people whose innocent blood was to be shed when one of the artists (in the soldier's role) pulled on the strings. While all this was happening, another performer would crawl along the base of the wall, representing the terrified marchers. Yet others, dressed as civil servants and Westminster politicians, would sweep the broken glass under a huge carpet.

The police arrived. Perhaps I had made a mistake in cordoning-off an area beneath the walls with a length of string to keep the public away from the crashing bottles. The demarcated area invited attention. But once we had explained to the police what we were going to do, they said they would have to stop us because of the danger to the public. They said that if one splinter of glass touched someone in the street, we could be sued for damage; they seemed as determined to prevent us from completing our journey as they'd been twenty years before. A strong confrontation followed but we held our ground. The performance took place, exonerating the past. It's not just where the law lies, but where power exists.

James King

As you know, I was wrongfully arrested and detained last year. As we drove in tense armed silence to Castlereagh, I made three key decisions. I'd deal with everyone I met courteously and clearly. I'd speak about no one other than myself. And I'd question those who questioned me, gently and supportively. In this way, I hoped to reclaim some power and humanity for myself, take advantage of my workshop skills and my 'difference', and reaffirm that mutilated, imprisoned and uniformed humanity that was pressed against me in the back of the car. By referring to no one other than myself, I'd place no one else at risk. I knew that engaging in dialogue could be dangerous within a sophisticated centre of practised and highly resourced interrogation. But I also knew that dialogue did not remove my option to remain silent at any point.

In one interrogation, plain-clothes officers asked me to comment on a particular IRA killing. The photos they showed me reminded me of a documentary I'd seen where a RUC [Royal Ulster Constabulary] officer had angrily denounced the NIO [Northern Ireland Office] for having offered him £300 for his daughter (a member of the RUC too), who'd been killed by an IRA mortar. First I asked my interrogators whether they had known either the father or the daughter. Each of them had known one or both. Then I asked them to describe their feelings when they'd heard of the death. Both responded, though I could see one was still more affected than the other. Finally, I asked what prevented them from venting their anger at home on the people they loved, or did they release it on those they questioned, like me?

I quietly reflected on how hard it must be to lose a daughter, and described how the RUC father had trembled when explaining why he'd turned down the £300. Suddenly the room was filled by an awful cry, more like a groan, and then commotion, as the senior officer tried to reassert his authority and the steely nerve of their profession. But the culture had cracked. I quickly declared that such emotional responses were important and human. When the notes of that session were read back to me, the whole dialogue had been edited to a single line: 'Baron Cohen was forthcoming in his views on terrorism.'

Dan Baron Cohen

QUESTIONS AND PRIORITIES

JAMES   Dan, you've been living and working in the Bogside since 1990, though your cultural work in that community goes back to 1988. As a dramatherapist who is convinced of the therapeutic value of artistic processes and the potential which these processes have for changing individuals and groups, I'd be interested to hear what you've learned from your community theatre and its therapeutic potential, and whether you think that protest and therapy can share the same stage.

DAN   There are many difficult debates about community, culture and therapy which cluster around your two questions, which have very different implications depending on where they are asked. For us, protest and therapy would share the same dialectical relationship as rhetoric and poetry in our political or *barricade* theatre, but before we talk about Derry Frontline I need to make it clear that, while I speak as someone who has been accepted as a writer, a cultural activist, a friend, and a son inside the Bogside, I'm still from 'across the water'; and over the years, I've become increasingly aware of how subtle and complex our cultural differences are, and how tentative my analysis therefore needs to be. I mention this partly to contextualise all that I'll be saying about the Bogside (where protest and therapy are inseparable in the *theatre of everyday life*), and partly because I believe my relationship to this community raises several key questions: Who is or should be the therapist? And who or what defines what is or is not therapy?

JAMES   Did Derry Frontline ever use dramatherapy?

DAN   No, at least not explicitly, though I believe the devising and production of a community play is itself profoundly therapeutic. Our theatre work has a dual, linked purpose: to speak out against the injustices of occupation, and to create a space *within the community* where painful experiences and contradictions (which are inhibiting progress), can be explored. In working with a nucleus of families over a number of years, we were forced to examine the psychological 'anatomy' of dependency and motivation; gradually we began to grasp the complexities of 'decolonising the mind'. As we debated the apparently conflicting needs of resistance and development, and advanced our definition of self-determination, we became convinced that dramatherapy needed to be integrated into our cultural liberation projects. To promote debate inside the community about the value of therapy, we staged Ariel Dorfman's *Death and the Maiden* in the Bogside earlier this year.

JAMES   That's useful. Will we begin with a definition of therapy?

DAN   You're the dramatherapist, James.

THERAPY IN CONTEXT: CLASS, COMMUNITY AND OCCUPATION

JAMES   Okay. I'll try one: the conscious and willing participation in a process of healing or change, for the better, in the participant's terms.

DAN   Conscious and willing participation can only be meaningful if it is based on *active consent*, and consent is only meaningful if it is based on self-confidence and access to information. People here are hardly going to risk abandoning that effective policy of resistance – 'whatever you say, say nothing' – passed down across the centuries, to consent to a process they associate exclusively with authority and privilege.

JAMES I accept that; does that invalidate my definition?

DAN Would it include informal therapeutic processes like writing, or even intimate conversations inside people's homes or prisons?

JAMES Yes, certainly therapy with a small 't'.

DAN And what is the therapeutic status of protest? How therapeutic is rioting, producing graffiti or agit-prop theatre; or smuggling 'comms' [communications] in and out the jails, the euphoric release of focused anger, in pursuit of change?

JAMES Does it change people for the better, or does it harden them, and reinforce their anger?

DAN I think that depends on the conditions of protest. Many people have acquired self-knowledge and self-confidence through years of sustained resistance, providing they've been able to find a space where they can reflect and open-up: out fishing, walking, even in the confinement of a prison cell. But for most people in the Bog, whose reflexes have been structured over decades by the violence of poverty and occupation, and who cannot afford that paratherapeutic refuge, the only way they survive the constant harassment by the British Army and the RUC in their streets and their homes is by hardening, barricading their vulnerability.

JAMES People who have to remain 'in control'.

DAN Exactly. And until they no longer *need* their anger to survive, when self-determination replaces self-defence, it may be rational to resist any kind of therapy.

JAMES Their resistence is likely to become rigid and uncreative –

DAN But people are aware that if they step outside the 'defined' or 'permitted' rituals of confrontation and resistance, they're likely to provoke even greater risk of violence or incarceration. In these conditions, people's anger can become explosive, tragically self-destructive, and mazed in shame and confused guilt. Any participation in an 'alternative' project risks exile within such a tightly-knit, self-policing community which is constantly scrutinising the world and itself as a reflex of self-protection and protest.

JAMES In the absence of the 'troubles', do you think such a close-knit community could be receptive to therapy?

DAN I think all impoverished communities live in a *permanent* state of crisis and war (which only becomes visible when mechanisms of 'normalisation' collapse), whether poverty is defined as such or not. In these circumstances, family unity and community support literally mean the difference between life and death, so it would be difficult to establish belief in the priority of therapy, let alone in the confidentiality of the

DAN   I'm sure that's the subjective cause of much post-colonial repression and what makes the arena of therapy such a significant realm of democracy and liberation.

JAMES   So the issue isn't one of whether therapy is valid?

DAN   No, providing that the therapeutic option is always politically framed, which for me is achieved by the metaphor of the barricade. The barricade reminds any therapeutic project that there is a dialectically-related 'interior' and 'exterior' to resistance, and situates its origins in the objective world. It also enables us to value the resistance to therapy, while at the same time to understand how such resistance can be fetishised as a complex act of compensation for loss. The barricade is not just a means of survival, the limit to your freedom and humanity; it can become a mirror, a way of life, the horizon beyond which it is frightening to look or even think, as with any rationality or faith.

JAMES   Do you not think people sometimes choose to construe their resistance as 'necessary', even choose to isolate themselves or the community, in fear of change? It's when our therapeutic needs are greatest that our resistance can be most extreme.

DAN   Yes, I think the most astute activists within this community realise that; the activists in our workshops intuitively explored those contradictions within the barricade culture: those unspeakable moments when the 'internal' colludes with the 'external' and it becomes impossible to distinguish between resistance and repression. Our workshops and performances became a space where the barricades questioned themselves and debated the circumstances in which they might be dismantled.

JAMES   Do you think that communities struggling to survive are unable to engage in therapy?

DAN   No, not necessarily. I am trying to identify the forces of inhibition within the cultures of survival and resistance which are frequently misunderstood and pathologised by predominantly middle-class therapists. How many therapists would be able to grasp that traumatic shudder when you realise you've *extended* the very violence you've been subjected to, *inside your home*, the one arena in which you have some illusion of control? What is the meaning of consent, participation or active choice, in *this* context? For any working-class person, the power-blindness reflected in such naive abstraction immediately situates therapy within the privilege of the middle class. Only by advocating a 'healing process' in terms of intervention, support, and people in control of their own time and choices, practised where they live and they work (the practicalities of self-determination), will it be possible for therapy to appear relevant to the people of the Bogside –

JAMES   The kind of people that middle-class therapists may not wish to encourage or support; people who in any case sense that, were their anger to be discharged or sublimated through therapy, they would be unable to remain at war.

DAN   This is more difficult. People here do not *choose* war, even if their patterns of protest have become rigid and planned. They all know, even intuitively, that the 'security forces' have greater difficulties dealing with the anarchic humanity of the clown than with the more confrontational, oppositional forms of protest. But they believe that anger is ultimately more effective in provoking the transformation of a profoundly *deaf* and unjust State.

JAMES   Would psychodrama reduce the power of an angry people?

DAN   It might initially allow people to respond more creatively and subversively. But the State knows how to marginalise the clown –

JAMES   It's that person in between that interests me. The free person who cannot be defined. The RUC eventually pigeon-holed streetperformers like myself as mad and probably harmless. The point is that we were more totally *sane* during these periods of 'creative protest' than at any other time! To recognise this is to stand society upon its head.

DAN   But there is a radical difference between clowning and 'active struggle'. The State permits therapy because, like performance or gallery art, it doesn't stray beyond acceptable spaces and speaks in specialist languages. Meanwhile, the creative project of self-determination which would transform every space, relationship and language we know, through the democratic use of power and all our resources, is actively opposed. And now that it's being advocated as an essential tool of 'peace and reconciliation', therapy is perceived by most people in the Bogside as a refined instrument for the blanding of working-class anger and dissent, not a method for the transformation of a structurally violent society.

THE DIALECTICAL RELATIONSHIP BETWEEN ANGER AND THERAPY

DAN   'Just anger' may be a necessary part of the process of change, just as it is in the individual's healing process. In the past twenty-five years, people here have found that only by rupturing institutionalised conventions and cultural constitutions *without permission* has it been possible to be heard. By entering and challenging the exclusive or policed centres of political and cultural authority (government buildings, theatres, chapels and schools), to perform sometimes rehearsed and sometimes spontaneous agit-prop protests, activists from the Bogside have been able to interrupt and expose the mechanisms of a *manufactured consent* which legitimises and sanitises the organised violence and terrorism of corporate capitalism. Now though these voices are angry and even exhilarated, they're also profoundly aware how much the divided communities of Derry need to be reconciled and healed. But to what? What for? By whom? And how? Is the process going to be genuinely determined by those directly involved?

JAMES These psycho-political issues are frequently unseen by the therapeutic profession, because of its own class identity.

DAN That's right, and because activists here will be influential in creating a climate of confidence and experiment, the suspicion that therapy will be used as a discreet form of containment needs to be allayed. We should also remember that precious therapeutic resources already exist within this community. Though the culture of resistance is both resilient and defiant, people also know how vulnerable they are and how fragile their unity is. They realise, profoundly, that their unity in adversity, based on necessity and anger, cannot risk confronting anything that threatens to shatter it. But though this culture of necessity may be far more fragile than any resourced culture of choice, it possesses great humanity and wisdom; people are painfully sensitive to suffering and are acutely aware of the nuances of oppression and manipulation. They possess a profound capacity for empathy and tolerance (undermined though these are by the contradictory emotional experience of obligation, gratitude, dependency and solidarity), essential assets in the therapeutic practice of everyday survival and protest.

JAMES I witnessed many of these paratherapeutic qualities during the production of *Threshold*. In saying that though, I also noted many wounded people who certainly were not able to find any refuge or support inside their community. Did Derry Frontline ever consider abandoning the pressures of theatre production to concentrate on the therapeutic needs of the drama workshop, as they became more revealed?

DAN During the past two years, the conflict between the interventionary and developmental priorities within our community projects became increasingly painful, prompting us to pause for a sustained period of reflection and evaluation. The contradiction seemed to be unavoidable. Without the (aesthetic) space to reflect, to become self-conscious, to experiment and to heal, people struggle to be human. But to begin and sustain the developmental work, the violence has to cease. People cannot be creative when their whole week is spent searching for milk tokens, and when they can't sleep or eat, without fear. Though there were those in Derry Frontline who argued our work ought to have been exclusively developmental, while our participants, their families and friends were literally being tortured and murdered, we had to campaign and speak out.

JAMES *Threshold* was much more than an agit-prop play though. What do you think will be its lasting effect upon its participants?

DAN Our workshop method, and the extended discussions about every aspect of community life, all of which have laid foundations for intimate, developmental work. Our plays may have been outspoken; but they also reflected on the psychological and emotional consequences of the conflict, dwelling on the ways in which violations can be inscribed into the body and culturally passed on from generation to generation. Slowly, this filtered out into the wider community. We'd learn that people were taking key insights and workshop skills into their homes and were launching their own developmental projects, with their children and lovers! Rather than diffusing decades of anger, we'd harnessed it to the exploration of key contradictions and found people taking risks based on more private quests for equality and justice. That's not to say everyone's life changed or that people weren't knocked back. But we've focused the priorities of the next phase of the long struggle for self-determination. There are many contradictions: the overlap of different stages of development within one community, between men and women, between different generations, and between the appeals of the dominant and dissident cultures. But new activists will be formed by these contradictions, and they will advance these paratherapeutic qualities into a radical community therapy, driven by a just anger and a personal need for justice.

I know a woman called Mary whose home has been repeatedly raided during the past twenty years. She has had two sons inside Long Kesh, both 'on the blanket' for five years (one of whom was on the 1980 hunger-strike), and has herself inspired or organised countless protests: she once stood outside the Cathedral with two other mothers, wearing nothing but a blanket, to force Derry to confront the hidden violation of the blanketmen in Long Kesh. That act of street-theatre still reverberates today!

This activist-grandmother recently returned from doing her shopping to discover her house being raided by a squad of armed British soldiers. Her arms full of carrier-bags, Mary squeezed past them into the kitchen and quite spontaneously handed different items of shopping to the soldiers. They had to rest their guns against the breakfast table while she directed them where to put away the tins, the fruit, and the vegetables. One of the soldiers cracked a joke about the absurdity of it all. Everyone laughed.

Mary had not only quickly reclaimed control over her own space; she had also rehumanised and subverted the situation, disarming the mercenaries, reconstructing them (even for two minutes), as sons and husbands. The story passed from mouth to mouth, house to house, and street to bar, empowering and inspiring everyone who heard it. Was this not dramatherapy?

Dan Baron Cohen

TOWARDS A RADICAL POPULAR THERAPY

DAN   My stories are just two from countless anecdotes here in the North which reveal what might be called the 'therapeutic reflex', appropriate cultural responses based upon 'empathetic insight and solidarity'. Both imply why it wouldn't be in the interests of an undemocratic State to promote therapy as a radical and empowering option, for how could authority function without the appropriate psychological and emotional 'constitution'? It would be interesting to know whether the therapeutic reflex is stimulated at times of crisis, in a bid for self-protection or self-empowerment. What is more interesting is that within communities where a 'humanity' based on solidarity and shared experience is still intact, such a reflex is a commonplace mechanism for diffusing tension and tendering support. Women here are constantly creating para-therapeutic spaces (inside toilets, corridors, kitchens and parks), to find a safe place where they cannot be overheard, be seen crying, even be seen meeting! When breaking down, reflecting, creating and adapting rituals, evolving methods and tactics, drawing upon one another and themselves to learn and transform their world, women are developing the methods and forms of what I would call a 'dialogic' therapy, appropriate to their needs and their resources.

JAMES   This is the therapeutic potential you see in your community.

DAN   That's right. Now once you systematise this 'reflex', once you pro-fessionalise and fund it, dont you risk transforming it into a new, more subtle, more benign form of authority?

JAMES   The authority of the expert –

DAN   Would systematising these paratherapeutic reflexes mystify and alien-ate them into an inert and hierarchical set of behavioural dogma?

JAMES   To be useful, they would need to be developed into a conscious and creative, therapeutic schema –

DAN   Providing the development and practice of such a process were carried out by the community itself –

JAMES   But if the therapist works with a client totally within the client's frame of reference and only responds to his or her desires and perceived needs, doesn't this inhibit the potential for therapy?

DAN   I think the most respected counselling within any 'community' inte-grates the internal/external perspectives in offering empathetic, *committed but detached* support. But I think you're right to focus on 'frame of reference', for this pinpoints what would be a fundamental priority within any liberation therapy: the rejection of 'neutrality' and the embracing of 'commitment' as the founding principle of therapeutic practice.

JAMES   Commitment to changing the world that damaged the individual?

DAN   Absolutely. The question is, of course, how far do you go? As a community therapist, do you endorse the politics of armed conflict for instance, not only because that is your community's own solution to injustice, but because you consider that to be the most rational and practical solution to global exploitation and suffering?

JAMES   A therapist can (and must) support a client emotionally, with-out necessarily supporting the actions of armed struggle.

DAN   But where does the therapist stand? We agree that the therapeutic space needs to lie 'outside and beyond' the anguish of the client, in a psycho-social sense, not merely a physical one. This is still always a *political space*. And for people here this sense of political space is fundamental –

JAMES   Which enables them to cloud the potential sympathy of their reaction to terrible acts of violence done in their name, outside their area.

DAN   I don't think that describes the majority. Contrary to what the media would have us believe, all the people I know empathise with the victims of this war, and their families. But let me approach this in another way: why does the Catholic Church deliberately appoint working-class priests to parishes well outside their own community? This severance of cultural bonds is explained in terms of distancing priests from relationships which might prejudice or undermine their judgement. Is it not more accurate to say that this act of deportation reinforces the authority of the church's judgement and its power over the community, depriving it of some of its most able, motivated and disciplined activists?

JAMES   Are you saying that only 'therapists from within' are capable of practising this more radical community therapy?

DAN   I am arguing for a committed therapy of liberation which only those who live and think in solidarity with the oppressed would be capable of practising: a therapeutic practice which places the methods and objectives of self-determination at its centre.

JAMES   But wouldn't such a therapy be subject to the prevailing community culture of survival, rather than independent of it?

DAN   I think that depends on the depth of confidence the community can invest in *every* therapist. The therapists will be trusted and supported as long as they respond to the needs of the individual and the community *consistently*; ground their method in a profound sensitivity to the community's knowledges and kinship structures; openly consult the community to resolve their difficulties; and ensure their methods and skills are popularised as part of a new, inclusive and dynamic culture. Though such work would need to be initially pioneered by activists (demonstrating and popularising their methods through *forum* and *legislative* theatre), their clear objective would be the evolution of an extensive network of community therapists within families and streets. This is all highly speculative, but I think it sketches the kind of dialogic therapeutic practice which would be effective in communities like the Bogside, and would make a radical contribution to debates about community policing in the post-ceasefire era.

JAMES   What exactly do you mean by dialogic?

DAN   I've seen both community groups and spontaneous gatherings in the home involved in intuitive therapeutic practices, using myth, story-telling, role-reversal and psychodrama to support and heal one another. But at one moment, one person facilitates another; at another, a group facilitates the original facilitator; in yet another situation, the original person mediates between two whole families. I don't want to idealise such community structures which can be manipulated to be fiercely reactionary and destructive. It simply strikes me that the potential exists within such community networks to evolve a *multivocal* model which celebrates dialogue and diversity rather than authority and conformity.

JAMES   Certainly, individual therapists (including myself), draw upon such 'natural' forms, which tend to evolve through client-centred workshops. But I don't think it would be easy for therapists like myself to enter your kind of community to facilitate those forms. I can't help thinking your personal relationship with someone from within the community also contributes to people's openness to the more experimental projects Derry Frontline has launched.

DAN   I think you may be right. Fundamentally though, people believe therapists are intent on pathologising the causes of all conflict – whether in the home or against the State – and writing off communities like the Bogside as psychotic and asocial. From without, the situation looks bleak, and to be honest, behind the proud defiant nationalist murals exists an appalling world of internalised violence and debt-inspired gambling and alcoholism. But there's so much more that's invisible to the outsider, living potentials which mustn't be allowed to be decimated by the ruthlessness of consumerism and its culture of cynical individualism.

JAMES   As we edge towards a ceasefire, people are talking about community policing and economic regeneration. Is there any word about counselling and healing?

DAN   You can understand why the question of policing and employment would be uppermost in people's minds. But behind the barricade of wise and angry cynicism, there's an emerging voice insisting that a 'therapy of liberation' needs to be a part of any post-conflict community development strategy. It's a voice which will grow in confidence and influence once activists start to read the therapeutic reports that are beginning to emerge from South Africa and Palestine. The ceasefire won't ease the pressure of poverty in the Bog, but it'll give people a little space and an impulse to think practically about the effects of this war, and the future.

JAMES   Very much the theme of *Threshold*.

DAN   That's right. Evidence that these ideas are already being explored behind the barricade. And as in *Threshold*, I suspect the most remarkable political change will now develop inside people's homes, through an intimate politics of *personal* conflict, towards a more profound model of

individual identity and community democracy. I'm sure dramatherapy
will be the political theatre of the future.

JAMES   Community-based dramatherapy?

DAN   Can there be any other?

Reconciliation

He didn't wear their uniform
You'll have to nail it to our backs, they said
You won't brand us with your crimes
Your shirt's already drenched in blood
and it's not even been worn

He didn't rot in the stench of his own shit
so you could trade in his dream
I didn't smuggle his wee notes of hope
inside this body for twelve years
for you to sign our land away to the banks

I didn't bury a son
and the sons of ten mothers before him
so you could hand this struggle over
on a plate
And I didn't walk with this knot of rage in my heart

from years of raids
stripsearches and uncried tears
to see my grandchildren grown up
afeared to hold up their heads
and say with pride

That's my father
He gave up his life
so I could be free

Threshold Derry, 1992

ACKNOWLEDGEMENT

Dan Baron Cohen and James King would like to thank Rosie O'Hara for her
assistance in editing these dialogues.

Chapter 20

Making the law – breaking the law

Tom Magill and Roisin Muldoon

INTRODUCTION

In January 1994 we undertook a drama project with a group of joyriders from West Belfast, having participated in a Social Action Groupwork course the previous summer. Given our prior knowledge of the Turas participant group we anticipated that the drama group might identify key issues of relevance and importance to their own lives, for example dealing with authority (police, paramilitaries, church, etc.), unemployment, joyriding, alcohol, drugs and women. Our initial title, 'Making the Law – Breaking the Law' was, we thought, wide enough to encapsulate whatever themes, issues and problems the potential group of young people might contribute. The project was designed to provide a practical introduction to theatre skills through groupwork and to build confidence and self-esteem by gradual stages towards presentation through dialogue. The six-month project developed into 'Oliver Twisted' and culminated in a video, based on the modern version of the Dickens story, through which the young people tell their own story.

CULTURAL AND POLITICAL CONTEXT

Catholic West Belfast comprises a large, sprawling area which stretches from the Divis flats near Belfast city centre to the newer open-planned estates of outer West Belfast – Lenadoon, Twinbrook and Poleglass. The population of the area is overwhelmingly working class.

Few communities have suffered as much violence over the past twenty-five years as Catholic West Belfast. Few communities have endured so much poverty and been deprived for so long of the resources necessary for a decent standard of living. The area has suffered historically from a chronic unemployment rate.

Most communities rely on the police to deal with crime in their localities. This is not the case in West Belfast. A substantial proportion of the community does not recognise the Royal Ulster Constabulary as a legitimate police force. Certainly prior to the IRA ceasefire declared on 31 August 1994 (and to a lesser extent at the time of writing), the police would have seen their priorities as combating politically motivated crime and protecting the security of their personnel. 'Ordinary' crimes, such as joyriding, would not be given the priority and immediate attention necessary to reassure the public as in other inner-city areas.

Feeling unprotected and vulnerable, many residents have developed a deep and unforgiving hostility towards joyriders. Many turn to the paramilitaries in their frustration, exerting pressure on them to deal with the problem. Consequently the paramilitaries have become the alternative police, the courts and the punishers.

THE JOYRIDING PHENOMENON

The joyriding phenomenon in West Belfast has been traced back to the hijacking of cars, orchestrated by the paramilitaries during the early to mid-1970s. Whilst this may have been one initial impetus, joyriding has for many years been a popular activity, not only in West Belfast but in many deprived inner-city areas in Britain and Ireland. Cars represent wealth, status and speed.

Northern Ireland does not suffer from a major joyriding problem. Statistics for car theft indicate rates of less than half the average for England and Wales. However, when West Belfast is examined in isolation a different picture emerges. In 1987 42 per cent of all cars stolen in Northern Ireland were recovered in West Belfast. By 1990 and 1991 the percentage of cars recovered had increased to 47.7 per cent and 47.2 per cent respectively.

Joyriders in West Belfast face a dual justice system. Those apprehended by the security forces are processed through the criminal justice system. Simultaneously, those identified and reported to the paramilitaries are beaten or exiled, or become victims of punishment shootings. Neither system is successful in deterring the persistent joyrider. Following lengthy negotiations between various voluntary and statutory agencies, funding was secured to tackle the problem of joyriding, and the Turas Project was set up in July 1991.

THE TURAS PROJECT: SETTING THE TASK

It was envisaged that Turas would supplement efforts already being made to engage and work with joyriders in West Belfast. One group of joyriders eluding the voluntary and statutory agencies were those most persistent offenders – a relatively small group of joyriders. From the outset it was agreed that Turas would adopt a unique approach. In addition to being offence/offender-specific it was agreed that the project would attempt to engage joyriders at times when they were most likely to offend – i.e. in the evenings and at weekends. Further, police statistics indicated that the vast majority of cars stolen in Northern Ireland were recovered in three estates located on the outskirts of West Belfast – Twinbrook, Poleglass and Lenadoon. In order to measure success and to be accountable to the community it was decided that the project would also be area-specific and so target these three estates deemed most high risk.

EMPOWERMENT

From the outset Turas staff have been committed to the notion of empowerment – giving the participant group a voice, control over the agenda and ownership of the programme. In working with persistent joyriders on a voluntary basis in a detached youth work mode it has always been acknowledged that to impose a staff agenda and ideas without consultation would be a recipe for disaster. However, pressure has been exerted on Turas staff from time to time to work with a high percentage of the targeted participant group, resulting in quantitative rather than qualitative contact.

THE INITIAL PROPOSAL

What we mapped out in our proposal was a *process* of working, based on group *ownership* of the material.

The model/design

The design or model for the structure or process is based on a Social Action Groupwork (SAG) model, applied from a sociological perspective and on adapting and applying the work of Augusto Boal[1] from a theatre perspective. Central to both is the concept of *change*.

SAG practice principles

Mullender and Ward (1990) outline the six practice principles which underpin the SAG model. Applied to the Turas participant group the six principles (illustrated in Figures 20.1–20.6) are as follows:

Principle 1

> We need to take a new view of the people we work with, refusing to accept negative labels and recognising instead that all people have skills, understanding and ability.

Figure 20.1 Social Action Groupwork practice principle 1

Principle 2

People have rights, including the right to be heard and the right to control their own lives. It follows that people also have the right to choose what kinds of intervention to accept in their lives. Service users must always be given the right to decide whether or not to participate in self-directed work, and the right to define issues and take action on them.

PRINCIPLE 2

'THE RIGHT TO CHOOSE'

GROUP WORK ······
or
ONE TO ONE ······

'CONTROL OVER THE AGENDA OF ACTION'

Figure 20.2 Social Action Groupwork practice principle 2

Principle 3

The problems that service users face are complex and responses reflect this. People's problems can never be fully understood if they are seen solely as a result of personal inadequacies. Issues of oppression, social policy, the environment and the economy are, more often than not, and particularly in the lives of service users, major contributory forces. Practice should reflect this understanding.

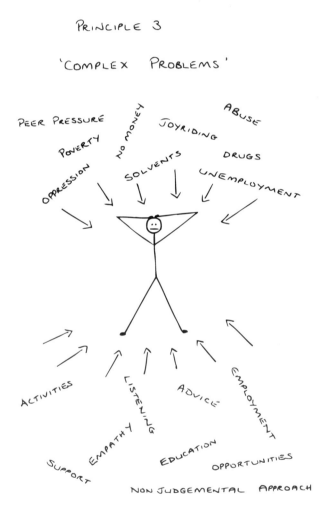

Figure 20.3 Social Action Groupwork practice principle 3

Principle 4

Practice can effectively be built on the knowledge that people acting collectively can be powerful. People who lack power can gain it through coming together in groups.

Figure 20.4 Social Action Groupwork practice principle 4

Principle 5

Practise what you preach. Methods of working must reflect non-elitist principles. Workers do not 'lead' the group but facilitate members in making decisions for themselves and in controlling whatever outcome ensues. Though special skills and knowledge are employed, these do not accord privilege and are not solely the province of the workers.

Figure 20.5 Social Action Groupwork practice principle 5

Principle 6

Our work must challenge all forms of oppression whether by reason of race, gender, sexual orientation, age, disability, class, or any other form of social differentiation upon which spurious notions of superiority and inferiority have historically been (and continue to be) built and kept in place by the exercise of power.

Figure 20.6 Social Action Groupwork practice principle 6

Evaluating the effectiveness of the project

Evaluating a creative piece of work can at best be difficult. For us, the workers, to evaluate the project would result in a subjective report, yet unless we ended up with a finished product it would be impossible for a third party to carry out a comprehensive evaluation. Usually when undertaking such a piece of work we would be confident of concluding with an end product. However, on this occasion, given our knowledge of the client group and the focus of the SAG model/principles, we were not so sure. We had grave doubts as to our participant group's ability to adhere to the task in hand and their ability to see the project through to the end. The SAG model reflects the view that it is not the product but the process that matters. Determined to cover ourselves and to satisfy our managers/funders we decided to record the entire process from beginning to end on videotape, pending the agreement of the participant group. As it transpired, the group were not opposed to the project's being videoed, and although we did not realise it at the time this aspect of the project was to become an all-important safeguard at a later stage, in relation to delivering a final product to the funding agency.

From our experience of using drama in the past we know that it can produce positive change in people. However, what methodology could we use to quantify, measure and evaluate the effectiveness of our work with this group? We settled on a form of participant observation, with a former joyrider operating the video camera to record the process of rehearsals.

Timescale and attendance

Initially we had thought the project would run from January to May; in practice it ran until July. We had weekly three-hour sessions, occasional weekends and one weekend residential; in total we had approximately 120 contact hours.

The group were predominantly male, aged 16–25; only 15–20 per cent of members were female. They had started joyriding between the ages of 11 and 16, and had been involved for five to ten years. The number attending each session ranged from two to twenty-two; average attendance per session was seven members.

THE SELF-DIRECTED GROUPWORK MODEL

Rationale

This model involves users taking collective action for mutual empowerment. We were attracted to the model for several reasons:

1 It is premised on groupwork and draws on Paulo Freire's 'problem-solving' approach to education (1972). Freire rejects the traditional 'banking'

concept of education, whereby information is deposited into a passive empty vessel, and believes instead in a liberating education that can lead people to take the initiative in acting to transform the society that has denied them the opportunity of participation. Uniting Freire, Boal (1979) and Social Action Groupwork (Mullender and Ward 1990) is the concept of social change through collective reflection and action based upon that reflection.

2 It resists negative labels.
3 It resists blaming the individual victim – e.g. seeing crime as a symptom not the cause of social ills.
4 It advocates users' taking control, with spectators becoming active – *spect-actors* in Boal's terminology (Boal 1992).
5 It insists that issues are dealt with in the open.

The five stages

There are five main stages, subdivided into twelve steps:

Stage a: The workers take stock: pre-planning stage.
Stage b: The group takes off: 'open planning' – the group sets its goals.
Stage c: The group prepares to take action:

- What are the problems to be tackled?
- Why do they exist?
- How can we produce change?

Stage d: Action – do it!
Stage e: Reflection on action.

(See Mullender and Ward, 1991, pp. 18–19.)

THE PROJECT: SIGNIFICANT EVENTS IN THE DIARY

There are three different strands to this story: the negative, the positive and the personal. All present different points of view. In the accounts that follow Tom's and Roisin's views are presented alternately (TM and RM).

The negative (TM)

January   People arrive drunk at the theatre venue; a fist fight breaks out in the venue over the definition of democracy and what constitutes a majority, in a vote as to whether people should be allowed to observe while others are participating.

February We are evicted from the venue because of the above behaviour.

Numbers drop from twenty-two to seven because 'Sundays are hangover days'.

We are stopped and searched by the British army because P and T were in the car; after they had given their names and addresses they were labelled as 'suspicious characters'.

The weekend residential: D is 'scooped' (picked up by the police) for having 'blow' (marijuana). A fight breaks out in the dormitory because people laugh at O's 'wounds'. (O had just been kneecapped by the IRA.) The majority are on a cocktail of 'bing' (cider), 'blow', and 'Eee's' (ecstasy). They rampage around the building setting off fire-alarms, soaking bedding with fire-extinguishers, shouting abuse at the girls, and so on, until 6.00 a.m. when they fall asleep exhausted. Next morning when confronted with their behaviour F pushes over the tripod with the camera on it, confronts R, our female worker, face to face and smashes the minibus window before leaving.

March Post-residential membership drops from ten to four.

April In our new venue, a bowling alley, we are there a few weeks when speakers are unscrewed and stolen from the wall. They deny the theft. We are evicted from the bowling alley.

May We are down to three members from an original twenty-two. We list where the others have gone over the four months:

- Five are in prison.
- Four are going steady or getting married.
- Three are 'ex-directory' (lying low because of IRA threats).
- Three are still 'hooding' (committing crimes for money).
- Two have emigrated.
- Two were 'swalling' (drinking very heavily).
- Two were homeless.
- One was 'exiled' by the IRA after a kneecapping.
- One was pregnant.
- One was working part time.

(We also gained four new members over this period.)

June We arrange for the group to see a play I had directed in Dublin. They fight in the bus on the way down, urinate on the road, fall down the steps drunk, try to start a fight in the foyer.

July The client group 'pull the plug' on the project because a member of staff will not collude in providing an alibi to help one person beat a car-theft charge.

The negative (RM)

January Overtly sexist behaviour and attitudes are demonstrated by one male participant, following which several young women participants opt out. Our delivery at the inaugural meeting is disjointed and uncoordinated. We (staff) had our own agenda.

February (residential) The group break the rules they themselves had agreed to by not restricting or limiting the amount of alcohol they had agreed upon.

March New participants arrive, openly roll up 'joints', breaking group rules. The group fail to challenge, and the staff are forced to police the group.

May Because of a drop in numbers several new members are recruited, creating difficulties for the staff since the new members do not fall into the Turas target participant group.

June Despite a final surge of energy and effort to complete the project, the sound does not come out on the video recording. The reshoot which is scheduled fails to take place.

The positive (TM)

January One lad's sexism is a catalyst in the young women's group, provoking rage and 'the best session yet'.
  F stays still and allows people to touch his face while they make a mask on him. (F is the loudest, most intelligent and most aggressive male in the group and also the most sexist.)
  F makes a personal discovery when I say we need to work on the opposite of ourselves – e.g. stillness and silence if we are always moving and talking. 'That's me,' he said quietly.
  F picks up all the litter from the floor that others have dropped at the end of the session. The girls look amazed!

February Those who stay after we have given the ultimatum on the residential – 'stay and work sober' – work positively together on common personal issues of oppression.

March Together we find a structure for distancing the compromising personal material they are generating (they force me to look at the *Oliver* musical), updating it to West Belfast today. *Oliver* deals with the story of an orphan's initiation into a marginalised criminal peer group, 'proving' himself through theft; it is a rite of passage from boyhood to manhood. The peer group becomes the parent who accepts people for what they are.

April   F sets himself up on the office computer to type fifteen scenes updating *Oliver*. This is seen both as 'empowering the user' and 'cluttering up the office'.

May   The cast share personal stories of running away from home, from beatings, from cruel parents. Everyone listens intently to each other. We now have respect and honesty.

We switch media from theatre to video, from delayed to instant gratification, much more in keeping with working-class values. People now can be present in their absence on video!

June   We prepare a production schedule; everyone is allocated a task. F designs a poster: a boy (Oliver), with a screwdriver twisting his head in one direction and a spanner on his neck twisting in the opposite direction. 'Who do the hands belong to?' I ask. 'The church and the Ra' (Irish Republican Army).

July   We find our locations and shoot the exterior shots – 'We constantly amaze ourselves with our own inventiveness and spontaneity. Everyone is pulling together as a team. It feels good' (TM field notes).

We discover a continuous hum over the interior shots and vote unanimously to reshoot them.

The positive (RM)

January   A large group of participants turn up for the first meeting in Poleglass Youth Centre.

Despite the overtly sexist behaviour of one male participant several young women continue to attend the sessions.

February   Following difficulties at the residential, the main protagonist apologises to the female member of staff (he had been abusive to her when he turned up at another Turas activity).

March   In spite of falling attendance figures a core group of four participants emerge who are determined to complete the project.

The personal (TM)

I imagined an instant rapport with this group: we shared many things in common – a working-class Belfast background, convictions for joyriding and imprisonment – but twenty years have passed since then and differences such as education outweigh the apparent similarities. I also imagined sectarianism would be a central issue. Sexism was in fact the major difficulty in the group initially. With the benefit of hindsight I would now place alcohol abuse at the centre, feeding out to four linked strands – violence, joyriding, sexism and imprisonment – linking the square around the circle.

The personal (RM)

In co-working on this project I was cautious from the outset. Both my colleagues, though having extensive experience in working with young people and drama, lacked direct experience of working with the Turas participant group. While the group were participating in the drama project they were simultaneously participating in other areas of the Turas programme. Adhering to the Social Action Groupwork model resulted in confusion and conflict at times for participants and staff alike. On occasions I felt that I was letting the participants down, that I had set them up to fail by not policing the group, not being more directive, and so on. The group were clearly not ready to take control of the agenda. They needed more guidance, support and direction.

THEATRE OR THERAPY: WHOSE CHOICE FOR CHANGE?

> The richest and most productive way to work with a group is to help them find their own voice, not to speak for them. When individuals don't express themselves emotionally for long periods of time they get sick; communities are the same. One way for our communities to heal is for all of us to take back our rights of healthy collective expression.
>
> (Schutzman and Cohen-Cruz 1994, p. 35)

'Therapy'

Since taking up my post as a probation officer in the Turas Project I (R.M.) have been wary of using the term 'therapy' to describe the work that I am doing. I am committed to working creatively with young people and have no doubt that much of what they undertake through drama, art, music, dance, writing, etc., is in itself therapeutic. Giving an alienated, disadvantaged young person a medium to vent their concerns and dreams, an opportunity to explain their anger and frustrations, can afford the worker an insight into where that young person is coming from and is at. The worker then has a responsibility to engage the young person in dialogue and to deal with what emerges from their contribution. Certainly this can be therapeutic for the individual, but therapy it is not.

The term 'therapy' can be alienating and patronising when one is working with a group of young people who are already alienated and whose experience of authority figures is of being patronised by them.

Motivation for change

We both agree that there are difficulties with the word therapy. Therapy for whom? Whose choice for change? We found in working with this group that any deviation from the peer-group norms – apathy, non-engagement, distrust – was viewed as a threat to the peer-group hegemony. This resulted in a tension between the group's desire for change and a distrust in their ability to effect change. Frustration was the outcome in this case.

POLICING THE GROUP: TO INCLUDE OR EXPEL?

At the outset of the project we agreed to resist expelling members, in accordance with the Self-Directed Groupwork model, as the participants already had a history of rejection and expulsion. In their own words: 'There's only one group lower than us – "touts"' (informers). We insisted that the group 'police' themselves. The result was that no one was ever sanctioned or expelled from the group, despite some appalling behaviour. The 'rebel' image has a very strong attraction in their community: for them, unlike the paramilitaries, who have very strict codes and rules, being 'rebellious' means breaking any rules that appear as rules, except the rules of the peer group, which don't appear as rules but as 'normal' or 'natural' behaviour, once inside the peer group. Having the power to make rules and follow them is an alien concept. Their creativity, imagination and inventiveness are limitless, however, when they are intent upon disrupting another agenda.

LIMITATIONS OF THE MODEL IN PRACTICE

Applying the Social Action Groupwork model for the first time in practice with a marginalised group we found that it favoured those who were already 'leaders' within the peer group – the dominant, the articulate, the aggressive, etc. Young women particularly, and some of the 'quieter' males in the group, would need to have their communication skills and assertiveness updated prior to their participation in the group. Likewise, some of the more dominant males would need their listening skills updated before they could participate on equal terms as a group member.

The SAG is a very demanding one, requiring participants to become and remain motivated in the project. A former joyrider who was working as a volunteer commented: 'They're not ready for this yet' – taking responsibility for themselves.

FEEDBACK ON THE PROJECT

Following the conclusion of the project feedback was gathered from several sources. We set out below the comments received from: Sam Fitzsimons, community youth leader and drama co-worker on the Turas project; Price Waterhouse, the project evaluators; participants who completed a post-project questionnaire; and Jean O'Neill, area manager.

The community youth leader and drama co-work

Never in twenty years of youth-work experience can I call to mind any process that has frustrated me as much as this particular project – based on the Social Action Groupwork Model. This model, I feel, is not dissimilar to that of the Social Education Model which most youth workers would be familiar with. The trouble that I had was that whilst I felt that empowerment and creating a sense of ownership was of vital importance, it only served to frustrate the group further.

Sam Fitzsimons

The videos demonstrate clearly the internal dynamics within the group and the self-supervising nature of much of the interaction. There is an evident hierarchy of status within the group. The workshops suggest that it is possible to engage this marinalized group in what might, at first, seem like an unlikely activity. The high skill level required to successfully undertake this task is also apparent.

(Price Waterhouse 1995)

The participants

(Some of the following information was collated by Anita Pannell, a former project worker with the Turas project.)

A number of the participants agreed to fill in a questionnaire about the project. Asked for their reasons for becoming involved in the project two-thirds said that they were interested in doing a play and one-third said that it was because they had heard that the group was making decisions rather than the leaders.

Two-thirds attended the workshop nearly every week and one-third every week. Two-thirds thought that the purpose of the workshop was putting on a play about your own life and owning the group, making your own rules, setting your own agenda. Everybody agreed that they had more of a say than usual in the group, and two-thirds thought that the group dealt with issues and problems of concern and interest to them, such as thieving, drinking, family arguments, getting into trouble. Two-thirds agreed that the group looked at ways of bringing about change in your life for the better, and wanted more of this; they also agreed that the group helped them learn drama and theatre skills.

Everyone agreed that the group made them aware that others had similar problems and they were not alone in their struggle. They also agreed that the group made them feel good about themselves. Two-thirds felt more comfortable with acting now and more able to talk in groups. Everyone agreed they were more able to make decisions with friends and more able to tell others what they thought. They also agreed that it was easier to understand why they faced some of the problems they did. Two-thirds thought that they were more able to take action with their friends to make their life better, and they liked belonging to the group, taking part in it, sharing interests and having a bit of responsibility. The same proportion didn't like the messing about and thought that some people were not ready to take responsibility for themselves, as demonstrated by behaviour such as coming in late, under the influence of drugs, or drunk.

All agreed that they would like to take part in a similar group again. Asked for suggestions and improvements for a similar course in the future they said: get more commitment from people; a bigger effort; a different venue; get the group to take responsibility for sorting people out.

The area manager

Drama is a safe way for young offenders to act out and describe their offending and experiences on the street, with family, peer group and the various organisations involved.

The initial response was positive, although staff reported back on some of the difficulties encountered in sessions. There was generally good attendance and an air of enthusiasm. The involvement of a sessional drama worker (Tom Magill) was useful in that it brought in new experiences and new skills, and it allowed staff members to concentrate on monitoring and organising the group. As the project progressed, concerns were expressed as to the effectiveness of the social action model with this particular group of young offenders. Progress was very slow, and it was difficult to maintain the interest of a group who are used to instant gratification. I was also aware that the staff involved had different views as to the validity of the model, although these difficulties were expressed and aired.

The final product (video) is disappointing, and is no reflection of the commitment and hard work of participants and staff members. Yet the process (which itself is recorded) shows the strength of using drama, and the dangers of sticking strictly to one model when concerns had been expressed about it. It was a difficult project, yet worthwhile in that it fitted well within the overall programme offered by Turas. It engaged a number of difficult young people and gave them an interest in fields outside cars and joyriding. Drama will continue to be used within the project.

Jean O'Neill

PROCESS AND PRODUCT: THE PRESSURE TO PERFORM

The criteria that funding agencies generally use to measure success are based on product. Product is visible; it can be viewed in public for all to see; it can portray change in a manifest form; it has a voice and speaks of itself; it has a beginning, middle and end. Product is easy to measure and judge in terms of its success or failure. Product can be weighed and priced. Product works on the premise of excluding those who won't measure up to be shown off. Product can be viewed in an evening. Product promises value for money.

Process, on the other hand, is virtually impossible to view. It finds it hard to portray itself in a manifest form. It is very self conscious and shy of the public. Its voice is uncertain and hesitant. It cannot be viewed in an evening. Process includes all of those who want to be involved, despite their past record. Process promises only participation.

In an era of temporary work contracts and competition amongst freelance workshop leaders for employment, the pressures to conform to the dictates of product are extreme.

The video: poor product or proof of process?

The video of 'Oliver Twisted' is virtually unedited, and there is a continuous hum over the interior shots from the local generator on the estate. But what we have is a record of the process of engaging in a dialogue with a very difficult and challenging group of young people, many of whom, in our opinion, have moved on significantly from where they were when they first arrived. Does this constitute therapy? From whose point of view? How do we evaluate it? How do we prove it? Who's listening anyway?

REFERENCES AND FURTHER READING

Boal, A. (1979) *The Theatre of the Oppressed*, London: Pluto Press.
—— (1992) *Games For Actors and Non-Actors*, London: Routledge.
—— (1995) *Playing Boal: Theatre, Therapy, Activism*, ed. M. Schutzman and J. Cohen-Cruz, London: Routledge.
—— (1995) *The Rainbow of Desire*, London: Routledge.
Chapman, T. (1993/4) 'The search for an effective community-based strategy for preventing the theft of cars: the West Belfast experience', *Social Action Journal* 1:4.

Freire, P. (1972) *Pedagogy of the Oppressed*, Harmondsworth, UK: Penguin.

Magill, T. (1994) 'Applying Boal in Belfast: two contrasting case studies', *Contemporary Theatre Review* (Autumn).

McCullough, D., Schmidt, T. and Lockhart, B. (1990) *Car Theft in Northern Ireland*, Cirac Paper 2.

Mullender, A., and Ward, D. (1990) Social Action Groupwork Theory.

—— (1991) *Self-Divided Groupwork: Users Take Action for Empowerment*, Nottingham: Whiting and Birch.

Prochaska, J. and Di Clemente, C. (1984) Daw-Jones-Irwin. The Transtheoretical Approach Crossing Traditional Boundaries of Therapy.

Poulter, C. (1988) *Playing the Game*, London: Macmillan.

Price Waterhouse (1995) *Turas Evaluation: Final Report*.

Chapter 21

Children of the Troubles

Crissiie Poulter

'I'm sick of Catholic and Protestant shows . . . they say we should talk about it but we don't talk about anything else!'

When people go to a psychotherapist they probably expect to discuss themselves and their lived experiences, and if they go to a dramatherapist they might expect to engage in dramatic activity based on such experiences. Is it safe to assume that they have gone to a therapist because they, or someone on their behalf, believes that their well-being is currently less than it could and should be? Is it believed therefore, that to talk about oneself and to come to terms with one's history can contribute to an improvement in one's well-being?

The reasons why people engage in community drama and, more particularly, community theatre are not so clear. Their relationship with their own lived experience and that of their families and friends is not always a valued site of exploration. If it's a comic sketch you want, or a funny story, . . . well, that's okay but if suggested as a serious subject of study it's a different matter altogether. . .

I live it; I don't want to play it and replay it . . .

As a result of the violent warring between the two main communities, the well-being of Northern Ireland could be said to be presently at risk and a number of initiatives have been developed over recent years which aim to reconcile its divided peoples. 'Education for Mutual Understanding' is a compulsory cross-curricular element in schools . . . 'Conflict Resolution' is high on the agenda of training needs for youth and community workers . . . The organisation 'Cooperation North' arranges exchange visits between North and South and between Catholic and Protestant youth groups, which always include a mandatory session with a facilitator whose role is to ensure that a discussion of self and other is included along the way. The 'Cultural Traditions' fund from the Community Relations Council is available only to projects which explore and express aspects of the two main, differing cultural traditions in Northern Ireland.

Many community drama projects have received support from such initiatives. Drama is, after all, such an effective way to explore different characters and situations. But the notion of reflection as a step towards reconciliation is not uppermost in everyone's list of motivations for involvement in drama.

'It's bad enough living here without doing plays about it. We want to give people a chance to get away from all that. . . to have a laugh . . .'

Yet Augusto Boal, a drama and theatre practitioner admired by so many others working in the field of community and educational development, is clear that we replay it to rework it, and to transfer that reworking from the aesthetic space of the drama to the real space of life.

In this chapter I shall discuss the therapeutic aspects of community drama and theatre in Northern Ireland, as demonstrated by two projects, one in inner-city Belfast and the other in rural Fermanagh. I shall also consider the problems posed by the word 'therapy' for those participating in work outside of the medical context.

WHERE AM I FROM? (1)

I was sitting out, by the flats, and a dirty nappy came flying down and landed beside me. Someone had just thrown it over their balcony. And that just made me think . . . the younger people round here don't care about the area . . . they take no pride in it . . . there's rubbish lying everywhere . . . they don't need anyone else to tell them they live in a lousy area. They think so themselves anyway. They've no respect for the older people . . . for their own grandparents. And then I thought I'd love to do something that would let them know just who their grandparents are . . . so they would be proud of them and of this place.

(adult; inner-city Belfast; joint instigator of the first community play in the area)

We don't want to do a bombs and bullets show . . . it's all they expect if you say you're from Northern Ireland . . . and we don't want to do one on the history of [our town] . . . it's boring.

(teenager; rural market town; engaged in devising youth theatre show to take to international festival of youth arts)

What's a shamrock?

(9-year-old; inner-city Belfast; creating a show in school to be shown to older residents, based on stories of the area gathered from home and from local history pages of the local newspaper)

WHERE AM I FROM? (2)

Northern Ireland has been the site of sectarian conflict for many years. The players change frequently, the scenario rarely. The island of Ireland comprises thirty-two counties and used to be part of the United Kingdoms of Great Britain. For most of this century only six of those counties have remained in the union with the UK. The other twenty-six were granted independence and are now known as the Republic of Ireland. Within the six counties now known as Northern Ireland, a bitter sectarian divide has occurred between those wishing to remain loyal to the union with the UK (Loyalists/Unionists – mainly Protestants) and those wishing to become part of the Republic and thus create an Irish nation once more, this time independent of British rule (Republicans/Nationalists – mainly Catholics). Before the ceasefire declared in 1994, sectarian killings had become an expected part of everyday life, together with sometimes fatal confrontations between the armed police, the British army and the paramilitaries within both communities. In twenty-five years, over three thousand people have lost their lives as a result of these most recent 'Troubles'.

TERRITORIES (PHYSICAL)

In many parts of the country, rural and urban, people live in areas defined by sectarian boundaries. In the rural areas such boundaries are known but not actual. In the inner city areas of Belfast they are enforced by so-called 'peace-lines', i.e. physical walls and railings which have been introduced since the current Troubles began over twenty-five years ago. Speed ramps (raised strips of road surface created to enforce a slower speed and therefore prevent fast escapes) are common, as are army checkpoints (where vehicles would regularly be stopped, the driver questioned and the vehicle sometimes searched). During the ceasefire the daytime checkpoints and street patrols were ceased and in some towns the speed ramps were removed.

TERRITORIES (CULTURAL)

As well as the imposed physical boundaries which delineate some of the areas, there are many cultural symbols and practices which distinguish Catholic from Protestant, Republican from Loyalist. The age-old religious distinctions remain, between the Catholic Church and those other Christian churches which were founded and have grown over the past five hundred years, protesting against the dictates of this Church of Rome and its leader the Pope yet still following the teachings of Christ and therefore still Christian. They are many and various (Anglican, Presbyterian, Church of England/Scotland/Ireland, etc.), yet all are united by their protest and hence known collectively as Protestant. The main visible distinction in present-day Ireland would probably be the prominence given to Mary, the mother of Christ, in Catholic ceremonies and decoration.

The most noticeably distinct ceremonies and symbols do not, however, relate to Church but to State and, more particularly, to events that have been major landmarks in the evolving, divided state of Northern Ireland. Thus, on 12 July every year, the Loyalists take to the streets with bands and banners to mark the anniversary of the Battle of the Boyne in 1690, a battle in which the Dutch King William of Orange triumphed over the Catholic armies of King James. Orange is now the symbolic colour of Protestant Loyalism and each area has its own 'Orange Lodge' and Orange Hall. It is these Lodges which produce most of the bands and the banners. The skill of the bands, the artistry of the banners and the military precision of the formations of each Lodge as it marches, reveal the importance of this event to the Protestant community. There has been criticism over recent years that some marches have been straying too far towards triumphalism and, in the choice of route, sometimes through Catholic areas, that tension and violence have been deliberately incited.

Meanwhile on 17 March each year there is St Patrick's Day, a celebration of the man credited with bringing Christianity to Ireland and using the three-part leaf of a native plant, the shamrock, to explain the Christian concept of the Trinity: the three gods in one, the Father, Son and Holy Spirit. St Patrick's Day is a public holiday throughout the island and tends to be celebrated with more of a carnival-style parade – people in costume, marching bands, decorated vehicles and a day of music and social events which move beyond the streets into the pubs and halls as night falls. The green of the shamrock is the symbolic colour of the Republic and therefore of Republicans in the North, and St Patrick's Day tends to be associated with them rather than with all the people of the island.

The difference in symbols goes beyond the colours of orange and green. The colours of the British (red, white and blue) and Irish (green, white and orange) flags are also significant, as are the flags themselves. In Loyalist areas the houses often have fittings attached to an outside wall for carrying flagpole and British flag in the July period. Both communities, in some areas, paint the kerbstones at the roadside in the colours of their respective flags. The flags themselves hang high on the telegraph poles and lamp-posts, out of reach of those who disapprove of such symbols. It is interesting to note that within the UK both Scotland and Wales have their own flag, anthem and floral symbol. Northern Ireland does not and remains frozen in a moment between two histories, British and Irish, unable to rewrite itself with new symbols, one side of the community dispossessed of their own history which included the Irish symbols at one time, symbols now associated with 'the enemy' and therefore lost – hence the ability of a young Protestant child to ask 'What is a shamrock?'

In recent years the Republicans have added another annual ritual, in August, the commemoration of the anniversary of internment (the arrest and jailing of people 'on suspicion of terrorism', without trial). This, and the commemoration of 'Bloody Sunday' (when civil rights marchers were shot by British soldiers in the city of Derry), has produced the equivalent of the

12 July marches, not in any sense of triumph over the other, but rather of defiance unto death.

In a country where rituals are so strongly evident in the way in which the divided community demonstrates its division, where the rituals of church are equally strong and attendance is high, where the forces of the state are visible on the streets, armed and paid to be suspicious of those who appear not to be, where the rituals of a surveillance society are imposed on all its citizens, there is a need to tread carefully with new rituals.

Yet there is a need for new rituals, for excuses to speak of ourselves in a moment of shared celebration, of public affirmation, in order to experience a positive reflection of self and the renewal which that brings with it.

It is not that the age-old rituals within personal and family life have disappeared. Far from it. They continue, strengthened by the strength of the family itself. The sense of locality, heightened by such constant reference to, and defining of, territory ensures that the more public family rituals of marriage and burial become moments when the whole community appears in order to show its support and presence. The frequency of violent death has been high as a consequence of the conflict, with the result that the rituals of death and burial have been extended to become events akin to public demonstration, with all the attendant policing and crowd control.

YOUTH: INNER CITY

With the daily news announcing shootings, explosions, arms finds, diffused bombs, punishment beatings, hijacks and more, not only the world, but also the people of Northern Ireland saw such images as a dominant reflection of themselves. In the inner city the neighbourhood became a prison, too dangerous to leave . . . always the chance of straying into enemy territory with the attendant risk of recognition and reprisal. So people stay at home, in a no-go area for the police, where local policing takes over, a system that can appear similar to the Mafia. The paramilitaries, whose main role is to engage in the struggle outside their immediate locality, become internal godfathers. Anti-social crimes, such as joyriding or drug-dealing, committed in the main by young people, are punishable locally by means such as shooting the culprits in the knee-caps or breaking their legs with iron bars and baseball bats.

And what of these children of the Troubles?

'It's boring round here. . . .'

In a forum theatre piece created and performed a few years ago by joyriders, the opening scene was a stylised 'Boredom Machine'. One person repeatedly flicked a remote control – 'There's nothing on the tele'; others echoed the same sense of nothing to do, nowhere to go and no money to be had, using other repeated gestures and phrases. The play then progressed on to a more recognisably naturalistic sequence concerning a young lad who is tempted to go out with his mates to steal a car. He is caught and his father becomes aggressively violent. The interventions from the spectactors were usually related to the naturalistic sequences: persuading his friends he didn't want to go, arguing with his father more persuasively. The interventions rarely took on the boredom machine. Yet if anything would prevent joyriding for the young man without relieving the poverty and inactivity trap – was it really an answer for him or had it simply contained him, made him more socially acceptable but still unable to contribute either to his own life or to those of the people around him. It may have been the style of the machine; it is possibly easier to intervene in a more naturalistic scene, but there are no rules which say that interventions must follow the acting style of the original. It seemed as if the self-diagnosis which produced the boredom machine was being ignored by some audiences and seen instead as simply a way of setting the scene, of saying 'this is a typical teenager really – just bored at home that's all – isn't it easy for things to get out of hand'. Yet it is this very condition of being a teenager which is so difficult to speak of when you're in it, and here theatre had been used to do just that.

YOUTH: IN THE MIDDLE OF NOWHERE?

In some rural areas there have been no killings. In others where one event has remained in the mind of the world, time can become one-dimensional to the point where the event almost becomes part of the name of the place. In Enniskillen, for example, a town in rural Fermanagh, a Republican bomb exploded near the route of a Remembrance Day parade, as local townspeople gathered to watch the parade. Eleven civilians were killed. It is known as the Poppy Day bomb, because of the poppies associated with the annual period of remembrance when British people remember those who died in the two World Wars of the twentieth century. That bomb was in 1987. When, five years later, a group of local teenagers were creating a show to take to an international theatre festival, they were adamant. 'We're not doing a bombs and bullets show – that's all they expect if you say you're from Northern Ireland.' Five years may be a short time to adults and may be a split second or an eternity to the families of those killed in the explosion, but to a 15-year-old the difference between age 10 and age 15 is enormous. They felt defined by the bomb if they travelled outside the island. Whereas other small market towns would be unheard of, everyone had heard of Enniskillen – 'Oh you poor children, that's where that terrible bomb was', as one of them said to me, mimicking a doubtless concerned adult met on a trip to America.

What are these trips and presents and money and peace initiatives and special funds? Attempts to end a war by investing in reconciliation and alternative possibilities? Unfortunately, one result of all this is that, if and when money becomes available for work with young people, it comes with strings of reconciliation attached, and very often this requires that the work focuses on the Troubles as a theme or that it involves cross-community participation. The young people in Enniskillen were funded by Cultural Traditions, an off-shoot of the Community Relations Council, to take a show to an international festival. The show was to reflect their lives and culture.

When asked what they would like to focus on for the show the teenagers were suspicious of a Cultural Traditions agenda, convinced that the international audience would expect 'a bombs and bullets show'. They also rejected the local heritage agenda: 'We're not doing the history of Enniskillen – it's boring.' They argued that these were not their troubles but rather those created by their parents' generation, and they wanted no part of it. This is inevitably difficult in towns where not only religious practices but also schooling is organised on sectarian lines, and where there is the attendant problem that public buildings tend also to be exclusive to one side or the other. This youth theatre project was taking place in the neutral territory of the local theatre, though the group was nevertheless predominantly Catholic.

Unlike the joyriders, these teenagers were not yet behaving in a manner likely to result in their social condition being identified, diagnosed or treated; they had chosen to spend their leisure time with the youth theatre project, but they were still disempowered in some ways. Not least because they lived in a town vigorously marketed as a tourist destination and therefore full of visitors, in a country avoided by just as many, if not more, who see it as a war zone. The reality for the teenagers came from neither of these pictures. They could not find themselves reflected in either scenario.

Rural and urban, these young people have little chance of employment locally. Yet they are children of families whose history has been tied to the experience of local work and the sense of community which that brings. The mills, the shipyards and the docks were the lifeblood of the Catholic and Protestant communities in the inner city areas of Belfast close to the docks. Farming, fishing and more mills serviced those in more rural towns and villages. All that has disappeared, and still that other historical Irish route is as well followed as ever: emigration. That may be internal migration – from the countryside to the metropolis of Belfast – or it may be from Northern Ireland to England or America, where every Irish family, North or South, has friends and relations. Those that stay will face unemployment, part-time and short-term jobs and, rarely, full-time work which will be in the city centre or 'the other side of town'.

Although the Enniskillen group wanted fun and flippancy in their show, in the end it reflected their very real concerns:

- boredom
- no work prospects
- inevitable emigration

- fear of 'the Big Apple' (New York)
- fear of London's 'cardboard city' (where homeless people sleep out, often in cardboard shelters)
- a town council at home which was overly concerned with tourism – lakes and mountains
- territorial violence around the disco and 'mixed' relationships.

And then there was the 'Troubles'. Despite the stated wish to avoid them they are an everyday part of life, and images cropped up in certain scenes, both humorous and serious, which reflected this. In fact the group chose to finish the show with the most serious 'Troubles' sequence, choreographed to reflect both the Poppy Day explosion and the wider situation in the North. When challenged by Northern Ireland arts *aficionados* who felt that the ending was too bleak, the teenagers stood firm: the audience had enjoyed themselves, had a laugh and then gone home with something to think about – just what they, as doctor, had ordered.

Using material produced by the group, the process of devising the show was an interesting example of drama and theatre being used as tools for diagnosis.

These were 'children of the Troubles', but whose definition of Troubles? Using image theatre and popular song lyrics to investigate sensitive areas of experience and memory – areas which the group avoided if asked to discuss them verbally – the process revealed not only a deeper malaise than that assumed by the outside world but one that the teenagers themselves had not previously articulated. Neither war nor religion but inevitable emigration from their rural homeland was at the top of their unspoken agenda, and a deep hurt and feeling of rejection and betrayal was revealed in relation to this.

To start with there was little said or acknowledged as we tried improvisations around the theme of the future. The question of where they thought they might be in five years time had produced only 'Not here', with no answers as to where might be the alternative to here. . .

Why might someone leave home for two days; weeks; months; years?

Holiday; holiday; holiday: they managed to find a holiday for every situation – a weekend at a friend's or the winner of a two-year round-the-world trip . . . everything was a holiday.

How far ahead did their ambitions lie? Next Friday . . . the disco . . . ten miles out of town . . . all the town discos are church or school . . . too close to home . . . inevitable division . . . identification as a stranger . . . ten miles away is the hotel disco . . . supposed to be for over-18s but who's turning away business for the sake of six months here or there?

What about the cathedral disco in the town? 'Get trouble if they know you're a Catholic,' say the lads. 'We don't get trouble,' reply the girls. 'That's cos you're a girl – fellas get trouble.' 'They don't like you going out with their girls.' 'I had to get a taxi to get me out of there once.'

I think of the Bacchae of Euripides, the women leaving the town to go up the mountain and dance. I bring in some masks from a production of Oedipus: who are the equivalent of the city fathers? the gods? the Bacchantes? Suddenly they are angry . . . about their own civic leaders.

'See the town council? . . . They only care about tourists – they don't care about us.' 'Go up the Diamond [the centre of the town] and see for yourself. . . . you can't even find a phone box . . . they've got hats on.'

Hats?

'Yeah – they've disguised them with hats to look nice for the tourists.'

Sure enough, each phone booth is crowned with wrought iron, to match the 'antiquating' approach to the signposts and rubbish bins . . .

So we get the tourist brochure. The language is almost melodramatic in its effusion. The young people create a pastiche,   'Fishing', and Tom, the co-devisor, writes a tourist sketch for them where the tourist guide trips over a soldier and tries to explain it away to the tourists . . . and to the soldier. . . . and Francis and Chrissie choreograph so that, as Madonna plays, the town planners decorate the Diamond, putting flowers in the teeth of the shoppers and in the barrel of the soldier plying war games on the floor, and everyone is led in a technically complex synchronised disco-routine by the three bored girls – the 'plastics' who also form part of the daily decoration of the Diamond.

It is the daydreaming Plastics who reveal the reality of emigration and the fears that go with it. They dream of leaving for London – or anywhere where there's a job. But the dream of London turns into a nightmare of racism, loneliness, drugs, drink and destitution in 'cardboard city'.

For some scenes the starting point was image work, the group creating static images in response to a theme or question. Sometimes these were animated into short scenes, usually no longer than a minute. Then the devisor would go away and work on an expanded sequence which would be further extended and refined in rehearsal. The street scene in the Diamond and the dream of New York started in this way, as did the final 'Troubles' sequence. For the latter they sculpted other members of the group into relevant images.

THE INTERNATIONAL LANGUAGE OF THEATRE

The fact that they were to travel to an international festival in another country with their show was very important to the whole process of devising. To travel and own the description of yourself; to speak because no one dare voice their preconceptions about you, because they never quite planned to meet you face to face – they meet you almost daily in their newspaper, victim or bully perpetrating or suffering. The group was determined that language shouldn't be a barrier between them and the international audience, so image and music became central to the piece.

All of this varies from approaches which use a group to explore and assist with an individual's situation or from one-on-one approaches. Here the group are exploring and expressing the group's experience – and using public expression, the opportunity to rewrite the possibilities of self away from the defining influence and expectations of home, is so important to them.

PREPARATION: READING THE IMAGE

In order to build up some essential skills for this way of working, many warm-up exercises which rely on visual image only, such as 'Picture Book' (see Poulter 1987), were used. In this simple exercise the group work in smaller groupings of four or five. Each group chooses a well-known story or play. They then prepare three group images which will communicate their chosen piece to the others, who must try to guess what it is. The idea is like a human cartoon-strip approach to storytelling. Although the exercise is a preparation for the use of image work in the later stages of the project, it also prepares them for the group processes involved in creating a piece of theatre which speaks for the whole group. In 'Picture Book' the players are engaging in a team exercise which involves them in negotiation, relating to other people, taking responsibility as part of a team, the generation of ideas, decision-making, planning, preparation, sharing and taking direction, meeting a deadline, giving and receiving support and group presentation.

LANGUAGE BARRIERS: THE WORD 'THERAPY'

Many professional theatre-workers in community and youth theatre would claim that the work is therapeutic in design, execution and results, though they might prefer a different word. 'Therapy' with its medical associations is not always a word with currency outside of clinical settings. It may have been Augusto Boal's use of the word in relation to his European work – the 'cop-in-the-head' techniques and others explained in his book *Rainbow of Desires* (Boal 1995) – which brought it into the current debates surrounding community, youth and educational drama. Yet there are no agreed guidelines.

In Belfast alone there are at least ten neighbourhoods producing community plays, and across the whole of Northern Ireland there are at least twenty youth theatre groups devising their own shows. The youth service is introducing drama training for its workers, and in schools Northern Ireland is ahead of England in introducing a formal course of drama as one of the examinable options at age 15/16. To my knowledge, though there have been one or two short courses in dramatherapy, there are no fully-qualified dramatherapists and there is no full-time professional training in the field.[1]

Meanwhile, as theatre practitioners operating in the field of community drama, do we need to learn some lessons from those whose professional title includes the word 'therapy'?

When we are writing about the work, what ethics and conventions should we be using? Theatre is such a public act that it is too easy to be public about everything – including place names and people's names. In sociological and psychological case studies, names and places are changed to protect the individuals concerned. Should we follow that practice? Yet if there was a public performance how could we disguise that? And how can what happened to Enniskillen be disguised and lent to another elsewhere? In Belfast the intensity of the 'Troubles' is common to a number of areas, and therefore they may recognise themselves in this but not feel named.

At least the invitation to discuss the work in this book is a step towards developing that debate.

NOTE

1 There was one dramatherapist: she's working in Scotland now, having spent the last few years stitching together a freelance programme in Northern Ireland between hospitals, colleges and a theatre-in-education company's Special Needs programme.

REFERENCES

Boal, A. (1995) *The Rainbow of Desires* (translated by A. Jackson), London: Routledge.
Poulter, C. (1987) *Playing the Game*, London: Macmillan.

Chapter 22

The drama has just begun

Mahnoor Yar Khan

INTRODUCTION

The year 1948 saw the formation of the state of Israel on a substantial part of land known as Palestine. A total of 780,000 Palestinians were displaced, some of whom came to live as refugees in the West Bank and Gaza, areas that were controlled by Jordan and Egypt respectively. Others were dispersed in the Diaspora to Lebanon, Jordan, Syria and elsewhere.

The educational system in the Occupied Palestinian Territories (OPTs) places great emphasis on rote learning, and very little opportunity is given to spontaneous participation. Children are not encouraged to be creative. Most schools do not have an art or drama program within the curriculum, and there are no community centers meeting these needs because of the ban imposed by the occupying forces. Classes are overcrowded and teachers still use severe methods of punishment including beating. Persistent closures of schools due to curfews and strikes have disrupted the education system. The loss of childhood that has been experienced by the children of the OPTs is in some cases compounded by long hours working in family businesses.

Research has shown that children are preoccupied with themes related to the Intifada (the popular uprising against Israeli occupation), and there seems very little free space in which to address objects and activity not related to conflict and war. There is growing concern among Palestinian professionals, parents and others about the effect of this relentless pressure on children's mental health, emotional lives and psychological functioning.

In 1992 I spent a year in the OPTs and witnessed the violence, both physical and psychological, that Palestinian children are exposed to both inside and outside the home. It was with this concern in mind that the pilot project "Children and Therapy through Theater and Video" was developed.

The use of drama/theatre has been recognized as an effective form of therapy for children in many parts of the world. It assists in helping children to understand themselves and the world they live in. It creates situations that help children to discover why people behave as they do, thus helping them reflect on their own behavior. It is a form by which actual incidents could be enacted under the guise of fiction. It creates an atmosphere and space where children can express themselves without feeling threatened. For Palestinians especially those born during the occupation, any creative art form is a new phenomenon.

It was felt that drama and video would give these children an alternative language; a language beyond the mere verbal; it would act as a means of exploring subjects and providing another perspective in their thinking beyond what they thought they already knew. It was the first time that the possibility of a form of alternative expression was introduced to these children.

It was intended to videotape the sketches enacted by the children and play them back to them, in order to enhance and further that process of reflection by allowing them to recall and analyze verbal, non-verbal, conscious and unconscious forms of expression.

THE SPACE

Finding space, both physical and mental is a major problem in the OPTs. Children are confined in overcrowded homes for long periods of time by curfews, strikes and violent activity on the streets, which is the only other place to be. In Palestinian society young girls (11–14 years) are expected to be home after school hours; interaction with boys outside school is un- common and to some extent socially unacceptable – this factor, though, is somewhat variable, depending on geographical areas. Our first concern was to give these children an acceptable space and a safe environment in which to perform; to explore their emotions and concerns chosen by themselves. The school is one such place.

A coeducational school in the Arab section of the Old City of Jerusalem was selected for the pilot. It is here that the occupier and the occupied live next door to each other, and there is ongoing tension and bouts of physical aggression between the two communities. It is here that the economic disparity of the two societies is so pronounced and where social, cultural and religious customs and norms differ so starkly.

THE PLANNING

Twelve sessions, of an hour and a half's duration, held twice a week over a six-week period, was what was planned. Because of curfews and strikes, during which we could not hold the sessions, the six weeks were extended to eight. These disruptions are a normal part of life in the OPTs and this was not regarded as a drawback.

The intention of the sessions was to sensitize the children to alternative forms of verbal and non-verbal expression through theatre games and sketches. In the course of the sessions the children would develop short sketches around areas of concern, choosing the characters and the roles they could play. Depending on the content of the sketches enacted, the facilitators would then open the floor for discussion, and encourage the children to talk about the different character roles they had played and whether they saw alternatives to these situations and characters. They would then put together sketches around the alternatives they had discussed, thus enabling them to interpret and enact roles and scenes as they saw and understood them.

The first two sessions were mapped out in detail before implementation; the remaining sessions took shape as we went along, depending on the children's participation and reactions and what the facilitators felt would be important and interesting for them.

Most sessions started with a warm-up in the open courtyard, after which we moved into a tiny classroom provided by the school. Here we did a relaxation exercise, and this was followed by the central core of the sessions.

THE CHILDREN

The children who attended were between the ages of 11 and 14 years. There were six girls and six boys. All of them belonged to two grades of the same school and knew each other. We had hoped to maintain the same group throughout the twelve sessions, but when word spread that the sessions were fun a couple of new children wanted to join in. We did not have the heart to turn the children away in the initial stages, but we did have to refuse subsequent requests by the children to join in.

There was initially a balance between Christian and Muslim and passive and active children. As the group began to evolve it was no longer possible to maintain such a balance.

THE TEAM

The team consisted of two local theatre persons and myself as coordinator/ facilitator. Working with children was a comparatively new experience for all three of us. For the two theatre persons it meant moving away from the traditional and conventional forms of drama that they were more familiar with. There was a group of five specialists: a child psychologist, a therapist, two counsellors and a psychiatrist. Drama as group therapy was a very new concept for them. Each session was recorded on video and audio tape. As theatre persons, we felt we were sensitive to children but were not qualified therapists and were therefore treading on unfamiliar ground; that's where the role of the specialists came in. The videotaping was mainly for the specialists who met once a week to view the video, and to discuss the sessions, the children's reactions and participation and the work of the three facilitators.

THE SESSIONS

Session 1

The first session involved games around trust-building, harmony, concentration, a release of energy and an attempt to break the traditional school mode. For us facilitators it was also a way of getting to know the children's names and to see how the girls and boys interacted with each other. The experience of girls and boys interacting with each other was novel for the children and as a result there was a great deal of nervous giggling.

In order to gauge the children's ability to verbalize and imagine, and to introduce them to the art of creating and developing stories, we placed some photographs on the floor. Each child was asked to select a photograph and weave a story around it; they were asked to avoid as far as possible merely describing the photograph.

It became obvious that the children's perceptions and reactions were greatly influenced by their surroundings. They were very shy while relating their stories and preferred to face the wall. The photographs all represented Palestine and Palestinians, yet the stories were about Somalia and Sudan, about being Bedouins and villagers. Bedouins and villagers are looked down upon as they and their lifestyles are considered uncivilized.

The central element in one of the photographs was a broken bicycle; the boy with this picture did not tell a story but described the photograph excluding the bicycle; when questioned about the surprising omission he refused to answer. After every story the group were allowed to ask the storyteller questions related to the story.

Voice, rhythm and harmony exercises proved too demanding for the group. Percussion sounds were most popular but beyond that the children were unable to move in rhythm to the sound or create any integration of sound, rhythm and harmony.

Session 2

The school has very little outdoor activity involving girls. We started session 2 with a game of tag. The child who was out had to hold onto that part of the body that was "tagged" and try to "tag" the other. For example if a girl was "tagged" on the knee she had to run holding onto her knee while attempting to "tag" the other. The group enjoyed the novelty of this. The game also introduced the idea of uninhibited touching, without specific attention being focused on it.

To create an awareness of the different parts of the body, their movement and control, we introduced "body talk," carried out in pairs and to music, in which partners had to ensure that some part of their body was touching a part of the other's body while in constant movement. Here, the boys and girls worked separately. There was a great deal of embarrassed giggling, discomfort and self-consciousness.

Back to the pictures: the group, sitting in a circle had to select just one picture from the cluster, taking turns to tell a story as they walked around the circle; the objective was to help enlarge the scope of their imagination and assist in the art of storytelling. As children who had grown up in a school system that does not encourage creativity or self-expression, they found it very difficult to let their imagination loose. The photograph selected showed a girl walking down steps of the Old City; behind her was a man. The children stuck to a fairly conventional story of a girl going to school, studying for her examination, going home and buying something on the way.

To reintroduce the use of harmony with sound and body movement each child had to select a machine and recreate the movement and the sound of the machine. There was hardly any imagination used in the selection of machines; they had to be prompted by the facilitators. The group were very distracted; perhaps because a new boy had joined the sessions and kept distracting the group, or because they had a series of tests scheduled for the next day and wanted to get back home to study.

Session 3

In this warm-up we asked each child to imitate the movement and sound of any animal, bird or thing. The facilitator introduced the session by imitating a tree in motion with the sounds of the leaves rustling and the tree creaking. Most of the children stood around shy and inhibited. Those that did try were fairly unimaginative in their selection; their actions were superficial with no attempt to become involved in the act.

During the relaxation exercise the group were asked to think about the picture selected in the previous session and create a different story around it.

The children mainly worked around recall. The facilitators encouraged the group to develop the story by asking certain pointed questions such as "What page is she on, and what's written on the page?" "What is she wearing, and what is the color of her dress?" The children did not try to develop the story further; the facilitator felt they needed to move away from the picture for a while.

Fantasy is regarded as an integral part of most children's stories, as it is obviously an integral part of their lives. In the Occupied Territories it often takes on an ominous form in which children tend to fantasize that they are unafraid of the soldiers, or unafraid when shot at or wounded. Children often relieve frustrations by solving problems through what could be termed as "wish fulfillment." It is said that children purge themselves of anxiety about desires that they know to be wrong or socially unacceptable through fantasy.

A fantasy about a rusty screw that had to be discarded, its trials and tribulations, was introduced by the facilitator. The children became fairly involved with the fantasy and brought up issues of being afraid, of being of no use any more, of being rejected, of the fear of not being able to support and feed oneself. The facilitator went one step further and introduced Hassna, the screw's girlfriend whom he missed very much. The group then talked about marriage, children and death.

By introducing the issue of the male–female relationship, the facilitator offered a certain legitimacy to talk about love, a subject that is hardly discussed in their society.

As a trust-building exercise, we asked the group to form a circle and placed one child blindfolded in the center of the circle. The child was gently pushed in all directions while attempting to keep his or her feet firmly rooted to one spot. The girls were uncomfortable when it was done with the boys, but were freer and seemed to enjoy it more when the group were segregated according to sex.

Back to the sound and movement exercise: this time the group had to select an instrument and create the sound of that instrument: it started with variety but soon all the children veered towards percussion sounds

Session 4

The children arrived half an hour late in this session. In order to introduce a certain sense of commitment and discipline, they were asked to explain why they were late. This took up a lot of time. There was a great deal of disturbance and distraction caused by a group of older boys outside. We had to dispense with the warm-up and relaxation exercises. The facilitators were unable to get to grips with the different elements of distraction.

Each child was handed a sheet of paper with different facial expressions on it. The children were asked to select one expression and try through facial and body movement to express the emotion of that expression; the rest of the group had to guess what expression the child was trying to enact. In retrospect it was felt that this exercise had been introduced too early; there had been no real development around body movement. Using the body to express a mood or emotion was a very new concept for these children; verbalization is predominant. The facilitators were eager to get somewhere with the children, so in turn were verbalizing too much. All in all this was not a well-planned or executed session.

Session 5

The theme of this session was the "souk" (market-place). In the warm-up each child was asked to select an activity that takes place in the "souk" in the early hours of the morning. There were sweepers, loaders, people opening up and cleaning their shops. Each one in the group was asked to select a character in the "souk" that they wished to play, spending some time on developing the character.

The group then created a "souk" in which they were asked to interact with each other. There was a man renting out video films. The seamstress cum garment salesgirl was rather self-conscious. The girls came requesting that measurements be taken for new outfits. The boys came in pairs, asking the price of the garments that were on sale, teasing each other as they tried them on. One of the boys had the group very amused as he enacted the part of a woman, requesting the seamstress to take his measurements and describing the sort of revealing dress he wanted her to stitch.

Then there was Um Khalil, played by a boy, selling lemons and vegetables, haggling, arguing and cursing her customers. Every action was well thought out, from weighing the vegetables, to picking up and putting them in a bag, to placing the money received in the front of her blouse. The group enjoyed interacting with Um Khalil.

Two girls took up the role of butchers. It was while the group were interacting with the butchers that we were asked by two in the group if they could play the role of the inspectors. The group developed the theme from there. The inspectors (in real life inspectors are Israelis) went up to the butchers and demanded to see their papers. They then smelt the meat, accused the butchers of selling rotten meat and threw them into prison. At this point a cordon of soldiers was set up around the prison. The accused were brought to trial in a court that had a judge, two assistants, lawyers and an usher who announced the case. The case was heard and after a brief discussion the accused were sentenced.

Back in prison, the families of the accused came to visit; they were separated from the prisoners by a row of tables; there was much shouting and wailing with the soldiers pushing and shoving them back.

Throughout, the reaction and interaction of the group were very spontaneous. In the discussion that followed the children commented that they enjoyed acting together and being allowed to say, do and act as they wanted.

It must be noted that the above scenario is a fairly common real-life occurrence for these children. It is possible that some of them had actually experienced parts of it. The prison scene is something that practically all families have been through. An interesting session.

Session 6

We decided to base this session on a popular TV cartoon series titled "Sanafar." For the warm-up, Sharshabbir, who is the bad man, and his friend Harhoor, the cat, try to catch the Sanafars. All those caught are locked up in a cell where they have to use their ingenuity to try to escape. The Sanafars manage to convince Harhoor who is guarding them that one of them is not feeling at all well and must get out. He believes the tale, opens the door, and the others charge out.

Sitting in a circle, the group were asked to select a Sanafar character they would like to enact. The facilitators then questioned each of them about the character they selected.

The Sanafars were asked by the facilitators to imagine that one of them was captured and locked in a cage. They had to find ways and means of getting the prisoner out. The plots were presented to the facilitator who challenged each idea, questioning all the loopholes and snags within the plot.

The facilitators decided to abandon this exercise. The group were having difficulty in developing their own plots and solutions; instead they were presenting the solutions of the TV serial.

Divided into two groups, each group was asked to create a picture and describe their individual characters in that picture. Each group then tried to recreate the other group's picture by imitating the facial expressions and body postures of their opponents.

The exercise was done in pairs. Each pair developed a picture by molding themselves into images. This was followed by the museum game. Here one of the boys from the group was selected to create a museum full of statues made from the other children; considering it was the first time, the boy showed great ingenuity, twisting and turning the statues (children's) hands, legs and bodies; with the girls he took recourse to verbal instruction rather than hands-on manipulation.

Session 7

The group were given the option of selecting the warm-up. They chose a relay race, much to the disappointment of the facilitators, who were expecting something more innovative.

The group were introduced to some basic mime: tugging at a rope, lifting a heavy suitcase, hanging from a rope and moving forward, trying to hold on to a bunch of helium balloons. The objective here was to create an awareness of body movements and set the imagination at play. The group showed lack of concentration and body tension while executing the exercise, and the facilitators had to demonstrate each exercise so that the group could imitate the action.

Back to the museum. This time the curator showed a visitor around, introducing and describing the finer points of each statue in nonsense sound rather than actual words; a dialogue ensued in this fashion. Each member of the group had a chance to be the curator and visitor. This was to introduce the importance of rhythm and sound in language as distinct from the spoken word, and to assist in creating characters. The facilitator along with one member of the group initiated this exercise. Surprisingly, after the initial bout of self-conscious giggling, the group became fairly well absorbed in the act.

There was one hitch: one of the boys refused to participate, saying he felt shy having to interact with the girls. This came as a surprise because he had had no problem interacting with the girls in the previous sessions. In the discussion that followed the group informed us that in their class, if a boy tried to talk with a girl he was accused of being a flirt or being effeminate.

They complained that theirs was the only class in the school in which the boys and girls never did things together, be it a project or planning for a school program. This fact bothered them, but this was the first time that the problem was raised, let alone discussed. It was interesting that not only was an issue as sensitive as male–female relationships being addressed but they were open to discussing it in this atmosphere. Since the negative elements of the class were not in the workshops, the group could afford to bring up such issues without feeling threatened.

Some of the children also complained that when they attempted to be less inhibited in the workshops, they were often teased later by others in the group.

They turned to the facilitator for advice, asking him what he would do in such a situation. The facilitator reiterated that he had attended an all-boys school and so had not had to face such a problem. Unfortunately there was no intervention by the facilitators in the area of feelings, prejudices, mockery and male–female relationships.

Session 8

The warm-up exercise was a race in which the children were each given two sheaves of newspaper on which they placed their feet. The idea was to ensure that the children's feet did not touch the ground while they moved forward but were always on the newspaper. The day was very windy; there were newspapers all over the place!

Coordination and cooperation were the objectives of the string exercise. The exercise was carried out in pairs. An imaginary string was tied to a part of the partner's body that was then moved in different directions by the one in control. The partner had to imagine and move that part of the body in the direction the controller was pulling the string. The children liked playing the part of the controller.

The objective of the mirror exercise in which the children imitated their partners was to sensitize the group on the issue of how people tend to operate in cliques and imitate each other, and the effect of it all. Strangely enough, this exercise developed quite differently: from imitating one another they began relating and enacting incidents that had taken place in the classroom. They took it in turns, imitating the teachers and how they behaved in class, much to the enjoyment of the rest of the group. It introduced us to the lack of respect and regard that the group had for their teachers, and the violence and aggression used by teachers against the children.

Feelings were the focus of the next exercise. The children worked in pairs, each partner taking turns to make the other go through a number of emotions

– sad, happy and angry, to name a few. They could do this through verbal and non-verbal expression. It was expected that children would use on their partners the same expressions (verbal and non-verbal) that would affect them. Unfortunately there was one boy in the group who disrupted the session and had to be asked to leave. By this time it was the group that was controlling the session and the facilitators were unable to retrieve it.

Session 9

The warm-up in this session was energizing. The objective was to coordinate body and sound. The members of the group had to run around the courtyard and, at the count of three, to jump, simultaneously creating the sound of the animal each one had selected.

In the chain-puzzle exercise the group had to collectively try to solve the puzzle. The group formed a circle with hands crossed in front; members of the group joined hands that they then had to unfurl, maintaining the circle and not letting go of each other's hands in the process. One group managed to solve the puzzle and then went on to help the second group.

In the relaxation exercise, the children, sitting on chairs, were asked to drop their hands between their legs and create a single monotonous sound. The members of the group found this a very strange way to relax, and giggled and disturbed each other. There were a few in the group who were trying to take the session seriously but it was not easy.

The children were divided into pairs. Each pair was asked to develop a short sketch. At the end of each performance a discussion followed with the group pointing out what they felt was right or wrong with the sketch and the acting. We only had time for two sketches.

The first one was a sketch with Oliver Twist (which was being taught in class) as the main character. The part of Oliver was played by a girl. In the scene, Oliver is informed that he has been sold and will have to leave the orphanage because it can no longer afford to look after him. Oliver refuses to leave his friends. The scenario was improvised on stage without prior planning. The girl said she had selected the part of Oliver because she felt a sort of empathy with him. The group liked the idea that Oliver had refused to leave his friends.

In the second sketch, "The Cat," a well-known sketch in which two neighbors who are constantly at loggerheads eventually decide to become friends, the group felt that the actors were uninhibited and acted well. They were happy that the quarreling neighbors had agreed to become friends.

Session 10

The warm-up was a game in which one person is "out" and tries to catch the others; whoever is caught joins hands with the first person and together they catch the next one till the chain gets longer and more unwieldy. A great deal of verbal and physical energy was expended in this game.

Indoors the group insisted on continuing, in pairs, with sketches that had been started in session 9. The performance of a short adaptation of a TV program, the idea of a lesson from the English reader and Red Riding Hood, did not elicit much enthusiasm from the group.

A sketch about cheating in class led to an involved discussion as to why children cheated. The group were quite open about why and how they cheated. To raise and discuss the issue with adults is quite unusual. It was obvious that the children were beginning to feel that this was a safe place in which they could discuss sensitive issues.

Session 11

A game of "catch the mouse" was introduced. The group formed a circle with a mouse inside the circle and a cat on the outside. It was up to the group to prevent the mouse from being caught by the cat. This was a popular game that the children did not want to stop playing.

The "person opposite" is a game played in pairs: one partner begins to question the other about his or her expression, stance and other related issues. The partner is not expected to reply verbally; the questions continue with the questioner noting the changing expressions in the partner and questioning him or her about them. In the second part of this game the partner had to enact the questions asked; for example, what does it feel like to have a stomach ache? or to be eating a delicious fruit?

Both these exercises make one aware of oneself and how facial and body expressions convey certain messages to the partner.

The questions here mainly centered on the partners' looks. There was a misunderstanding in regard to what was expected of the partner in response to the questions being asked, which ended up being verbalized, as a result of which the objective of the exercise was lost. The facilitators did not intervene but allowed the verbalization to continue.

One of the boys was disturbing the group. The facilitator stopped the exercise, asked the group to sit in a circle and questioned each as to why they thought the boy was behaving as he was and what should be done. The boy's argument was that if they all did not laugh at what he was doing he would eventually be quiet. All this took up a great deal of time; the group was bored and distracted. It was badly handled.

Action and reaction were the theme of the exercise that followed. The exercise was carried out in pairs with partners developing sketches that involved action and reaction. The sketches included the following: the partner is kicked in the shin, and reacts by holding on to the injured part and crying out in pain; a mother is constantly telling her daughter to clean the house and the daughter complains about all the work she is made to do; a mother is rushed to hospital and the daughter reacts – this we learnt was an actual incident.

It was during this interplay that we learnt that a boy and girl in the group were not talking to each other. The problem had started in the classroom. Unfortunately, owing to lack of time, the issue could not be discussed.

Session 12

The group were asked if they wanted to discuss the issue of the girl and boy not being friends. The facilitators were informed that both were class prefects; there had been some conflict between them, nasty and rude remarks had been exchanged and now they were not talking. The group seemed uninterested in the fact that there was a rift between the two; it didn't seem to bother them at all. The boy was an enthusiastic participant at the sessions; he had joined the school recently and was doing quite well. The girl was intense and very earnest about what was being done in the sessions; she remained aloof and seemed to have very few friends among the group.

The group were then asked to enact what had actually happened in class through changing roles. We found that they enacted the argument but did not look into the cause of it. The idea of a mediator was introduced to patch things up. Each one took it in turns to act as mediator. There was a lot of aggression between the mediator and the two individuals, who stood at different ends of the room. An attempt was made by one girl to reason with the two, who after a while grudgingly shook hands. I think this was more to please the facilitators. The facilitators at this point could have subtly talked about feelings, trust and mistrust but preferred to remain on the outside of the circle.

In the last half of the session we screened and discussed certain sections of the twelve sessions that we had videotaped. There was great excitement and self-conscious giggling; some were shy. Some in the group referred to how they had looked or acted; not all were happy with their performance!

CONCLUSION

The classroom that had been allotted to us was very small. At one session, settlers who had access to the wall that runs around the school playground had thrown stones at the children during school recess; that evening we had to abandon the warm-up outside because the children were apprehensive.

Two of the boys dropped out halfway. One of them had to help his father in his bakery while the other who was the main cause of distraction and disrupting the sessions decided to stay away. Two boys who seemed to enjoy the sessions were absent for a couple of sessions. The group informed us that these two had witnessed some trouble in the Old City and had been taken in for questioning by the Israeli military. When they returned to the group they did not broach the subject and we did not press them to do so.

All six girls stayed with us throughout. One commented: "This is the first time that I have been out of the house after school hours. I have enjoyed being here." During one of the sessions when some of the participants were feeling too shy to act, one of the girls, in a very matter-of-fact manner, said: "We are here to participate, so stop feeling shy and inhibited." It was this very same girl who was having problems with one of the boys in class, who was also part of our group.

The drama had only just begun; before we knew it the twelve sessions were over. It was felt that the work would have to carry on for at least a year before the effects on the children could be gauged. The area of work was very new for all of us and we were only just beginning to consolidate our positions.

It was not easy to tell the children that we would not be conducting any more sessions. The relationship between the group and the facilitators was beginning to be defined more clearly. The children and the facilitators were becoming more comfortable with and sensitive to each other. This was a place where the children were beginning to feel "safe." In a society that does not address issues of sexuality, here were young adolescents eager to discuss and be "enlightened" on the issue. It was an area of concern that they wanted to deal with and did not know how to. As facilitators and specialists it was still too early for us to gauge whether the sessions had in any way had a therapeutic effect on any of the children.

Because the sessions were held on the school premises, the children initially presumed that the usual classroom controls would apply. It took them a while to get used to the idea that here facilitators didn't "talk down" but talked to them; that the interaction was on a level of mutual respect and that one worked within those parameters. They soon realized that they were not going to be instructed all the time but it was up to them to present their own ideas and feelings that were acknowledged and accepted. It was here that physical and verbal activity were encouraged rather than suppressed. In a discussion at the end of session 12 one child commented that "You have allowed us to say and do as we pleased without stopping us."

Initially, the two local theatre persons were not comfortable with the so-called criticism or expectations of the specialists. I felt that too much was being read into every act of the children by the specialists and there were too many sweeping generalizations. For instance, the child psychologist after viewing the first two sessions commented that these children seemed to be the privileged ones who were not directly affected by the Intifada and were therefore not addressing it! The idea was to give these children a space where they didn't have to address the Intifada if they didn't want to (something they are doing among themselves all the time). Moreover, it is understandable that these children would in fact not address issues that are most painful to them in front of strangers. We had provided a platform where they could address other issues and concerns, and that's what they were doing. It took time for them to understand that the intention of the drama experiment was to allow the children to prioritize their concerns.

Some of the specialists' insights into the children's reactions to what we were doing and "vice versa" made us more aware of the children and the way in which they were interacting, in addition to allowing us to see what and where our weak spots were. It also helped in the planning of the sessions.

All Palestinians living and working in the Occupied Territories are under constant pressure related to the occupation. Concentration levels are low and inconsistent. It was not easy to keep the children's interest constant, to prevent them from completely controlling the sessions, and to deal with some of the disruptive elements in the sessions. The facilitators learnt that control was one of the most difficult areas they had to deal with. The boys at times took advantage of the lack of aggressive discipline. The facilitators were tempted to resort to traditional methods of reprimand, but refrained.

In retrospect, as facilitators, we were not always "on the ball." We were not intervening at the right time, but were allowing issues to pass with the intention of taking them up later; but that later did not come because there was always something new to deal with.

The video element which was originally planned was not realized. We only had the group for an hour and a half over twelve sessions, which is a very short time, and we felt that it would be unsuitable to introduce a totally new element. Another factor was the difficulty of bringing a TV into the classroom; the school had one but the authorities were reluctant to shift it from the laboratory. Although in session 12 we did play back some of the material we had videotaped, this was more because the children were eager to see themselves on TV. It should be noted, however, that all the sessions were videotaped. After the first session, the group was quite oblivious to the camera.

Not all the sessions were carried out as planned. Because of the different elements that were part of the group experience some of the sessions had to be changed and improvised on the spot.

This was the first time in the OPTs that an attempt had been made to use drama as therapy for children who have lived in a situation of war for an extended period. The children who were part of the drama experience were all considered "normal." The question that still remains is whether being able to address areas of concern and looking at alternatives are therapeutic. Not all the specialists we worked with agreed. Do we use the word "therapy" in its clinical sense or do we take the liberty of using it because it conveys the idea that any form of externalization and addressing of internal concerns is positive and therefore can have a therapeutic effect? These are major issues that need to be grappled with elsewhere.

I returned to the OPTs in October 1994 to set up and develop a more intensive program. The realization of the important need for dramatherapy for children within the OPTs is growing. Apart from hands-on work a series of dramatherapy workshops has been scheduled for the next two years. I am presently working in two centers in Khan Younus in the Gaza Strip. We hope to produce a working manual that can be used in other parts of the Arab world. Life under occupation for children in Gaza has been a very different experience from that of the children living in the West Bank. The curtain has just risen and the drama has just begun, for us and for the children of Palestine.

ACKNOWLEDGMENTS

I would like to thank Dr. Sue Jennings for encouraging me to write this chapter, and Angela who edited the drafts.

BIBLIOGRAPHY

Barker, C. (1977) *Drama Games*, London: Methuen.
Blatner, A. (1988) *Acting In Practical Application of Psycho-Dramatic Methods*, 2nd edn, New York: Springer.
Boal, A. (1979) *Theatre of the Oppressed* (translated by C.A. and M.L. McBride), New York: Urizen Books.
——— (1992) *Games for Actors and Non-Actors* (translated by A. Jackson), London: Routledge.
——— (1994) *Playing Boal: Theatre, Therapy, Activism*, ed. M. Shutzman and J. Cohen-Cruz, London and New York: Routledge.
El Sarraj, E. (1993) *Peace and the Children of Stone*, Report of the Gaza Community Mental Health Centre.
Jennings, S. (ed.) (1987) *Dramatherapy: Theory and Practice 1* and *2*, London: Routledge.
——— (1990) *Dramatherapy with Families, Groups and Individuals: Waiting in the Wings*, London: Jessica Kingsley.
Kanaaneh, M. and Netland, M. *Children and Political Violence: Psychological Reactions and National Identity Formation among the Children of the Intifada*, parts 1 and 2, Report of the ECRC, East Jerusalem.
Moreno, J.L. (1987) "The role concept: a bridge between psychiatry and sociology," in J. Fox (ed.) *The Essential Moreno*, New York: Springer.
Nixon, A. (1992) *State of Palestinian Children*, volumes 1, 2 and 3, Report by Sweden Save the Children, Stockholm.
Quotq, S., Punamaki, R.L, and El Sarraj, E. (1993) *The Relation between Traumatic Experiences Activity and Cognitive and Emotional Responses among Palestinian Children*, Report of the Gaza Community Mental Health Centre.
Spolin, V. (1985) *Theatre Games for Rehearsal*, Ill.: Northwestern University Press.
Stanislavski, C. (1936) *An Actor Prepares*, New York: Theatre Arts.
Warren, B. (1990) *Using the Creative Arts in Therapy*, London: Routledge.

Chapter 23

The Trinidad Carnival

A cross-cultural drama of seduction and communal therapy

Terrence Brathwaite

INTRODUCTION

This chapter attempts to address the healing potentials of the Trinidad Carnival as a foundation of self/communal therapy, negating the need for psychotherapists in the country. With special emphasis on dance, music and theatre/oral tradition, the first section reviews the relationship of these art forms to the Trinidad individual and society. Of particular importance here is the freedom to adapt body movement, rhythms and role-plays which have originated elsewhere, in addition to the facility of improvisation in performance.

The second section looks at the sensous flow of uninhibited movement; counter-tension; effort study and effort conceptual elements involved in the Trinidad Carnival, and how theatre and music influence and drive the movement patterns. Therapists may find the results of this particular examination useful in understanding the meaning of their African, Asian or Latin American clients' movements, for diagnosis and follow-up therapy evaluation during counselling.

In the third and final section I attempt to justify the benefits of the Trinidad Carnival as an interracial expression of positive characterisation and a possible coping system for psychic tension. The focus here is on the therapeutic modes of anticipatory psychic management (Hanna and Hanna 1968), alternative catharsis and paradox meditation (Hanna 1976, 1979) in this communal venture, which has the effect of submerging ethnic and social divisions.

EMANCIPATED AESTHESIA

In tracing the genesis of the Trinidad Carnival, we can explore the ancient and symbiotic pathways of all the intercultural traditions of humanity. Gradually, we realise that the origins of the festival aesthetics are essentially at the heart of the momentum of Caribbean life. Such is a life of transformed traditions, worked by a 'creole' aesthesia; a renewed life born of both ancient pan-European sensibilities and of well-tested Afro-Asian artistic institutions, celebrated from the cradle to the grave.

The momentum of life in Trinidad is a dynamic rhythm which expresses a composite world – self-consistent and assumptive with an independent sense of approval and value. This momentum supports the ebb and flow of life in Trinidad and cements the symbiosis of the healing arts. It turns work into a mixed-media production (involving movement, music, costume and song), physical communication into intimate relationships, and trance into a glance of altered consciousness.

From the lullaby, the calypso ballad, 'sow and reap' celebrations, street theatres and communal integrative dances of growth to the funeral procession, the eclectic rhythms of Caribbean life wield their influencing power. The people of Trinidad share an intimacy with the curative, transcendental energy of this rhythm, particularly through the annual creative, emancipative events of the Trinidad Carnival. Such events not only shape the Trinidad Festival, but also maintain socio-cultural patterns, provide individual stability for the people, and empower them in a way which no form of American or European psychotherapy can approximate.

It is highly amusing therefore, that when American and European media reporters go to the Caribbean, all they see is poverty and underdevelopment. They don't see the ever-increasing family of foreign tourists, religiously shadowing local or expatriate Trinidad nationals who return home annually for the 'greatest show on earth'. They don't see the joy and creativity of the celebration as it unites revellers of diverse backgrounds, while showing them at their best – vibrant, inventive and committed to seizing the glory of the day. They don't see, for that matter, many Caribbean people needing psychiatrists.

The latter phenomenon results mainly from the fact that our Carnival serves both as a celebration and as a communal therapy, with the unusual effect of submerging, for the duration of the festival, ethnic, social and mental health divisions, in an attempt to make each Carnival the greatest annual theatrical spectacle of all time. The word theatre is significant here, because to experience Carnival is to experience a dance-play of rhythmic seduction, geared to evoking free-movement response.

The concept of the Carnival celebration as a communal therapy is further echoed in the belief of the Bakongo of West Africa, that ritual processioneers ideally transmit fortune and spiritual rebirth to a village that they circle. The Bakongo also believe that the wearing of masks and head-dresses adorned with feathers establishes the possibility of curing illness by rising out of oneself, and emerging from one's physical situation into a full spiritual awareness and potentiality.

Finding oneself in our composite world

The cross-fertilisation of dance, theatre, music and the plastic arts in the Trinidad Carnival is truly representative of the diverse cultural attitudes, expressions and aspirations of the nationals. Thus it makes the festival a synthesis between old and new, between folk, popular and high art forms, between native and alien traditions.

From a helicopter view, even the sacred colours of the country's national flag – red, black and white – seem to effectively come alive during the celebrations. Interpenetrating their respective symbolic elements of fire, earth and water, which encompass the people's past, present and future, the colours sensitise and inspire the society as one united, vital, free and dedicated nation 'under a groove'. In a real and meaningful way, the Trinidad Carnival evolves as a mode of indoctrination about the people's role, their individual sense of self-worth, and group support against mental ill health.

It is worthwhile to note here that in psychotherapy, where mental illness is conceptualised as expressing disorders of communication resulting from past experience, the major psychotherapeutic tools are communicative modalities. This means that the therapy must include the individual's past and present relations to the persons close to her or him (Frank 1973, p. 318).

The dance-play of the Trinidad Carnival can therefore be perceived as both a form of group psychotherapy – to prevent communicative disorders and demoralisation – and a remediative process for personal wars. Carnival dance-play phenomenology harmonises with the purview that psychotherapy cannot stop with the individual, but must also include the individual's past and present social–cultural relations.

To better appreciate this dramatic microcosm of multicultural Trinidad, a basic understanding of the country's history is necessary. Trinidad is the southernmost island in the Caribbean, encountered by Christopher Columbus in 1498. With a population today of 1.3 million, Trinidad, more than any other Caribbean island, can be described as a 'palette of peoples', who come from every single ethnic group, perhaps except Eskimos.

African descendants and East Indians, each comprising approximately 42 per cent of the population, form the base of the multiethnic stew, while smaller groups sprinkle their own flavour to taste. These groups include the mixed races (14 per cent), whites (1.2 per cent), Chinese (0.86 per cent), Syrian/Lebanese (0.11 per cent) and others (1.83 per cent) (Brathwaite 1992, p. 15).

It is not unusual, therefore, for a foreign visitor to Trinidad to be introduced to a national whose racial background is a cultural kaleidoscope. The words of a bouncy calypso ballad aptly emphasise this phenomenon, portraying a beautiful female Trinidadian 'reveller' on a Carnival day as 'So Cosmopolitan ... A Negro girl with Chinese eyes, Red Indian, Spanish and Portugese ... A Syrian, Scot and Lebanese' who is 'English French and German too . . . mix up just like callaloo' (McCollin 1987).

'Callaloo' is a metaphor for the diverse racial heritage of the island. Essentially a soup which eventually became the country's national dish, it is a combination of soft-shell crab, hot peppers, the meat and milk of a coconut, curry and the green leaf of a tropical ground plant called 'dasheen'. The more sundry the components, the tastier the soup; the more varied the racial and cultural heritage of its people, the more powerful and healthier is said to be the nation.

A former Spanish colony, Trinidad was inundated with Roman Catholic French planters at the end of the eighteenth century. It was they who originally brought Carnival to the country. The festival itself evolved in three stages. From about 1780 to 1834 it was kept alive by the white French Creole plantocracy and the free coloureds. Following Emancipation from 1834 to about 1880, the middle and upper classes withdrew and the festival became more of a ritual and celebration of freedom by the black urban classes. This culminated in the Camboulay Riots[1] of 1881 and finally the post-1880s, when the festival was purged of some of its indecency and violence and moved towards the middle-class domination which has characterised it since the 1920s (Lee 1990, p. 22).

The Trinidad Carnival therefore began as a Latin cultural celebration, a stage of fantasy. During the eighteenth century, the free persons of colour were subjected to very stringent regulations, and although not forbidden to wear masks, were yet segregated from and never allowed to join in the amusements of the privileged class. In the post-Emancipation period, the Carnival further evolved as a focal point for the elaboration of African cultural retentions in drama, music, dance, costume and ritual, and for a celebration of freedom. Of particular significance was the freedom to adapt body movement, rhythms and role-plays which have originated elsewhere, in addition to the facility of improvisation in performance.

The propensity of the Trinidadians to adapt and innovate in drama, music, song and dance is a strong factor in the development of their cultural arts forms. This factor is consistent with the Government's policy of socio-cultural, political and religious freedom enshrined in the country's con-stitution, and so eloquently expressed in its national anthem by the words 'where every creed and race find an equal place'. Early acknowledgement and understanding of this factor would be extremely advantageous for those open-minded creative arts therapists who wish to explore the psychotherapeutic values of the Trinidad Carnival, and the rich process of creative change, within the contextual reality of a socially and culturally diverse Trinidad.

In his essay 'The development of Carnival in Trinidad and Tobago' (1990, p. 23), Simon Lee describes the elite of the society as usually masked or disguised. The chosen costume of the ladies was the graceful and costly dress of the mulattress of the period, while gentlemen adopted that of the garden negro, in creole *negue jadin*, or black field slave. At Carnival time the *negue jadin* united in bands and proceeded in the evenings to the *cannes brûlées*.

They marched with torches through the town streets imitating what actually took place on the estate when a plantation was on fire. In such situations, labourers on neighbouring estates were conducted to the plantation, alternately day and night, to assist in grinding the burned canes before they went sour; hence the origins of the *cannes brûles*.

The early use of satirical imitation among the elite became an integral feature of Carnival after Emancipation. At this stage, public Carnival was a time of illusion for the free: a time when white men could pretend to be black men; a time when white women by dressing as blacks could fantasize that their husbands desired them as much as their mulatto mistresses.

For the free coloureds with their Republican leanings Carnival represented a disavowal of rigid racial, economic and social divisions which were clearly evident in Trinidadian society, for a central aspect of French Republican ideology was the concept that colonials were not black or white or coloured, but French (Lee 1990, p. 23).

According to Lee, the festival became a flashpoint here for the frustrations and resentments which simmered, boiled and sometimes erupted as the colony plunged into recession and urban unemployment. Set against tensions between Roman Catholic and Anglican, creole and immigrant, black and coloured, the struggle between the black working class eclipsed all and culminated in the Camboulay Riots of the 1880s.

The combative quality of most of nineteenth-century Carnival, Lee further points out (p. 24), stems directly from the ex-slaves' desire to shock and offend a society which they held responsible for the horrors of their past. Carnival for them had a ritualistic significance rooted in the experience of slavery. Carnival was no longer a European-inspired nature festival. Adapted by the Trinidad people, it became a deeply meaningful anniversary of deliverance from the most hateful form of human bondage.

THE PSYCHOTHERAPEUTIC VALUES OF DANCE-PLAY IN THE TRINIDAD CARNIVAL

The significance of the Caribbean people's freedom to adapt foreign art forms, to come to terms with aggressive emotions and instincts, and to openly express their innate sense of creative urgency without guilt, is critical to their mental well-being. The question that arises is how beneficial is this to a practising creative arts therapist? For the answer, let us turn to a discussion of the psychological values of the drama of seduction that is the Trinidad Carnival, and its interrelationship with folk dance and music. Special emphasis will be placed on the creative and artistic work which can change the lives of individuals experiencing personal conflicts.

Life's meaning might be perceived as the joy or satisfaction of successfully meeting each obstacle or challenge – of overcoming, developing, growing, achieving; constantly drawing on and extending one's resources. The crux of life's meaning in Trinidad is its folklore, whenever and wherever we find it. The greatness of this unique cultural heritage is that it helps to make the whole individual and the whole society.

The concept of 'whole' here is easily eroded, when the human potential is threatened by personal wars, which translate into socio-communual conflicts. As hinted previously, the therapeutic use of dance-plays in the Trinidad Carnival approximates the human potential of the self-actualisation model of therapy and the preventive medicine model rather than the medical model as such.

Gradually, the festival has evolved as a cement of society, with ritualised excitements, deep competitive feeling among the bands, and a blend of tradition and novelty, promoting a saturnalian release of emotions, smothering for a time divisions within the body politic and providing an invaluable catharsis for all (Wood 1968, p. 243). This evolution is even more significant when one thinks of the genesis of the Trinidad Carnival as a lawless, noisy festival of the urban lower class.

The dance-play is staged by revellers who are usually inspired to portray heroic figures in their festival bands. For instance, warriors dressed in armor reminiscent of ancient Rome, with glowing white plumes of feathers over metal African masks, depict the call of ancestral forebears. The concept of war and warriors is linked to the Roman armour, while the pure white feathers suggest the revellers' yearning to fly back to the motherland and use their suit of armour to battle against the evil of Africa – for example elements of apartheid and colonialism.

Afro-Trinidadians strongly believe that Europe had conquered Africa using the bible, the gun and germ infection against bows, arrows and spears. The revellers' stance here is to promote the stage of the dance-play as more of a level playing-field, upon which the battles of old can be revisited, refought and manipulated, this time with matching artillery on both sides.

Here the Carnival dance-play helps the reveller or group of revellers to identify and cope with their respective personal or communal war zones, through a celebrated simulation exercise, which helps individuals to adapt to the social environment, and change distasteful aspects of the social milieu.

Bearing in mind that the social relations in which individuals are engaged affect their mental health, the Carnival dance-play reflects, influences and is part of many aspects of the society and culture to which it belongs. Drama, like music and dance, can be viewed as a language of command and control, i.e. a vehicle of power – defined as the ability to influence others' predispositions, feelings, attitudes, beliefs and actions (Hanna 1979).

Folklore as healing force

In Trinidad, several legendary characters exist, around whom are spun interesting tales according to their attributes in personal and social 'healing'. They may originate from elsewhere, but the action of the characters takes place in Trinidad. Three key characters are Africa's Anancy (a spider), La Diablesse (French for she-devil), and Papa Bois (French for father of the woods or forest). Let us explore these characters in the dramatic context of personal and communal therapy.

Anancy, the spider, is a witty, cunning character who invariably overcomes his enemies by placing them in a ludicrous situation; stories of his exploits on bullies, greedy people and 'show-offs' therefore create much entertainment.

La Diablesse appears as a beautiful woman dressed all in white. Her dress is usually long, reaching right down to the ankles in order to hide one of her feet which is cloven. When she supposedly walks the dark country roads at night, the cloven hoof is always on the grass edge of the road to avoid recognition by the sound of her steps. La Diablesse usually appears to inebriated or adulterous males on their way home late at night after leaving functions such as dances. She hypnotises her victims, leads them astray and disappears after emitting peals of chilling demonic laughter. When confrontation takes place between couples in Trinidad, it is not unusual to hear the wife of a humiliated 'cheating husband' expressly refer to his extra-marital partner as a La Diablesse.

Papa Bois is a father figure who is sometimes incorrectly acknowledged as King of the Forest. Unlike a King who rules, more often than not by show of force, Papa Bois is in fact a gentle and caring paternal character. He lives in the depth of the forest, but appears to be everywhere at the same time, to lend assistance wherever animals are hurt or injured. He is that benign, gracious character imbued with a strong desire to protect and save the creatures of the forest. Legend has it that many a trapped animal, whose capture or death was certain, escaped, leaving the hunter without an explanation, save that at the time he heard the plaintive notes of a horn coming from the deep woods. Papa Bois fights cruelty to animals, and the pollution and indiscriminate waste of Nature's rich resources.

When incorporated into the dynamics of the Trinidad Carnival dance-play, these characters lend themselves in a real and meaningful way to fulfilling manifest or latent functions, the latter in particular being deduced from the dance-play's socio-cultural settings, as well as from wider settings than the experience that one culture provides. Denis Dutton in his 'Art, behaviour, and the anthropologists' (1977) clarifies the idea of latent function in a functional way, by suggesting a concept of implicit intention, which he defines as 'those consequences that actors do not recognise in the same way that outsiders do, but that may be equivalent; and those that actors do not recognise, but are implied by the regular recurrence and systematic consequences of their behaviour' (p. 387).

The York University experience: a framework

The following is a description of a framework in which I effectively used this concept with a team of selected underprivildeged adolescents, who volunteered for a series of private workshops at the Faculty of Fine Arts, York

University in Canada. While not a model, it provides a valid system for exploring the specific behaviour patterns of seven young adults, who, though born in Canada, were the offspring of immigrants. These participants were deemed mentally disoriented by their Canadian schoolteachers and peers, because they seemed to have problems 'fitting in'. Communication of their feelings was thus often inaccurate or even misleading. What looked to many like an expression of anger, for example, often turned out to reflect hurt feelings resulting from racial harassment or fear of anomy.

The following criteria were established for the selection of these adolescents:

1 That they were aged between 14 and 17
2 That they had been identified by a senior registered social worker as 'underprivileged', i.e. members of a welfare-dependent or single-parent family residing within an underdeveloped inner city environment
3 That they were not and had not been subject to any organic condition such as brain damage, brain injury or epilepsy.

I initiated this project with a two-fold aim. First, through the Trinidad Carnival dance-play and music, I was determined to sensitise these young adults to the profound physiological and psychological changes which normally occur during adolescence, and help them to manage some of the problems they experienced during this transition. Such problems included confusion of self-image and sexual identity, low esteem, unstable body image, poor impulse control and difficulties with interpersonal relationships. Second, I intended to focus on the participants' movement dynamics, body rhythms, body forms and space perception, and design a prototype baseline for developmental dance-theatre in therapy, for these and other 'underprivileged' adolescents.

The system of 'Labananalysis'[2] was chosen as the movement notation method. The participants included young adults of Afro-Caribbean parentage, and my teaching assistants included persons of Chinese, Canadian, Afro-Caribbean and East African nationalities. Using the medium of the Trinidad Carnival dance-theatre and rhythms, I attempted and succeeded to a considerable degree in providing a safe, appropiate forum of self-discovery and analogical induction, in which areas of conflict were identified and enacted through a 'theatre of the oppressed'.

The challenge I encountered with these young adults demonstrated how crucial it is for a practising creative arts therapist to understand and relate to the urgency of a multiethnic people; to culturally reinterpret and rearrange with unwavering passion. I stress this because the challenge I refer to was one which I was obliged to come to terms with quite early in the exercise. As a group leader objectively managing a creative therapeutic project, it was my duty to advocate and determine the types of movement, actions and interactions that would promote easier stabilisation of body and self-images, so that participants' feelings of confusion could be safely expressed. That was the intended code of practice. Interestingly, I was also bound, by that same code, to break the rules of my own exercise.

More often than I expected, I was compelled as a matter of cultural principle to encourage the participants to deviate from the norms of American schools of thought and vocabularies of movement, which, through osmosis, these young adults were taught to adhere to for survival within the Canadian system. It was only through engineering such deviation that I was able to woo the participants to freely explore and fulfil manifest or latent functions, by symbolically 'trying on' culturally appropriate adult roles and behaviours, based on their colourful ancestral heritage. The study also helped both the participants and the teaching assistants to review and rearrange their attitudes to the social environment and to distasteful aspects of their social mileu.

The study, entitled 'Theatre Dance Workshop KAIRIB', evolved around the central idea that a young adult was a young adult, not a disabled or coloured young adult, and certainly not an upper-, middle- or lower-class adult. The following methodology was adopted:

1 observation and analysis of the selected young adults in a social meeting-place, outside York University's Dance Department (which many of them were told and believed was beyond their reach, academically)
2 observation and analysis of the young adults in the university's Modern Dance studio
3 comparison and evaluation of the group's behaviour and movement patterns in both situations
4 design and development of suitable therapeutic programmes based on the Trinidad Carnival dance-play.

To complement this scheme of work, the special needs of the group were assessed in terms of the Caribbean folk norms. One fact identified by this assessment was that many of the young people did not have the benefit of a positive adult role model at home. The project therefore incorporated positive role models, who performed collectively as benevolent guardians in a concrete jungle (i.e Papa Bois), moral disciplinarians (La Diablesse) and creative dance/play motivators, challenging the students to overcome their personal/communal enemies with brain, not anger or brawn (e.g. Anancy, the cunning spider). In addition, they were further supported by prominent mixed-race personalities in the community, who were specially invited to discuss current controversial socio-political issues relevant to their development.

The living stage

Each two-hour class began promptly at 4.00 p.m. at the York University Dance Department on Friday evenings. A thirty-minute discussion on cross-cultural history (i.e. Africa, Europe, Asia and the Americas) gave the participants food for thought and material to work with physically, when they were encouraged to let go and simply express themselves.

They were called together by the joyous pulsating rhythms of the drums and flute, and encouraged to form a circle, so as to transmit the energies through each other and into the centre of the ring. They were also encouraged to explore the sensation of touching each other's hands and to say a prayer (to their own spiritual creator) asking for blessing and the pure energy to release and positively create. In Africa there is an old saying: 'You want to dance, but did you ask the drummer?' The participants adhered to this principle by walking past the drummer and gently touching the drum's goatskin at its centre, as a gesture of goodwill and connection.

At the barre, the participants were taken through a rigorous 'balletcise' routine, as practised in the school of the Dance Theatre of Harlem. This was in keeping with my aim of helping them to increase their flexibility and strength, while recognising the relevance of European classical movement to their culture. Once the barre exercises were completed, the participants moved centre-studio to continue their routines for increasing flexibility in their movement and constructively building the strength of their muscles. While centre-studio, their exercises included stretches on the floor (Martha Graham influenced), correctives (Irmgard Bartenieff), progressions (Katherine Dunham's methods and technique) and Carnival-style body-awareness routines (Beryl McBurnie) across the floor.

These routines across the floor were structured around spirited locomotion (stepping, running, galloping, skipping, etc.); elevation (mainly high jumps, which both boys and girls relished); turns (right-angle turns, circling, and whirling with the whole body or parts of the body leading); rising and sinking; opening and closing; advancing and retreating. The dual purpose of these movements was to help the participants to further expand their sensory awareness, together with their capacity of character or abstract movement. These two purposes were of course interrelated with the need to increase strength and flexibility, while introducing the participants to the real 'feel' of Carnival fever.

As I demonstrated the movements, postures and gestures, I observed the participants trying to digest every colloquialism, every expression and every celebratory, enlightening, joyful, inspirational motion. Their enthusiasm made me reflect on the drama of seduction that is the Trinidad Carnival, which energises you with its teasing message to live once and die forever in a grand release. The famed Calypso balladeer David Rudder captured the actuating emotions of the participants in these words, reprinted in the *Trinidad Guardian* Carnival Magazine:

Does your spirit do a dance to this symphony?
Does it tell you that your heart is afire?
And does it tell you that your pain is a liar?

Does it wash away all the unlovely?
                    (Rudder 1992, p.27)

An added dimension to what the participants were already learning was the special classes in North African dance – a part of their heritage about which they knew very little. They normally experienced movement and mime which were not formal in structure, but restless, unanchored, untamed and untrapped. So this was what they needed to 'touch base' with their regressed or hyperactive urges. No doubt, the participants' discussion on their way out after classes revolved around whose hips oscillated the most and who were more hypnotised by the alluring rhythms of the drums.

These highly spontaneous movements are still a living force, particularly in the Afro-Asian indigenous cultures, not dominated by technology. They are also still used for forming and regulating group and individual relationships, interaction, and definition of roles. By comparison, in Western cultures, such music-driven theatrical displays have been almost shelved. When we are aware of these traditions we can better understand the dilemma young adolescents face when they become caught in such a cultural lag in a foreign environment, and are socially demoted for it.

MODES OF DANCE PLAYS AS GROUP THERAPY

Upon completion of the York University study, certain facts emerged clearly. These 'underprivileged' young adults selected for testing were quite capable of reaching their fullest potential – if provided with the right impetus. They were not limited in movement range, sporadic space awareness and two-dimensional body rhythms. Their metaphoric body patterns were rather broad and loosely held. They did not move with straight unbendable spines and did not restrict their expressions to repetitive gestural motions. Rather they preferred to integrate earthbound motions with elevated ones at will.

They were not comfortable with just walking mainly on tiptoes or twirling ritualistically in one spot as their American peers were inclined to. When travelling from one spot to another, they did so without abruptness, without erratic darting and stopping movements, and they usually moved with buoyancy, with the upper part of their bodies meandering in polyrhythmic counterpoint. They did not mindlessly bump into each other, trip or fall in space without apparent reason. Most of all, they were more open to touch. This was not the case when we first began the dance-play study.

They integrated because they felt comfortable with the challenge of voluntarily 'trying on' personal and community roles which stretched their imagination. According to Dean (one keen participant), they felt they could explore and spontaneously enact their true feelings, because 'they were not obstructed by insecure adults with petty criticisms, or peer pressure to stay in their low-class corner'.

This became quite evident during one of the group's attempt to enact a mutually agreed story-line, which was based on a human being wanting to reach his highest potential through flight – quite similar to the story of Jonathan Livingstone Seagull (Bach 1973). This signified the need in these young adults to be winners. With the theme 'The ground-dove has no say with the eagle', that particular dance-play was accompanied by a Calypso ballad entitled 'Education', written and sung by the current Calypso king of the world, Trinidadian Dr Slinger Francisco of the University of the West Indies[3] (Francisco 1987). Better known by his sobriquet 'The Mighty Sparrow', he urged Caribbean children to shake off the shackles of colonial oppression, attend school and learn as much as they can, as otherwise later on in life they would pay the penalty. The participants were baptised by the essence of his lyrics, which translated:

> Without an education in your head, your whole life will be pure misery, you're better off dead;
> For there is simply no room in this whole wide world, for an uneducated little boy or girl;
> Don't allow idle companions to lead you astray, to earn tomorrow you got to learn today.

Through this dance-play, Dean was encouraged to show his emotional frustrations, and to keep his goals and ideals well in sight, while waiting for the right moment to soar. His attempts to progress were downplayed by his female companions, who each characterised a threatening La Diablesse, dancing circles around him with mocking laughter, while a male colleague pretended to chain his ankles, anchoring him to the ground. As the group leader and 'father-figure', I continually encouraged Dean to disregard the mindless jeers of his 'fairweather' friends and hold on to his dreams. The use of heavy bass drum-rolls also played a significant part in sensitising the participant to the rhythm of his heartbeat, while the sound of Papa Bois's horn urged him on, beyond the wilderness of the concrete jungle in which he felt a misfit.

This dance-play was rehearsed until its potentially destructive emotional impact was reduced to manageable proportions, in a process of 'systematic desensitization' (Wolpe 1958) or 'anticipatory psychic management' (Hanna and Hanna 1968). This method prepares an individual for a threatening experience, by strengthening the mastery for which that individual strives (Freud 1955, pp. 43, 14–17), through proactive propagation and meta-morphosis through varied mechanisms, which are characteristic of artistic production (Kohut 1955).

At an early age, I accepted that simplicity in communication is the essence of exactitude. I have since learnt from my experiences with these young adults that communication is merely a web, and our minds a spider. We do not express what our true feelings really are. Instead we communicate only what we know of our true feelings (based on the limitations of our consciousness), in a shallow attempt to win friends and influence our community. The buzz-word 'keep it simple stupid' (acronym KISS) aptly describes how we have devalued our ability to communicate, so that we use only about ten per cent of our mental and creative capabilities.

Nature is not simple. Human beings are not simple creations. Expressions of emotions take many different forms, and feelings can express themselves in bodily changes, in action, and in words. Today, we are still trying to grapple with these different forms in the Western world. Yesterday Westerners encountered, sought and colonised the rest of the world for material gain, the control of human capital and suppression of any culture which seemed different. We now have the result of all this: a synthetic colonial world of poverty – not just material, but also emotional poverty, because no attempt was made to communicate, only to conquer.

Ironically, cross-cultural communication is the current 'flavour of the year'. Like spiders we are trying to make scientific inferences from this web of information – a person's words, non-verbal cues, the situational context, and one individual's expectations of another. This natural process is being systematically simplified for human consumption, by humans, who still have not come to terms with the complex nature of true folkloric communications within interpersonal relationships, much less the intercultural community. We still fail to unravel the 'chicken and egg' phenomenon.

The Trinidad Carnival dance-plays essentially integrate the scientific with the folkloric, while maintaining a cathartic nature. The revellers enter the two-day festival with 'excess emotional baggage'. The tension-reducing traditional rituals of rebellion or dramatised conflicts (Gluckman 1954), coupled with enervative movements, movement patterns of defiance, and/or transgressional criticism, are characteristic of cathartic behaviour.

The York University dance-play study, like the Trinidad Carnival experience, provided a healthy fatigue or distraction, which abated a temporary anxiety crisis, and thus allowed more enduring personality patterns to regain ascendancy (Munroe 1955, p. 630). Even more so it encapsulated certain critical issues and phases of social dramas, adjusting imbalances and helping the participants to work through the discourse of their social life. One major aspect of this experience is the fact that these young adults were constantly sidelined from formal decision-making activities in their daily experiences. Therefore, within the study, the dance-play values catalysed social action, and involved the participants in a process of paradox mediation, or the absolving of conflicting opposites.

Victor Turner in his book *Drama, Fields and Metaphors: Symbolic Action in Human Society* describes four essential phases of social dramas, for which the dance-play provides a mediation, or reconciliation by restorative action. These four phases are (1) a breach of the regular norms of a social group, (2) a mounting crisis, (3) a legal or ritual redressive process, and (4) public and symbolic expression of an irreparable schism or conciliation (Turner 1974, p. 38). Using Turner's formula, the York University initiative could be seen to have interpreted the breach, fostered the crisis, ameliorated the conflict and avoided serious discord, while celebrating Dean's reintegration with his true role as an individual and sense of self-worth with the support of the team.

The dance-play also contributes to mediating several paradoxes within the dialectic of one's social life. There is, for example, the paradox of individualism and competition as juxtaposed with the need for community spirit and group solidarity. There is the paradox of change and innovation countered to the principle of respect for the status quo. There is also the paradox of respect and obedience to one's elders, versus the irreverent and mocking rebellion against assertive authority, or '"transparent living"' (Uchendu 1965). A microcosm of the Trinidad Carnival, the dance-play permits the participants to let go and become purified and revitalised through emotional communication prohibited in everyday life.

The Trinidad Carnival, itself a 'ritual of rebellion' (Gluckman 1954), has been known to baptise its 'children of frolic' in a feverish experience of grand release, not to be bypassed. Sean Drakes, a photo-editor of the *Trinidad Guardian*, describes the baptism of this drama of seduction when he writes:

> Trying hard not to look like a foreigner, I started chipping and waving my Kentucky Fried Chicken jug in the air like the folks beside me. From time to time, I stopped to document the fun and frolic, the pranks and merriment, and the few rarities woven in between: one woman with her legs straddling a man's waist was so lost that she didn't realise she had somehow busted a wound on her forehead until folks standing nearby pointed at her blood-drenched tank top.
>
> (Drakes 1992, p. 39)

Trying unsuccessfully to analyse the intriguing power, hypnotic spirit and exciting mystery of the dance-play that is Trinidad Carnival, he eventually concludes: 'Who cares! as long as it stays alive. Frankly, I'll leave analysis to the next first timer, 'cause I've been baptised' (ibid.).

In reflecting on his experience at York, Dean also spoke of his baptism, and the opportunity it gave him to wash away the negatives, by venting his strong emotions without feeling guilty or expecting someone to rebuke him for 'being too ambitious for his race'. Mead (1946) calls this 'expression in counterpoint'. The female members of the cast on the other hand felt that they were able to assert themselves in 'danger zone' arenas – La Diablesse is seen as a demonic whore – without feeling debased. They used their roles in an alternative communal arrangement of benevolence, which dug at the hypocrisy of ethnic and social division, while reinforcing how extremely beneficial the dance-play of Trinidad Carnival can be, as a creative cross-cultural healing medium.

CONCLUSION

Through a ritualistic form of self/collective therapy, the Trinidad Carnival and York dance-players were able to disregard their inhibitions, become totally entranced in their roles and use the related events as functional escape routes from their personal wars and communal conflicts. In conclusion, we can accept that the cross-fertilisation of dance, theatre, music and plastic arts in the Trinidad Carnival is truly representative of the diverse cultural attitudes, expressions and aspirations of the nationals, making the festival a synthesis between old and new, between folk forms and high art forms, between native and alien traditions (see Figure 23.1).

The festival is internationally acknowledged as the greatest 'healing' theatrical spectacle ever seen and experienced. It provides us with invaluable insights into the psyche of several cultural mindsets, which can be used in drama and other creative arts therapy settings, while serving as an effective intercultural coping system for psychic tension.

NOTES

1 Revellers clashed with Trinidad police on Carnival Monday 1881, fearing suppression of the festival.
2 'Labanalysis': a composite method of movement observation, analysis and notation created by Rudolf Laban.
3 Dr Francisco, D. Litt. (honoris causa), was honoured by the University of the West Indies for his contribution to the Calypso art form worldwide.

REFERENCES

Bach, R. (1973) *Jonathan Livingstone Seagull*, London: Turnstone Press.
Brathwaite, B. (1992) *Teaching Inside Out*, Trinidad and Tobago: Gloria Ferguson.
Drakes, S. (1992) 'Baptism Of Pan', *Trinidad Guardian* Carnival Magazine, 4 March, p. 39.
Dutton, D. (1977) 'Art, behaviour, and the anthropologists', *Current Anthropology* 18(3): 387–407.
Francisco, S. (1987) 'Education', *Trinidad Junior Express*, 12 July, p. 5.
Frank, J. (1973) *Persuasion and Healing: A Comparative Study Of Psycho-Therapy*, revised edn, Baltimore: Johns Hopkins University Press.
Freud, S. (1955) *Beyond the Pleasure Principle*, London: Hogarth Press.
Gluckman, M. (1954) *Rituals of Rebellion in South-East Africa*, Manchester, UK: Manchester University Press.
Hanna, J. L. (1976) 'The anthropology of dance ritual: Nigeria's Ubakala Nkwa di Iche Iche', Ph.D thesis, Columbia University; Ann Arbor, Mich.: University Microfilms.
—— (1979) *To Dance is Human: A Study of Nonverbal Communication*, Austin: University of Texas Press.
Hanna, J. L. and Hanna, W. J. (1968) 'Nkwa di Iche Iche: dance plays of Ubakala', *Presence Africaine* 65: 13–18; also *Anthropologica* 11: 243–273.
Kohut, H. (1955) 'Some psychological effects of music and their relation to music therapy', *Music Therapy* 5: 17–20.

Theatre/Oral tradition

Afro-centric

Talk Tent (dialect plays) Canboulay Speech Band Calypso Tent 'Kalinda'/Stick-fight Meet
Traditional Mas (e.g. Anancy, Warriors, Dame Lorraine, Midnight Robber, King Sailor, Jab-Jab)

French

Pre-Carnival Dame Lorraine Shows

East Indian

Indar Sabha Phagwa Ramleela Kheesas Divali Mohurrum/Hosay

Trinidad dance

Afro-centric

Shango Limbo King Sailor Bongo 'Easy Chipping' 'Saga Ting' 'Break-away'

N. American

Tap Jazz Pop Soul Ballroom

Spanish

French

Bele Pique Quadrille Joropo Castillian Juarap

British/Scotish

Reel Jig Ballet

East Indian

Kathak/Odissi Nagara Holi Dance The Jharoo Gatka Banaithi

Trinidad music/instruments

Afro-centric

Steelband Tamboo bamboo Drum (Boolay/Cutter)

Spanish

French

Flute Violin Drums Quatro Guitar Maracas Parang

British

Semi-classical songs

East Indian

Tassa/Nagara Drums Dholak Sarangee Majeera (cymbals) Dhantal Tabla

Figure 23.1 Cross-cultural influences of the Trinidad Carnival

Lee, S. (1990) 'The development of Carnival in Trinidad and Tobago', Introduction to N. Norton, *Twenty Years of Trinidad Carnival*, Trinidad and Tobago: Paria.

McCollin, R. (1987) 'The calypso as oral tradition in Trinidad and Tobago', taped presentation at the University of the West Indies, School of Continuing Studies, St Augustine Campus, Trinidad, 6 August.

Mead, M. (1946)'Dance as an expression of culture patterns', paper prepared for the Second Seminar on the Function of Dance in Human Society, New York.

Munroe, R.L. (1955) *Schools of Psychoanalytic Thought: An Exposition, Critique and Attempt at Integration*, New York: Holt, Rinehart & Winston.

Rudder, D. (1992) 'The spirit Of Calypso', *Trinidad Guardian* Carnival Magazine, 4 March, p. 27.

Turner, V. (1974) *Dramas, Fields and Metaphors: Symbolic Action in Human Society*, Ithaca: Cornell University Press.

Uchendu, V. (1965) *The Igbo Of Southeast Nigeria*, New York: Holt, Rinehart & Winston.

Wolpe, J. (1958) *Psychotherapy by Reciprocal Inhibition*, Stanford: Stanford University Press.

Wood, D. (1968) *Trinidad in Transition*, London: Oxford University Press.

Index